HADITH COMMENTARY

HADITH COMMENTARY

Continuity and Change

EDITED BY
JOEL BLECHER AND
STEFANIE BRINKMANN

EDINBURGH
University Press

Edinburgh University Press is one of the leading university presses in the UK. We publish academic books and journals in our selected subject areas across the humanities and social sciences, combining cutting-edge scholarship with high editorial and production values to produce academic works of lasting importance. For more information visit our website: edinburghuniversitypress.com

Edinburgh University Press Ltd
13 Infirmary Street,
Edinburgh, EH1 1LT

First published in hardback by Edinburgh University Press 2023

Typeset in 11/13 Minion Pro by
IDSUK (DataConnection) Ltd, and
printed and bound by CPI Group (UK) Ltd, Croydon, CR0 4YY

A CIP record for this book is available from the British Library

ISBN 978 1 4744 6104 7 (hardback)
ISBN 978 1 4744 6105 4 (paperback)
ISBN 978 1 4744 6106 1 (webready PDF)
ISBN 978 1 4744 6107 8 (epub)

Contents

Part II   Modern Recollections and Reimaginings

Figures

Notes on Contributors

Ali Aghaei is a Research Associate at the Institute of Islamic Theology of the University of Paderborn. He received his PhD from the Islamic Azad University in Tehran. He has worked as a Member of the Academic Board in the Encyclopedia Islamica Foundation in Tehran, contributing to writing and editing entries in *Dāneshnāmeh-ye Jahān-e Eslām*, as Research Fellow at the Corpus Coranicum project at the Berlin-Brandenburg Academy of Sciences and Humanities, and as Research Associate and director of the Irankoran project, funded by the Federal Ministry of Education and Research in Germany and hosted by the Berlin-Brandenburg Academy of Sciences and Humanities.

Maroussia Bednarkiewicz is a Research Fellow at the University of Tübingen. She studied German and Russian at the University of Geneva and obtained an MA in Islamic studies and History at the University of Oxford. Her PhD dissertation delves into the history of the Islamic call to prayer in Hadith literature. To develop further the computational analysis of large Hadith corpora is the aim of her current project.

Joel Blecher is Associate Professor of History at the George Washington University in Washington, DC, the author of *Said the Prophet of God: Hadith Commentary Across a Millennium* (2018), and co-translator of Ibn Ḥajar al-ʿAsqalānī's *Merits of the Plague* (2023) with Mairaj Syed. His other writings have appeared in the *Journal of Near Eastern Studies*, *Islamic Law & Society*, *Oriens* and several edited volumes. His work has been supported by the National Endowment for the Humanities, the American Council of Learned Societies, the Kluge Center at the Library of Congress, and the Institute for Advanced Study in Princeton.

Stefanie Brinkmann is Research Fellow at the Bibliotheca Arabica project at the Saxon Academy of Sciences and Humanities in Leipzig. Trained in Arabic, Persian and Roman Studies, she had acting professorships at the universities of Freiburg and Hamburg, and was member and principal investigator of a number of manuscript projects. She has published in the fields of manuscript studies, especially on hadith manuscripts, material culture in hadith and classical Arabic poetry.

Samer Dajani is an Independent Researcher. He received his BA in Arab and Islamic Civilizations from the American University in Cairo, followed by an MA and PhD in the field of Islamic Studies from SOAS, University of London. He was Research Fellow and Lecturer at the Muslim College in Cambridge. His research interests include Hadith, Sufism and Jurisprudence. He is the author of *Sufis and Sharīʿa: The Forgotten School of Mercy* (Edinburgh University Press, 2022) and the translator of *Reassurance for the Seeker: A Biography and Translation of Ṣāliḥ al-Jaʿfarī's al-Fawāʾid al-Jaʿfariyya* (2014).

Mohammad Gharaibeh is Professor of Islamic Intellectual History at the Berlin Institute for Islamic Theology at the Humboldt-Universität zu Berlin. In his research, he focuses on the history and development of Islamic theological ideas and concepts, the circulation and reception of texts, and the spread of scholarly networks as well as their impact on the production and regulation of Islamic knowledge. He is the editor of *Beyond Authenticity: Alternative Approaches to Hadith Narrations and Collections* (2023).

Susan Gunasti is Professor of Religion at Ohio Wesleyan University, specializing in Islam in the Ottoman period. She is the author of *The Qur'an between the Ottoman Empire and the Turkish Republic: An Exegetical Tradition* (2019). Her writings have appeared in the *Journal of Islamic Studies* and *Islamic Law and Society*.

Ali Altaf Mian is Assistant Professor of Religion and the Izzat Hasan Sheikh Fellow in Islamic studies at the University of Florida. His peer-reviewed articles have appeared in numerous journals, including *Islamic Law and Society, History of Religions, ReOrient, Journal of Urdu Studies, Religion Compass, Journal of Islamic Studies* (Oxford), and *Journal of Shiʿa Islamic Studies*. He is presently working on completing several manuscripts, including *Surviving Modernity: Muslim Ethics and Politics in Colonial India* and *Embodying the Sunnah: Ḥadīth Studies in Modern South Asia*.

Shadi Nafisi is Associate Professor at the University of Teheran. She received her PhD in 2002 and her MA in 1994 from the University of Tarbiat Modarress in Teheran. Before coming to the University of Teheran in 2012, she worked as Assistant Professor at the University of Qur'an and Hadith in Ray (1999–2012). She also served (2001–12) as Research Fellow in the Department of Qur'an and Hadith Studies of the Encyclopedia of Islam Foundation in Teheran.

Aslisho Qurboniev is a Post-doctoral Fellow of the Islamic West at the KITAB (Knowledge, Information Technology, and the Arabic Book) project at Aga Khan University (Institute for the Study of Muslim Civilizations, International, London). Aslisho obtained his PhD (2020) from the University of Cambridge with a dissertation titled 'Traditions of Learning in Fatimid Ifriqiya (296–362/909–973): Networks, Practices, and Institutions'. Previously he read Islamic Studies and History (MPhil, 2014) at the University of Oxford. His research interests also include medieval Islamic learning, knowledge transmission, Shi'i Islam and digital humanities.

Youshaa Patel is Associate Professor of Islamic Studies at the department of Religious Studies at Lafayette College and the author of *The Muslim Difference: Defining the Line between Believers and Unbelievers from Early Islam to the Present* (2022). His research explores how Islam shaped and was shaped by Muslim encounters with Christians, Jews and others in the Middle East and beyond.

Sajjad Rizvi is Professor of Islamic Intellectual History at the University of Exeter. He is the author of *Mullā Ṣadrā Shīrāzī* (2007), *Mullā Ṣadrā and Metaphysics* (2009), and most recently with Scott Davison and Shira Weiss of The Protests of Job: *An Interfaith Dialogue* (2022), co-editor with Feras Hamza and Farhana Mayer of *An Anthology of Qur'anic Commentaries* (2008), co-editor with Annabel Keeler of *The Spirit and the Letter: Approaches to the Esoteric Interpretation of the Qur'an* (2016), and co-editor with Kazuo Morimoto of *Knowledge and Power in Muslim Societies: Approaches in Intellectual History* (2023). His three main research interests are Islamic philosophical traditions in the East up to the present day, Qur'anic Studies (*tafsīr* and hermeneutics) and Shi'i philosophical theology.

Gowaart Van Den Bossche obtained his PhD in history at Ghent University in January 2019 for a dissertation on early Mamluk historiography, chancery practice and literary culture. Between 2019 and 2022 he worked as Post-doctoral Research Fellow with the KITAB project at Aga Khan University Institute for the Study of Muslim Civilisations in London. He is currently a post-doctoral research fellow funded by the Research Foundation Flanders (FWO), working on universal historiography in early eighth/fourteenth century Egypt and Syria. He has published articles in *al-Masaq*, *Annales Islamologiques* and Islamic Law and Society on various aspects of late medieval Islamic history and society.

Preface

The idea for this volume was first conceived during a workshop on hadith commentaries at the Centre for the Study of Manuscript Cultures in Asia, Africa and Europe at Hamburg University (CSMC) in December 2017, organised by Stefanie Brinkmann and Ali Zaherinezhad. The workshop was part of a project on a heavily annotated Tīmūrid-era manuscript of *Ṣaḥīḥ al-Bukhārī*.[1] Joel Blecher was the keynote speaker, and his book, *Said the Prophet of God: Hadith Commentary across a Millennium*, had just been released in the United States – he brought the first bundle of copies to Europe with him in his briefcase. The diversity and range of presentations, and the vivid discussions about the practice of hadith commentary made clear the many aspects of the tradition that remained unstudied. By the end of the workshop, we imagined a volume – *Hadith Commentary: Continuity and Change* – that would bring new scholars into the field and introduce new voices to cover an array of topics covering a variety of time periods, regions, methodological approaches and sectarian divisions.

We first thank Ali Zaherinezhad, whose inspiration and efforts were critical in the conceptualisation and preparation of this volume at its early stages. In a way, this book is also his. We would also like to thank the Centre for the Study of Manuscript Cultures in Asia, Africa and Europe at Hamburg University for the support and infrastructure that enabled us to pursue our research. Furthermore, we thank our current hosting institutions, which have facilitated our ongoing research in the field of hadith commentary and supported this edited volume in terms of funding and infrastructure. They are (in alphabetical order): the Bibliotheca Arabica Project at the Saxon Academy of Sciences and Humanities in Leipzig (www.saw-leipzig.de/bibliotheca-arabica); and the George Washington

---

1 The project was part of the Centre for the Study of Manuscript Cultures in Asia, Africa and Europe at Hamburg University, funded by the Deutsche Forschungsgemeinschaft; Stefanie Brinkmann was the principal investigator, and Ali Zaherinezhad was the research fellow.

University's Department of History and the GW Columbian College of Arts and Sciences' Humanities Facilitating Fund. We owe a special thanks to Daniel B. Schwartz, Sam Nohra and Michael Weeks for moving mountains to make these funds available.

We thank the contributors of this volume for their commitment and for their new insights. We also thank the anonymous reviewers who gave useful advice and constructive criticism on the individual chapters. We owe a debt to Nicola Ramsey, Kirsty Woods and Louise Hutton at Edinburgh University Press, as well the series editor, Ramon Harvey, for their support and efforts in bringing this volume to print. Special thanks go to Valerie Joy Turner for copyediting and indexing the book, work which immensely improved its intelligibility and usability.

We also thank our families and friends for their support as we spent many long hours away from them working on this book. Joel in particular would like to dedicate his work on this project to Summer, Aria and Hawthorn.

The transliteration of Arabic, Persian and Turkish names, technical terms, and other phrases into Latin characters follows the *International Journal of Middle Eastern Studies*, except for the elision of al- and compound names with Allāh, which we write as one word (e.g. ʿAbdallāh, Hibatallāh, versus other compound names such as ʿAbd al-Raḥmān) according to the system used by Brill. Well-established terms, such as Qurʾan, hadith, imam and geographic regions are given in their common contemporary forms. We have left Sunni and Shiʿi without diacritics in the introduction for the benefit of a wider readership, but have employed diacritics for these terms in the other chapters. Dates appear in the Hijrī and Common Era forms (e.g. 436/1044) up to the eighteenth century. We employ the following abbreviations:

EI² *Encyclopaedia of Islam, Second Edition.* Edited by P. Bearman, Th. Bianquis, C. E. Bosworth, E. van Donzel, and W. P. Heinrichs. 12 vols. Leiden: Brill, 1960–2004. Brill Online.

EI³ *Encyclopaedia of Islam, THREE.* Edited by Kate Fleet, Gudrun Krämer, Denis Matringe, John Nawas and Everett Rowson. Leiden: Brill, 2007–. Brill Online.

EQ *Encyclopaedia of the Qurʾān.* Edited by Jane McAuliffe Dammen. 6 vols. Leiden: Brill, 2001–6. Brill Online.

EIr *Encyclopaedia Iranica.* Edited by Ehsan Yarshater. New York: Columbia University. <http://www.iranicaonline.org>.

Introduction
What is Hadith Commentary?

Joel Blecher and Stefanie Brinkmann

The tradition of hadith commentary has been a central site of Islamic intellectual life for more than a millennium, yet it has only recently attracted scholarly attention among Islamicists.[1] Building on this recent work, *Hadith Commentary: Continuity and Change* is the first book to collect a range of scholarly essays on key texts and critical themes of hadith commentary across a variety of periods and areas. Addressing the diversity of sects, periods and regions in which hadith commentary developed, this volume demonstrates that novel intellectual activity did not decline following the so-called 'golden age' of Islam, and that in fact the medium of commentary thrived. This edited volume pushes the field of hadith studies to expand beyond analyses of hadith transmission, and into the vast and understudied world of the hadith's normative significance to those communities that held them to be authentic.

The present volume is designed for specialists in the field of Islamic studies, but may also appeal to non-specialists working on commentary traditions in other religions and cultures of learning. This volume aims to expand the boundaries of the nascent field of hadith commentary by covering a broad time frame, from the beginnings of commentarial activity in the second/eighth century to the modern voices of the twentieth and twenty-first centuries, by traversing a vast geographical area from regions across the Islamic world, by combining different methodological approaches, and by examining commentary traditions from Sunni, Shi'i and Sufi traditions.

Before we embark on this ambitious task, a fundamental question must first be addressed: What *is* a hadith commentary? Many might answer the question

---

1 Blecher, *Said the Prophet of God*; for a bibliography of recent articles related to hadith commentary, see Blecher, 'Ḥadīth Commentary'.

by simply pointing to line-by-line commentaries (*sharḥ*, pl. *shurūḥ*) explicating hadiths in a collection such as *Ṣaḥīḥ al-Bukhārī*. Yet this is just one kind of hadith commentary, albeit an important one.

Joel Blecher describes the range of hadith commentary as follows:

> Construed broadly, the term could include any formal or informal oral or written gloss on a given *ḥadīth*. Narrowly defined, the practice of *ḥadīth* commentary refers to a cumulative and transregional tradition of line-by-line Muslim scholarly exegesis on individual *ḥadīth* and *ḥadīth* collections, from the late Islamic formative period to the present day.[2]

As we see, at the broadest end of the spectrum, hadith commentary may be defined even more widely than Blecher's passage above suggests. Indeed, we might even point to the placement of an epigraphic inscription of a hadith on the Dome of the Rock as a loose form of commentary on the importance and use of hadith.[3] In this sense, we may consider any reference to a hadith, whether in architecture or a quotation in a poem or a sermon, as commentarial activity or as commentarial gesture. In a more narrowly defined sense, we may speak of a genre of hadith commentary in which a later author tries to systematically elucidate an earlier text containing hadith. Such hadith commentaries can encompass many approaches to linguistic, legal or theological matters, chains of transmission, variants and issues of reliability, but not all commentaries cover this range of content, and some are limited to one or a few elements of these issues. This volume, for example, deliberately includes the genre of commentary on obscure terms (*gharīb al-ḥadīth*) as part of the commentary tradition, though this genre is largely dedicated to lexical issues.

What, then, are the range of textual (or even non-textual) forms hadith commentary can feature? What are the various methodological approaches by which we can define the practice of hadith commentary? Many academic studies discussing commentary literature characterise it as secondary. That is, the commentary is a secondary text added at a later stage; it annotates and elucidates a primary text, mediating between the primary text and the reader. This derivative quality is thus, first, a chronological relationship, and scholars should be cautious not to consider it derivative in a hierarchical or evaluative sense. After all, some commentaries even eclipse the so-called primary text they were intended to elucidate. As Jonathan Brown

---

2 Blecher, 'Ḥadīth Commentary', in *EI³*, online: http://dx.doi.org/10.1163/1573-3912_ei3_COM_32080 (accessed 20 February 2022).

3 Lucas, 'An Efficacious Invocation'.

states, the primary text 'acted as a medium for a much more expanded discussion in which the author could express his own vision of the Islamic worldview'.[4]

But the production of commentary on hadith was not limited to rereading centuries-old texts in new contexts, or attempting to preserve the meaning of primary texts for future generations (or contesting who has the power to preserve this transmission); nor should hadith commentary be viewed solely as a vessel in which to propagate certain worldviews external to it. Rather, hadith commentary is a tradition that cultivates certain unique virtues and practices, and links participants to a transgregional and transtemporal forum for intellectual exchange.[5] It was in this far-reaching scholarly network that students and masters could realise religiously defined aims and gain social status and recognition.

And yet, how does one draw the line between a hadith, a hadith collection, a hadith commentary and other forms of commentary? If Muhammad or one of the Imams explained what he meant by a certain utterance in the textual content (*matn*) of a hadith, is this a form of hadith commentary within the hadith itself? And if the compiler of a hadith collection carefully selected reports for incorporation into his compilation and left out others – is this act of inclusion and exclusion a form of commentary? And if a compiler chose to arrange hadiths into chapters and subchapters – is this an act of commentary as well?[6] If the compiler then added chapter titles, or additional textual material (e.g. *tarājim*, headings or rubrics) to guide the reader to and through the following chapters, or after citing a tradition, added statements about its reliability, its chains of transmission (*isnād*), or its variants – should these additions be considered commentarial activity? And why did many post-canonical hadith compilers select traditions from the primary collections and rearrange the material under chapter headings, if not to say something new, or address new audiences with their collections?

On the one hand, as the preceding paragraph suggests, we can make a strong argument for these examples to be considered 'commentary'

---

4 Brown, *Hadith*, 52.

5 Assmann and Gladigow, in *Text und Kommentar*, offer insight into the complex matters of commentary, on a theoretical level, and regarding the range of regional commentary cultures stretching from India and China to mediaeval Europe. Gregor Scholer offers an overview of commentary in the 'classical-Islamic tradition' (Schoeler, 'Text und Kommentar').

6 In the case of *muṣannaf* works, compilers organised hadith into chapters (*kitāb*, pl. *kutub*) and subchapters (*bāb*, pl. *abwāb*). Canonical and redaction criticism (from the field of Biblical Studies) has long shown the potential of examining the authorial voice or the compiler's attitude and the aim behind this conscious arrangement of material. See Burge, 'Reading between the Lines'.

worthy of more intensive study. On the other hand, there may also be good reasons to distinguish these practices from the genre of hadith commentary. After all, these examples cannot be properly characterised by chronological principles as secondary, in which a hadith, or groups of hadiths are commented upon and elucidated through an intentionally separate and chronologically later text (be it in written or oral form) – a hypotext and a hypertext.[7] And yet, if our definition is guided by the principle of chronology alone, we would have to consider, by logical extension, many other textual forms, such as *fatwās*, legal or theological treatises (*rasā'il*), Qur'an commentary (*tafsīr*), sermons, prophetic medicine and many others as forms of hadith commentary, since their explanations and interpretations represent explications of hadiths for present and future purposes.[8] Still, many scholars prefer to treat *fatwās*, *rasā'il* and others as genres unto themselves.

But what, then, can we identify as the decisive principle that distinguishes a hadith commentary from a *fatwā* elaborating on a hadith? One possible reply to this question is simply to define a hadith commentary as what commentators claimed was a hadith commentary, explicitly embedding themselves in that tradition. In this view, a book that the commentators themselves classified as hadith commentary is simply considered part of the tradition. Commentators might deliberately emphasise that they are part of this tradition by giving their commentary a corresponding title, such as a *sharḥ* of al-Bukhārī or a *ḥāshiya* on al-Nawawī's *Arba'īn* ('forty [hadith]'). But even if they did not give their works such denotative titles (and in the past, it was not uncommon for authors to leave their works untitled, or to allow their works to be referred to by a variety of appellations), then later scholarly communities might have done so, simply by referring to the book as a *sharḥ* of *Ṣaḥīḥ al-Bukhārī*, or a *ḥāshiya* on the forty hadith.[9] Similarly, an author's announcement in the work's preface of his intention to elucidate hadith – *sharaḥa* (commenting), or *fassara* (interpreting) – likewise signals to readers that the book should be taken as a contribution to the hadith commentary tradition.

And yet, in our attempt to define this category of hadith commentary, the fluidity of the genre's boundaries has persisted, and, in a sense, any fixed definition is beside the point. A definition is a tool that, when calibrated

---

7 Compare Gérard Genette's concept of hypertextuality with Eric van Lit's application for the Islamic commentary tradition, e.g. in van Lit, 'Commentary and Commentary Tradition'. See also Chapter 10 of this volume by Bednarkiewicz, Qurboniev and Van Den Bossche.

8 On the terminology of commentary in the field of logic, see Gutas, 'Aspects of Literary Form'.

9 Gladigow calls these groups 'textual communities'. See Gladigow, 'Der Kommentar als Hypothek des Textes', 35.

and configured in various ways, can offer scholars new insights into shared problems. The scholars in the present volume define hadith commentary in a wide range of ways that go well beyond the line-by-line *sharḥ*. These varieties include a lexical commentary of *gharīb al-ḥadīth*, a translation of al-Bukhārī's *Ṣaḥīḥ* into Turkish, and the hadith criticism laid out by the Imāmī scholars al-Sharīf al-Murtaḍā (d. 436/1044) in his *Kitāb al-Āmālī* (Book of dictations), and by Ṭabāṭabā'ī (d. 1402/1981) in his Qur'an commentary *al-Mizān*.

This variety and fluidity of definitions of hadith commentary also come to the fore when we consider the diverse ways that scholars tend to classify hadith commentaries. Regardless of how useful such classifications are to readers, they allow us to map the variety of hadith commentaries and help us analyse how commentators approach their base texts, what they thought deserved commentary, for whom and why.

The most common way of classifying hadith commentaries is to differentiate them by disciplines: legal, linguistic and theological, among others, depending on the primary aim of the commentary. Another common method of classifying hadith commentaries is to refer to the sectarian affiliation of the commentator within the Islamic intellectual tradition; these include, for example, Shi'i, Sufi, Mālikī or Ḥanbalī hadith commentaries, among others. This classification suggests that the interpretation of hadiths is primarily related to the commentators' legal and theological commitments and that the commentary reflects the hermeneutical approach taken by the author and his audience. It may also point to the various texts that are commented on; for example, a commentary on a Shi'i hadith collection. And yet, many works primarily concerned with legal matters also touch on issues of grammar and theology, just as a commentary authored by a Ḥanbalī may focus on matters that, on the surface, have little to do with Ḥanbalī law, and may relate more to Sufism or other schools of law.

Another way of classifying hadith commentary relates to the work's format. This mode of classification primarily assesses the length of the commentary, in terms of dimension but also detail.[10] While some commentaries discuss each hadith of a collection, others provide only a partial commentary on a collection; that is, they discuss selected hadith, though they might still follow the arrangement of the collection.[11] Such a selection (and its omissions) necessitates a study of the ways in which the traditions were chosen, and the possible motivations of the commentator.

10 For instance, under this rubric, Ibn Ḥajar al-'Asqalānī's (d. 852/1449) *Fatḥ al-Bārī* would be considered a detailed and comprehensive line-by-line commentary.
11 For instance, Badr al-Dīn al-Damāmīnī's (d. 827/1424) *Maṣābīḥ al-Jāmi'*.

These formal categories of length and comprehensiveness can be applied to the aforementioned types of commentary as related to discipline and sectarian affiliation. A fourth category relates to the mode of transmission. A commentary performed orally can be viewed virtually, as a streaming video, or it can be experienced live during a hadith session (*majlis al-ḥadīth*, a gathering related to the publication, recitation or study of hadith). Similarly, written commentaries can be accessed in manuscript form, as edited texts or digitally.

While the most common classifications are by discipline, sectarian affiliation and format, another possible method of classifying the varieties of hadith commentary relates to the kinds of texts that are commented upon. This is a rather technical approach and does not relate to discipline, sectarian affiliation, content or the like. Rather, what matters is the type of textual material that is explained.[12]

Regarding hadith collections, or hadith texts as a point of reference, this categorisation can be split into the following two groups. The first group consists of commentaries on identifiable hadith collections; that is, collections titled by their compilers who are usually known by name. The second group includes commentaries that treat a selection of traditions from various sources, or a general pool of hadiths.[13] This group could include lectures, commentaries on a single hadith,[14] or texts in a question-and-answer format. This last category particularly exemplifies the porous boundary of what constitutes a hadith commentary. Commentaries on abridgements (*mukhtaṣar*s) or versifications of identifiable works straddle the two groups, since they are both identifiable, but are also, typically, an expression of the commentator's selective editing choices.

The first group – those commentaries on collections that can be identified as separate works – can be further divided into primary and secondary collections. Primary collections are those in which the compiler is part of the original chain of transmission; these include the pre-canonical and canonical collections, both Sunni and Shi'i. Secondary collections can

12 This classification, developed by Friederike S. Schmidt, was a result of her survey on hadith commentaries in the Berlin manuscript catalogue of Wilhelm Ahlwardt (1889); her work was conducted as part of the research module 'Macro-Perspective' (supervised by Stefanie Brinkmann) at the Bibliotheca Arabica Project, Saxon Academy of Sciences and Humanities, Leipzig, Germany.

13 If we take the lexicographic *gharīb al-ḥadīth* subgenre as an example, then the *gharīb al-ḥadīth* commentary attributed to 'Abd al-Qāhir al-Suhrawardī (d. 563/1168) on al-Baghawī's *Maṣābīḥ al-sunna* would be considered part of the first group, while Abū 'Ubayd al-Qāsim b. Sallām's (d. 223/837 or 224/838) *Gharīb al-ḥadīth* would belong to the second group, since Abū 'Ubayd collected traditions from various sources and does not refer to a reference text in the sense of a specific collection.

14 For instance, 'Abd Allāh ibn Muḥammad Shinshawrī's (d. 999/1591) *Sharḥ ḥadīth Umm Zar'* (Cairo: Dār al-Risāla, 2019).

be classified as later adaptations. The most prominent of these are post-canonical works in which the compilers selected traditions from primary collections and arranged them as a new collection, on which numerous commentaries were composed.[15]

We should reiterate that these various modes (and others not mentioned here) by which scholars classify hadith commentary often overlap and intersect, and no one mode is sufficient to describe the phenomenon. But being explicit about the use of these competing modes of classification and not taking them for granted as fixed categories allows scholars working on the academic study of hadith commentary to choose and develop the most advantageous frameworks for their own case studies.

In the past, those who sought to understand a hadith would have to seek out a shaykh who could deliver a commentary in a crowded study circle, or consult a manuscript in classical Arabic filled with his annotations,[16] or free-standing comments. While hadith masters and handwritten codices can still be consulted today, now hadith commentaries are available in many languages and have been mass-produced in print, uploaded electronically and can be streamed on video on laptops and smartphones. And yet, even as the tradition of hadith commentary has navigated dramatic changes across time and place, it has also preserved, if selectively, important continuities and patterns of interpretation.

Thus, following the abstract question of 'What is a hadith commentary?', we are confronted with a rich constellation of questions that bear on the sociohistorical dimension of commentaries and the religious experiences they elicit in historical practice. What intellectual milieu was a commentary produced in; and what social, political and religious purposes did these commentaries serve for their communities? And, relatedly, what material rewards and religious excellences were at stake in the contestation over the direction of the tradition? What roles have patronage and the endowment of educational institutions played in sustaining the practice of hadith commentary?

And how has the historical exclusion of women from positions of commentarial authority on hadith (even while women have been included as authoritative transmitters of hadith in certain locales and during specific

---

15 On so-called digest collections with truncated *isnāds*, see Brown, *Ḥadith*, 57–58. Examples include al-Ṣaghānī's (d. 650/1252) *Mashāriq al-anwār* with traditions taken from the *Ṣaḥīḥayn* of al-Bukhārī and Muslim, or al-Baghawī's (d. 510/1117 or 516/1122) *Maṣābīḥ al-sunna*, for which he chose traditions from the canonical collections and al-Dārimī's (d. 255/869) *Sunan*.

16 Brinkmann, 'Marginal Commentaries in Hadith Manuscripts'.

eras) influenced the practice and audience of hadith commentary?[17] How do constructs like ethnicity and race operate in the spaces and media where hadith commentary is practised?[18] What other social dynamics and political considerations were at work in specific scholarly communities engaged in the production of commentaries?

Lastly, are there social, economic or political forces that might explain why some hadith compilations attracted numerous commentaries, while others withered in obscurity? And if the 'medium is the message', as Marshall McLuhan famously stated, what social and political messages has the *medium* of hadith commentary sent? And have these messages gone beyond any single explanation of a particular hadith or a select commentarial work?

As Blecher argues in his introduction to *Said the Prophet of God*, the practice of hadith commentary cannot be reduced to competition over social capital and political power, though social and political forces are an important part of the puzzle. Stipends, tax advantages, prestige, status and fame were just some of the social and material rewards that could be attained in the setting of a hadith commentary session. It is important to understand the way commentary sessions allow seekers to resolve contradictions in their understandings of Islam, and to perfect certain excellences of character modelled by Muhammad that Muslims sought to bring into their daily lives. Furthermore, the commentary sessions also allowed some seekers to attain ecstatic experiences and visions of Muhammad. This suggests that the purpose of hadith commentary goes far beyond elucidating arcane grammatical points or advancing a hadith scholar's career. In this way, scholars may benefit from analyses informed not only by hermeneutics and history, but also by 'thick' phenomenologically informed ethnographic descriptions of commentary practices.[19]

The academic study of hadith commentary requires a deep understanding of the genesis of hadith scholarship and its entrenchment with other disciplines in the various legal and theological schools, in addition to a comprehension of local and global political developments and social phenomena, in order to compare them across broad temporal and spatial distances. While

---

17 Although women were active as hadith transmitters since the early period, their commentarial activity has not been collected or passed on, apart from the notes in the texts of hadith by figures such as ʿĀʾisha. For the period prior to the twentieth century, women do not appear as the authors of commentaries, nor do we know of women that are quoted in hadith commentaries. For some examples of their possible peripheral participation in the exegetical activity of hadith, see Sayeed, *Women and the Transmission of Knowledge*. Compare Davidson, *Carrying on the Tradition*. Only in modern times have women started to compose hadith commentaries. In this respect, hadith commentary resembles the *tafsīr* tradition.

18 Blecher and Dubler, 'Overlooking Race and Secularism'.

19 Blecher, *Said the Prophet of God*, 1–18.

some of these elements are addressed in this volume, the task ahead is so ambitious and the lacunae so gaping that some elements will have to await future research. In arranging our current volume chronologically rather than by theme, we hope to draw out the important continuities and changes in the practice of hadith commentary as commentators and their audiences of patrons and students have responded to local social and political realities and religious experiences.

A historical overview of the practice of hadith commentary has already been undertaken,[20] thus, the aim of the present work is somewhat different. This book unfolds chronologically in two parts: 'Formations and Developments in the Early and Middle Periods' and 'Modern Recollections and Reimaginings'; this gives readers a sense of the development of this tradition over time and place. That said, readers should take care to note that the broad periodisation is not absolute, and contributions may cover more than one period. For instance, Stefanie Brinkmann's article on *gharīb al-ḥadīth* begins with the third/ninth century and reconstructs the development of this genre through the Mamlūk period and into the twentieth century. Likewise, Youshaa Patel's contribution on apocalyptic hadith is grounded in the Mamlūk period, but also addresses the use and reuse of these traditions in modern militant movements in the Middle East. The digital humanities project devised by Bednarkiewicz, Qurboniev, and Van Den Bossche is included in the section on the modern period, but delves into the tradition's past to uncover new insights. To that end, readers specialising in a single period may find it beneficial to consult chapters from both parts of this book.

In Part I, readers discover continuities and changes in several chapters that illuminate early Sunni and Shi'i attempts to comment on hadith prior to the crystallisation of the genre during the middle periods. Stefanie Brinkmann examines the origin and development of the lexical commentary of *gharīb al-ḥadīth*. This genre is the earliest form of hadith commentary; thus reconstructing its historical development and exemplifying basic structural patterns lay the groundwork for the subsequent chapters. Ali Aghaei discusses Shi'i intellectual thought and the hermeneutical approach to isolated traditions (*akhbār al-āḥād*) of the fifth-/eleventh-century luminary al-Sharīf al-Murtaḍā. Aghaei shows that al-Murtaḍā developed a distinct methodology to interpret hadith by applying a combination of Mu'tazilī and Shi'i principles.

In the middle chapters of Part I, the volume explores the texts, people, and practices that circulated in the context of the socially competitive post-classical Sunni and Shi'i scholarly milieux, and examines the critical

20 Blecher, *Said the Prophet of God*, 4–13; Blecher, 'Ḥadīth Commentary', in *EI³*; Karagözoğğlu, 'Commentaries'.

themes in mysticism, theology and law that are addressed across various regions of the Islamic world. Youshaa Patel surveys the interpretations of the hadith of *al-ghurabā'* ('blessed are the strangers') in a range of texts from the fourth/tenth to eighth/fourteenth century to show that modern militant interpretations of the hadith that stress its connection to jihad are a departure from the dominant ascetic virtues that Sufi interpreters associated with it in earlier times. This chapter is a case study of how hadith commentary can be used to illuminate the contours of an important moral and religious concept in the evolving landscape of Islamic thought. Samer Dajani's chapter takes up the influence of Sufism on the hadith commentary tradition more broadly and more explicitly; in it he explores whether and to what extent we can speak of a Sufi hadith commentary tradition. In doing so, this chapter also represents the first attempt to collect and introduce some of the most important works of hadith commentary written by Sufis and focusing on Sufi themes.

Part I concludes first with Mohammad Gharaibeh's chapter, which discusses the form of hadith commentary by examining Ibn Rajab al-Ḥanbalī's extensive commentary on al-Nawawī's renowned *al-Arbaʿīn* (Forty hadith). Gharaibeh shows that Ibn Rajab played with the form of the commentary in novel ways, in response to the intellectual and social context in which he was working. Lastly, Sajjad Rizvi's chapter offers readers the first comprehensive introduction in English to the flowering of Shiʿi hadith commentary in the Ṣafavid period. Rizvi depicts a tradition of commentaries in conflict with each other over the very nature of Shiʿi traditions. The Akhbārī commentaries were a return to scripture (as opposed to legal and theological reasoning), while philosophers and mystics deployed hadith to confirm and corroborate their intellectual insights. The chapter concludes with a case study of how the notion of intellect (*ʿaql*) arising in hadith was understood by various Shiʿi interpreters in this period.

Part II, 'Modern Recollections and Reimaginings', addresses hadith commentaries in the context of colonialism and the birth of the nation state in Turkey, Iran and India. Susan Gunasti's chapter examines an early twentieth-century effort – approved by the Turkish parliament – to complete a Turkish translation and commentary of *Ṣaḥīḥ al-Bukhārī*. In doing so, Gunasti illustrates how religious authority was articulated in the genre of hadith commentary and in Islamic print culture, and how the legacy of Ottoman-era religious ideas and institutions endured in Turkish-language hadith commentaries after the fall of the Ottoman empire. Ali Mian's chapter addresses modern South Asian debates on authority, authenticity and the question of unity and diversity. He examines modern Deobandī Ḥanafī commentators, and notes that they do not follow the lead of the twelfth-/eighteenth-century reformer and hadith scholar, Shāh Walī Allāh of Delhi (1114–1176/1703–1762), to reconcile legal differences in the service of a unified, ecumenical approach to the normative order. Rather, Deobandī Ḥanafī scholars used both 'content-based' (*matn*) and 'transmission-based' (*isnād*) forms of criticism to display their interpretive excellences and to defend the Ḥanafī tradition against criticism from Salafī detractors. Next, Shadi Nafisi brings to light the exegetical work of Muḥammad Ḥusayn Ṭabāṭabāʾī (d. 1981), a paragon of modern Shiʿi thought in twentieth-century Iran. Nafisi examines how Ṭabāṭabāʾī assesses the authority of a given hadith by paying particular attention to the *matn* of the hadith and its relationship to the Qurʾan. This opens the possibility of intertextual and comparative work that crosses the boundaries between *sharḥ al-ḥadīth* and *tafsīr al-Qurʾān*.

The last chapter, by Maroussia Bednarkiewicz, Aslisho Qurboniev and Goowart Van Den Bossche, breaks new ground by modelling the potential of large digital corpora for the analysis of hadith commentary. These authors show that the tool of text reuse particularly (i.e. counting citations and excerpts of commentaries across generations of the textual tradition) speaks volumes about commentators' processes and their relationship to their predecessors.

The book closes with Joel Blecher's afterword entitled 'More Comments, Further Questions', in which he explores the themes of continuity and change in the hadith commentary tradition across time and place, and points to avenues that could be fruitfully pursued in future studies.

Finally, we must add that even as accessibility to hadith commentaries has increased over the past centuries, many catalogued manuscripts that best attest to the hadith commentary tradition remain unedited; this is in addition to what must be a bevy of uncatalogued, unknown or lost material. Many spaces in which contemporary hadith commentary are delivered live are likewise inaccessible to researchers due to political instability, travel restrictions and gender segregation, among other factors. Therefore, our understanding of the hadith commentary tradition is preliminary and will require revision and adjustment as the full corpus of texts comes to light. It is our hope, then, that this first collection of scholarly essays will not be the last. In an echo of the title of this book's afterword, we hope that this volume will not mark the final word in this field, but will spur further questions and scholarly commentary.

Bibliography

Assmann, Jan and Burkhard Gladigow (eds). *Text und Kommentar. Archäologie der literarischen Kommunikation IV*. Munich: Wilhelm Fink Verlag, 1995.

Blecher, Joel. 'Hadith Commentary.' In Andrew Rippin (ed.), *Oxford Bibliographies in Islamic Studies*. New York: Oxford University Press, 2016. Available at doi: 10.1093/obo/9780195390155-0192.

Blecher, Joel. 'Ḥadīth Commentary', in *EI³*, 4:61–68.

Blecher, Joel. *Said the Prophet of God: Hadith Commentary across a Millennium.* Oakland: University of California Press, 2018.

Blecher, Joel and Josh Dubler. 'Overlooking Race and Secularism in Muslim Philadelphia.' In Vincent Lloyd and Jonathan S. Kahn (eds), *Race and Secularism in America*, 122–150. New York: Columbia University Press, 2016.

Brinkmann, Stefanie. 'Marginal Commentaries in Hadith Manuscripts.' In Marcus Stock and Christine Lechtermann (eds), *Practices in Commentary*, 6–44. Frankfurt a.M. 2020 [special issue of *Zeitsprünge, Forschungen zur Frühen Neuzeit*, Sonderband 24].

Brown, Jonathan A. C. *Hadith: Muhammad's Legacy in the Medieval and Modern World.* Oxford: Oxford University Press, 2009.

Burge, Stephan R. 'Reading between the Lines: The Compilation of *Ḥadīt* in the Authorial Voice.' *Arabica* 58 (2011): 168–197.

al-Damāmīnī, Badr al-Dīn. *Maṣābīḥ al-Jāmiʿ*, ed. Nūr al-Dīn T. ālib, 10 vols (Qatar: Wizārat al-Awqāf, 2009).

Davidson, Garrett. *Carrying on the Tradition: A Social and Intellectual History of Hadith Transmission Across a Thousand Years.* Islamic History and Civilisation, vol. 160. Leiden and Boston: Brill, 2020.

Gladigow, Burkhard. 'Der Kommentar als Hypothek des Textes. Systematische Erwägungen und historische Analysen.' In Jan Assmann and Burkhard Gladigow (eds), *Text und Kommentar. Archäologie der literarischen Kommunikation IV*, 35–49. Munich: Wilhelm Fink Verlag, 1995.

Gutas, Dimitri. 'Aspects of Literary Form and Genre in Arabic Logical Works.' In Charles Burnett (ed.), *Glosses and Commentaries on Aristotelian Logical Texts: The Syriac, Arabic, and Medieval Latin Traditions*, 31–43. London: The Warburg Institute, 1993.

Karagözoğğlu, Mustafa Macit. 'Commentaries.' In Daniel Brown (ed.), *The Wiley Blackwell Concise Companion to the Hadith*, 159–186. Hoboken, NJ: John Wiley & Sons, 2020.

Lit, Eric van. 'Commentary and Commentary Tradition: The Basic Terms for Understanding Islamic Intellectual History.' *Mélanges de l'Institut Dominicain d'Études Orientales (MIDEO)* 32 (2017): 3–26.

Lucas, Scott. 'An Efficacious Invocation Inscribed on the Dome of the Rock: Literary and Epigraphic Evidence for a First-Century *ḥadīth*.' *Journal of Near Eastern Studies* 76, no. 2 (2017): 215–230.

Sayeed, Asma. *Women and the Transmission of Knowledge in Islam.* Cambridge: Cambridge University Press, 2013.

Schoeler, Gregor. 'Text und Kommentar in der klassisch-islamischen Tradition.' In Jan Assmann and Burkhard Gladigow (eds), *Text und Kommentar. Archäologie der literarischen Kommunikation IV*, 279–292. Munich: Wilhelm Fink Verlag, 1995.

Shinshawrī, ʿAbd Allāh ibn Muḥammad. *Sharḥ ḥadīth Umm Zarʿ.* Cairo: Dār al-Risāla, 2019.

PART I

Formations and Developments in the Early and Middle Periods

CHAPTER 1

Between Philology and Hadith Criticism: The Genre of Sharḥ Gharīb al-Ḥadīth

Stefanie Brinkmann*

Introduction

Some time at the beginning of the third/ninth century in the eastern Iranian province of Khurāsān, the future caliph al-Ma'mūn argued with one of the earliest authors of a *gharīb al-ḥadīth* book, Naḍr b. Shumayl (d. c. 204/820), about the vocalisation of a word in a hadith (*ḥadīth*, pl. *aḥādīth*). In the version of the hadith as it was transmitted by Hushaym b. Bashīr b. al-Qāsim (d. 183/799), the word was vocalised with a *fatḥa* (a); in another version, this one transmitted by 'Awf al-A'rābī (d. 146/763–764), it was read with a *kasra* (i). Naḍr considered the version with a *kasra* (i) to be the correct version and gave Hushaym's dialect as the reason for his different vocalisation: *wa-hādha laḥn Hushaym.*[1]

In the early Islamic empire, understanding differences in vocalisation and the meaning of unfamiliar or unusual words was an essential require-ment for the proper reading of the Islamic sources, Qur'an and hadith alike. Again and again in later centuries, it was stressed that a proper knowledge of the Arabic language should precede any examination of the content of a text. Majd al-Dīn b. al-Athīr (d. 606/1210), author of the famous and widely disseminated *al-Nihāya fī gharīb al-ḥadīth wa-l-athar*, stated that in order to understand hadith properly, one must first comprehend its language (lit., *alfāẓ*),[2] and second, its meanings (*ma'ānī*). 'And without a doubt, the

---

* This research has been carried out within the Bibliotheca Arabica Project, based at the Saxon Academy of Sciences and Humanities in Leipzig (www.saw-leipzig.de/bibliotheca-arabica). I would like to thank (in alphabetical order) the following persons for their sup-port: Joel Blecher, Hannah-Lena Hagemann, Boris Liebrenz, Nadine Loehr, Friederike Schmidt, Anne Weber and Ali Zaherinezhad.

1 Al-Zubaydī, *Ṭabaqāt*, 55–56.

2 The term *lafẓ*, pl. *alfāẓ*, can range in meaning from 'phoneme', to 'word' or 'expression'. In this chapter I usually translate it as 'word', but note that *lafẓ* can have other meanings as well.

knowledge of its words comes first.'[3] In his sixth chapter of the *Muqaddima*, on knowledge and teaching (*al-ʿilm wa-l-taʿlīm*), Ibn Khaldūn (d. 808/ 1406) points out that 'the study (*naẓar*) of the Qurʾān and Ḥadīth necessarily has to be preceded by the sciences of language (*ʿulūm al-lisāniyya*) because it [i.e. *naẓar*] is based on them'.[4]

Issues of vocalisation and the proper understanding of words and expressions, as well as the complexity of grammatical structures, were of key importance in the early period of the Islamic empire (and beyond). With the Qurʾanic revelation and the emergence of an Islamic state in the first/seventh to second/eighth centuries, the Arabic language became the underpinning of religion, politics and administration, and an integrative element in future multi-ethnic and multi-lingual Islamic culture.[5] Thus, collecting linguistic data and standardising the Arabic language (including orthography) was of utmost importance during the first three to four centuries, when major works in the fields of grammar (*naḥw*) and lexicography (*lugha*) were composed. These ambitions were aimed at the standardisation and control of the Arabic language in the Islamic empire, as a basis for administration and trade, and as the official language of communication, as much as they were focused on a religious agenda, that is, for recording (and explaining) the religious scriptures. Qurʾanic Arabic and its cultural environment were considered an ideal model, and accordingly, the major sources for the standardisation of Arabic were the Qurʾan itself, pre-Islamic poetry, the language of tribes from the central Arabian Peninsula[6] and, to a lesser extent, hadith.

Among these main sources for linguistic data collecting, hadith was perhaps the most controversial. The reasons were manifold. Not all transmitters were native speakers of Arabic, and thus their transmissions carried the potential threat of corrupt language. Since hadith transmitters had been active in different geographical regions for many decades, their wide-ranging network was much less limited and controllable as a linguistic source than the Qurʾan. Furthermore, the transmission of hadith was not necessarily verbatim but was sometimes based on content (*riwāya bi-l-maʿnā*); this led to different versions of the same text. Hence, some grammarians and lexicographers were hesitant to use hadith as a source, while others were more comfortable doing so. The grammarian Sībawayhi (d. 180/796),

---

3 Ibn al-Athīr, *al-Nihāya*, 3.
4 Ibn Khaldūn, *Muqaddima*, 2:172.
5 On Arabic and Arab identity from the early to the contemporary period, see Suleiman, *Arabic in the Fray*, and his article 'Ideology'.
6 The idea of a 'pure Arabic' even involved excluding certain tribes as sources for 'language data mining', namely, tribes who, based on their geographic settlement area, were thought to use Arabic corrupted by neighbouring cultures; Suleiman, *Arabic in the Fray*, 52.

for example, quotes only a very few traditions, compared to his teacher, the lexicographer al-Khalīl (d. 175/791), who cites numerous hadiths in his *Kitāb al-ʿAyn*. Despite this reluctance to use hadith as a linguistic source, by the late second/eighth century scholars had started to collect obscure words in hadith. At times these oddities were illustrated and documented with further evidence, such as with cross-references to poetic verses (*shawāhid*). By explaining such obscure words, expressions and different vocalisations, *gharīb al-ḥadīth* represents the first stage of hadith commentary, a stage that took place long before the extensive, multi-thematic hadith commentaries were composed. Notably, in *gharīb al-ḥadīth* texts the explanation of words is usually expressed with either or both of the two terms later used for commentary: *fassara* (*tafsīr*) or *sharaḥa* (*sharḥ*).

This chapter presents *gharīb al-ḥadīth* as a nucleus for the hadith commentary that was to come and reconstruct its lines of transmission for the subsequent centuries. Although its linguistic data had been absorbed by the two traditions of lexicography and hadith sciences, *gharīb al-ḥadīth* books continued to be written far into the middle period and beyond – a fact much neglected by contemporary research. After a discussion of the issue of defining *gharīb al-ḥadīth* and the state of research, I examine the genre under two main rubrics: first, I take a historical approach and briefly sketch the development of *gharīb al-ḥadīth* and concentrate on the authors' provenance and the centres of production in a historical context; second, I examine the arrangement of the books, specifically as it relates to passages that deal with the names of beverages. For this article, I consulted many reference works and historical sources in order to register *gharīb al-ḥadīth* works that are attributed to specific authors.[7] The process of identifying and attributing a *gharīb al-ḥadīth* book to a particular author poses a few challenges: First, many books have not been preserved or are not accessible as manuscripts. Thus, one sometimes must accept an attribution without being able to consult the text. Second, reference works and sources list partly diverging titles, or the title referred to remains uncertain.[8] Third,

---

7 Among them, I collected sources and reference works from *EI²* and *EI³*; C. Brockelmann's *Geschichte der arabischen Litteratur* (*GAL*); Fuat Sezgin's *Geschichte des arabischen Schrifttums* (*GAS*); Kaḥḥāla, *Muʿjam*; al-Ziriklī, *al-Aʿlām*; [Ibn] al-Nadīm, *al-Fihrist*; al-Zubaydī, *Ṭabaqāt*; al-Qifṭī, *Inbāh*; *al-Fihris al-Shāmil*; the *muqaddima* of al-Khaṭṭābī, *Gharīb al-ḥadīth*; the *muqaddima* of Ibn al-Athīr, *al-Nihāya*; and al-Ḥibshī [al-Ḥabashī], *Jāmiʿ al-shurūḥ*. Among Shīʿī books, I have utilised al-Ṭihrānī, *al-Dharīʿa*. The sources I referred to include more than eighty *gharīb al-ḥadīth* titles attributed to different authors from the second/eighth to the twentieth century.

8 For example, the attribution of Ibn Ḥajar al-ʿAsqalānī's (d. 852/1449) *Gharīb al-ḥadīth* is uncertain. His inclusion in the list of *gharīb al-ḥadīth* authors is based on the attribution of a *gharīb* work to him in *Kashf al-ẓunūn* (1:464, where the title is given as *Taqrīb al-gharīb*); a manuscript listed in the *Fihris al-Shāmil*, 1133 (where the title is given as *Gharīb al-lugha fī Ṣaḥīḥ al-Bukhārī*); and the list of authors in Demirel, *ʿUlūm al-ḥadīth*, 136

there is the problem of how to define a *gharīb al-ḥadīth* work. Boundaries between related genres are sometimes fluid, especially regarding works on *mushkil al-ḥadīth* or proper multi-thematic commentaries.[9]

Definition

The term *gharīb* can apply to a specific type of *isnād* (chain of transmission), and to the philological issue of rare and obscure words and expressions. As a category of *isnād*, *gharīb* denotes a tradition with a limited corroboration, that is, a hadith in which one single authority is transmitted for at least one link in the chain. Thus, such a hadith is part of the *āḥād* category, as opposed to *mutawātir* hadiths, which are transmitted by a larger number of reporters. As a single-strand hadith, *gharīb* is often used synonymously with *fard*.[10] The term *gharīb* can also refer to the text of a tradition (*matn*) as a unique text (version). The authoritative value of such *gharīb* traditions has been widely discussed, particularly in relation to which context (e.g. law or creed) such terms may be of value.[11] In this chapter, I do not consider *gharīb* as a category of the *isnād*, rather I discuss it as a lexical term that denotes uncommon and rare words. It can be used synonymously with *nādir* (pl. *nawādir*; rare), *shādhdh* (pl. *shawādhdh*; anomalous), or sometimes *ḥūshī* or *waḥshī* (odd, unusual, vulgar). To varying degrees,

(where the title is given as *Gharīb al-ḥadīth al-Bukhārī*). The title *Taqrīb al-gharīb* is mentioned, e.g. in al-Sakhāwī, *al-Jawāhir wa-l-durar*, 677, and by ʿAllūsh, *al-Jāmiʿ*, 21. Whereas al-Sakhāwī cites this as a commentary on al-Bukhārī, Isḥāq, *Muʿjam*, 296, relates it to the Qurʾan. We cannot be certain if the references above are citations of the same text, but we might assume that this *gharīb al-ḥadīth* work, or one of those mentioned above (if indeed they represent different texts), is not itself a book but the fifth chapter of Ibn Ḥajar's *Hadi al-sārī*, which is the introduction of his commentary entitled *Fatḥ al-Bārī* (which is a commentary on al-Bukhārī's *Ṣaḥīḥ*). This chapter is entitled ʿal-Faṣl al-khāmis fī siyāq mā fī al-kitāb min al-alfāẓ al-gharība ʿalā al-tartīb al-ḥurūf mashrūḥan' (Ibn Ḥajar, *Hadi al-sārī, muqaddima Fatḥ al-Bārī*, 73–208).

9 Such a borderline case is, for example, Ibn Qutayba's (d. 276/889) *Taʾwīl mukhtalif al-ḥadīth*. As a counterpart to his *Taʾwīl mushkil al-Qurʾān*, it deals specifically with problems in lexicography, though his main aim is to argue against hadith-critical attitudes of Muslim groups, above all Muʿtazilīs. Another example would be Ibn Furak's (d. 406/1015) *Mushkil al-ḥadīth* (with its variant titles), which includes lexicographic explanations but focuses on issues of theology. A third borderline case is Qāḍī ʿIyāḍ's (d. 544/1149) *Mashāriq al-anwār*, which is a commentary on the *Ṣaḥīḥayn* and Mālik's *Muwaṭṭaʾ* (with the aforementioned focus); for a brief overview, see https://www.sifatusafwa.com/en/hadith-collections-explanations/mashariq-al-anwar-ala-sahih-al-athar-al-qadi-iyyad.html (accessed 26 October 2022). The third borderline case goes beyond the strict treatment of lexicographic problems and thus is an example of a fluid border between *gharīb al-ḥadīth* and a multi-thematic commentary.

10 Al-Ṭībī, *al-Khulāṣa*, 56–57.

11 Brown, *Hadith*, 94–95, 235.

works on *gharīb* are collections of rare, obscure and foreign words, dialectic variants, unfamiliar synonyms and differences in pronunciation and vocalisation. The works might also extend to rare idiomatic expressions or unusual syntactic structures.[12] *Gharīb* books list monothematic vocabularies or explain words from the Qur'an (*gharīb al-Qur'ān*) or hadith (*gharīb al-ḥadīth*).

Over time, *gharīb al-ḥadīth* came to be integrated into both lexicography (that is, dictionaries) and hadith sciences. In lexicography, *gharīb al-ḥadīth* works fell under the category of topical vocabularies (*mubawwab*), which were quite popular during the early centuries of Islam, offering vocabularies on topics such as camels, humans, weapons or the rain and other natural phenomena.[13] The data from these collections came to be integrated into multi-thematic dictionaries, such as Abū 'Ubayd al-Qāsim b. Sallām's (d. 223/837 or 224/838) *al-Gharīb al-muṣannaf* and Abū al-Ḥasan 'Alī b. [Aḥmad] b. Ismā'īl b. Sīda's (d. 458/1066) *al-Mukhaṣṣaṣ*, and dictionaries arranged by formal criteria (*mujannas*), such as Muḥammad b. Mukarram b. Manẓūr's (d. 711/1311) *Lisān al-'Arab*. In the field of hadith, data from *gharīb al-ḥadīth* collections were useful in the critical analysis of a tradition's text (*matn*) in the wider context of hadith sciences (*'ulūm al-ḥadīth*) and hadith criticism (*jarḥ wa-ta'dīl*); the data also became an essential part of the developing genre of hadith commentary. Nearly all hadith commentaries include some philological information on lexicography and grammar; in fact, philological elements usually represent the first part of a commentary section. As far as we can determine at this time (given the limited research that has been dedicated to this phenomenon thus far), notes on lexicography and grammar are the dominant marginal (and interlinear) annotations in manuscripts of hadith collections. Thus, lexicography (and grammar) constitutes the nucleus from which further commentary and exegetical activity arose.

This oscillation between lexicography and hadith sciences is reflected in the various classifications of the genre. Aḥmad al-Anṣārī, the seventh-/thirteenth-century cataloguer of the Ashrafiyya library in Damascus, assigned works of *gharīb al-ḥadīth* to the thematic category of transmitted sciences/hadith.[14] And in the endowment list of the Damascene Ḥanbalī scholar Ibn 'Abd al-Hādī (d. 909/1503), *gharīb al-ḥadīth* books are also clearly considered part of a hadith-oriented library, even though few volumes

---

12 Baalbaki, *Arabic Lexicographical Tradition*, on *gharīb* in general: 36–45, especially 84–99. In some cases, *gharīb* works contain familiar words, which were apparently included because of their unusual usage in specific contexts.

13 On these topic-centred vocabularies, see Naṣṣār, *Ma'ājim*; Baalbaki, *Arabic Lexicographical Tradition*, 132ff.

14 Hirschler, *Medieval Damascus*.

are dedicated to the topic.[15] The palace library of the Ottoman ruler Bayezid
II (r. 886–918/1481–1512), for which the librarian ʿAṭūfī compiled the catalogue in 908/1502–3, differs from these two libraries in Syria.[16] In Bayezid's
library, *gharīb al-ḥadīth* books were kept in the section on Arabic philology;
namely, with books on Arabic lexicography and linguistics. In the fourth/
tenth century, the bibliographer Ibn al-Nadīm (d. 380/990) listed works
on *gharīb al-ḥadīth* in the philological section (*al-maqāla al-thāniyya*),[17]
while in the *Muqaddima* Ibn Khaldūn (d. 808/1406) addressed the issue
of *gharīb al-ḥadīth* in the chapter on the sciences of hadith.[18] We find such
shifting classifications throughout the centuries; indeed, they mirror the
multifaceted genre of *gharīb al-ḥadīth*.

The State of Research

The *gharīb al-ḥadīth* genre has received comparatively little attention. To
my knowledge, no monograph on the subject has yet been written in a
Western language.[19] With regard to other types of publications that treat
gharīb al-ḥadīth in the context of other disciplines in Arabic and Islamic
studies (e.g. works on lexicography, hadith, etc.) in Western languages,
the genre has received more attention in the field of lexicography than in
books related to hadith, since *gharīb al-ḥadīth* is but one part of the larger
gharīb strand of scholarship. In such works of lexicography, the stress
is on citing (known) authors and their texts, explaining the arrangement of the lexicographic material, and describing the interrelations of
these works.

In contrast to the state of research in Western languages, publications
in Arabic are more numerous, though relevant scholarship only increased
significantly after the year 2000. Many studies also discuss a single *gharīb
al-ḥadīth* author and his method in organising the *gharīb* material; clearly
most works are dedicated to Ibn al-Athīr's (d. 606/1210) *al-Nihāya fī gharīb
al-ḥadīth*, and fewer to Abū ʿUbayd al-Qāsim b. Sallām and Ibn Qutayba

---

15 Hirschler, *Monument*.

16 Necipoğlu, Kafadar, Fleischer (eds), *Treasures of Knowledge*. See the articles by Recep
    Gürkan Göktaş for hadith, and Tahera Qutbuddin's contribution on Arabic philology.

17 Following authors from the Basran and Kufan schools, Ibn al-Nadīm has a chapter
    called 'Tasmiyyat al-kutub al-muʾallafa fī gharīb al-ḥadīth', *Fihrist*, 1:270–271. It is
    followed by the chapter on *nawādir*. Note that books on *gharīb al-Qurʾān* are part of
    the section on the Qurʾan and the Qurʾanic sciences (*ʿulūm al-Qurʾān*).

18 Ibn Khaldūn, *Muqaddima*, 177ff.

19 The first edition of the *Encyclopaedia of Islam* did not include a separate entry on
    gharīb al-ḥadīth; *EI²* has a short general entry on *gharīb* by S. A. Bonebakker; *EI³*, still
    in its beginning stages, does not yet have an entry on *gharīb*, *gharīb al-ḥadīth* or *gharīb
    al-Qurʾān*.

(d. 276/889).[20] Thus, research is often based on known published works from the third/ninth to the sixth/twelfth century, with later adaptations of *gharīb* works rarely mentioned. General studies on *ʿulūm al-ḥadīth* (hadith sciences) in Arabic include a chapter on *gharīb al-ḥadīth*, since it represents an essential part of reading, critically assessing and analysing the text of a tradition. In the same vein, and like publications in Western languages, Arabic works in the field of lexicography include a chapter on the genre of *gharīb al-ḥadīth*.[21] New and revised compilations of 'classical' works and indices are still being published today.[22]

The common approach of listing authors and titles chronologically and describing the arrangement of the linguistic material and the interrelation of the books (both in Arabic and Western languages) neglects three notable aspects. First, regardless of whether the secondary literature is dedicated to lexicography or hadith, most studies by far are restricted to 'Sunnī' authors; that is, the *gharīb* material is collected from Sunnī hadith and refers to traditions from the Prophet, his Companions (*ṣaḥāba*) and their Successors (*tābiʿūn*). Books on *gharīb al-ḥadīth* from the Shīʿī Imāmī tradition are usually not mentioned. For example, the two scholars who have written survey chapters on *gharīb al-ḥadīth*, R. Baalbaki and Ḥ. Naṣṣar, do not mention the Twelver Shīʿī traditionist Ibn Bābawayh (Ibn Bābūya al-Qummī, d. 381/991), who is said to have written a *gharīb al-ḥadīth* work. Ibn Bābawayh's book is supposed to be a collection of difficult vocabulary from traditions attributed to the Prophet and to the first Shīʿī Imam, ʿAlī b. Abī Ṭālib (*gharīb al-ḥadīth al-nabī wa-amīr al-muʾminīn*).[23] Apart from Ibn Bābawayh's book, the other Imāmī *gharīb al-ḥadīth* studies were written recently, in the period from the eleventh/seventeenth to the twentieth century. The Ṣafavid period (907–1135/1501–1722) is thus a clear starting point for the production of Shīʿī *gharīb al-ḥadīth*, and in this sense, *gharīb al-ḥadīth* and Imāmī hadith commentary share a common origin.[24] As recently as 1421/2000–2001, Ḥusayn al-Ḥasanī al-Bīrjandī published a *gharīb al-ḥadīth* work on the collection entitled *Biḥār al-anwār* by the Ṣafavid scholar Muḥammad Bāqir al-Majlisī (d. 1111/1700);[25] but it should be stressed that Shīʿī scholars used the known 'Sunnī' *gharīb al-ḥadīth* books in their studies throughout the centuries.[26]

---

20 See, for example, Shalabī, *al-Khaṭṭābī*; Zaydī, *Manhaj Abī ʿUbayd*; al-Suḥaybānī, *al-Taʾwīl fī gharīb al-ḥadīth*; Badr al-Dīn, *Ibn al-Athīr al-muḥaddith*.

21 See Naṣṣar, *al-Muʿjam*.

22 ʿAllūsh, *al-Jāmiʿ*; Mīrah, *Fihris gharīb al-ḥadīth*.

23 Al-Ṭihrānī, *al-Dharīʿa*, 16:46.

24 See Chapter 6 in the present volume.

25 This book is not mentioned in Demirel's study of Sunnī and Shīʿī hadith sciences, which lists the most recent publications up to the nineteenth century.

26 See Chapter 2.

A second aspect that is neglected in most publications on *gharīb al-ḥadīth* concerns the social and political context of production. Who were the authors of these *gharīb al-ḥadīth* works? What regions did they come from and what were their fields of study? What were the centres of production for *gharīb al-ḥadīth* works? A third neglected issue reflects a common narrative in the history of Arabic literature; namely, the focus on the early Islamic period to the seventh/thirteenth century (and possibly including the eighth/fourteenth century), and the neglect of works from later centuries (apart from the 'modern period'). Studies on hadith literature produced in the middle period have only recently become more vivid, as is reflected in the growing interest in the commentary genre. Hence, most studies on *gharīb al-ḥadīth* end with Ibn al-Athīr's *al-Nihāya*. Naṣṣār mentions the two abridgements (*mukhtaṣar*) of Ibn al-Athīr's (d. 606/1210) *al-Nihāya* by Jalāl al-Dīn al-Suyūṭī (d. 911/1505) and ʿAlī b. ʿAbd al-Malik al-Hindī al-Muttaqī (d. 975/1567), while ʿAllūsh adds Ibn Ḥajar al-ʿAsqalānī's (d. 852/1449) *Taqrīb al-gharīb*.[27]

The History of the Genre

It is not entirely clear who wrote the first *gharīb al-ḥadīth* collection. Often (for example, by Ibn al-Athīr),[28] Abū ʿUbayda Maʿmar b. al-Muthannā (d. 209/824) is credited with being the first. In his *Gharīb al-ḥadīth*, al-Khaṭṭābī (d. 386/996 or 388/998) refers to Abū ʿUbayd al-Qāsim b. Sallām as the first author of such a work,[29] while Naṣṣār points out that it may have been Abū ʿAdnān ʿAbd al-Raḥmān b. ʿAbd al-Aʿlā al-Sulamī (d. c. 250/864).[30] While Abū ʿUbayd's *Gharīb al-ḥadīth* has survived,[31] as far as we know, many of the early works are lost. According to Ibn al-Athīr, Abū ʿUbayda Maʿmar b. al-Muthannā's *Gharīb al-ḥadīth* was a small booklet consisting of a few pages. Ibn al-Athīr mentions two reasons for its limited length; since it was the first book written in this genre, the author could not build on earlier material (subsequent authors tended to integrate their predecessors' data and added to it, so collections grew over time). Second, Abū ʿUbayda's contemporaries were still familiar with the vocabulary of the first/seventh and second/eighth centuries, meaning that fewer words and expressions required

---

27 See n. 8. Naṣṣār, *al-Muʿjam*, 51–52; ʿAllūsh, *al-Jāmiʿ*, 21.
28 Ibn al-Athīr, *al-Nihāya*, 1:5.
29 Al-Khaṭṭābī, *Gharīb al-ḥadīth*, 1:47.
30 Naṣṣār, *al-Muʿjam*, 1:42; Baalbaki, *Arabic Lexicographical Tradition*, 72.
31 The *Fihris al-Shāmil* lists thirteen manuscripts (1131). On the Leiden manuscript as early preserved evidence for Iraqī scholarship, see Brockopp, *Muhammad's Heirs*, 151–154; Witkam, 'The Oldest Known Dated Arabic Manuscript'; on the reception of this work, see also Lecomte, 'A propos de la résurgence des ouvrages d'Ibn Qutayba'.

explanation.[32] Following these earliest collections was al-Naḍr b. Shumayl al-Māzanī's (d. between 203/818 and 204/820) *Gharīb al-ḥadīth*, of which no manuscript has been preserved, as far as we know today.

The best known, most quoted and best preserved *gharīb al-ḥadīth* works up to and including that of Ibn al-Athīr are the following.

1. Abū ʿUbayd al-Qāsim b. Sallām (d. 223/837 or 224/838): *Gharīb al-ḥadīth*.
2. The following works by Ibn Qutayba (d. 276/889): *Gharīb al-ḥadīth*; *Iṣlāḥ al-ghalaṭ fī gharīb al-ḥadīth li-Abī ʿUbayd al-Qāsim b. Sallām*; *al-Masāʾil wa-l-ajwiba fī al-ḥadīth wa-l-tafsīr*; *Taʾwīl mukhtalif al-ḥadīth*.
3. Abū Isḥāq al-Ḥarbī (d. 285/898): *Gharīb al-ḥadīth*.
4. Abū al-Qāsim Thābit (father, d. 313/925 or 314/926) and Abū Muḥammad Qāsim b. Thābit (son, d. 302/914) al-Saraqusṭī: *al-Dalāʾil fī gharīb al-ḥadīth*, or *al-Dalāʾil fī sharḥ mā aghfala Abū ʿUbayd wa-Ibn Qutayba min gharīb al-ḥadīth*.
5. Abū Sulaymān al-Khaṭṭābī (d. 386/996 or 388/998): *Gharīb al-ḥadīth*.
6. Abū ʿUbayd al-Harawī (d. 401/1011): *Kitāb al-Gharībayn fī al-Qurʾān wa-l-ḥadīth*.
7. Al-Zamakhsharī (d. 538/1144): *al-Fāʾiq fī gharīb al-ḥadīth*.
8. Qāḍī ʿIyāḍ (d. 544/1149): *Mashāriq al-anwār ʿalā ṣaḥīḥ/ṣiḥāḥ al-āthār*.
9. Ibn al-Jawzī (d. 597/1201): *Gharīb al-ḥadīth*.
10. Ibn al-Athīr (d. 606/1210): *al-Nihāya fī gharīb al-ḥadīth wa-l-athar*.

Regardless of the identity of the first scholar to collect linguistic data from hadith, Abū ʿUbayd's *Gharīb al-ḥadīth* was certainly a model for later works.[33] As a lexicographer, Abū ʿUbayd also wrote a topical dictionary, his *al-Gharīb al-muṣannaf*. The second constitutive *gharīb* work is Ibn Qutayba's *Gharīb al-ḥadīth*. Ibn al-Athīr refers to these two books by Abū ʿUbayd and Ibn Qutayba, together with al-Khaṭṭābī's *Gharīb al-ḥadīth*, as 'the foundations (lit. *ummuhāt*) of the books [of this genre]'.[34] Later authors basically built upon these early works, revising, criticising and/or complementing their content. Some switched from an *isnād*-based structure that follows the *musnad* type of hadith collections to an alphabetical system, and some differed in the material adduced, but these later works can still be characterised, principally, as completions and critical revisions.

<hr>

32 Ibn al-Athīr, *al-Nihāya*, 1:5.
33 See also Ibn al-Athīr, *al-Nihāya*, 6.
34 Ibn al-Athīr, *al-Nihāya*, 8.

24 STEFANIE BRINKMANN

The tradition of *gharīb al-ḥadīth* reached its apex with Ibn al-Athīr's *al-Nihāya*. After Ibn al-Athīr it seems that the constitutive linguistic data had been collected, and in the seventh/thirteenth century the production of *gharīb al-ḥadīth* slowed down. From the seventh/thirteenth century on, two types of *gharīb al-ḥadīth* books dominate: first, *gharīb* works on post-canonical hadith collections, such as sixth-/twelfth-century 'Abd al-Qāhir al-Suhrawardī on al-Baghawī's *Maṣābīḥ al-sunna*, or Yūsuf b. 'Abdallāh al-Urmayūnī (d. 958/1551) on al-Suyūṭī's *al-Jāmiʿ al-ṣaghīr*; and second, adaptations, such as abridgements (*mukhtaṣar*) or versifications (*naẓm*).

Shīʿī collections follow a different timeline regarding *gharīb al-ḥadīth*. After the *gharīb al-ḥadīth* work attributed to the fourth-/tenth-century scholar Ibn Bābawayh, there was a gap of several centuries before new *gharīb* works were written in the eleventh/seventeenth century. At that point, Fakhr al-Dīn 'Alī b. Muḥammad al-Najafī al-Ṭurayḥī (d. 1085/1674)[35] wrote his *Majmaʿ al-baḥrayn wa-maṭlaʿ al-nīrayn fī gharīb al-Qurʾān wa-l-ḥadīth*[36] and *Gharīb aḥādīth al-khāṣṣa*.[37] Serdar Demirel mentions the book entitled *Ghāyat al-āmāl* by Maḥmūd 'Alī b. Aṣghar al-Ṭabāṭabāʾī (d. 1310/1892) as a *gharīb al-ḥadīth* work,[38] while al-Ṭihrānī simply refers to it as '*sharḥ al-aḥādīth wa-tafsīr al-āyāt*'.[39] Muḥammad Riḍā b. Qāsim al-Najafī's (d. 1303/1885) *Lubb al-lubāb fī gharīb al-ḥadīth wa-l-kitāb* is seemingly equally focused on hadith and Qurʾan.[40] To my knowledge, no recent *gharīb al-ḥadīth* work on Sunnī hadith has been published, while Shīʿī scholars continue to produce in this field today; for example, al-Bīrjandī's *Gharīb al-ḥadīth fī Biḥār al-anwār* was published in Tehran in 1421/2000–2001.[41]

Gharīb al-ḥadīth in History: Centres of Production

The histories of various literary genres often present them as if all these works were produced, transmitted and used equally or to the same extent from al-Andalus, sub-Saharan Africa, to India and Southeast Asia. Even though it is self-evident that this was not the case (naturally some texts and genres were more popular and/or available in certain regions than in others), there

---

35 According to al-Ṭihrānī, *Dharīʿa*, 20:22, al-Ṭurayḥī died in 1085/1674; al-Bīrjandī, *Gharīb al-ḥadīth*, has 1087/1676 or 77.

36 Al-Ṭihrānī, *Dharīʿa*, 20:22.

37 Al-Ṭihrānī, *Dharīʿa*, 16:46.

38 Demirel, *ʿUlūm al-ḥadīth*, 137.

39 Al-Ṭihrānī, *Dharīʿa*, 16:6.

40 Al-Ṭihrānī, *Dharīʿa*, 18:290; Demirel, *ʿUlūm al-ḥadīth*, 137.

41 While al-Bīrjandī's alphabetically organised *gharīb al-ḥadīth* book on al-Majlisī's Shīʿī hadith collection *Biḥār al-anwār* is available online, the aforementioned books were not accessible to me and their inclusion here is based on al-Tihrānī's *Dharīʿa* and Demirel's study on *ʿUlūm al-ḥadīth*.

is still a remarkable lack of geographical and social differentiation in the mapping of Arabic literature. Hence, I attempt to map the genre of *gharīb al-ḥadīth* and contextualise regional shifts in political and social events.

For the formative period, that is, the first/seventh to the fourth/tenth century, the identification of regional centres of production also addresses the social-ethnic dimension of the impact of the *mawālī* in the production of *gharīb al-ḥadīth* books.[42] By the late fourth/tenth and fifth/eleventh centuries, we can speak of such an advanced state of Arabisation and Islamisation, and such a broad and established tradition of *gharīb al-ḥadīth* that questions of ethnicity and language seem to matter less, though the acquisition and knowledge of Arabic remained a challenge for most non-Arab Muslims. Hence, while I raise the issue of ethnicity for the earliest authors of *gharīb al-ḥadīth*, the focus of this section is on their geographical provenance and their main centres of activity.

Mawlā status usually signifies a non-Arab convert to Islam who is 'adopted' by an Arab tribe, clan or patron. This system was important in the transition process from an Arab tribal society to the establishment of the Islamic civilisation, as it crystallised in the 'Abbāsid period. The term *mawlā* is complex and lacks a clear-cut definition. Although it is applied mainly to non-Arab converts who become clients of an Arab patron, it was also applied to freedmen regardless of their ethnicity, especially in the first centuries; and while it is sometimes used as a synonym for a Persian, others use the term to refer to any non-Arab ethnic group.[43] The fluid definition is met by the difficulties of attributing an ethnic descent to an author, given the multi-ethnic nature of many areas and widespread geographical mobility, and sometimes also because of the lack of information, or inconsistent information in the sources.

Still, the concept of being non-Arab seems to be a key factor in the *mawlā* designation. In the first centuries, non-Arabs had to learn Arabic if they wanted to serve in any official capacity and they had to decide whether to convert; if they did convert, they needed it to gain status in this new political and religious order, for example, through military service or scholarship.[44] Even second- or third-generation *mawālī* still recalled these enormous upheavals.

---

42 'Ethnic' and 'ethnicity' are problematic, ambiguous terms because they encompass concepts of shared ancestry, language, social practices, etc. These concepts must be studied as dynamic and socially constructed identities in specific historical contexts. In this subchapter, ethnicity takes the Arabic sources as a starting point and implies an Arab or non-Arab background.

43 John Nawas speaks about a socio-ethnic designation. Nawas, 'The Birth of an Elite', 74–75 n.1.

44 See also Lecker, 'Biographical Notes', 74, with reference to second-/eighth-century Basra. On the role of elites in the establishment of political, economic, and administrative control over the vast regions of the early Islamic empire, see Hagemann and Heidemann (eds), *Transregional and Regional Elites*.

Already in the nineteenth century, the role and importance of non-Arab scholars in the formation of Islamic civilisation (in terms of quantity as well as quality) were subjects of discussion. Influential Islamicists, including Ignaz Goldziher, Josef Schacht and Alfred von Kremer, claimed that the development of Islamic civilisation was largely the achievement of non-Arabs, most of Persian descent. In 1996, Rina Drory stressed the role of an urbanised second generation of Persian converts in the construction of an Arab past and as a link between the local tribal transmitters and the future scholars.[45] Although this view has since been challenged, or at least modified, it is evident that non-Arab converts played an important role. Thus, the impression given in some publications, that 'Arabs' standardised the Arabic language, should be met with caution.[46]

In the field of Islamic law, Harald Motzki demonstrated the participation of Arab scholars in the first two centuries.[47] A much broader statistical approach was taken by the *'Ulamā'*-Project, carried out from 1994 to 2000 by Monique Bernards and John Nawas. In order to determine the share of Arabs and *mawālī* in the fields of hadith, jurisprudence, exegesis, Qur'anic readings and grammar, they analysed ninety classical Arabic biographical dictionaries that covered the first four centuries. Throughout this period, the share is nearly equal (*mawlā*: 23.9 per cent, Arab: 23.3 per cent), with 52.8 per cent unknown. When this is broken down by century, it shows the overwhelming preponderance of Arabs in the first/seventh century, compared to the nearly equal share in the second/eighth century, and finally, a clear preponderance of *mawālī* in the third/ninth century. At the same time, the number of unknown designations rose continually over these four centuries, reflecting the above-mentioned fading of socio-ethnic differences during the development of a pan-Islamic civilisation. The dominance of Arabs in the first/seventh century is clearly explained by their role in transmitting the prophetic traditions.[48]

These results tie in with the findings of this chapter on *gharīb al-ḥadīth* production, as I illustrate below. The *mawālī* had a great influence on *gharīb* production during the period from the second/eighth to the third/ninth century (and even beyond). Before turning to the biographies of the authors of *gharīb al-ḥadīth*, I offer a few insights into the authors' perceptions of the development of language and non-Arab ethnicity.[49]

Ibn Qutayba gives examples of the difficulty of some expressions, stresses the need to ask lexicographers for explanations and speaks of

45 Drory, 'Abbasid Construction'.
46 See, for example, Carter, 'Arabic Lexicography', 106–108.
47 Motzki, 'The Role of Non-Arab Converts'.
48 Nawas, 'The Birth of an Elite'.
49 As the vast majority of *gharīb al-ḥadīth* works have not been preserved and remain unedited or unstudied, I can only present a few voices from the authors of these works.

students (*ṭālibīn*) using *gharīb al-ḥadīth*.[50] We do not have a structured narrative of how the Arabic language developed or how the growing contact and commingling between native Arabic speakers and non-Arabs took place. Al-Khaṭṭābī remarks that by the third/ninth century, there were a growing number of non-Arab (*ʿajam*) hadith transmitters, and this led to the spread of incorrect expressions or pronunciations.[51] While al-Zamakhsharī does not dwell on incorrect expressions or pronunciations, apart from stressing Muḥammad's excellent Arabic,[52] Ibn al-Jawzī offers a clear narrative. According to him, the Prophet, his Companions and their Successors were Arabs who communicated with one another in a common language. Over time, the increased interaction with non-Arabs led to a corruption of the Arabic language. Consequently, most people became ignorant of it and required explanation (*tafsīr*).[53] In contrast to this simplistic narrative, Ibn al-Athīr refers to various levels of vocabulary – common (*ʿāmm*) and specialised or distinguished (*khāṣṣ*) – and the different tribal dialects in the Prophet's time, although he, too, stresses the correctness of the language of the Companions (*ṣaḥāba*). During the conquests (*futūḥ*), however, the Arabs had intermingled with non-Arabs (Byzantines, Persians, Ethiopians, Nabateans and others), such that by the time of the Successors (*tābiʿūn*) foreign languages had begun to influence Arabic.[54]

Turning to the biographies, for the first four centuries, the designation of *mawlā* was taken as key information; this was complemented by the category of the name. But note that many *mawālī* adopted Arab names and an Arab genealogy upon conversion, a point that creates difficulties in identifying lineages.

Biographical analysis shows that many of the early authors were second- or third-generation *mawālī*: Muḥammad b. Aḥmad al-Mustanīr Quṭrub (d. 206/821) was probably a *mawlā*, though his exact ancestry is not known. Abū ʿUbayda Maʿmar b. al-Muthannā was a *mawlā* of the second generation, his grandfather was apparently a Persian Jew.[55] Abū al-ʿAbbās Aḥmad b. Yaḥyā Thaʿlab (d. 291/904), a scholar from and active in Baghdad, was a *mawlā*. In the West, ʿAbd al-Malik b. Ḥabīb was likely of *mawlā* origin.[56] In some cases, authors may have had Nabatean forebears (e.g. the mother of Abū ʿAmr Isḥāq al-Shaybānī, d. between 205/820 and 213/828), or Byzantine (e.g. the father of Abū ʿUbayd

---

50 Ibn Qutayba, *Gharīb al-ḥadīth*, 147–152.
51 Al-Khaṭṭābī, *Gharīb al-ḥadīth*, 1:47.
52 Al-Zamakhsharī, *al-Fāʾiq*, 1:11.
53 Ibn al-Jawzī, *Gharīb al-ḥadīth*, 1:1.
54 Ibn al-Athīr, *al-Nihāya*, 1:4–5.
55 Lecker, 'Biographical Notes'; Madelung, 'Abū ʿUbayda'.
56 Fierro, 'Introduction of Ḥadīth in al-Andalus', 75.

al-Qāsim b. Sallām[57]), or Berber ancestors (e.g. Abū al-Qāsim Thābit and his son Abū Muḥammad Qāsim al-Saraqusṭī). Most non-Arab authors had Persian, often Khurāsānī family backgrounds like Ibn Qutayba, who was born in Kufa into an Arabicised Persian family from Khurāsān that probably went to Iraq in the early ʿAbbāsid period. Muḥammad b. Aḥmad b. Kaysān may have been of Persian descent, since the Iranian name Kaysān came from his grandfather. Many authors of the third/ninth and fourth/tenth centuries were born and grew up, in part, in greater Khurāsān.[58] This is the case, for example, for Abū ʿUbayd al-Qāsim b. Sallām (from Herat), Ghulām Thaʿlab (d. c. 345/956–957, from Abīward, Khurāsān), al-Khaṭṭābī (from Bust, Khurāsān), and Abū ʿUbayd Aḥmad al-Harawī (from Herat). Other places of origin in Iran include Fasā, in the province of Fārs; this was the birthplace of Abū Muḥammad ʿAbdallāh b. Durustawayh (d. 347/958).[59] The prominence of those of often Persian provenance continued well into the sixth/twelfth century: Yaḥyā b. ʿAlī al-Tibrīzī (d. 502/1109)[60] was born in Tabrīz; Ibn Fūrak al-Iṣbahānī (d. 406/1015)[61] was from Isfahan; ʿAbd al-Qāhir al-Suhrawardī (d. 563/1168) was born in Suhraward, in the province of Jibāl; ʿAbd al-Ghāfir al-Fārisī (d. 529/1134)[62] hailed from Nishapur; and al-Zamakhsharī (d. 538/1144) was from Zamakhshar, in Khwārazm.

It should come as no surprise that scholars from greater Khurāsān played an important role, since it was a centre for many branches of early scholarship. The presence of Khurāsānī figures in early hadith scholarship in general is noteworthy, and *gharīb al-ḥadīth* can be seen as part of this early preoccupation with hadith among scholars from this region.

Bulliet assumes that 80 per cent of the population of Iran had become Muslim by the end of the fourth/tenth century.[63] A rapid increase in conversions could be observed following the ʿAbbāsid revolution in 132/750. There were many reasons for this phenomenon, among them the ambition to gain status in the newly established political rule, though economic issues, such as tax and inheritance laws, also played a role.[64] A considerable number of Khurāsānīs came to Iraq during the early ʿAbbāsid caliphate.[65] While this

---

57 Ibn Khallikān, *Wafayāt al-aʿyān*, 4:60, no. 534: ʿwa-kāna abūhu ʿabdan rūmiyyanʾ.

58 On this region that stretches over parts of modern Iran, Turkmenistan, Afghanistan, and Tajikistan, see Rante, *Greater Khorasan*, 2015.

59 Sezgin, *GAS*, 8:106.

60 Kaḥḥāla, *Muʿjam*, 13:214; al-Ziriklī, *al-Aʿlām*, 8:157f.

61 Al-Ziriklī, *al-Aʿlām*, 6:83.

62 Kaḥḥāla, *Muʿjam*, 5:267.

63 Bulliet, ʿConversion to Islamʾ, 31.

64 See Drory, ʿAbbasid Constructionʾ; Paul, ʿIslam in Iranʾ.

65 Bulliet, ʿConversion to Islamʾ; Paul, ʿIslam in Iranʾ; Daniel, ʿConversion IIʾ; Khan, ʿAn Empire of Elitesʾ.

may explain, in part, the social mobility between Iraq and Khurāsān, it does not necessarily explain the huge impact of scholars from those areas. Given that greater Khurāsān was a centre of learning, with a great number of scholars and madrasas even before the Niẓāmiyya was established in Baghdad,[66] it is easy to see that this prosperous scholarship formed the ideal conditions for the development of Islamic thought. The central role its location played in trade with the East resulted in somewhat wealthy cities, and only added to this situation. Hence, Khurāsānī scholars travelled or moved to Baghdad, and Arab scholars relocated to Khurāsān. The Arab Naḍr b. Shumayl (d. c. 204/820), an early *gharīb al-ḥadīth* author, is a typical figure who illustrates the mobility between Khurāsān and Iraq. He was born in Marw, grew up in Basra, studied lexicography (under Khalīl b. Aḥmad), grammar, hadith and *fiqh* in Iraq, and later returned to his hometown of Marw, where he acted as judge (*qāḍī*) and joined the *majālis* of al-Ma'mūn.[67]

Let us now turn to the production centres of *gharīb al-ḥadīth*. Regardless of their descent and birthplace, nearly all *gharīb al-ḥadīth* authors, at some point in their careers, studied in Iraq with famous scholars in the fields of grammar and lexicography, as well as hadith and *fiqh*.[68] As expected, Kufa and Basra initially had pride of place, since they were the centres of grammar (and the respective grammar schools) and lexicography. By the third/ninth century, Baghdad had gained importance in these fields. As the seat of the 'Abbāsid caliphate it witnessed enormous growth and became a centre of scholarship; it was simply 'the place to go'.[69] This shift in importance from Kufa and Basra to Baghdad is evident from the activities of the *gharīb al-ḥadīth* authors. Early second-/eighth- to third-/ninth-century authors were closely connected with Kufa or Basra,[70] and were often affiliated with the school of grammar they adhered to. But from the fourth/tenth century on, many were centred in Baghdad.[71]

Even in the fifth/eleventh and sixth/twelfth centuries, with Baghdad under Būyid and Saljūq rule, scholars still travelled to Baghdad. In 447/1055, the Turkish Saljūqs invaded the city, brought an end to the Shīʿī Būyid dynasty (334–447/945–1055) and promoted a 'Sunnisation' of the city.

---

66 Mottahedeh, 'The Transmission of Learning'.

67 Al-Zubaydī, *Ṭabaqāt*, 55–61.

68 One of the exceptions was 'Abd al-Ghāfir al-Fārisī (d. 529/1134), who remained in the East and travelled to Khwārazm, Ghazna and India (Hind) before returning to his hometown, Nishapur, where he died.

69 Scheiner and Janos (eds), *The Place to Go*, 1–45.

70 For example, Naḍr b. Shumayl, al-Asmaʿī, Muḥammad b. Aḥmad al-Mustanīr Quṭrub, al-Shaybānī, Abū ʿUbayd al-Qāsim b. Sallām, Abū ʿUbayd b. al-Muthannā and al-Mubarrad.

71 Among these, we can list Ibn Thaʿlab, al-Anbārī, Ibn Kaysān, Abū al-Ḥusayn ʿUmar b. Dirham, Ghulām Thaʿlab, al-Khaṭṭābī, al-Dāraquṭnī and Ibn Durustawayh.

Part of this endeavour involved the establishment (by the vizier Niẓām al-Mulk) of the Niẓāmiyya madrasa, which became a centre of Sunnī scholarship. Thus, Baghdad remained the place to go under Saljūq rule and many *gharīb al-ḥadīth* authors studied and taught there. The author Yaḥyā b. ʿAlī al-Tibrīzī (d. 502/1109) grew up in Baghdad, travelled to Syria, stayed in Damascus for a while and visited Cairo, before returning to Baghdad to work at the Niẓāmiyya madrasa. Roughly a generation later, ʿAbd al-Qāhir al-Suhrawardī (d. 563/1168) taught hadith at the Niẓāmiyya. Among his many travels, al-Zamakhsharī (d. 538/1144) stayed in Baghdad before returning to his home, Khwārazm, where he died. The Ḥanbalī Arab Ibn al-Jawzī (d. 597/1200) was native to Baghdad and a highly influential scholar of the city. When Saljūq rule disintegrated, it reformed into individual atabeg domains, such as the Zangid dynasty that ruled in parts of Syria and northern Iraq (521–649/1127–1250). The peak of *gharīb al-ḥadīth* activity, namely Ibn al-Athīr's *al-Nihāya fī gharīb al-ḥadīth*, happened in Mosul under Zangid rule.

Baghdad remained a centre of scholarship into the seventh/thirteenth century, under Sunnī ʿAbbāsid and Ayyūbid power. Political constellations allowed for travel between Iraq, Egypt, Syria and even Turkey, then under the dynasty of the Rum Saljūqs. Muwaffaq al-Dīn ʿAbd al-Laṭīf al-Baghdādī's biography is rather typical; he wrote the *gharīb al-ḥadīth* book *al-Mujarrad li-lughat* [or *gharīb*] *al-ḥadīth*. ʿAbd al-Laṭīf al-Baghdādī, who was born and died in Baghdad, travelled to Egypt, Syria, Jerusalem (then under Ayyūbid rule) and the territories of the Rum Saljūqs. With the end of the ʿAbbāsid caliphate in 656/1258, political constellations in the Near and Middle East changed and new centres of scholarship arose.

Beside greater Khurāsān and Iraq, the West, or more precisely al-Andalus, was another site of early *gharīb al-ḥadīth* scholarship. The emirate of Cordoba (138–317/756–929) and the succeeding caliphate of Cordoba (317–422/929–1031) ushered in a period of cultural blossoming. Hadith studies were introduced to al-Andalus from the second half of the second/eighth century, through works such as Mālik b. Anas's (d. 179/795) *Muwaṭṭaʾ*. One of the central figures in the introduction of hadith to al-Andalus was ʿAbd al-Malik b. Ḥabīb al-Qurṭubī (d. 238/852), who was born in Ḥiṣn Wāṭ, close to Granada, and flourished in Cordoba, where he also died. By the first half of the third/ninth century, Mālikī law was established as the predominant *madhhab* in al-Andalus, and in this context ʿAbd al-Malik b. Ḥabīb wrote a *gharīb al-ḥadīth* book on Mālik's *Muwaṭṭaʾ*. Like other early hadith scholars, he travelled to the East, namely to Mecca, Medina and Egypt, in order to study with local scholars and collect books from the East (*mashriq*) to bring back to his native land.[72] There was a clear dominance of Egyptian

---

72 See the preface to ʿAbd al-Malik, *Tafsīr gharīb al-Muwaṭṭaʾ*, 1:23. Fierro, 'Introduction of Ḥadīth', 77–78. See also Akmaluddin, 'Epistemology of *Sharḥ Ḥadīth*'.

and Medinese traditionists in al-Andalus at this earliest stage – it was only in the second half of the third/ninth century that Andalusī (hadith) scholars began to train in Iraq, too.[73] Egypt and Arabia remained important destinations for Andalusī scholars, however. Abū al-Qāsim Thābit and his son Muḥammad Qāsim b. Thābit al-Saraqusṭī followed the Ḥijāzī and Egyptian route for their *riḥla*. In around 288/900 they travelled from Saragossa to the east and studied in Egypt and Mecca with known scholars. They returned to al-Andalus in 294/906 as experts in language (*lugha*) and hadith, and jointly produced the well-known *gharīb al-ḥadīth* book entitled *al-Dalāʾil fī sharḥ mā aghfala Abū ʿUbayd wa-Ibn Qutayba min gharīb al-ḥadīth*. The book merges, critically revises and complements the works of Abū ʿUbayd and Ibn Qutayba.

Under Almoravid (al-Murābiṭ) rule (mid-fifth/eleventh century to 541/1147), Qāḍī ʿIyāḍ (d. 544/1149, fl. Ceuta, Granada, Marrakesh) produced his *Mashāriq al-anwār ʿalā ṣaḥīḥ al-āthār (fī tafsīr gharīb al-ḥadīth)*, a work that reflects the aforementioned fluid boundary between *gharīb* and commentary. The influential *Maṭāliʿ al-anwār ʿalā ṣiḥāḥ al-āthār (fī fatḥ mā staghlaqa min kitāb al-Muwaṭṭaʾ wa-kitāb Muslim wa-kitāb al-Bukhārī)* by Ibn Qurqūl (Ibrāhīm b. Yūsuf, d. 569/1173) was likewise produced under the Almoravid (al-Murābiṭ) and Almohad (al-Muwaḥḥid) dynasties, which stretched from parts of the Maghrib to al-Andalus. Nūr al-Dīn b. al-Khaṭīb al-Dahsha al-Ḥamawī's (d. 834/1431) *Tahdhīb al-maṭāliʿ* and *Tuḥfat dhawī al-arab fī mushkil al-asmāʾ wa-l-nasab*, and al-Ḥusāmī al-Qirīmī's *Muntakhab maṭāliʿ al-anwār* (written in 757/1356) all include excerpts from Ibn Qurqūl's *Maṭāliʿ*; al-Suyūṭī is supposed to have used it for his *Tuḥfat dhawī al-adab*.[74] The *Maṭāliʿ* was apparently versified by Muḥammad b. Muḥammad al-Baʿlī al-Mawṣilī (d. 774/1372).[75] The reception of Ibn Qurqūl's *Maṭāliʿ* thus continued far into eighth-/fourteenth- and ninth-/fifteenth-century Egypt and Syria. Apart from al-Andalus and parts of Morocco, however, *gharīb al-ḥadīth* books are largely absent from the Maghrib.

To sum up, regarding the centres of *gharīb al-ḥadīth* production up until the seventh/thirteenth century, we know that the biographies of *gharīb al-ḥadīth* authors mention travels to Egypt, Mecca, Medina, Mosul, and Syria (Aleppo and Damascus), although these cities and regions do not appear to have been important production centres for *gharīb al-ḥadīth* works until the seventh/thirteenth century. While Motzki identifies several centres of Islamic law in the first two centuries (Mecca and Medina, Kufa and Basra, Yemen, Syria, Egypt, and Khurāsān), it seems that there were

---

73 Fierro, 'Introduction of Ḥadīth', 77–78.
74 Brockelmann, *GAL*, 1:370–371, 2:66, Suppl. 1:633, 2:70–71.
75 Kaḥḥāla, *Muʿjam*, 11:235–236; al-Ziriklī, *al-Aʿlām*, 7:39–40.

far fewer places of production for the *gharīb al-ḥadīth* works. Iraq was defi-
nitely the centre of *gharīb al-ḥadīth* activity from the Umayyad period until
the seventh/thirteenth century; work then began in Basra and Kufa, and
then continued in Baghdad from the third/ninth century. Other regions
of *gharīb al-ḥadīth* activity include greater Khurāsān in the east and al-
Andalus (including Morocco, in the case of Qāḍī ʿIyāḍ and Ibn Qurqūl) in
the west.

This pattern of *gharīb al-ḥadīth* production and its scholarly network
changed during the seventh/thirteenth and eighth/fourteenth centuries.
Apart from ʿAbd al-Laṭīf al-Baghdādī's *al-Mujarrad*, we do not know of any
major work of *gharīb al-ḥadīth* that was composed in the seventh/thirteenth
century.[76] There were many reasons for this. The most obvious is that Ibn
al-Athīr's *al-Nihāya* had collected everything that needed to be said about
obscure and foreign words in hadith, and so there was no need to add anything further. In addition, Iraq and the regions to the east suffered from
political turmoil. The Mongol invasion of Baghdad in 656/1258 ended the
ʿAbbāsid caliphate, destroying important economic infrastructures. Baghdad lost a large proportion of its population during this invasion. It ceased
to be a central political power under Mongol rule, which was characterised
by multiple urban centres such as Tabriz, Sultaniyya and Maragha. Even
though Mongol and post-Mongol rule stimulated its own distinct cultural
and scientific activities, it seems that religious scholarship on the Qurʾan
and hadith found less patronage than before the conquest – at least until
Ghazan Khān's conversion to Islam in 694/1295. Sunnī scholarship found
support further to the west, in the Mamlūk Empire. The centres of *gharīb
al-ḥadīth* production thus shifted to Egypt and partly to Syria. While until
then many authors had hailed from the east (Iran and Central Asia) and
the west (mainly al-Andalus), from the eighth/fourteenth century on most
authors were from Syria or Egypt.[77]

The beginnings of Mamlūk rule were characterised by power struggles;
they were not firmly established in Egypt until the rule of Sultan Baybars
(r. 658–676/1260–1277). Syria remained a contested region throughout the
seventh/thirteenth century; finally, Egypt and Syria were united under the
Mamlūks in the eighth/fourteenth century. At this point, some limited *gharīb
al-ḥadīth* activity resumed, in the figures of Muḥammad b. Muḥammad

---

76 Aḥmad b. ʿAbdallāh al-Ṭabarī (d. 694/1295), born and active in Mecca, with ties to
    Rasūlid Yemen, wrote two alphabetical rearrangements of Abū ʿUbayd al-Qāsim's
    Gharīb al-ḥadīth: *al-Durr al-manthūr li-l-Malik al-Manṣūr* and *Taqrīb al-marām
    fī gharīb al-Qāsim b. Sallām* (see ʿal-Ṭabarī', in *EI²*, 10:16).
77 Examples include Muḥammad b. Muḥammad al-Mawṣilī al-Baʿlī (d. 774/1372),
    Ismāʿīl b. Shams al-Dīn Muḥammad b. Birdis al-Baʿlbakī (d. 786/1384), Maḥmūd b.
    Muḥammad al-Dahsha al-Ḥamawī (834/1430), Ibn Ḥajar al-ʿAsqalānī (d. 852/1449)
    and Qāsim b. Quṭlūbughā (d. 879/1474).

al-Mawṣilī al-Baʿlī,[78] who was born in Baalbek, active in Damascus and Hama, and died in Tripoli in 774/1372, and Ismāʿīl b. Muḥammad b. Bardis al-Baʿlbakī (d. 786/1384), from Baalbek.[79] These two authors wrote versifications of earlier *gharīb al-ḥadīth* books: al-Mawṣilī al-Baʿlī's *Lawāmiʿ al-anwār fī naẓm gharīb al-Muwaṭṭaʾ wa-Muslim* seems to be a versification of Ibn Qurqūl's *Maṭāliʿ al-anwār*, while Ibn Bardis al-Baʿlbakī's [*al-Kifāya fī*] *naẓm al-Nihāya* is a versification of Ibn al-Athīr's *al-Nihāya*. The ninth/fifteenth century saw an expansion of the Mamlūk Empire via the Hijaz to Yemen, but internal strife and war expenditures weakened Mamlūk power during this time. In the eighth/fourteenth and ninth/fifteenth centuries, vast regions of the Middle East (and beyond) were also ravaged by the plague, which led to a substantial decrease in population and severe economic crises. Further to the north, in Turkey, the first Ottoman sultans established and expanded their power in the eighth/fourteenth century, as rivals (and sometimes allies) of the Mamlūks, before defeating them in the early tenth/sixteenth century by invading Syria (in 922/1516) and conquering Egypt (in 923/1517).

One would think that such periods of political instability and socioeconomic crisis were not necessarily favourable to intellectual productivity. But even in times of crisis, we can sometimes observe an impressive output of cultural production, a paradox that Carl Petry pointed out with regard to patronage during the later Mamlūk period.[80] Apart from the fact that some people actually profited from the crisis, the cultural heyday of late Mamlūk Egypt is to a large extent due to the complex nature of Mamlūk society, which comprised roughly three groups: the Turkish Mamlūk elite, civil officials (often *ʿulamāʾ*) and the mainly Arabophone population. The complex relationship between the Mamlūk elite and civil officials was one of interdependence: members of the military elite offered patronage, often through salaried positions (*manṣib*, pl. *manāṣib*), while civil officials acted as mediators between the partly detached Turkish elite and the population.[81] Ibn Ḥajar al-ʿAsqalānī, to whom some sources attribute a *gharīb al-ḥadīth* book, is an example of this Mamlūk-*ʿulamāʾ* bond.[82] Born in 773/1372 in Egypt, he held a number of positions, including the chief Shāfiʿī judge (*qāḍī*) in Egypt in 827/1424. Furthermore, amidst the weakening of political and economic power, many *amīr*s and sultans, as well as their

---

78 Kaḥḥāla, *Muʿjam*, 11:235–236 (he does not mention a specific title, only that al-Baʿlī al-Mawṣilī wrote a versification of the *Maṭāliʿ al-anwār*); al-Ziriklī, *al-Aʿlām*, 7:39–40; *GAL* has him as al-Baladī, *GAL* 2:25, 161; Suppl. 2:20–21.

79 Kaḥḥāla, *Muʿjam*, 2:290 (has the title as *al-Kifāya fī ikhtiṣār al-Nihāya*); al-Ziriklī, *al-Aʿlām* 1:324; *GAL* 1:358 (has a date of death 764/1362).

80 Petry, 'A Paradox of Patronage'.

81 Petry, 'A Paradox of Patronage', 184–185.

82 See n. 8.

wives and children, established pious endowments (*waqf*) in the form of madrasas, mosques, *khānqāh*s and other places of scholarship, and public welfare. Hence, the relationship between elites and civil officials, as well as the practice of *waqf*, enabled scholars to gain influential positions and made Cairo (and also Mamlūk Syria) into a centre of scholarship.[83] Besides Ibn Ḥajar (a Shāfiʿī), his contemporary Ḥanafī colleague Ibn Quṭlūbughā (d. 879/1474) also turned his attention to *gharīb al-ḥadīth*, but in Ibn Quṭlūbughā's case in the context of the Ḥanafī legal tradition: his *Gharīb al-aḥādīth al-madhkūra fī sharḥ mukhtaṣar al-Qudūrī li-l-Aqṭaʿ* seems to be a *gharīb* work based on al-Aqṭaʿ's commentary on the widely disseminated *Mukhtaṣar fī al-fiqh al-Ḥanafī* by Aḥmad b. Muḥammad al-Qudūrī (d. 428/1037).[84] And al-Suyūṭī (d. 911/1505) composed *al-Durr al-nathīr fī talkhīṣ Nihāya Ibn al-Athīr*, one of the many abridgements of Ibn al-Athīr's *al-Nihāya*.

In 922/1516, the Ottoman sultan Selim invaded Syria and then Egypt in 923/1517. Ottoman power expanded to the Hijaz and into parts of Yemen, where they secured control over the holy sites and harbours important for the Indian Ocean trade. By way of these established trade and pilgrimage routes, three scholars to whom *gharīb al-ḥadīth* works have been attributed arrived from the Indian Sultanate of Gujarat: ʿĪsā b. Muḥammad Quṭb al-Dīn al-Safawī (d. 953/1546), ʿAlī al-Muttaqī al-Hindī (d. 975/1567)[85] and a certain ʿAlī al-Hindī (lived around 952/1545).[86] All three are said to have composed abridgements of Ibn al-Athīr's *al-Nihāya*, all with the same simple title *Mukhtaṣar al-Nihāya*. In Mecca, ʿAlī al-Muttaqī was the Sufi master of another scholar who hailed from Gujarat, Muḥammad Ṭāhir ʿAlī al-Patanī (d. 986/1578). In al-Patanī's *Majmaʿ biḥār al-anwār fī gharāʾib al-tanzīl wa laṭāʾif al-akhbār* he examined uncommon words in the *Ṣaḥīḥ*s of al-Bukhārī and Muslim.[87] But in general, production of Sunnī *gharīb al-ḥadīth* had slowed down decisively by the tenth/sixteenth century. This contrasts with an increase in Twelver Shīʿī commentary production under Ṣafavid rule, with its patronage of Shīʿī scholarship and Shīʿī *gharīb*

---

83 Since scholars often depended on the patronage of the ruling elite, there was competition to receive support. See Blecher, *Said the Prophet of God*, 49–79; Broadbridge, 'Academic Rivalries'.

84 Al-Ziriklī, *al-Aʿlām*, 1:213. Al-Qudūrī's *Mukhtaṣar* was a standard work in Ḥanafī law, and al-Aqṭaʿ's commentary on it, the *Sharḥ Mukhtaṣar al-Qudūrī*, was widely used in teaching and learning contexts. On different titles, see Sezgin, *GAS*, 1:452; in his edition of Ibn Quṭlūbughā's *Gharīb al-Qurʾān*, the editor ʿAlī al-Ḥafīsha (1971) names a certain *Sharḥ gharīb aḥādīth sharḥ al-Aqṭaʿ ʿalā al-Qudūrī* (54); al-Kattānī, *Fihris al-fahāris*, 2:973.

85 Hosein, 'al-Muttaḳī al-Hindī', in *EI²*, 7:800–801.

86 Kaḥḥāla, *Muʿjam*, 7:258.

87 On him see Chapter 8 in this volume.

al-ḥadīth publications, both of which continued under the ensuing dynasties and into the twentieth century.[88]

The Structure of the *Gharīb Al-ḥadīth* Works

Since most of the early *gharīb al-ḥadīth* works have not been preserved, it is difficult to assess to what extent they all adhered to the same structure. It is clear from what has been preserved, however, that the arrangement of *gharīb al-ḥadīth* works until the fourth/tenth century (and possibly beyond) was based on the *isnād*. Hence, it followed principles of hadith sciences and the *ṭabaqāt* system. Abū 'Ubayd al-Qāsim b. Sallām, Ibn Qutayba, al-Saraqusṭī and al-Khaṭṭābī structured their material according to the transmitters and *isnād* system, while al-Ḥarbī's *Gharīb al-ḥadīth* displays an *isnād* arrangement in combination with formal criteria. Later authors, for example, al-Zamakhsharī and Ibn al-Athīr, rearranged the material and used a system based on formal criteria, that is, some type of alphabetical arrangement. In this chapter, I examine the different types of arrangements, exemplifying structure and content with an excursis on words for (alcoholic) beverages and their containers in selected *gharīb al-ḥadīth* works.

The alphabetical system may have been advantageous in a time of better public education and increased participation of scholars and laymen from various scientific fields and with diverse interests in the study of hadith texts.[89] Since *gharīb* books were widely used in teaching, it was easier for students to navigate through a formally arranged dictionary when searching for a word rather than to sort through *isnād*s. Another basic difference between the various *gharīb al-ḥadīth* works is the use of linguistic evidence to help explain words; this linguistic evidence came from poetry, Bedouin sayings and expressions, and the Qur'an. While Abū 'Ubayd al-Qāsim b. Sallām quotes poetry to a limited extent, later authors sometimes quote linguistic and literary evidence (*shawāhid*) more extensively and digress in part from lexical explanations to a more elaborate treatment of the linguistic data, for example by discussing derivation (*ishtiqāq*) or citing proverbs and anecdotes.

The *gharīb* material in books following the *isnād* structure can be divided into three groups of traditions: those attributed to the Prophet, those from his Companions and those from the Successors. Apart from this division, there seems no further clear arrangement of the material,

---

88 The biographies and historical contexts of Shī'ī authors must be the object of another study. See also Chapter 6.

89 The more user-friendly alphabetical arrangement was also stressed by Ibn al-Athīr, *al-Nihāya*, 1:8.

but this does not exclude logical thematic complexes in minor clusters
entirely. Ramzi Baalbaki argues that, apart from Abū ʿUbayd's *isnād*-based
structure, '[t]here is no further internal arrangement within this general
division'.[90] Overall, Baalbaki's claim seems valid. But this does not mean
that the text is completely devoid of any internal structure, as the discussion of alcoholic beverages shows.

Abū ʿUbayd uses the occasion of a single prophetic hadith to cover the
whole topic of alcoholic beverages; in a passage over roughly seven pages,
he even includes a discussion of the vessels connected to these beverages.[91]
Instead of treating the various appellations scattered over various traditions
separately, Abū ʿUbayd collects them in one place. In doing so, he also disregards the division between prophetic, Companion and Successor hadiths.
In fact, most traditions relating to (alcoholic) beverages are attributed to
Companions or Successors and not to the Prophet. Here content dominates
the otherwise higher order of the *isnād* arrangement.

Abū ʿUbayd treats the topic in three sections: beverages with specific
names, beverages without specific appellations and the vessels that contain
potentially alcoholic beverages. He structures the material as follows: the
starting point is a prophetic hadith, introduced as: 'And Abū ʿUbayd said:
In the hadith of the Prophet, may he be blessed, he was asked about the *bitʿ*
[a honey wine], and he answered: "Any beverage that intoxicates is forbidden."'[92] Although at first glance the question seems to relate to one specific
beverage, the Prophet's general statement that any intoxicating beverage
is forbidden frames the following explanation of appellations. Abū ʿUbayd
then discusses *khamr, sakar, bitʿ, jiʿa, mizr, sukurka, faḍīkh, muṣannaf, ṭilāʾ,
bādhaq, bukhtuj, jumhūrī, naqīʿ (al-zabīb), maqdhī, muzzāʾ* and *ṣaf*.
The section opens as follows:

> With regard to the beverages (*al-ashriba*), there are numerous tradi-
> tions (*āthār*) from the Prophet (may God be pleased with him) and
> his Companions with different beverage appellations, and for each
> [there is] an explanation (*tafsīr*). And the first of them is *khamr*; this
> is what is fermented from grape juice (*wa-hiya mā ghaliya min ʿaṣīr
> al-ʿinab*).[93]

Abū ʿUbayd stresses that there is no disagreement among Muslims
about the prohibition of *khamr*, but there is disagreement about other
beverages. This applies, for example, to *sakar*, made from dates that are

90 Baalbaki, *Arabic Lexicographical Tradition*, 74.
91 Abū ʿUbayd, *Gharīb al-ḥadīth*, ed. Khān, 2:175–183.
92 Abū ʿUbayd, *Gharīb al-ḥadīth*, ed. Khān, 2:175.
93 Abū ʿUbayd, *Gharīb al-ḥadīth*, ed. Khān, 2:176.

not boiled (*lam tamassahu al-nār*). Abū ʿUbayd then quotes ʿAbdallāh b. Masʿūd as stating that *sakar* is *khamr* – and this equivalency makes it a forbidden drink.

The remainder of this section adheres to the same structure: Abū ʿUbayd cites the individual terms and then gives a brief explanation. For example:

> And among these is *al-bitʿ* (*wa-minhā al-bitʿ*), this is the one that was mentioned in the Prophet's (may God be pleased with him) hadith, and it is a wine made from honey (*nabīdh al-ʿasal*). And among these [drinks] is *al-jiʿa*, and this is a wine made from barley (*nabīdh al-shaʿīr*). And among these in *al-mizr*, and it is made from sorghum (*wa-huwa min al-dhura*).[94]

This section on specific appellations concludes with the remark that all these names should be subsumed under the term *khamr* and that the author compiled them in one place because of a prophetic hadith: 'Some people of my *umma* drink wine (*khamr*), whatever they might call it' (*inna nāsan min ummatī yashribūna al-khamr bi-ismi yusammūnahā bihi*).[95]

The next short thematic section deals with beverages for which Abū ʿUbayd does not have specific designations, such as a *naqīʿ* (made from raisins), a wine (*nabīdh*) made from wheat (*ḥinṭa*) or figs (*tīn*), or a condensed *dibs*, from the juice of dates. In sum, Abū ʿUbayd refers to the well-known hadith by ʿUmar b. al-Khaṭṭāb stating that *khamr* is anything that cloaks or changes the rational mind (*al-khamr mā khāmara al-ʿaql*).

This pattern of a general introduction, followed by a hadith that outlines the topic, and a conclusion can also be found in the next section, the last one related to beverages, about vessels. In hadith collections the chapters on beverages (*bāb/abwāb al-ashriba*) contain traditions related to specific vessels that the Prophet had supposedly forbidden. Accordingly, Abū ʿUbayd adds these vessels to his section on (alcoholic) beverages. He starts again with a reference to a prophetic hadith in which Muḥammad prohibited the use of *dubbāʾ*, *ḥantam*, *naqīr* and *muzaffat*. Abū ʿUbayd then explains these terms, for example, by giving other (non-prophetic) traditions. The *dubbāʾ* (gourd) is mentioned with reference to people in Taif, who use gourds as vessels for grapes; they left grapes in them to ferment (lit. until they boil, or bubble, *hadara*). The *naqīr* is a kind of vessel

---

94 On ingredients and appellations, see also Brinkmann, 'Beer in Early Islam'; Brinkmann, 'Wine in Ḥadīth'; Kueny, *Rhetoric of Sobriety*. For the pre- and early Islamic period, see Maraqten, 'Wine Drinking'. For the Mamlūk period, see Lewicka, *Food and Foodways*, 457–550.

95 Abū ʿUbayd, *Gharīb al-ḥadīth*, ed. Khān, 2:180.

made by people in Yemen, who hollowed out the stump of a date tree, and placed various types of dates in it until they started to boil (that is, ferment). The *ḥantam* is explained as a green ceramic vessel that was used to transport wine (*khamr*), and the *muzaffat* is a vessel that was treated with pitch. Following these explanations, Abū 'Ubayd again sums up their relevance: these vessels were forbidden by the Prophet if they contained alcoholic beverages or types of juice, fruit or grain that could undergo fermentation in them, but there is no harm in using these vessels if there is nothing fermenting or alcoholic in them. Part of this conclusion is a tradition from Ibn 'Abbās: 'Anything *ḥalāl* remains *ḥalāl* [regardless of what] kind of vessel [it is in], and anything *ḥarām* remains *ḥarām* [regardless of what] kind of vessel [it is in].'[96]

The section on beverages and vessels is followed by a section on blessings after someone sneezes and then by a section on fasting in winter, both introduced by prophetic hadiths. Thus, major topics might not always show a logical arrangement, but it is noteworthy that within these sections a systematic structure does appear, as is clearly shown by the chapter on beverages and vessels. In explaining various words, Abū 'Ubayd quotes other traditions and occasionally cites poetic evidence (*shawāhid*). Interestingly, Qur'anic verses are not cited, even though the prohibition of intoxicating beverages is addressed in a number of (in part seemingly diverging) Qur'anic verses. Abū 'Ubayd also notes when he is not familiar with a particular term but has been informed about its existence.

This earliest preserved *gharīb al-ḥadīth* book clearly shows why we can see this genre as a starting point for more extensive commentaries: not only does it transgress pure word-by-word explanations and include the historical and geographic contexts for some beverage appellations, but Abū 'Ubayd also frames these appellations in a larger interpretative effort. His way of introducing and concluding thematic sections is a commentary on the legal question of alcoholic beverages (and the vessels that contain them). Hence, he goes beyond a lexicographical explanation, beyond a definition of vocabulary, and discusses the (legal) relevance of related traditions. This is not necessarily true for all topics treated in his *Gharīb*; rather it depends largely on the legal or theological implications of single traditions. But Abū 'Ubayd clearly shows that his ambition was to comment on hadith more broadly, not exclusively on lexicographical grounds.

Al-Ḥarbī (d. 285/898) was perhaps the first to combine the *isnād* arrangement and formal criteria. Only the fifth and last volume of his *Gharīb al-ḥadīth* has survived. This fragment of the fifth volume of his work spans three volumes in the modern edition; we can speculate that the complete work was an extensive *gharīb al-ḥadīth* compilation. Al-Ḥarbī

---

96 Abū 'Ubayd, *Gharīb al-ḥadīth*, ed. Khān, 2:182–183.

complemented the specific lemma of one hadith with other possible permutations of that root found in other hadith. For instance, the subchapter on the lemma m-s-k is supplemented by the lemmata *m-k-s* and *s-m-k*. *Sh-ʿ-r* is supplemented by *r-ʿ-sh*, *ʿ-r-sh*, *sh-r-ʿ*, *ʿ-sh-r*. While the roots do not follow a specific order, al-Ḥarbī usually quotes the hadith alongside the *isnād*, and he occasionally digresses into other semantic fields. The difficulty in navigating his book, in terms of looking up a specific word, was mentioned by Ibn al-Athīr[97] and subsequent authors did not adopt al-Ḥarbī's system.

As mentioned earlier, there is a strong interrelation between the *gharīb al-ḥadīth* books. Abū ʿUbayd and Ibn Qutayba's works constitute the foundation of this genre; all subsequent works were built on them. Abū ʿUbayd's book may be considered the starting point. In his *Gharīb al-ḥadīth* Ibn Qutayba usually does not repeat Abū ʿUbayd but adds details where he thinks information is missing. In his critical reassessment of Abū ʿUbayd's material, his treatment of the linguistic data is also more elaborate. Ibn Qutayba's work follows the tripartite system of traditions from the Prophet, Companions and Successors,[98] and is preceded by six introductory chapters.[99] In these chapters, he discusses words related to jurisprudence (*fiqh*) and judicial decisions (*aḥkām*), namely purification, prayer, almsgiving and taxes, selling and buying, marriage and divorce. This is followed by a collection of words relating to various fields of jurisprudence. These chapters are a separate book, like a small compendium for legal experts. Ibn Qutayba's critical revision of Abū ʿUbayd's material is also evident in his second book, *Iṣlāḥ ghalaṭ Abū ʿUbayd fī Gharīb al-ḥadīth*, in which Ibn Qutayba criticises fifty-three traditions from Abū ʿUbayd. His *Masāʾil wa-l-ajwiba fī ḥadīth wa-l-tafsīr* follows another arrangement, namely 190 discussions (*masʾala*) related to hadith, with a special focus on *gharīb* words.[100] As noted, Ibn Qutayba's fourth book, *Taʾwīl mukhtalif al-ḥadīth*, is a border case.

Regarding beverages, Ibn Qutayba does not repeat those mentioned by Abū ʿUbayd, but he adds further evidence, for example, additional traditions or Qurʾanic verses. In this practice, he is followed by most later scholars. In addition to his *Gharīb al-ḥadīth*, Ibn Qutayba published a separate work on the issue of beverages: *Kitāb al-Ashriba wa-dhikr ikhtilāf al-nās*

---

97 Ibn al-Athīr, *al-Nihāya*, 1:8.

98 Female transmitters have a separate section under the Companions (*ṣaḥāba*).

99 Ibn Qutayba, *Gharīb al-ḥadīth*, 153–240. Baalbaki mentions only five, without further information.

100 This work was written after his *Gharīb al-ḥadīth*, as is evident from a reference of the assumed interlocutor, who refers to traditions that would not be included in the *Gharīb al-ḥadīth* (*masʾala* 21).

fīhā.[101] As the title (The book of beverages and the people's differing views on them) suggests, the book discusses beverages, including their legal impact. It includes poetic evidence, anecdotes and proverbs, and presents and discusses diverging attitudes that concern both the explanation of an appellation and the legal status of beverages. In this sense, it is less a straightforward lexicographical work and more a mixture of *adab* and *fiqh*.

'Abd al-Malik b. Ḥabīb's *Tafsīr gharīb al-Muwaṭṭa'* also refers to Abū 'Ubayd but is completely different in structure. It frames the commentary in question-and-answer sequences. This narrative structure is typical for other legal traditions as well. Thematic chapters, such as that on prayer or purity, have anonymous interlocuters who ask 'Abd al-Malik about specific hadiths: *wa-sa'alnā 'Abd al-Malik b. Ḥabīb 'an sharḥ ḥadīth Mālik*, and are then followed by the *isnād* and quotation of the relevant hadith, and end with 'Abd al-Malik's answer (*qāla 'Abd al-Malik*). Dealing with juridical issues, the *Tafsīr gharīb al-Muwaṭṭa'* digresses from lexicographic commentary to other topics.

Many later authors include less linguistic material on beverages than Abū 'Ubayd or Ibn Qutayba. In his *gharīb* book on Mālik's *Muwaṭṭa'*, the Andalusian 'Abd al-Malik b. Ḥabīb dedicates a few pages to the topic of prohibited beverages under the thematic section entitled *Sharḥ gharīb kitāb al-ashriba*.[102] The interlocutors ask about the prohibition of vessels (*dubbā'* and *muzaffat*) in producing *nabīdh*, as articulated in a hadith transmitted by Ibn 'Umar. 'Abd al-Malik b. Ḥabīb offers several answers in reply to this query about vessels and beverages; these replies are always introduced by *qāla 'Abd al-Malik*. After a brief explanation of *dubbā'*, *muzaffat*, and *ḥantam*, he comments that these vessels are forbidden if they contain a prohibited beverage. He then explains *bit'*, *al-ghubayrā'* (*al-sukurka*, made from wheat, *qamḥ*) and *mizr*, which is made from sorghum (*dhura*), and adds that Muḥammad forbade these beverages if they were intoxicating. The third thematic complex refers to *faḍīkh*, which was known as a beverage of mixed substances (*khalīṭayn*). 'Abd al-Malik points out that in contrast to these beverages, *faḍīkh* would be prohibited even if it were not intoxicating. In short, there is less material on beverage names; rather the key issue is their legal status.

Later authors switched to more user-friendly arrangements based on formal criteria. Al-Zamakhsharī's *al-Fā'iq* is arranged according to the first two radicals of the word. If a lemma is not discussed under its radicals, al-Zamakhsharī usually offers a cross-reference to the hadith in which it appears. Qāḍī 'Iyāḍ's *Mashāriq al-anwār* is arranged by all the radicals of the word.

---

101 Ibn Qutayba, *Kitāb al-Ashriba*.
102 'Abd al-Malik, *Tafsīr gharīb al-Muwaṭṭa'*, 2:428–431.

Further east, in sixth-/twelfth-century Baghdad, Ibn al-Jawzī expressed his criticism of many of the founding fathers of the *gharīb al-ḥadīth* genre by accusing them of leaving out a large body of material. In this, he differs here from other authors who pointed out flaws and lacunae in previous works, but also praised the merits of the founding authors. Ibn al-Jawzī's criticism of al-Harawī might be the harshest, but even Abū ʿUbayd al-Qāsim b. Sallām is not exempt from his reproof: 'Then came Abū ʿUbayd al-Qāsim b. Sallām and authored this scattered and miscellaneous information and added to it and expanded the book until he thought that nothing was left of [noteworthy] *gharīb*. But in this, he failed in many ways.'[103] Ibn al-Jawzī promises to make up for all these flaws by leaving out nothing, so that his book, which follows an alphabetical order, may serve as a substitute for previous works. This presumptuousness is criticised by his contemporary Ibn al-Athīr. Ibn al-Athīr quotes Ibn al-Jawzī's claim to make up for his predecessors' flaws verbatim and then states, regarding Ibn al-Jawzī's book, '... and I recognised that it is merely an abridgement (*mukhtaṣar*) of al-Harawī's book, picking from bits and pieces of its chapters, adding nothing more than some scattered words or isolated formulations'.[104] In fact Ibn al-Athīr's *al-Nihāya* became the pinnacle of the *gharīb al-ḥadīth* genre, with most successor works being adaptations of some kind. A standard work in madrasas for hadith study and a reference book for jurists or theologians, its detailed introduction (*muqaddima*) is a source for the history of the genre until today. Alongside Abū ʿUbayd and Ibn Qutayba's *Gharīb al-ḥadīth* and al-Harawī's *Gharībayn*, *al-Nihāya* is the most widely disseminated *gharīb al-ḥadīth* book and the work that inspires the most adaptations (abridgements, versifications, etc.).

The later, alphabetically arranged *gharīb al-ḥadīth* books usually contain fewer vocabulary terms on beverages – they repeat some terms that were mentioned by Abū ʿUbayd, but not all the names registered in his *Gharīb*, nor do they add new names. For example, al-Zamakhsharī only briefly explains *bādhaq* by quoting Ibn ʿAbbās's answer to a question regarding it: 'Muḥammad was before the *bādhaq*', meaning that Muḥammad lived before the name of this beverage became known in the region, and that 'whatever intoxicates, that is forbidden'.[105] Al-Zamakhsharī then explains that *bādhaq* is an Arabicised Persian word, *bādha* (*bāde*, wine), and that this corresponds to *khamr*. The only other word he discusses from Abū ʿUbayd's list is *mizr* (beer). He quotes a hadith in which people from Yemen complain that their work cultivating the land and the cold is so difficult that they could not manage their labour without this beverage, to

---

103 Ibn al-Jawzī, *Gharīb al-ḥadīth*, 1:2.
104 Ibn al-Athīr, *al-Nihāya*, 1:9–10.
105 Al-Zamakhsharī, *al-Fāʾiq*, 1:90.

which the Prophet said: 'Everything intoxicating is forbidden.'[106] In sum, al-Zamakhsharī has far fewer terms and for those he does list, he differs from Abū ʿUbayd by quoting different hadith material.

Ibn al-Jawzī only discusses *bādhaq*[107] as a kind of (intoxicating) beverage, and *sukurka*,[108] for which he cites Abū Mūsā as stating that it is the wine (*khamr*) of the Abyssinians (al-Ḥabasha). He quotes Abū ʿUbayd's statement that it is made from sorghum (*dhura*) and al-Azharī's claim that the word is not Arabic. Thus, he includes less lexicographic material, and it is not related to any kind of legal commentary.

In contrast to al-Zamakhsharī and Ibn al-Jawzī, Ibn al-Athīr includes most of the beverages Abū ʿUbayd addresses, although some, such as *ṭilāʾ*, are missing. He also discusses *bukhtuj*,[109] *mizr*[110] and *sukurka*,[111] and quotes further traditions to identify the ingredients of the beverages and the etymologies of their names. In doing so, he cites predecessors from other fields of knowledge, such as the lexicographer al-Jawharī and al-Harawī, the author of a *gharīb al-ḥadīth* book. While Abū ʿUbayd and Ibn Qutabya abandoned the lexicographic approach in favour of legal commentary, Ibn al-Athīr's commentary has an outwardly lexicographic function. This might be because of the ongoing formation of Islamic law during the lifetimes of Abū ʿUbayd and Ibn Qutabya, while later scholars such as Ibn al-Athīr could concentrate more on lexicography, since by Ibn al-Athīr's time there were many legal treatises on beverages and the Qurʾanic prohibition of alcohol. Notably, the *gharīb al-ḥadīth* books of the later scholars lack discussions of other aspects of hadith as a science; that is, discussions of specific transmitters, variants, ways of transmission and such. It is the later, more extensive hadith commentaries that merged these issues.

Conclusion

In his edition of Ibn Quṭlūbughā's (d. 879/1474) *Gharīb al-Qurʾān*, the editor ʿAlī al-Ḥafīsha states that '*gharīb al-Qurʾān* books can be considered the first module for the composition of the extensive commentaries (*tafāsīr muṭawwala*)'.[112] In a similar vein, *gharīb al-ḥadīth* books can be considered the starting point for more detailed, multi-thematic hadith commentaries that encompass, to varying degrees, issues of language (lexicography and grammar), variant readings, chains of transmission and

---

106 Al-Zamakhsharī, *al-Fāʾiq*, 3:363.
107 Ibn al-Jawzī, *Gharīb al-ḥadīth*, 1:62.
108 Ibn al-Jawzī, *Gharīb al-ḥadīth*, 1:488.
109 Ibn al-Athīr, *al-Nihāya*, 1:101.
110 Ibn al-Athīr, *al-Nihāya*, 4:324.
111 Ibn al-Athīr, *al-Nihāya*, 2:383.
112 Ibn Quṭlūbughā, *Gharīb al-Qurʾān*, 4.

transmitters, the significance and meaning of legal reasoning, theology and other topics, as well as diverging attitudes among scholars. As noted, the boundary between studies dedicated to hadith lexicography and those that also address further issues of explanation or interpretation can be fluid at times. While many of these works remain unpublished and inaccessible even as digitised manuscripts, the exact categorisation of specific works called *gharīb al-ḥadīth* requires further research. As the nucleus of more extensive hadith commentary and a specialised dictionary for the study of traditions, *gharīb al-ḥadīth* works were widely transmitted, read and studied from al-Andalus to the Balkans, to India and throughout the Middle East. In addition to the transmission and reception of individual books, their content has also survived through other paths of transmission; it has been incorporated into thematically or alphabetically organised dictionaries, such as *al-Mukhaṣṣaṣ* and *Lisān al-'Arab*, in works of *'ulūm al-ḥadīth* and hadith criticism, and in proper, more extensive hadith commentaries.

Gharīb al-ḥadīth works can be classified roughly as follows: the first and basic works were written in the second/eighth and third/ninth centuries, and critical revisions and supplements were composed from the late third/ninth to the fourth/tenth century and up to the early seventh/thirteenth century (for this era, Ibn al-Athīr represents the example par excellence). After the seventh/thirteenth century, a few *gharīb al-ḥadīth* compilations were based on later, post-canonical hadith collections, but most books were adaptations of the books of the second/eighth to seventh/thirteenth centuries (usually abridgements, extracts or versifications). While the production of 'Sunnī' *gharīb al-ḥadīth* had slowed down by the tenth-/sixteenth century, Shīʿī books of this genre were produced from the Ṣafavid period on (907–1135/1501–1722); this activity endured at least into the twentieth century. The only early Shīʿī *gharīb* book is attributed to the fourth-/tenth-century scholar Ibn Bābawayh. Note that, just as it is almost impossible to map geographical borders for the transmission of these texts due to the transregional dissemination of most works, a sharp divide between 'Sunnī' and 'Shīʿī' *gharīb al-ḥadīth* texts is artificial, as most Shīʿī scholars used the books of Sunnī authors when discussing lexicography of the *matn*.

During the Umayyad and 'Abbāsid period, Iraq was the production centre for *gharīb al-ḥadīth* books. This is no surprise, given that Kufa and Basra were early philological centres and Baghdad became the centre for scholarship from the third/ninth century on. In terms of the authors' provenance and their production of *gharīb al-ḥadīth* works, Iran and especially greater Khurāsān in the east, and al-Andalus in the west, can be considered particularly important for the genre in 'Abbāsid times. Due to political and economic developments, the centre of *gharīb al-ḥadīth* production was transferred to Mamlūk Egypt and Syria in the eighth/fourteenth and ninth/ fifteenth centuries. Patronage and the complex interrelations between the

Turkish elite, scholars as civil servants and the Arabophone population enabled a vivid cultural and intellectual life, despite political and economic crises and recurrent waves of the plague. In the Ottoman period, no major noteworthy work was written in this genre, but many earlier works were preserved as references for the study of hadith, law and lexicography. They were studied in madrasas and kept in most libraries, representing a key source for teaching and learning. Already at the time of the founding figures of the genre, *gharīb al-ḥadīth* texts were transmitted from al-Andalus to Iran; this enormous dissemination of *gharīb al-ḥadīth* books continued throughout the following centuries. Future research in libraries in India and sub-Saharan Africa will surely add to this picture.

Gharīb al-ḥadīth works share certain characteristics with other, more extensive commentaries; they build upon each other, intertextuality is often strong, and the goal of both this genre and the commentaries is to explain the content to the contemporary public. In this sense, *gharīb al-ḥadīth* books represent a continuous 'rereading' of previous texts as an adaptation to contemporary needs and serve as a control over this tradition.

Bibliography

Primary Sources

'Abd al-Malik b. Ḥabīb b. Sulaymān al-Sulamī. *Tafsīr gharīb al-Muwaṭṭa'*. Edited by 'Abd al-Raḥmān b. Sulaymān al-'Uthmaynīn. 2 vols. Riyadh: Maktabat al-'Abīkān, 1421/2001.

Abū 'Ubayd al-Qāsim b. Sallām. *Gharīb al-ḥadīth*. Edited by Ḥusayn Muḥammad Muḥammad Sharaf and 'Abd al-Sallām Muḥammad Hārūn. 6 vols. Cairo: al-Hay'a al-'Āmma li-Shu'ūn al-Maṭābi' al-Amīriyya, 1404–15/1984–94.

Abū 'Ubayd al-Qāsim b. Sallām. *Gharīb al-ḥadīth*. Edited by Muḥammad 'Abd al-Mu'īd Khān. 4 vols. Hyderabad: Dā'irat al-Ma'ārif al-'Uthmāniyya, 1384/1964. Reprint of Beirut: Dār al-Kitāb al-'Arabī.

Bīrjandī, Ḥusayn al-Ḥasanī. *Gharīb al-ḥadīth fī Biḥār al-anwār*. Tehran: Markaz-i Buḥūth-i Dār al-Ḥadīth, 1421/2000–01.

Ḥājjī Khalīfa = Kātib Čelebī, Ismā'īl Bāshā. *Kashf al-ẓunūn*. Beirut: Dār Iḥyā' al-Turāth al-'Arabī, n.d.

al-Harawī, Abū 'Ubayd Aḥmad. *Kitāb al-Gharībayn fī al-Qur'ān wa-l-ḥadīth*. Edited by Aḥmad Farīd al-Mazīdī. 6 vols. Mecca and Riyadh: Maktaba Nizār Muṣṭafā al-Bāz, 1419/1999.

Ibn al-Athīr, Majd al-Dīn. *al-Nihāya fī gharīb al-ḥadīth wa-l-athar*. Edited by Ṭāhir Aḥmad al-Zāwī and Maḥmūd Muḥammad al-Ṭanāḥī. 5 vols. Beirut: al-Maktaba al-'Ilmiyya, 1399/1979.

Ibn Fūrak, Muḥammad b. al-Ḥasan al-Iṣbahānī. *Mushkil al-ḥadīth wa-bayānuhū*. Edited by Mūsā Muḥammad 'Alī. Beirut: 'Ālim al-Kutub, 1405/1985.

Ibn Ḥajar = al-'Asqalānī, Aḥmad b. 'Alī b. Ḥajar. *Fatḥ al-Bārī fī sharḥ Ṣaḥīḥ al-Imām Abī 'Abdallāh Muḥammad b. Ismā'īl al-Bukhārī*. Edited by 'Abd al-'Azīz b.

'Abdallāh b. Bāz, Muḥammad Fuʾād 'Abd al-Bāqī, and Muḥibb al-Dīn al-Khaṭīb. 13 vols. Cairo: al-Maktaba al-Salafiyya, n.d.

Ibn Ḥajar = al-'Asqalānī, Aḥmad b. 'Alī b Ḥajar. *Hadi al-sārī*. Edited by 'Abd al-Qādir Shayba al-Ḥamad. Riyadh: Maktabat al-Malik Fahd al-Waṭaniyya, 2000.

Ibn al-Jawzī, Abū al-Faraj 'Abd al-Raḥmān. *Gharīb al-ḥadīth*. Beirut: Dār al-Kutub al-'Ilmiyya, 1425/2004.

Ibn Khaldūn, Walī al-Dīn 'Abd al-Raḥmān b. Muḥammad. *Muqaddima Ibn Khaldūn*. Edited by 'Abdallāh Muḥammad al-Darwīsh. Damascus: Dār Ya'rib, 1325/2004.

Ibn Khallikān, Aḥmad b. Muḥammad. *Wafayāt al-a'yān wa-anbā' abnā' al-zamān*. Edited by Iḥsān 'Abbās. 8 vols. Beirut: Dār Ṣādir, 1397–98/1977–78.

[Ibn] al-Nadīm, Abū al-Faraj Muḥammad b. Isḥāq. *al-Fihrist*. Edited by Ayman Fuʾād Sayyid. 4 vols. London: al-Furqān Islamic Heritage Foundation, 1430/2009.

Ibn Qutayba, Abū Muḥammad 'Abdallāh b. Muslim al-Dīnawarī. *Gharīb al-ḥadīth*. Edited by 'Abdallāh al-Jabūrī. 2 vols. Baghdad: Maṭba'a al-'Ānī, 1397/1977.

Ibn Qutayba, Abū Muḥammad 'Abdallāh b. Muslim al-Dīnawarī. *Kitāb al-Ashriba wa-dhikr ikhtilāf al-nās fīhā*. Edited by Yāsīn Muḥammad al-Sawwās. Damascus: Dār al-Fikr, 1420/1999.

Ibn Qutayba, Abū Muḥammad 'Abdallāh b. Muslim al-Dīnawarī. *al-Masā'il wa-l-ajwiba fī al-ḥadīth wa-l-tafsīr*. Edited by Marwān al-'Aṭiyya and Muḥsin Kharāba. Beirut: Dār Ibn Kathīr, n.d.

Ibn Qutayba, Abū Muḥammad 'Abdallāh b. Muslim al-Dīnawarī. *Ta'wīl mukhtalif al-ḥadīth*. Edited by Ibn Usāma Salīm b. 'Ulyad al-Hilālī. Riyadh: Dār Ibn Qayyim and Cairo: Dār Ibn 'Afān, 1430/2009.

Ibn Quṭlūbughā. *Gharīb al-Qur'ān*. Edited by 'Abd al-Mu'min Abū al-'Aynayn 'Alī al-Ḥafīsha. Beirut: Dār al-Kutub al-'Ilmiyya, 1971.

al-Khaṭṭābī, Abū Sulaymān Ḥamd b. Muḥammad. *Gharīb al-ḥadīth*. Edited by 'Abd al-Karīm Ibrāhīm al-'Uzbāwī. 2 vols. Mecca: Jāmi'a Umm al-Qura, 1402/1982.

Qāḍī 'Iyāḍ, Mūsā. *Mashāriq al-anwār 'alā ṣiḥāḥ al-āthār*. 2 vols. Tunis: al-Maktaba al-'Atīqa and Cairo: Dār al-Turāth, 1975.

al-Qifṭī, Jamāl al-Dīn Abū al-Ḥasan 'Alī b. Yūsuf. *Inbāh al-ruwāt 'alā anbāh al-nuḥāt*. Edited by Muḥammad Abū al-Faḍl Ibrāhīm. Cairo: Dār al-Fikr al-'Arabī and Beirut: Mu'assasa al-Kutub al-Thaqāfiyya 1406/1986.

al-Sakhāwī, Shams al-Dīn Muḥammad. *Jawāhir wa-l-durar fī tarjama Shaykh al-Islām Ibn Ḥajar*. Edited by Ibrāhīm Bājis 'Abd al-Majīd. Beirut: Dār Ibn Ḥazm, 1999.

al-Ṭībī, al-Ḥusayn b. Muḥammad Sharaf al-Dīn al-Dimashqī. *al-Khulāṣa fī ma'rifat al-ḥadīth*. Edited by Abū 'Āṣim al-Shawāmī al-Atharī. Cairo: al-Maktaba al-Islāmiyya, 1430/2009.

al-Zamakhsharī, Maḥmūd b. 'Umar. *al-Fā'iq fī gharīb al-ḥadīth*. Edited by 'Alī Muḥammad al-Bajāwī and Muḥammad Abū al-Faḍl Ibrāhīm, 4 vols. Cairo: 'Īsā al-Bābī al-Ḥalabī, 1971.

al-Zubaydī, Abū Bakr b. Muḥammad al-Andalusī. *Ṭabaqāt al-naḥwiyyīn wa-l-lughawiyyīn*. Edited by Muḥammad Abū al-Faḍl Ibrāhīm. Cairo: Dār al-Ma'ārif 1984.

Secondary Literature

Akmaluddin, Muhammad. 'The Epistemology of *Sharḥ* Hadith in al-Andalus in the Second to the Third Century AH: A Book Study of *Tafsîr Gharîb al-Muwaṭṭa* by 'Abd al-Malik bin Ḥabîb.' *Jurnal Ushuluddin* 26, no. 2 (2018): 113–129. doi: <http://dx.doi.org/10.24014/jush.v26i2.5374>.

'Allūsh, 'Abd al-Sallām Muḥammad. *Al-Jāmiʿ fī gharīb al-ḥadīth, wa-yashtamalu al-matn ʿalā al-Nihāya li-Ibn al-Athīr, wa-l-ḥāshiya ʿalā Gharīb al-ḥadīth li-Ibn ʿUbayd, wa-Gharīb al-ḥadīth wa-Iṣlāḥ ghalaṭ Abī ʿUbayd kullayhimā li-Ibn Qutayba, wa-Iṣlāḥ ghalaṭ al-muḥaddithayn li-l-Khaṭṭābī, wa-l-Fāʾiq li-l-Zamakhsharī, wa-Iʿrāb al-ḥadīth li-l-ʿUkbarī.* 5 vols. Riyadh: al-Maktaba al-Rushd, 1422/2001.

Baalbaki, Ramzi. *The Arabic Lexicographical Tradition. From the 2nd/8th to the 12th/18th century.* Leiden: Brill, 2014.

Badr al-Dīn, Umaymah Rashīd. *Ibn al-Athīr al-muḥaddith: wa-manhajuhu fī itab (al-Nihāya fī gharīb al-ḥadīth wa-l-athar).* Beirut: Dār al-Nawādir al-Lubnāniyya, 2014.

Bauden, Frédéric. 'al-Ṭabarī, Aḥmad b. 'Abd Allāh.' In *EI²*, 10: 16–17.

Blecher, Joel. *Said the Prophet of God: Ḥadīth Commentary across a Millennium.* Oakland, CA: University of California Press, 2018.

Brinkmann, Stefanie. 'Beer in Early Islam. A Ḥadīṯ Perspective.' *Arabist* 36 (2015): 3–34.

Brinkmann, Stefanie. 'Wine in Ḥadīth. From Intoxication to Sobriety.' In Bert G. Fragner, Ralph Kauz, Florian Schwarz (eds), *Wine Culture in Iran and Beyond.* Österreichische Akademie der Wissenschaften, Philosophisch-Historische Klasse, Sitzungsberichte, 852. Band. Veröffentlichungen zur Iranistik. Herausgegeben von Bert G. Fragner und Florian Schwarz 75, pp. 71–135. Vienna: Verlag der Österreichischen Akademie der Wissenschaften, 2014.

Broadbridge, Anne. 'Academic Rivalries and the Patronage System in Fifteenth-Century Egypt: al-'Aynī, al-Maqrīzī, and Ibn Ḥajar al-'Asqalānī.' *Mamlūk Studies Review* 3 (1999): 85–107.

Brockelmann, Carl. *Geschichte der arabischen Litteratur (GAL)*, vol. 1: Weimar: Felber 1898; vol. 2: Berlin: Felber 1902; Suppl. 1, Leiden: Brill, 1937; Suppl. 2, Leiden: Brill, 1938; Suppl. 3, Leiden: Brill, 1942.

Brockopp, Jonathan. *Muhammad's Heirs: The Rise of Muslim Scholarly Communities, 622–950.* Cambridge: Cambridge University Press, 2017.

Brown, Jonathan A. C. *Hadith: Muhammad's Legacy in the Medieval and Modern World.* Oxford: Oxford University Press, 2009.

Bulliet, R. 'Conversion to Islam and the Emergence of a Muslim Society in Iran.' In N. Levtzion (ed.), *Conversion to Islam: A Comparative Study of Islamization*, pp. 30–51. New York: Holmes and Meier, 1979.

Carter, M. G. 'Arabic Lexicography.' In M. J. L. Young, J. D. Latham, and R. B. Serjeant (eds), *Religion, Learning and Science in the 'Abbasid Period*, pp. 106–117. Cambridge: Cambridge University Press, 1990.

Daniel, E. L. 'Conversion II: of Iranians to Islam', in *Eir*, 6:229–232.

Demirel, Serda [Sardār Dimīrl]. *ʿUlūm al-ḥadīth bayna ahl al-sunna wa-l-jamāʿa wa-l-shīʿa al-imāmiyya al-ithnā ʿashariyya.* Beirut: Dār al-Kutub al-'Ilmiyya, 1434/2013.

Drory, Rina. 'The Abbasid Construction of the Jahiliyya: Cultural Authority in the Making.' *Studia Islamica* 83 (1996): 33–49.

Fierro, Isabel. 'The Introduction of Ḥadīth in al-Andalus (2nd/8th–3rd/9th centuries).' *Der Islam* 66, no. 1 (1989): 68–93.

Al-Fihris al-shāmil li-l-turāth al-ʿarabī al-islāmī al-makhṭūṭ. Vol. 2. *Al-Ḥadīth al-nabawī al-sharīf wa-ʿulūmuhu wa-rijāluhu*. Edited by Muʾassasa Āl al-Bayt, pp. 1130–1131. Oman: Muʾassasa Āl al-Bayt, 1991.

Göktaş, Recep Gürkan. 'On the Ḥadīth Collection of Bayezid II's Palace Library.' In Gülru Necipoğlu, Cemal Kafadar and Cornell H. Fleischer (eds), *Treasures of Knowledge: An Inventory of the Ottoman Palace Library (1502/3–1503/4)*. Vol. 1: *Essays*, pp. 309–340. Leiden and Boston: Brill, 2019.

Hagemann, Hannah-Lena and Stefan Heidemann (eds). *Transregional and Regional Elites: Connecting the Early Islamic Empire*. Vol. 1: *The Early Islamic Empire at Work*. Studies in the History of Culture in the Middle East 36. Berlin: De Gruyter, 2020.

Al-Ḥibshī [al-Ḥabashī], ʿAbdallāh Muḥammad. *Jāmiʿ al-shurūḥ wa-l-ḥawāshī: Muʿjam shāmil li-asmaʾ al-kutub al-mashrūḥa fī al-turāth al-islāmī wa-bayān shurūḥihā*. Abu Dhabi: al-Majmaʿ al-Thaqāfī, 1425/2004.

Hirschler, Konrad. *Medieval Damascus: Plurality and Diversity in an Arabic Library. The Ashrafiya Catalogue*. Edinburgh: Edinburgh University Press, 2016.

Hirschler, Konrad. *A Monument to Medieval Syrian Book Culture: The Library of Ibn ʿAbd al-Hādī*. Edinburgh: Edinburgh University Press, 2020.

Hosein, M. Hidayet. 'al-Muttaḳī al-Hindī.' In *EI*[2], 7:800–801.

Isḥāq, ʿAlī Shawwākh. *Muʿjam muṣannafāt al-Qurʾān al-karīm*. Vol. 3. Riyadh: Dār al-Rifāʿī, 1404/1984.

Kaḥḥāla, ʿUmar ar-Riḍā. *Muʿjam al-muʾallifīn*. Edited by Maktabat al-Muthannā. 15 vols. Beirut: Maktabat al-Muthannā, 2010.

Al-Kattānī, ʿAbd al-Ḥayy b. ʿAbd al-Kabīr. *Fihris al-Fahāris wa-l-athbāt wa-muʿjam al-maʿājim wa-mashyakhāt wa-musalsalāt*. Edited by Iḥsān ʿAbbās. Beirut: Dār al-Gharb al-Islāmī, 1402/1982.

Khan, Ahmad. 'An Empire of Elites: Mobility in the Early Islamic Empire.' In Hannah-Lena Hagemann and Stefan Heidemann (eds), *Transregional and Regional Elites: Connecting the Early Islamic Empire*. Vol. 1: *The Early Islamic Empire at Work*, pp. 147–169. Series: Studies in the History of Culture in the Middle East 36. Berlin: De Gruyter, 2020.

Kueny, Kathryn. *The Rhetoric of Sobriety: Wine in Early Islam*. Albany: State University of New York Press, 2001.

Lecker, Michael. 'Biographical Notes on Abū ʿUbayda Maʿmar al-Muthannā.' *Studia Islamica* 81 (1995): 71–100.

Lecomte, Gérard. 'A propos de la itabence des ouvrages d'Ibn Qutayba sur le Hadit aux Vie/XIIe et VIIe/XIIIe siècles. Les certificats de lecture du K. Garib al-Hadit et du K. Islah al-Galat fi Garib al-Hadit li-Abi ʿUbayd al-Qasim b. Sallam.' *Bulletin d'Études Orientales* 21 (1968): 347–409.

Lewicka, Paulina. *Food and Foodways of Medieval Cairenes: Aspects of Life in an Islamic Metropolis of the Eastern Mediterranean*. Leiden and Boston: Brill, 2011.

Madelung, Wilferd. 'Abū ʿUbayda Maʿmar b. al-Muthannā as Historian.' *Journal of Islamic Studies* 3 (1992): 47–56.

Maraqten, Muhammad. 'Wine Drinking and Wine Prohibition in Arabia before Islam.' *Proceedings of the Seminar for Arabian Studies* 23 (1993): 95–115.

Mīrah, Maḥmūd Aḥmad. *Fihris gharīb al-ḥadīth li-Abī ʿUbayd al-Qāsim b. Sallām al-Harawī (157–224H)*. Beirut: Dār al-Bashāʾir al-Islāmiyya, 1987.

Mottahedeh, Roy. 'The Transmission of Learning: The Role of the Islamic Northeast.' In Nicole Grandin and Marc Gaborieau (eds), *Madrasa: La transmission du savoir dans le monde Musulman*, pp. 63–72. Paris: Editions Arguments, 1997.

Motzki, Harald. 'The Role of Non-Arab Converts in the Development of Early Islamic Law.' *Islamic Law and Society* 6, no. 3 (1999): 293–317.

Naṣṣār, Ḥusayn. *Maʿājim ʿalā al-mauḍūʿāt*. Kuwait: Maṭbaʿa Ḥukūma al-Kuwayt, 1405/1985.

Naṣṣār, Ḥusayn. *Al-Muʿjam al-ʿarabī: Nashʾatuhu wa-taṭawwuruhu*. Cairo: Dār Miṣr li-l-Ṭibāʿa, 1408/1988.

Nawas, John. 'The Birth of an Elite: Mawālī and Arab ʿUlamāʾ.' *Jerusalem Studies in Arabic and Islam* 31 (2006): 74–91.

Necipoğlu, Gülru, Cemal Kafadar, Cornell H. Fleischer (eds). *Treasures of Knowledge: An Inventory of the Ottoman Palace Library (1502/3–1503/4)*. Vol. 1: *Essays*. Leiden and Boston: Brill, 2019.

Paul, Jürgen. 'Islam in Iran von 632–1500.' In Ludwig Paul (ed.), *Handbuch der Iranistik*. Bd. 2, pp. 253–265. Wiesbaden: Reichert Verlag, 2017.

Petry, Carl. 'A Paradox of Patronage during the Later Mamluk Period.' *Muslim World* 73 (1983): 182–207.

Qutbuddin, Tahera. 'Books on Arabic Philology and Literature: A Teaching Collection Focused on Religious Learning and the State Chancery.' In Gülru Necipoğlu, Cemal Kafadar, Cornell H. Fleischer (eds), *Treasures of Knowledge: An Inventory of the Ottoman Palace Library (1502/3–1503/4)*. Vol. 1: *Essays*, pp. 607–634. Leiden and Boston: Brill, 2019.

Rante, Rocco (ed.). *Greater Khorasan: History, Geography, Archaeology and Material Culture*. Berlin: De Gruyter, 2015.

Scheiner, Jens and Damien Janos (eds). *The Place to Go: Contexts of Learning in Baghdad 750–1000 CE* Studies in Late Antiquity and Early Islam. Princeton, NJ: Darwin Press, 2014.

Sezgin, Fuat. *Geschichte des arabischen Schrifttums (GAS)*. 17 vols. Leiden: Brill, 1967–2015.

Shalabī, ʿAbd al-ʿĀṭī. *Al-Khaṭṭābī wa-gharīb al-ḥadīth*. [Egypt?]: al-Maktab al-Jāmiʿ al-Ḥadīth, 2006.

al-Suhaybānī, ʿAlī b. ʿUmar. *Al-Taʾwīl fī gharīb al-ḥadīth: min khilāl itab al-Nihāya li-Ibn al-Athīr*. Riyadh: Maktaba al-Rushd Nāshirūn, 2009.

Suleiman, Yasir. *Arabic in the Fray: Language Ideology and Cultural Politics*. Edinburgh: Edinburgh University Press, 2013.

Suleiman, Yasir. 'Ideology, Grammar-Making and the Standardization of Arabic.' In Bilal Orfali (ed.), *In the Shadow of Arabic: The Centrality of Language to Arabic Culture. Studies Presented to Ramzi Baalbaki on the Occasion of His Sixtieth Birthday*, pp. 3–30. Studies in Semitic Languages and Linguistics 63. Leiden: Brill, 2011.

al-Ṭihrānī, Muḥammad Muḥsin b. ʿAlī Āqā Buzurg. *al-Dharīʿa ilā taṣānīf al-Shīʿa*. 25 vols. Beirut: Dār al-Aḍwāʾ, 1403–06/1983–86.

Witkam, Jan Just. 'The Oldest Known Dated Arabic Manuscript on Paper (dated Dhu al-Qaʿda 252 (866 AD).' <http://www.islamicmanuscripts.info/E-publications/witkam_oldest_dated/index.html>, accessed July 2020.

Zaydī, Kāṣid Yāsir. *Manhaj Abī ʿUbayd fī tafsīr Gharīb al-ḥadīth*. Leeds: Majallat al-Ḥikma, 1999.

al-Ziriklī, Khayr al-Dīn Ibn Maḥmūd. *al-Aʿlām: Qāmūs tarājim li-ashhar al-rijāl wa-l-nisāʾ min al-ʿArab wa-l-mustaʿribīn wa-l-mustashriqīn*. 8 vols. Beirut: Dār al-ʿIlm al-Malāyīn, 2002.

CHAPTER 2

The Hermeneutics of al-Sharīf al-Murtaḍā: The Interpretation of akhbār al-āḥād *in* Kitāb al-Amālī

*Ali Aghaei**

Introduction

For Shīʿīs, hadiths (often rendered as 'traditions') and *akhbār* (sg. *khabar*, 'reports') that describe words, actions or habits of infallible figures, including the Prophet Muhammad and the Shīʿī Imams, are considered the most important sources on theological and legal issues because they are seen to hold divine knowledge.[1] Therefore, it has long been an essential challenge for Shīʿī scholars to determine the authenticity of traditions and reports. A common criterion involves examining whether the tradition is a 'concurrent report' (*khabar mutawātir* or has been narrated by a limited number of transmitters, thus a 'single, isolated tradition' (*khabar al-wāḥid*, pl. *akhbār al-āḥād*).[2] If it is a concurrent report, the tradition is well attested and thus considered authentic, but what about a single, isolated tradition? Among the leading scholars of the Būyid period, two distinct attitudes toward isolated traditions are discernible: A 'traditionalist' attitude and a 'rationalist' position. Proponents of the traditionalist view endorsed the

---

* This is a revised version of an article that I published in Persian together with my colleague Mehrdad Abbasi as 'Principles and Method of al-Sharīf al-Murtaḍā in Understanding of *Akhbār al-Āḥād*: The Case of *al-Amālī*', Ṣaḥīfa-yi Mubīn 46 (2010–11): 175–195. I have significantly improved the former article in various ways, particularly in terms of source material and argumentation, and I have contextualised al-Murtaḍā's ideas in the wider scope of early theories of Islamic hermeneutics. I am grateful to Devin J. Stewart for his meticulous reading and correcting my English text, to Ramon Harvey for his valuable comments, and Andreas Ismail Mohr for his careful proofreading.

1 See Kohlberg, 'Introduction', 165.

2 In short, *khabar al-wāḥid* is a report that falls short of the predicate *mutawātir* in that it has only one or a few transmitters at each stage (*ṭabaqa*) of its *isnād*; see Juynboll, 'Khabar al-Wāḥid'; Pavlovitch, 'Ḥadīth: 7.1.1. *Mutawātir/khabar al-wāḥid*'.

authority of *khabar al-wāḥid*, while proponents of the rationalist view regarded it as inadmissible.[3]

Al-Sharīf al-Murtaḍā rejected the traditionalist attitude and adopted Muʿtazilī ideas regarding the fundamental place of reason (*ʿaql*) in the establishment of religious knowledge. He did not accept the authority of *khabar al-wāḥid*; in fact, he rejected them with both rational and scriptural arguments. Yet in his works he interpreted these kinds of reports and traditions. In this chapter I explore al-Sharīf al-Murtaḍā's hermeneutical approach to *akhbār al-āḥād* to present his principles and methods of interpreting traditions. In order to address his theoretical principles, I first investigate al-Murtaḍā's views on the authority of *khabar al-wāḥid* and then discuss some examples of his interpretations of traditions.

The focus of this chapter is al-Murtaḍā's magnum opus, *Ghurar al-fawāʾid wa-durar al-qalāʾid*, known as *Amālī al-Murtaḍā*. This book belongs to the dictations (*amālī*) genre[4] in Arabic literature; it contains eighty dictation sessions (*majlis*, pl. *majālis*) in addition to a sizeable appendix (*takmila*). In each session, al-Murtaḍā discusses the interpretation of a Qurʾanic verse and/or a prophetic tradition that poses a challenge to his theology, explains a rare linguistic occurrence or presents a compelling stylistic case.[5] In each instance, al-Murtaḍā lists a variety of views to provide a vivid image of the scholarly debate on the question, and then presents his own interpretation, which he supports with evidence from Arabic literature and poetry. In this study, I examine twenty-eight traditions in sections entitled 'interpretation of a tradition' (*taʾwīl khabar*) and six additional traditions in al-Murtaḍā's appendix under the general title 'question' (*masʾala*) in al-Murtaḍā's *Amālī*.[6]

---

3 The authority of *khabar al-wāḥid* as a source of religious knowledge was a topic of contention between the Muʿtazilīs and *ahl al-ḥadīth*. While the *ahl al-ḥadīth* assumed that *khabar al-wāḥid* was an authority from which religious knowledge could be derived if it was verified by an unbroken *isnād* of trustworthy transmitters that went back to the Prophet, the Muʿtazilīs rejected the authority of *khabar al-wāḥid* and instead ranked reason (*ʿaql*) as a source for knowledge and interpreting the Qurʾan and hadith. For an overview of early and classical views and thoughts on hadith, see El-Omari, 'Accommodation and Resistance'; Melchert, 'The Theory and Practice of Hadith Criticism'.

4 *Amālī* (sg. *imlāʾ*, 'dictations'), usually followed by the name of the person whose dictations to his disciples and students in various occasions and sessions were gathered, hence also called *majālis* (sg. *majlis*, 'sessions'), is a widespread title in Arabic literature in a variety of fields, including hadith. See Kohlberg, 'Introduction', 168.

5 The book contains interpretations of more than 140 Qurʾanic verses, 34 hadiths, 31 proverbs, approximately 1,350 lines of poetry and biographical information on 65 individuals.

6 I do not examine the traditions that al-Murtaḍā cited as evidence or proof for his argumentations in other sections of his *Amālī*.

Al-Sharīf al-Murtaḍā's Life[7]

Abū al-Qāsim ʿAlī b. al-Ḥusayn al-Mūsawī, commonly known as al-Sharīf (al-Sayyid) al-Murtaḍā ʿAlam al-Hudā (355–436/965–1044), was born in Baghdad to a prominent family of high religious, social and political standing. His father, Abū Aḥmad al-Ḥusayn b. Mūsā (d. 400/1009), was a descendant of Mūsā b. Jaʿfar al-Kāẓim (d. 183/799), the seventh Imam of the Twelver Shīʿīs; he was appointed syndic of the ʿAlid nobility (*naqīb al-ʿAlawiyyīn*) several times. His mother, Fāṭima bt. al-Ḥusayn (d. 385/995), was the granddaughter of the Zaydī Imam Abū Muḥammad al-Ḥasan b. ʿAlī al-Uṭrūsh (d. 304/917), a descendant of the fourth Imam, ʿAlī b. al-Ḥusayn Zayn al-ʿĀbidīn (d. 95/712), and ruler of Ṭabaristān under the title al-Nāṣir al-Kabīr (r. 300–4/913–17).

Al-Murtaḍā's younger brother Muḥammad, known as al-Sharīf al-Raḍī (d. 406/1015), was widely recognised for his literary skills and known as the compiler of *Nahj al-balāgha*, the famous anthology of sermons, letters and aphorisms attributed to ʿAlī b. Abī Ṭālib (d. 40/661). Al-Raḍī was more inclined to politics, and after their father's death, he took on most of his titles and responsibilities in the social and political domain. In contrast, his brother, al-Murtaḍā, was more interested in scholarship and mainly known for his accomplishments as a jurist and theologian. He was also a skilled poet, literary critic and Qur'an commentator. After the premature death of his brother in 406/1015, however, al-Murtaḍā assumed all the religious, administrative and political duties his father and brother had held. He was appointed chief syndic of Ṭālibids (*naqīb al-nuqabāʾ*), leader of the pilgrimage (*amīr al-ḥajj*), and supervisor of the grievance council (*walī al-maẓālim*). When his teacher Muḥammad b. Muḥammad b. Nuʿmān, known as al-Shaykh al-Mufīd, died in 413/1022, al-Murtaḍā became the leading Imāmī jurist in Baghdad.

Al-Sharīf al-Murtaḍā studied language and rhetoric with the well-known poet ʿAbd al-ʿAzīz b. ʿUmar Ibn Nubāta al-Saʿdī (d. 405/1014), poetry and *adab* with Abū ʿUbaydallāh Muḥammad b. ʿImrān al-Marzubānī (d. 384/994), grammar with the grammarian and Muʿtazilī theologian Abū al-Ḥasan ʿAlī b. ʿĪsā al-Rummānī (d. 384/994), and hadith with Ḥusayn b. ʿAlī b. Bābūyah (Ibn Bābawayh), the brother of al-Ṣadūq (d. 381/991–92); he also studied theology (*kalām*), law (*fiqh*) and legal theory (*uṣūl al-fiqh*)

---

7 For his biographical information, I consulted the following secondary sources: Ahmad Muhammad al-Matouq, 'Al-Sharīf Al-Murtaḍā's Contribution', 100–128; Madelung, "Alam-al-Hodā'; Stewart, *Islamic Legal Orthodoxy*; Stewart, 'al-Sharīf al-Murtaḍā (d. 436/1044)'; Abdulsater, 'The Climax of Speculative Theology', 11–60; Abdulsater, *Shiʿi Doctrine*, 16–51. For a comprehensive list of primary sources on al-Murtaḍā's biography, see Madelung, "Alam-al-Hodā', bibliography; Stewart, 'al-Sharīf al-Murtaḍā', 169 n.12; Abdulsater, 'The Climax of Speculative Theology', 15 n.37.

with al-Shaykh al-Mufīd. It is unclear whether he studied with the leading scholar of the Muʿtazila at the time, al-Qāḍī ʿAbd al-Jabbār b. Aḥmad
al-Hamadhānī (d. 415/1024); if he did, it would have been for a short period,
because al-Hamadhānī moved from Baghdad to Rayy around 380/990–991.

The Imāmī Shīʿa widely recognised al-Murtaḍā as their most authoritative scholar of the time. This fact is reflected by the numerous legal and
theological questions submitted to him from Imāmī communities from
many distant cities and regions in Iran, Syria and beyond. His enormous
wealth also enabled him to allocate considerable resources to his studies
and teachings. At the Dār al-ʿIlm,[8] an institution dedicated to studying
and teaching that he administered and probably located at his house, he
received his students and other scholars, convened assemblies for scholarly discussions (*majālis*) and held debates (*munāẓarāt*). In addition to
giving his students access to his extensive library, he distributed quite
generous stipends and provided them with paper. Most of the prominent
Imāmī scholars of the next generation were among his students; for example, Abū al-Ṣalāḥ al-Taqī b. Najm al-Ḥalabī (d. 447/1055), Abū al-Fatḥ
Muḥammad b. ʿAlī al-Karājakī (d. 449/1057), Abū al-ʿAbbās Aḥmad b.
ʿAlī al-Najāshī (d. 450/1058), Abū Jaʿfar Muḥammad b. al-Ḥasan al-Ṭūsī
(Shaykh al-ṭāʾifa, d. 460/1067), Abū Yaʿlā Ḥamza b. ʿAbd al-ʿAzīz Sallār
al-Daylamī (d. 463/1071), and Abū al-Qāsim ʿAbd al-ʿAzīz b. Niḥrīr Ibn
al-Barrāj (d. 481/1088). Al-Murtaḍā was known for his broad-mindedness
as well. His close friends included intellectuals of varying denominational
and religious affiliations, including the famous Sabian litterateur, Abū
Isḥāq al-Ṣābī (d. 384/994).

Along with his teacher al-Shaykh al-Mufīd and his student and colleague al-Shaykh al-Ṭūsī, al-Sharīf al-Murtaḍā was one of the great
Imāmī jurists of Būyid Baghdad; he established the doctrinal, literary and institutional basis of the Shīʿī legal school in the late fourth/
tenth and early fifth/eleventh centuries. He is one of the forerunners
of *ijtihād* in Shīʿī jurisprudence and one of the founders of its legal
theory. With al-Murtaḍā, the rationalist trend of the Imāmī school of
Baghdad reached its peak. His teacher al-Shaykh al-Mufīd maintained
that reason is unable to reach any religious knowledge without the aid
of revelation. In contrast, al-Murtaḍā affirmed that the fundamental
truths of religion must be established by reason alone, in agreement
with the Muʿtazilī thesis. In theology, he adopted the doctrine of the
Basran Muʿtazilīs, a position that was prevalent in Baghdad in his time,
with some modifications concerning Twelver Shīʿī positions on the

---

8 Lit., 'house of knowledge'. The institution was a library founded by the Būyid vizier Abū
   Naṣr Sābūr b. Ardashīr in 381/991 or 383/993. After Sābūr's death, al-Murtaḍā took
   over its administration; see Sourdel, 'Dār al-ʿIlm'.

imamate, the infallibility of prophets, *al-manzila bayn al-manzilatayn*[9] and God's will. Al-Murtaḍā's anti-traditionalist tendency is well known. Most notable here is his total rejection of *akhbār al-āḥād*. Again, he went beyond his teacher al-Mufīd, who accepted the validity of *akhbār al-āḥād* when there was additional evidence for their truthfulness.[10] I discuss this issue in more detail below.

Rejection of the Authority of *Akhbār Al-Āḥād*

Prior to the Būyid period, the dominant trend among the Imāmīs was to look to traditions narrated by the Imams, often *akhbār al-āḥād*, as the basis for theology as well as law, because an infallible Imam was recognised as the only possible source of certain religious knowledge. This 'traditionalist attitude' is best represented by traditionists (*aṣḥāb al-ḥadīth*) in Rayy and Qum, such as Aḥmad b. Muḥammad b. Khālid al-Barqī (d. 274/887), Muḥammad b. al-Ḥasan al-Ṣaffār al-Qummī (d. 290/ 903) and Abū Jaʿfar Muḥammad b. Yaʿqūb al-Kulaynī (d. 329/941). Muḥammad b. ʿAlī b. Bābūyah al-Ṣadūq, the leading scholar of the Būyid period, endorsed the use of *khabar al-wāḥid* as a valid basis for both law and theology. In the works of al-Shaykh al-Mufīd we find growing dissatisfaction with the traditionalist school. This dissatisfaction was mostly related to the development of a Shīʿī doctrine in line with the standards of certainty set by the Muʿtazilīs of the time.[11] For al-Mufīd, isolated traditions provide only 'presumption' (*ẓann*) and not 'certainty' (*yaqīn*). They had to be excluded as sources of law, not to speak of theology. Therefore, al-Mufīd rejected many of the traditions that Ibn Bābūyah collected in his books on the grounds that they were isolated traditions. However, al-Mufīd accepted isolated traditions when they were supported by additional proof (*dalīl*), such as a rational argument (*ḥujja min ʿaql*), evidence from customary usage (*shāhid min ʿurf*) or consensus without dissent (*ijmāʿ bi-ghayr khulf*).[12]

In his discussion of legal hermeneutics, al-Murtaḍā followed his teacher in what we can label 'the certainty school'. Certainty was of crucial importance to al-Murtaḍā, not only in theological issues[13] but also in legal arguments. In his doctrine on legal theory, al-Murtaḍā's 'materialist approach'

---

9 A theological term used by the Muʿtazila for designating the salvation status of the mortal sinner (*fāsiq*); see van Ess, 'al-Manzila Bayn al-Manzilatayn'.

10 McDermott, *The Theology*, 298–299.

11 See Madelung, 'Imāmism and Muʿtazilite Theology', 13–29.

12 McDermott, *The Theology*, 298–299.

13 See al-Murtaḍā, *al-Dhakhīra*, 341. In his view, the issue of whether traditions provide certainty is of primary importance because discussions of the imamate and prophethood are dependent on traditions.

is evident.[14] In his reply to the legal questions he received in 420/1029, al-Murtaḍā provided a clarification of the way that leads to knowledge for all rules of law.

> Know that for the rules of law one must have a source that leads to knowledge (*ʿilm*), for as long as we do not have knowledge of the rule and are not certain that it is beneficial (*maṣlaḥa*), we must allow for its being harmful (*mafsada*). And it is wrong (*yaqbuḥu*) for us to proceed to act based on it, because to proceed to act based on something that may be harmful is like proceeding to act based on what we know is harmful.[15]

To realise this aim, al-Murtaḍā needed criteria for judging source materials that would enable him to have certain knowledge and not mere presumption. Thus, for endorsing or rejecting the authority of a *khabar*, al-Murtaḍā's fundamental criterion is whether it provides certainty. Therefore, he classifies *akhbār* into three categories; namely, those *akhbār* whose truthfulness is known (*maʿlūm al-ṣidq*), those whose falsehood is known (*maʿlūm al-kidhb*) and those whose truthfulness or falsehood is not known (*ghayr maʿlūm al-ṣidq aw al-kidhb*).[16] He puts *al-khabar al-mutawātir* in the first category, because its authenticity is certain, and thus it provides certainty. By contrast, he places *khabar al-wāḥid*, whose truthfulness or falsehood, and thus its authenticity, cannot be endorsed, in the third category.[17] That is, *khabar al-wāḥid* provides no certainty, and at best, if the report is narrated by a trustworthy (*thiqa*) transmitter, it gives rise only to the presumption that it is true, while we must still doubt its authenticity.[18] As a result, al-Murtaḍā does not accept the authority of *khabar al-wāḥid*, even if 'its narrator be one of the most trustworthy'.[19] The critical point in his argument for the rejection of *khabar al-wāḥid* is the possibility of its falsehood, which prevents it from meeting the criterion of certainty.

In sum, action must be based on knowledge, and since *khabar al-wāḥid* is not a source of knowledge, it cannot serve as a basis for action. Therefore al-Murtaḍā, in his various works, frequently states: '*khabar al-wāḥid* imposes neither knowledge nor action.' Thus, 'action on the basis of

---

14 I follow the terminology used by Zysow in his *The Economy of Certainty*, 3: 'For the materialist jurist, probability has no place in the formulation of the rules of law. Every rule of law must be certain in order to be valid.' This contrasts with what he labels the 'formalist approach'.

15 Al-Murtaḍā, 'Jawābāt al-masāʾil al-mawṣiliyyāt al-thālitha', in *Rasāʾil*, 1:203.

16 Al-Murtaḍā, *al-Dharīʿa*, 2:6–8.

17 Al-Murtaḍā, *al-Dharīʿa*, 2:39.

18 Al-Murtaḍā, *al-Dharīʿa*, 2:41.

19 Al-Murtaḍā, *Rasāʾil*, 3:270.

khabar al-wāḥid is not accepted' and '*khabar al-wāḥid* has no authority (*ḥujja*) in law'.[20]

Al-Murtaḍā not only rejects the authority of *khabar al-wāḥid*, but he also explicitly states, 'According to the Imāmī scholars, acting on the basis of *akhbār al-āḥād* is not accepted in law',[21] that is, basing legal behaviour on isolated traditions is not permissible. His rejection of acting based on *khabar al-wāḥid* is as apparent as his rejection of acting based on *qiyās* (analogy).[22] He also claims that there is a consensus (*ijmāʿ*) among Imāmī scholars on this issue.[23] Thus he regards the rejection of acting based on *qiyās* and *khabar al-wāḥid* as distinguishing features of Imāmī legal hermeneutics. In his treatise titled *Ibṭāl al-ʿamal bi-akhbār al-āḥād*, al-Murtaḍā unequivocally states,

> The certain knowledge is acquired by every opponent or adherent of the Imāmīs that in law they do not act on the basis of any report that does not impose knowledge, and that this has become a slogan which they are known by, just as the rejection of analogy is their slogan, and everyone who is in contact with them knows this.[24]

Considering al-Murtaḍā's rejection of the authority of isolated traditions, the following question arises: If the Imāmī scholars unanimously agree to reject the authority of *khabar al-wāḥid*,[25] why are so many *akhbār*

---

20 See al-Murtaḍā, *Rasāʾil*, 1:117, 126, 235, 261, 302, 403, 417; 2:13, 30–31, 47, 60, 123, 129–130, 351; 3:125; al-Murtaḍā, *al-Intiṣār*, 111, 117, 120, 138, 149, 182, 217, 235, 269, 303, 305, 311, 344, 346, 376, 391, 408, 414, 422, 424, 427, 432, 435, 464, 483, 500, 529, 554.

21 Al-Murtaḍā, *Rasāʾil*, 1:24–25; see also 1:203.

22 It is known that the Shīʿī Imams issued strong warnings against the use of analogy, but al-Murtaḍā's argument against analogy is formulated to pursue his demand for certainty: 'We reject analogy ... as a source of legal rules because analogy provides probability not certainty'; al-Murtaḍā, *Rasāʾil*, 1:203.

23 See al-Murtaḍā, *Rasāʾil*, 1:7, 24–27, 206, 211; 3:309.

24 Al-Murtaḍā, *Rasāʾil*, 3:309.

25 Surprisingly, his student and colleague, al-Shaykh al-Ṭūsī claims the opposite, namely a consensus among Imāmī scholars on acting upon *akhbār al-āḥād* in legal issues when they are transmitted in Imāmī books and collections; see al-Ṭūsī, *al-ʿUdda*, 1:126–129. Needless to say, these two opposing consensus claims in almost the same generation of scholars indicates that there was a substantial difference between their doctrines of Shīʿī legal theory, that is, 'the materialist approach' of al-Murtaḍā vs. al-Ṭūsī's 'formalist approach'. See Zysow, *The Economy of Certainty*, 283–284. For a comprehensive discussion on this issue, see Ḥubballāh, *Naẓariyyat al-sunna*, 130–152. Note that al-Ṭūsī's doctrine was not immediately adopted by Imāmī scholars and a line of prominent Shīʿī jurists including al-Qāḍī ʿAbd al-ʿAzīz b. al-Barrāj (d. 481/1088), Abū ʿAlī al-Faḍl b. al-Ḥasan al-Ṭabrisī (d. c. 548–552/1153–1158), Ḥamza b. ʿAlī b. Zuhra (d. 585/1189), and Muḥammad b. Idrīs al-Ḥillī (d. 598/1202) followed al-Murtaḍā's position regarding *akhbār al-āḥād*. Al-Murtaḍā radical rejection

al-āḥād in Imāmī sources, and why are they frequently cited in legal and theological discussions? Is it not because some Shīʿī scholars accept and act based on *khabar al-wāḥid*?

This question often appears in al-Murtaḍā's treatises (*rasāʾil*), and he approaches it from several perspectives. First, he disregards the claim that Shīʿī scholars supposedly act based on *khabar al-wāḥid*. In his argument, he distinguishes between two groups: (1) those scholars on whom one can rely because they comprehend what they transmit and what they leave aside, and (2) those who simply transmit what they have heard and narrate what they have received from their predecessors. According to al-Murtaḍā, the first group, whom he refers to as *mutakallimūn* (scholars of *kalām*, theologians),[26] never act based on *akhbār al-āḥād*. Only the second group, whom he calls *aṣḥāb al-ḥadīth* (traditionists),[27] would argue based on an uncertain hadith for a legal rule. He states: 'These people [*aṣḥāb al-ḥadīth*] argue for the principles of religion (*uṣūl al-dīn*) – such as the uniqueness of God, justice, prophethood and imamate – on the basis of *akhbār al-āḥād*, while it is known to every sane person that they [*akhbār al-āḥād*] do not provide any proof for that.'[28] In his view, traditionists' books and collections do not provide proof for legal arguments and therefore should be set aside.[29]

Nevertheless, al-Murtaḍā acknowledges that in their discussions with non-Imāmī Muslims, Imāmī scholars may refer, particularly, to *akhbār al-āḥād* of non-Imāmīs (not *akhbār al-āḥād* in general), but this is done merely for rhetorical and polemical purposes; they do not cite them in these cases as legal proofs.[30] Nevertheless, according to al-Murtaḍā, one can act based on some *akhbār al-āḥād* when Imāmī scholars unanimously agree on their truthfulness because they find evidence attesting to their authenticity.[31] Interestingly, al-Murtaḍā regards most of the traditions in Imāmī

of *akhbār al-āḥād* was later set aside in favour of a dominant tendency among Shīʿī scholars to follow al-Ṭūsī, who held that the legal reports transmitted by the traditionists of Qum were valid, since they were covered by the consensus of the Imāmī community. See also Madelung, "Alam-al-Hodā'.

26 Al-Murtaḍā, *Rasāʾil*, 1:23–24, 26.

27 Al-Murtaḍā, *Rasāʾil*, 1:26–27, 211. By *aṣḥāb al-ḥadīth*, al-Murtaḍā is referring to the traditionists of Rayy and Qum, whom he considers anthropormorphist and predestinarian, except for Ibn Bābūyah al-Ṣadūq (d. 381/991); see al-Murtaḍā, *Rasāʾil*, 3:310. Al-Murtaḍā does not exclude Abū Jaʿfar Muḥammad b. Yaʿqūb al-Kulaynī (d. 329/941) from this negative assessment; he states that al-Kulaynī's *al-Kāfī* is full of forgeries; see al-Murtaḍā, *Rasāʾil*, 1:410. See also Madelung, "Alam-al-Hodā'.

28 Al-Murtaḍā, *Rasāʾil*, 1:211.

29 Al-Murtaḍā, *Rasāʾil*, 1:26–27, 211.

30 Al-Murtaḍā, *Rasāʾil*, 1:27. Examples of this behaviour can be found in *al-Intiṣār*, where time and again he refers to Sunnī traditions as support for an Imāmī rule.

31 Al-Murtaḍā, *Rasāʾil*, 1:19.

sources as *mutawātir*, even though they are transmitted through a limited number of transmitters and are usually considered *akhbār al-āḥād*. Again, his evidence for this claim is that Imāmī scholars unanimously agree on their truthfulness.[32] In other words, according to al-Murtaḍā, most Imāmī hadiths provide certainty, either because of their *tawātur* status or because of strong evidence indicating their authenticity, namely Imāmī scholars' consensus, which renders them equivalent to *mutawātir* reports.[33]

In brief, we can conclude that al-Murtaḍā takes for granted Shīʿī scholars' rejection of acting based on *khabar al-wāḥid*. In his view, this fact should not be doubted merely because of the existence of *akhbār al-āḥād* in Shīʿī literature. By rejecting the authority of *khabar al-wāḥid*, al-Murtaḍā indeed puts aside one of the most significant sources of Twelver Shīʿī law and replaces it with the concept of the consensus of Imāmīs. As a result, whenever legal inference (*istinbāṭ*) cannot be performed by referring to the Qurʾan or *mutawātir* reports, one should rely on consensus.[34] With regard to disagreements, however, al-Murtaḍā takes reason as the ultimate standard on which arguments ought to be based.

Interpreting *Akhbār Al-āḥād*

Despite his categorical rejection of the authority of *akhbār al-āḥād*, in many of his works, and especially in his *Amālī*, al-Murtaḍā often cites isolated hadiths from both Shīʿī and Sunnī sources and interprets them. Why does he trouble himself so much with (often) figurative/non-literal interpretations (*taʾwīl*) of isolated traditions? According to al-Murtaḍā,

> As far as beliefs are concerned, one can rely on anything proofs lead to. Therefore, whenever the apparent meaning of a tradition runs counter to our beliefs, we must interpret it … We apply this rule to the Qurʾan, whose authenticity is unquestionable, let alone to *akhbār al-āḥād*, about which we have no certainty … In case interpretation (*taʾwīl*) of traditions fails, however, there remains no other option than to reject them.[35]

He also states, 'Each *khabar* whose apparent meaning implies determinism (*jabr*), anthropomorphism (*tashbīh*), or the like, and which necessitates excessive exertion (*takalluf*) to be correctly interpreted should thus be rejected.'[36] Despite its *prima facie* meaning (i.e. al-Murtaḍā's tendency

---

32 Al-Murtaḍā, *Rasāʾil*, 1:26.
33 Al-Murtaḍā, *Rasāʾil*, 1:25–26, 211.
34 Al-Murtaḍā, *Rasāʾil*, 1:11–20, 89, 204–205; 3:312–313.
35 Al-Murtaḍā, *Amālī*, 2:350; see also al-Murtaḍā, *Rasāʾil*, 1:408–411.
36 Al-Murtaḍā, *al-Dharīʿa*, 2:40.

to reject all traditions that imply determinism, anthropomorphism and the like), his statement suggests that these traditions must be interpreted in such a way that they do not contradict Imāmī principles and doctrines unless figuring out appropriate meanings for them requires exertion and arbitrariness.

However, we must not think that al-Murtaḍā resorted to figurative interpretations of traditions whose authenticity he did not endorse. In *al-Shāfī fī al-imāma*, he makes the statement,

> He who [figuratively] interprets (*ta'wīl*) a certain tradition not only would not regard it as inauthentic but also would not even have the slightest doubt about its authenticity. For, if it were otherwise, then he would try to show its falsehood and to prove its inauthenticity rather than to interpret it figuratively.[37]

In another place, he explicitly states, 'It is compulsory upon us to interpret [in a meaningfully correct way] the traditions whose authenticity we are certain of.'[38] We can conclude here that when al-Murtaḍā interprets reports and dedicates himself to elaborating on their various meanings, he has already conceded the legitimacy of these traditions and accepted them as authentic. This agrees with what has already been stated about al-Murtaḍā's position on isolated traditions: he does not accept *akhbār al-āḥād* on their own and does not interpret traditions unless he accepts them as certain, because he sees them as *mutawātir* or as corroborated by strong evidence; this is basically the consensus (*ijmā'*) of Imāmīs.

A cursory look at al-Murtaḍā's elaborations regarding the traditions that are discussed in his *Amālī* reveals that he pays little attention – if any at all – to chains of transmission (*isnāds*) and deals almost exclusively with their texts (*matns*). He does not usually mention the *isnāds* of traditions, and even when he does occasionally, he rarely uses the *isnād* in his evaluation or criticism of the tradition transmitted through it.[39] This manner is fully consistent with his view on *khabar al-wāḥid*. In his view, if the tradition is isolated, then it does not have any legal authority and is invalid for theological issues. Therefore, there is no need to investigate the *isnād* and its transmitters. Moreover, if the tradition is *mutawātir*, or supported by firm evidence, then it is regarded as authentic, and again there is no need to investigate its *isnād*. This explains why, in his book *al-Dharī'a ilā uṣūl al-sharī'a*, he explicitly refuses to go further in discussing the common secondary topics related

---

37 Al-Murtaḍā, *al-Shāfī*, 2:262–263.
38 Al-Murtaḍā, *Rasā'il*, 2:125.
39 For a limited number of examples, see al-Murtaḍā, *Amālī*, 1:304, *majlis* 26, 454, *majlis* 34; 2:172, *majlis* 65. In rare cases, he mentions the weakness of the *isnād*. Interestingly, he interprets these cases as well; see, for instance, al-Murtaḍā, *Amālī*, 2:5, *majlis* 49.

to *khabar al-wāḥid*, including the endorsement or rejection of *al-khabar al-mursal*, or the criteria for preferring some traditions over others while dealing with contradictory traditions. This is contrary to what al-Ṭūsī does when he dedicates a section of his *al-ʿUdda fī uṣūl al-fiqh* to these issues. Al-Ṭūsī accepts the authority of isolated traditions whereas al-Murtaḍā does not. 'Only those who endorse the authority of *khabar al-wāḥid*', al-Murtaḍā says, 'should busy themselves with these secondary issues'.[40]

What remains is to interpret the tradition so that its meaning does not contradict beliefs that are based on solid proofs. Here, al-Murtaḍā's rule regarding the interpretation of traditions is as follows:

> Any probable meaning which has evidence in the Arabic language and literature could be suggested. Whoever is confronted with an odd statement should mention all the semantic possibilities of that statement, because it could be that the speaker intended one of those possibilities. However, we cannot acquire certainty regarding his intended meaning; it is hidden from us.[41]

This shows that whereas al-Murtaḍā requires certainty in accepting a tradition, he opens the door to much speculation regarding its meaning. In defining the meaning of a tradition, therefore, al-Murtaḍā never puts aside any proposed semantic possibility, and he tries to classify traditions by comparing them to one another. In some instances, given the variety of interpretations, he does not prioritise any of them, because there is evidence for each of them in the Arabic lexicon and literature. None has priority over the others. For instance, there are two variants of the prophetic tradition on 'the prohibition of earning money through prostitution'.[42] After citing various Sunnī works in *gharīb al-ḥadīth*, including that of Abū ʿUbayd al-Qāsim b. Sallām (d. 224/838),[43] Abū

---

40 Al-Murtaḍā, *al-Dharīʿa*, 2:78–79. Compare to al-Ṭūsī, *al-ʿUdda*, 1:146–155.

41 Al-Murtaḍā, *Amālī*, 1:18–19. His view resembles what is referred to in literary theory as 'authorial intentionalism', according to which an author's intentions should determine or constrain the proper interpretation of the literary work. Nevertheless, intentionalism does not necessarily countenance only one meaning for a literary work. There are many ways in which it can accept multiple or disjunctive interpretations. If the goal of interpretation is to consider the meanings a work will sustain when approached in the conventions of literature and language within and against which it is created, then many interpretations of the work will be available to the reader, for all that is required is compatibility. For further discussion, see Davies, *Philosophical Perspectives on Art*, ch. 11: 'Authors' Intentions, Literary Interpretation, and Literary Value', 166ff.

42 *Nahā ʿan kasb al-zammāra/al-rammāza*. Both *rammāza* and *zammāra* signify prostitution. See Lane, *Arabic-English Lexicon*, 1:1153 and 1250, respectively.

43 Abū ʿUbayd, *Kitāb Gharīb al-ḥadīth*, 3:356–358. According to Abū ʿUbayd, only one variant is correct, i.e. *al-zammāra*; he maintains that the other variant (*al-rammāza*) does not make sense here.

Muḥammad ʿAbdallāh b. Muslim Ibn Qutayba (d. 276/889)[44] and Abū Bakr Muḥammad b. al-Qāsim (Ibn) al-Anbārī (d. 328/940),[45] al-Murtaḍā states that neither of the two variants has priority over the other, because there is evidence for each in the Arabic language, and each can be interpreted in an entirely valid way.[46]

He does not mind if different semantic possibilities of a given statement contradict or conflict with each other, if they do not run counter to beliefs that are based on solid proofs. For instance, in interpreting the prophetic tradition, 'If you feel no shame, then do what you want',[47] he mentions three semantic possibilities as the intended meaning behind the hadith:[48]

1. It may be an expression of appreciation of an act done for God, meaning that if people know what they are doing is for God's sake, then they should not be concerned with what others might say or ascribe to them (e.g. accusing them of hypocrisy).[49]
2. It may exaggerate the refutation of a wrong act, meaning that if people do not feel ashamed of being insolent, they may do whatever they like.[50]
3. It may clarify the fact that if people are not involved in wrongdoing for which they might be ashamed, then they can proceed with doing [that act].[51]

---

44 Ibn Qutayba, *Iṣlāḥ ghalaṭ Abī ʿUbayd*, 59–62. Ibn Qutayba refutes Abū ʿUbayd's view about the second variant by providing supporting evidence from the literature.

45 Al-Murtaḍā apparently quoted this from Ibn al-Anbārī's *Gharīb al-ḥadīth* (which is not extant), though citations from his book are found in later sources. For this case, see al-ʿAskarī, *Taṣḥīfāt al-muḥaddithīn*, 1:177–178. Ibn al-Anbārī, here and in many other places, rejects Ibn Qutayba's view, though in some cases his criticisms of Ibn Qutayba's ideas, as noted by al-Murtaḍā, are not well-argued and relate to personal rather than scholarly motives; see al-Murtaḍā, *Amālī*, 1:334–335.

46 Al-Murtaḍā, *Amālī*, 1:454–457, *majlis* 34.

47 *Idhā lam tastaḥyi fa-fʿal mā shiʾta*. See Ibn Ḥanbal, *Musnad*, 4:121; 5:273, 383; al-Bukhārī, *Ṣaḥīḥ*, 4:152; for a variant of the tradition with a Shīʿī *isnād*, see Ibn Bābūyah al-Ṣadūq, *ʿUyūn akhbār*, 2:59.

48 Al-Murtaḍā, *Amālī*, 1:75–76, *majlis* 6.

49 This interpretation is attributed to Jarīr b. ʿAbd al-Ḥamīd (d. 188/804). For Abū ʿUbayd, it is close to the tradition that says, 'If Satan comes to you during your prayer and says: "you are practicing hypocrisy", make your prayer longer'. See Abū ʿUbayd, *Kitāb Gharīb al-ḥadīth*, 2:328–330.

50 Abū ʿUbayd suggests this interpretation, which considers *ifʿal* an indicative rather than an imperative verb. This means, one who is not ashamed of what he/she is doing can do anything, however disgusting; Abū ʿUbayd, *Kitāb Gharīb al-ḥadīth*, 2:330–332. See also Ibn Qutayba, *Taʾwīl mukhtalif al-ḥadīth*, 346. For a similar interpretation attributed to Abū al-ʿAbbās Aḥmad b. Yaḥyā Thaʿlab (d. 291/904), see al-Khaṭṭābī, *Gharīb al-ḥadīth*, 1:156.

51 See also al-Khaṭṭābī, *Gharīb al-ḥadīth*, 1:156.

These three interpretations are not compatible with each other. The hadith cannot simultaneously describe the situations of someone doing good and someone (else) doing wrong, just as it cannot encourage the good deed while it condemns the wrong deed. However, this incompatibility does not constrain al-Murtaḍā from proposing three different interpretations of the hadith.

Hermeneutical Tools for Interpreting Traditions

By drawing on his knowledge of Arabic lexicography, grammar, and rhetoric and by applying Muʿtazilī-Shīʿī principles in theology, al-Murtaḍā created a distinctive methodology for the interpretation of the Qurʾan and hadith.[52] He often interprets hadiths as a Muʿtazilī-Shīʿī theologian, and in doing so, he makes use of the Qurʾanic verses as a skilled exegete. Traces of al-Murtaḍā's multi-dimensional character are evident in his interpretations. Literary criticism and rational analysis are essential tools in al-Murtaḍā's hermeneutics, to such an extent that we can label his approach 'literary-theological'. At the time of his work, the major hadith compilations – both Shīʿī and Sunnī – and a variety of secondary works on hadith, such as rare traditions (*gharīb al-ḥadīth*), difficult or problematic traditions (*mushkil al-ḥadīth*), and disputed traditions (*mukhtalif al-ḥadīth*), had already been produced.[53] Therefore, he had an abundant source of hadith literature at his disposal, and he benefited from this tremendously.

Here, by studying the traditions al-Murtaḍā used in his *Amālī*,[54] I explore the hermeneutical tools he employed to understand and interpret traditions. He cited these traditions for specific interpretive reasons, and his commentaries on these traditions are intended to address one or more

---

52 For an outline of the characteristics of Muʿtazilī exegesis of the Qurʾan, see Goldziher, *Schools of Koranic Commentators*, 65–95. In recent years, the Muʿtazilī tradition of Qurʾanic exegesis has started to receive more scholarly attention. For some reflections on the approach, methodology and hermeneutical principles employed by Muʿtazilī exegetes, see Mourad, 'Why Do We Need Tafsīr?', particularly 121 n.1, for some recent studies that examine Muʿtazilī *tafsīr*. In my contribution to the *Handbook of Qurʾānic Hermeneutics* (ed. Georges Tamer, forthcoming), I explore the hermeneutical principles and methods of al-Sharīf al-Murtaḍā in his interpretation of the Qurʾan.

53 For a general overview on the formation and development of hadith literature, see Robson, 'Ḥadīth: II. Collections of Ḥadīth', in *EI²*, online: http://dx.doi.org/10.1163/1573-3912_islam_COM_0248 (accessed 20 February 2022); Pavlovitch, 'Ḥadīth: 6. Muṣannafs, Musnads, and the Formation of the Six-Book Canon'; Blecher, 'Ḥadīth Commentary', in *EI³*, online: http://dx.doi.org/10.1163/1573-3912_ei3_COM_32080 (accessed 13 April 2019).

54 Of course, he interprets traditions in other places; for other instances; see al-Murtaḍā, *Rasāʾil*, 1:113–115, 120, 350–354, 408–411 (also below), 441–443; 2:20–21, 46–47; 3:133–134 (also below), 233–239.

such interpretive issues, whether (1) difficult vocabulary; (2) odd or ambiguous senses; (3) inconsistency or contradictions with the text of the Qur'an, agreed-upon hadiths, reason or his theological or legal opinions. In what follows, I examine each of these issues in detail, and reveal al-Murtaḍā's hermeneutical approach to traditions and his methods of resolving the problems raised.

Commenting on Difficult Vocabulary

The most common issue that occupies al-Murtaḍā is the difficult vocabulary. Some of these are cases of odd words that are key to the traditions, while others appear in selections of poetry or in other evidence al-Murtaḍā cites in defining or interpreting a particular Qur'anic verse or tradition.[55] To interpret traditions with odd vocabulary, he usually refers to the statements of Arab lexicographers and philologists and to the poetry of outstanding Arab poets. Regarding certain traditions, however, he finds it sufficient to elaborate on their vocabulary rather than to interpret them.[56]

In addition to mentioning various interpretive aspects of a tradition, al-Murtaḍā occasionally suggests a new meaning for a difficult term; in these cases, he refers to the Arab lexicon, but interprets it in a novel manner. Indeed, through such cases, al-Murtaḍā demonstrates his skills in Arabic literature and philology. For instance, in commenting on a tradition transmitted from 'Alī b. Abī Ṭālib, 'Whoever loves us, the people of the house, should prepare to be wrapped in poverty',[57] he mentions two distinct interpretations suggested by Abū 'Ubayd al-Qāsim b. Sallām and Ibn Qutayba al-Dīnawarī, respectively. According to Abū 'Ubayd, in this case, 'poverty' should be interpreted as applying to 'the other world' (*al-ākhira*); that is, one should provide good deeds as provision for the afterlife, because one will require them on the day of judgement.[58] By contrast, Ibn Qutayba believes that poverty should be interpreted as applying to 'this world' (*hādhihī al-dunyā*), and one should practice patience, as mentioned in the tradition that compares patience in poverty to a veil that covers poverty in this world.[59] While endorsing both statements, al-Murtaḍā presents a

55 For a long list of difficult vocabulary taken from traditions or poetry, explained and clarified by al-Murtaḍā, see the index prepared by the editor of *Amālī*, 2:460–474: *fihris al-lugha*.

56 The editor of *Amālī*, however, has also labelled them *ta'wīl khabar*; for instance; see al-Murtaḍā, *Amālī*, 1:95–98, *majlis* 7; 1:107–112, *majlis* 8; 1:219–220, *majlis* 15; 1:368–370, *majlis* 27; 2:172–174, *majlis* 65; 2:285–286, *majlis* 79; 2:398, *mas'ala*.

57 *Man aḥabbanā ahla al-bayti fa-l-yu'idda li-l-faqri jilbāban aw tajfāfan*; see also *Nahj al-balāgha*, 4:26.

58 Abū 'Ubayd, *Kitāb Gharīb al-ḥadīth*, 4:358–359.

59 Ibn Qutayba, *Iṣlāḥ ghalaṭ Abī 'Ubayd*, 117–118.

third meaning arising from a philological reflection; he claims this meaning is new. According to al-Murtaḍā, one definition of *faqr* is 'to pierce the
nasal bones of a camel to bridle it through those holes, so that the camel
may be controlled using this halter'. Following this definition, the intended
meaning of the tradition is that the advocate of *ahl al-bayt* should harness
his soul and lead it to obedience, distract it from the desires that its nature
inclines to and make his soul submit to patience regarding what he hates
and the hardship of what he is supposed to do.[60]

According to al-Murtaḍā, the difficulty in understanding a certain
hadith is often due to its vocabulary. Thus, a misconception or a poor
understanding of such vocabulary can result in strange and unreliable
interpretations of traditions. In such cases, after mentioning the various
semantic possibilities of the odd term, al-Murtaḍā reveals the intended
meaning of the tradition. Without fail, he takes into account the statements of other experts on vocabulary in hadith – usually the works of
Abū 'Ubayd, Ibn Qutayba and Ibn al-Anbārī – and then either supports
and corroborates their opinions with his own ideas or criticises their
understanding.[61] For instance, in interpreting the prophetic tradition,
laysa minnā man lam yataghanna bi-l-Qur'ān,[62] he brings forward three
interpretations that his predecessors proposed for the verbal phrase *lam
yataghanna*:[63] (1) *lam yastaghni bi-l-Qur'ān* ('is not satisfied with the
Qur'an'),[64] (2) *lam yuḥassin ṣawtahū bi-l-Qur'ān* ('does not recite the
Qur'an with a pleasant voice'),[65] or (3) *lam yataladhdhadh bi-l-Qur'ān*
('does not enjoy reciting the Qur'an').[66] Each interpretation provides a
possible meaning of the tradition and thus removes its ambiguity. Since
al-Murtaḍā is convinced that all the semantic possibilities of a statement
are plausible and that none should be ruled out, he merely seeks to prioritise some of these meanings and singles out the most and least likely
understanding, based on evidence from Arabic literature. Using philological evidence, he also offers a fourth meaning for this tradition. Just
as *ghaniya al-qawm bi-l-makān* means 'The people tarried and dwelt

60 Al-Murtaḍā, *Amālī*, 1:17–18, *majlis* 2.
61 For example, see al-Murtaḍā, *Amālī*, 1:5–8, *majlis* 1; 1:17–18, *majlis* 2; 1:75–76, *majlis*
    6; 1:405–407, *majlis* 30.
62 Ibn Ḥanbal, *Musnad*, 1:172, 175, 179; al-Bukhārī, *Ṣaḥīḥ*, 8:209.
63 Al-Murtaḍā, *Amālī*, 1:31–34.
64 Abū 'Ubayd, *Kitāb Gharīb al-ḥadīth*, 1:384–387.
65 The opinion is attributed to an anonymous authority; see al-Murtaḍā, *Amālī*, 1:32ff.,
    majlis 3. See also Abū 'Ubayd, *Kitāb Gharīb al-ḥadīth*, 1:386.
66 This opinion, attributed to Ibn al-Anbārī, is only found in al-Murtaḍā's *Amālī*, 1:34.
    Cf. Ibn al-Anbārī, *al-Zāhir*, 2:7, where he says: *qad taghannā idhā jahara*. This indicates
    that Ibn al-Anbārī understood the tradition as *lam yajhar bi-l-Qur'ān* ('does not recite
    the Qur'an aloud').

long in the place',[67] *lam yataghanna bi-l-Qur'ān* means (4) *lam yuqim 'alā al-Qur'ān* ('does not take Qur'an as his dwelling [while looking for something else to adopt as his abode, resort, and residence]').[68]

In his interpretation of hadiths, al-Murtaḍā also pays attention to rhetorical aspects in his exploration of their meaning. For instance, in discussing the prophetic hadith, 'If the Qur'an were put in a hide (*ihāb*), fire would not burn it',[69] he first mentions the remarks of Ibn Qutayba and Ibn al-Anbārī on the hadith. Ibn Qutayba suggested three interpretations for this hadith: (1) the word *ihāb* (skin, hide) is used metaphorically for the body, meaning that if a Muslim learns the Qur'an, he or she will not burn even when they are thrown into hell; (2) the word *ihāb* is used in a literal sense, meaning that, at the time of the Prophet, when the Qur'an was written on parchment and thrown into fire, it did not burn, and this was a testament to the truth of his proclamation; and (3) the immunity to fire is attributed to the Qur'an itself, not to the parchment on which it is written. That is, fire burns parchment, but not the Qur'an itself.[70] After rejecting these interpretations, Ibn al-Anbārī offers a fourth interpretation. If the parchment on which a Qur'anic verse is written falls into fire and burns, the Qur'an is not destroyed, because God preserves it in the hearts of the righteous.[71] After quoting and criticising the opinions of earlier scholars, al-Murtaḍā stresses the rhetorical feature of the prophetic saying, and voices his own opinion, that this hadith is an exaggerated pronouncement to commemorate the status of the Qur'an and inform us of its value. According to al-Murtaḍā's interpretation, the hadith implies that if the Qur'an written on a piece of parchment is thrown into fire, and given that fire is supposed not to burn something of high value, then fire should (according to the theory) not burn the Qur'an. But indeed, this is not the case – when the Qur'an is placed in fire it burns. In order to substantiate his rhetorical interpretation, he brings forth evidence from the Qur'an[72] and Arabic literature.[73]

---

67 Cf. Q. 7:92, *ka-an lam yaghnaw fīhā* ('as though they had not dwelt therein') as referring to the punishment of those who denied Shu'ayb: the earthquake seized them and left them motionless in their homes as if they had never been there.

68 Al-Murtaḍā, *Amālī*, 1:34–36, *majlis* 3. For similar instances, see al-Murtaḍā, *Amālī*, 1:354–358, *majlis* 26; 1:492–494, *majlis* 37; 1:630–635, *majlis* 48.

69 *Law kāna al-Qur'ānu fī ihābin mā massathu al-nār*; Ibn Ḥanbal, *Musnad*, 4:151, 155.

70 Ibn Qutayba, *Ta'wīl mukhtalif al-ḥadīth*, 290–292.

71 See al-Murtaḍā, *Amālī*, 1:427–428.

72 Cf. Q. 59:21: 'Had We sent this Qur'an down on a mountain, you would have seen it trembling, crumbling in awe of God. These parables We cite for the people, so that they may reflect.'

73 Al-Murtaḍā, *Amālī*, 1:428–429, *majlis* 32. For other examples, see al-Murtaḍā, *Amālī*, 1:6–7, *majlis* 1; 2:316–317, *takmila*.

Removing Contradictions with the Literal Meaning of the Verses of the Qur'an or with Sound Traditions

Sometimes al-Murtaḍā explains traditions in which the apparent meanings contradict Qur'anic verses or other traditions. For instance, the prophetic tradition, 'The dead person is tortured (*yuʿadhdhabu*) in his grave by [his relatives'] wailing for him',[74] seems to violate the Qur'anic principle that people are held responsible for their own works and not for those of others (e.g. Q. 6:164: 'No one bears the burdens of another'). This verse indicates that the deceased are punished in the afterlife for their own works and offences, not for those of others. Therefore, the apparent meaning of the tradition must be interpreted in a way that accords with the Qur'an. Al-Murtaḍā offers the following interpretations:

1. This hadith refers to people who request that their relatives wail for them after their death, and states that such wailing does not serve any purpose, rather it only causes them to be punished in the grave. Therefore, deceased people are punished not for the mourners' wailing, but for their own request.[75]
2. It is said that this report was due to an error in transmission by Ibn ʿUmar, who cited this tradition in relation to his sister Ḥafṣa (Muḥammad's wife) when she was crying for her father ʿUmar b. al-Khaṭṭāb, the second caliph. The correct version should be: The Prophet passed by a dead Jew and witnessed his family wailing for him. He addressed them, saying, 'You are wailing for him while he is being punished (*yuʿadhdhabu*) in the grave for his sins.'[76]
3. Another interpretation, which is supported by some evidence in Arabic literature, states that *ʿadhāb* means 'suffering', not 'punishment'. When the deceased see that their beloved ones are wailing for them and afflicted by distress after their death, they 'suffer' in their grave. Thus, suffering in this sense does not imply being

---

74 *Inna al-mayyita yuʿadhdhabu fī qabrihī bi-l-niyāḥati ʿalayh.* Other variants include *inna al-mayyita la-yuʿadhdhabu bi-bukāʾi ahlihī ʿalayh, man nīḥa ʿalayhi fa-innahū yuʿadhdhabu bi-mā nīḥa ʿalayhi,* etc. See Ibn Ḥanbal, *Musnad,* 1:26, 36, 42, 54; 2:38; 6:107; al-Bukhārī, *Ṣaḥīḥ,* 2:80–81; Muslim, *al-Jāmiʿ al-ṣaḥīḥ,* 3:41–45.

75 According to al-Murtaḍā, it was a common pre-Islamic custom for people to request that their families wail over them after they die. He provides poetry as evidence. See al-Murtaḍā, *Amālī,* 1:341.

76 A series of traditions ascribed to ʿĀʾisha, Muḥammad's wife, contends that Ibn ʿUmar is neither a liar nor someone accused of lying, but the sense of hearing does err (*al-samʿu yukhṭiʾu*). According to ʿĀʾisha, the Prophet never said what Ibn ʿUmar transmitted, and certainly not regarding Muslims. See Mālik b. Anas, *Muwaṭṭaʾ,* 2:329; al-Shāfiʿī, *al-Umm,* 10:216–217.

'tortured' or 'punished' by God, but only experiencing 'grief' and 'sorrow'.[77]

Removing a Conflict with Legal Rulings

Sometimes the apparent meanings of traditions seem incompatible with legal rulings, and thus al-Murtaḍā tried to interpret and justify the meanings of these traditions in order to reconcile them with the rulings. For instance, the prophetic tradition (given that the hadith is correct) 'May God damn the thief who steals an egg (*bayḍa*) or a rope (*ḥabl*), and thus has his hand cut off!'[78] led the Khawārij to infer that cutting off the hand of a thief is not restricted by the value of the item stolen. They argued that the Qur'an itself confirms this generality (*ta'mīm*), for Q. 5:38 states, 'As for the thief, whether male or female, cut off their hands',[79] and does not mention any restrictive condition or specification (*takhṣīṣ*). Moreover, some regarded the apparent meaning of the hadith as contradicting another tradition that says, 'Cutting off the hand [of a thief] is not allowed except for a quarter of a dinar [or more]',[80] in which a minimum amount is specified as a condition for cutting off the hand of a thief. To remove these contradictions, some scholars[81] have stated that in this hadith, *bayḍa* signifies 'a sword' and not an egg, and *ḥabl* refers to 'a ship's rope', not an ordinary, inexpensive rope, and both items exceed the minimum value mentioned in the tradition. In rejecting this view, Ibn Qutayba says that the one who voiced such an interpretation was not familiar with Arabic. He maintains that, because the statement contains a curse, 'the more pejorative the interpretation, the more fitting it would be to the context'.[82] According to Ibn Qutayba, the hadith was uttered after the revelation of the Qur'anic verse and was compatible with its literal meaning, but the Qur'anic verse is what was specified by the determination of the minimum value necessary for the cutting off of a thief's hand.[83] Al-Murtaḍā rejects Ibn Qutayba's interpretation, and points

---

77 Al-Murtaḍā, *Amālī*, 1:340–343, *majlis* 25. For another example of removing discrepancies between traditions, see al-Murtaḍā, *Amālī*, 2:200–204, *majlis* 68.

78 *La'ana Allāhu al-sāriqa yasriqu al-bayḍata fa-tuqṭa'u yaduhū wa-yasriqu al-ḥabla fa-tuqṭa'u yaduh.* See Ibn Ḥanbal, *Musnad*, 2:253; al-Bukhārī, *Ṣaḥīḥ*, 8:15, 18; Muslim, *al-Jāmi' al-ṣaḥīḥ*, 5:113.

79 *Al-sāriqu wa-l-sāriqatu fa-qṭa'ū aydiyahumā.*

80 *Lā qaṭa illā fī rub'i dīnār.*

81 Sulaymān b. Mihrān al-A'mash (d. 148/765) attributes the idea to some anonymous scholars; see al-Bukhārī, *Ṣaḥīḥ*, 8:159. But al-Murtaḍā states that Ibn Qutayba heard this interpretation from the Shāfi'ī jurist (*faqīh*) Yaḥyā b. Aktham (d. 242/857) in his session (*majlis*) in Mecca. See al-Murtaḍā, *Amālī*, 2:6; cf. Ibn Qutayba, *Ta'wīl mukhtalif al-ḥadīth*, 246, where he did not name that *faqīh*.

82 Ibn Qutayba, *Ta'wīl mukhtalif al-ḥadīth*, 246.

83 Ibn Qutayba, *Ta'wīl mukhtalif al-ḥadīth*, 245.

out a rhetorical aspect of the tradition; he clarifies that the Prophet did not intend to articulate a legal ruling, but rather pronounced it to humiliate the thief. This removes the contradiction and repudiates the misgivings of the Khawārij.[84]

Removing Antinomy with Theological Principles

Al-Murtaḍā's primary goal in interpreting hadiths was to defend Muʿtazilī-Shīʿī theological principles and to respond to critiques raised in this regard. Since many traditions are authoritative sources for the theological tenets of various groups, following his own theological principles, al-Murtaḍā first questions their understanding of these traditions, and in doing so, corroborates and justifies his articles of faith. Indeed, this is al-Murtaḍā's dominant goal in comprehending and interpreting hadiths. Even in cases in which he elaborates on the vocabulary of traditions, his rational and theological approach is evident in his mode of argumentation. And even in his reaction to theological debates, he uses his literary skills a great deal.[85]

A revealing example is his interpretation of the prophetic hadith, 'The hearts of humans are between two fingers (sg., iṣbaʿ) of God, and He turns them however He desires'.[86] With regard to this hadith, the question arises as to how to interpret it in a way that is compatible with Muʿtazilī-Shīʿī theological principles and does not fall into the trap of anthropomorphism.[87] Al-Murtaḍā mentions two possibilities to interpret this tradition. First, he suggests that finger (iṣbaʿ) here does not refer to a part of the body, rather it indicates 'a positive effect' (al-athar al-ḥasan), as when we are surprised by something, we point to it with our finger. Thus, the tradition implies that the human heart is placed between two divine gifts (niʿmatayn), the gift of this world and that of the other world.[88] The second interpretation is that the word iṣbaʿ refers to the possibility of penetrating

<hr>

84 Al-Murtaḍā, Amālī, 2:5–9, majlis 49.

85 For example, see al-Murtaḍā, Amālī, 2:50–53, majlis 53; 2:83–85, majlis 56.

86 *Inna qulūba banī Ādama kullahā bayna iṣbaʿayni min aṣābiʿi al-raḥmāni yuṣarrifuhā kayfa yashāʾu*; al-Murtaḍā, Amālī, 1:318. He cites other variants of the tradition as well. See also Ibn Ḥanbal, Musnad, 2:168; 3:112; 4:182; 6:91, 251, 302, 315; Muslim, al-Jāmiʿ al-ṣaḥīḥ, 8:51; Ibn Bābūyah al-Ṣadūq, ʿIlal al-sharāʾiʿ, 2:604.

87 Al-Murtaḍā, Amālī, 1:318. The same question was posed to his brother al-Sharīf al-Raḍī, al-Majāzāt al-nabawiyya, 346.

88 Ibn Qutayba cited this interpretation and criticised it; he questioned why, if the heart is placed between two divine gifts, should the Prophet pray to God to strengthen his heart in His religion (*thabbit qalbī ʿalā dīnik*)? Ibn Qutayba, Taʾwīl mukhtalif al-ḥadīth, 302–303. Cf. also Ibn Bābūyah al-Ṣadūq, ʿIlal al-sharāʾiʿ, 2:604–604, who interprets the two fingers as the two ways, good and evil (*ṭarīq al-khayr wa-ṭarīq al-sharr*).

hearts; in this manner, *iṣbaʿ* is a kind of hyperbole (*mubālagha*) to describe divine power. To substantiate these two interpretations, al-Murtaḍā quotes Q. 39:67[89] and provides additional evidence from Arabic literature.[90]

Another example is al-Murtaḍā's interpretation of the tradition,

> The most favourable deed in the eyes of God is the one that you pursue with perseverance, no matter how meagre it might be. Therefore, perform those deeds for which you have the strength (*mā tuṭīqūna*), for God will not get exhausted (*lā yamallu*) until you do (*ḥattā tamallū*).[91]

To justify the last part of the tradition, which seems to attribute 'exhaustion' to God, al-Murtaḍā suggests four possible interpretations; for each he provides evidence from poetry and numerous examples from Arabic literature to substantiate its different meanings. For instance, he tries to explain the meaning of the hadith as follows: 'God does not cut off His bounty and benevolence from you until you are tired of asking Him.' To justify this understanding, he refers to a rhetorical feature in the Qur'an, namely *izdiwāj* (pairing) and *mushākala* (resemblance), and says, 'The human action is literally "weariness," whereas the divine action is called "weariness," not in the literal sense but only on account of pairing and verbal resemblance, though their meanings are different.' To support this idea, he provides evidence of a similar rhetorical feature in Q. 2:194, 'Whoever commits aggression against you, retaliate against him in the same measure as he has committed against you',[92] and Q. 42:40, 'The repayment of a bad action is one equivalent to it'.[93] Al-Murtaḍā maintains that using such paired expressions, one with a literal meaning and the other in a figurative sense, is common in Arabic, particularly in reference to human acts *vis-à-vis* divine acts.[94] In addition, he points to the possibility of an error on the part of the narrator in transmitting the tradition. In his view, the correct

---

89 'The entire earth will be in His grip on the day of resurrection, and the heavens will be folded in His hand (*maṭwiyyātun bi-yamīnihī*).

90 Al-Murtaḍā, *Amālī*, 1:318–321, *majlis* 22. See also Ibn Qutayba, *Taʾwīl mukhtalif al-ḥadīth*, 303; Ibn Fūrak al-Iṣbahānī, *Kitāb Mushkil al-ḥadīth*, 118–121.

91 *Inna aḥabba al-aʿmāli ilā Allāhi ʿazza wa-jalla adwamuhā wa-in qalla fa-ʿalaykum min al-aʿmāli bi-mā tuṭiqūna fa-inna Allāha lā yamallu ḥattā tamallū.* According to al-Murtaḍā, Abū Hurayra narrated this tradition from the Prophet. For variants of this tradition from ʿĀʾisha, see Ibn Ḥanbal, *Musnad*, 6:40, 61, 84, 122, 128, 189, 199, 212, 233, 241, 244, 250, 268; al-Bukhārī, *Ṣaḥīḥ*, 2:48, 244; 7:50; Muslim, *al-Jāmiʿ al-ṣaḥīḥ*, 2:188–189; 3:161.

92 *Fa-man iʿtadā ʿalaykum fa-tadū ʿalayhi bi-mithli mā iʿtadā ʿalaykum.*

93 *Wa-jazāʾu sayyiʾatin sayyiʾatun mithluhā*; al-Murtaḍā, *Amālī*, 1:56–57, *majlis* 5.

94 Al-Murtaḍā, *Amālī*, 1:57. For other examples of figurative interpretations, see al-Murtaḍā, *Amālī*, 1:6–7, *majlis* 1; 1:426–431, *majlis* 32.

reading is *lā yamullu* (instead of *lā yamallu*),[95] which can mean either 'God does not punish you with fire unless you are tired of worshipping Him and refrain from obeying Him' or 'God does not hasten to punish you, but He is patient and deliberate with regard to you, until you become weary of His patience and hasten His torment [upon you] by committing forbidden acts and sins'.[96]

To remove some theological misconceptions, al-Murtaḍā employs grammar as well as rhetoric. For instance, regarding the prophetic tradition, 'The believer's intention is better than his deed',[97] and in response to the question of how it is possible for 'an intention to be better than a deed and deserve more merit', the sixth Imam, Jaʿfar b. Muḥammad al-Ṣādiq (d. 148/765), replied, 'For the deed may have been a hypocritical show for people, but the intention is sincerely for God'.[98] Ibn Qutayba explains this to mean that the intention, and not the deed, is the cause of eternal bliss in paradise.[99] Al-Murtaḍā mentions two other interpretations: (1) The believer's intention is better than a deed devoid of intention (*ʿamalihī al-ʿārī min niyya*); and (2) The believer's intention in doing a good deed is better than his act of transgression (*ʿamalihī alladhī huwa maʿṣiyatuhū*). None of these interpretations satisfies al-Murtaḍā. Moreover, in all these interpretations, *khayr* is considered a 'comparative adjective', which, as al-Murtaḍā maintains, is only acceptable when two things of the same category are compared. Here, however, intention and action are not of the same category; thus, the comparison is pointless. Therefore, he suggests that *khayr* is used here as a 'verbal noun' in the sense of 'being good'. In this case, the hadith implies that the believer's intention is regarded as being among his virtuous deeds.[100]

It is no exaggeration to claim that al-Murtaḍā is brilliant in his interpretation of traditions. For example, note his interpretation of the tradition attributed to Jaʿfar al-Ṣādiq: 'The Prophet made a "pact of brotherhood"

---

95 For the root *m-l-l*, he suggests the pattern *malla/yamullu* intead of *malla/yamallu*, which changes the meaning. As evidence, he cites *al-malla* with the meaning of 'a bread oven' and mentions that if one says *malla al-rajulu al-khubzata yamulluhā*, it means 'he bakes the bread in the oven'.

96 Al-Murtaḍā, *Amālī*, 1:57. For other examples in which he suggests a probable error in the wording of the tradition, see 1:341, *majlis* 25; 2:201–202, *majlis* 68; 2:394, *takmila*.

97 *Niyyatu al-muʾmini khayrun min ʿamalih*; see al-Kulaynī, *al-Kāfī*, 2:84; Ibn Qutayba, *Taʾwīl mukhtalif al-ḥadīth*, 224, *niyyatu al-marʾi khayrun min ʿamalihī*; al-Ṭabarānī, *al-Muʿjam al-kabīr*, 6:185–186; al-Iṣbahānī, *Kitāb al-Amthāl*, 33–34, *niyyatu al-muʾmini ablaghu min ʿamalihī*.

98 Ibn Bābūyah al-Ṣadūq, *ʿIlal al-sharāʾiʿ*, 2:524.

99 Ibn Qutayba, *Taʾwīl mukhtalif al-ḥadīth*, 224–225.

100 Al-Murtaḍā, *Amālī*, 2:316–317, *takmila*. See also al-Murtaḍā, *Rasāʾil*, 1:120; 3:233–239.

(*mu'ākhāt*)[101] between Salmān al-Fārisī and Abū Dharr al-Ghifārī, but if Abū Dharr had found out what was hidden in Salmān's heart *he* would have killed *him*.'[102] This hadith is clearly problematic – how is it possible for the Prophet to establish such a 'pact of brotherhood' between two persons, while if one of the two had known about the secret in the other's heart, he would have regarded it as permissible to murder his brother? Al-Murtaḍā first presents two interpretations of the phrase '*he* would kill *him*': (1) The pronoun 'him' refers to what is hidden in Salmān's heart (i.e. 'it'), that is, Abū Dharr would oppose Salmān's secret if he knew it; and (2) The pronoun 'him' refers to Abū Dharr himself, that is, knowing the secret in Salmān's heart would disturb Abū Dharr in his heart and mind. In both interpretations, the verb 'would have killed' is considered hyperbole (*mubālagha*). Al-Murtaḍā, however, is not satisfied with these two interpretations, because both run counter to the fact that Salmān and Abū Dharr were sincere Companions of the Prophet and not dishonest or hypocritical. Thus, he suggests an interpretation of the tradition that accounts for their sincerity: The pronoun 'him' refers to Abū Dharr rather than Salmān, and the subject of the verb 'to kill' (the pronoun 'he', in English translation) is the hidden secret (i.e. 'it') in Salman's heart and not Abū Dharr. Thus, the tradition means that if Abū Dharr were to conceive of the hidden content of Salmān's heart and to realise the true extent of his devotion to God, his affection toward Salman would be intensified beyond what he could stand, and he would be overwhelmed.[103]

Removing the Contradiction with Reason

For al-Murtaḍā, reason is one of the most significant tools with which to understand and interpret hadith. He believes that one should first examine hadiths against the standard of reason and then against the Qur'an and other sound hadiths. Only after the hadith passes these tests can one declare

---

101 A 'pact of brotherhood' is an agreement between two Muslims, to the effect that they consider each other brothers. According to Muslim sources, the Prophet made pacts of brotherhood among his Companions (though there are disagreements regarding their number and names). See Watt, 'Mu'ākhāt'.

102 *La-qad ākhā rasūlu Allāhi bayna Salmān wa-Abī Dharr wa-law iṭṭala'a Abū Dharr 'alā mā fī qalbi Salmān la-qatalahū.* Cf. al-Ṣaffār al-Qummī, *Baṣā'ir al-darajāt al-kubrā,* 45; al-Kulaynī, *al-Kāfī,* 1:401, where the context of the tradition is religious dissimulation (*taqiyya*). This means, even among close Companions of the Prophet such as Abū Dharr and Salmān, there was an overwhelming danger of loss of life if *taqiyya* was not practised. In Sunnī sources the pact of brotherhood was said to have been made between Salmān and Abū al-Dardā'; e.g. al-Bukhārī, *Ṣaḥīḥ,* 2:243.

103 Al-Murtaḍā, *Amālī,* 2:396–397, *takmila.*

it to be sound.[104] Al-Murtaḍā sought to provide a reasonable interpretation of hadiths whose apparent meanings do not seem to be compatible with reason. For instance, in his interpretation of a tradition about the poem attributed to ʿAlī b. Abī Ṭālib and addressed to his Companion al-Ḥārith al-Hamdānī,[105] which indicates the presence of the Imam at the deathbed of any moribund person,[106] al-Murtaḍā states, 'how can every dying person see him (ʿAlī), when it is not possible for a body to be present at the same time in different places'.[107] Thus, he follows the rational approach of his teacher al-Mufīd[108] and suggests, given that the hadith is correct, that

> the meaning is that in that moment near to death, he [the dying person] realises the result of his loyalty and allegiance to him [ʿAlī] or his deviation from him, for it has been narrated that when a person approaches death and is close to death, he will be shown in that moment what indicates whether he is going to be among the people of paradise or among the people of hell.[109]

When no such possible interpretation exists, al-Murtaḍā rejects the authenticity of the hadith altogether. For example, in a tradition that mentions the virtues and vices of various fowl, beasts, foods and lands, it is also stated that praiseworthy species worship God, love His friends and curse the enemies of God's friends, while reprehensible species insult God's friends. Rejection of the *wilāya* (guardianship) of the Shīʿī Imams is even cited as the reason for which eating some food is forbidden (*ḥarām*).[110] Al-Murtaḍā considers it irrational to attribute correct belief to some

104 Al-Murtaḍā, *Rasāʾil*, 1:410.
105 *Yā Ḥāri Hamdāna man yamut yaranī / min muʾminin aw munāfiqin qabalā / yaʿrifunī ṭarfuhū wa-aʿrifuhū / bi-naʿtihī wa-smihī wa-mā faʿalā* ('O al-Ḥārith al-Hamdānī, whoever dies will see me / be a believer or hypocrite before [his death] / his eyes know me and I know him / by his nickname, his name, and what he did'). See Ibn Abī al-Ḥadīd al-Muʿtazilī, *Sharḥ Nahj al-balāgha*, 1:299.
106 For traditions referring to a similar idea, see al-Majlisī, *Biḥār al-anwār*, 27:157ff.
107 Al-Murtaḍā, *Rasāʾil*, 3:133. See also al-Murtaḍā, *Rasāʾil*, 1:281. Al-Mufīd states that there is consensus among Imāmīs on this issue. See the next note.
108 See al-Mufīd, *Awāʾil al-maqālāt*, 73–74.
109 Al-Murtaḍā, *Rasāʾil*, 3:133. See also al-Murtaḍā, *Rasāʾil*, 1:280–281.
110 See al-Ṣaffār al-Qummī, *Baṣāʾir al-darajāt al-kubrā*, 373–374, on a toad cursing ʿAlī b. Abī Ṭālib; al-Kulaynī, *al-Kāfī*, 6:223, on a swallow grieving over what happened to the People of the House (*ahl al-bayt*); 6:225, on a skylark cursing whoever hates the Prophet's family; and 6:547–548, on doves cursing the killers of al-Ḥusayn b. ʿAlī. Ibn Bābūyah al-Ṣadūq, *Kitāb al-Khiṣāl*, 493–495, provides a list of animals, including a monkey, pig, bat, lizard, bear, elephant, maggot, eel, rabbit, scorpion, spider, catfish, as well as stars like Canopus and planets such as Venus, which were originally human but were transformed into animals because of their various sins. For a comprehensive list of these traditions in early Shīʿī literature, see al-Majlisī, *Biḥār al-anwār*, 27:261–284.

beasts and wrong belief to others; and because these living beings have no legal responsibility (*mukallaf*), we cannot speak of their believing in truth or falsehood.[111]

Nevertheless, he does not entirely put aside these traditions, and he tries as much as possible to interpret them. For example, in a tradition in *Kitāb al-Tawḥīd* in al-Kulaynī's *al-Kāfī*, Hishām b. al-Ḥakam relates to Jaʿfar al-Ṣādiq a trick question raised by one of the heretics (*zanādiqa*) to put God's omnipotence into doubt:

> Is God capable of fitting the entire world into an egg without enlarging the size of the egg or diminishing the size of the world?
>
> The Imam responds, 'If someone is capable of placing all that you see into the pupil of your eye, He [God] is also capable of performing this action.'[112]

Although the falsehood of this tradition is evident to al-Murtaḍā, as he believes that there is a plethora of such wrong and irrational hadiths even in Imāmī collections and that one should disregard them categorically, he provides an interpretation of the tradition contrary to its apparent meaning, though he confesses that it is an arbitrary interpretation (*taʾwīl mutaʿassif*). He states,

> The *zanādiqa* probably did not distinguish between what is possible (*mumkin*) and what is impossible (*muḥāl*). Thus, the Imam was worried that if he said that this was something logically impossible, they would regard it as an inability on God's part. He thus responded in a way which implies that if something is logically possible, then it is within God's power to do that.[113]

Conclusion

In contrast to most later Imāmī scholars, al-Murtaḍā is one of the pioneering Shīʿī scholars who did not recognise the authority of *akhbār al-āḥād* and claimed that there was a consensus among Imāmī scholars on this issue. However, al-Murtaḍā's rejection of the authority of *akhbār al-āḥād* did not mean that he disregarded them altogether. In his works, particularly his *Amālī*, al-Murtaḍā often mentions traditions that, according to their *isnād*s, are in the category of isolated traditions. He does not reject

---

111 Al-Murtaḍā, *Amālī*, 2:349–353, *takmila*. For another example, see al-Murtaḍā, *Amālī*, 2:392–395, *takmila*.
112 Al-Kulaynī, *al-Kāfī*, 1:79.
113 Al-Murtaḍā, *Rasāʾil*, 1:410–411.

them; rather, he deliberately interprets them such that their meanings do not contradict his doctrinal views or legal opinions. Instead of rejecting isolated traditions whose apparent meanings seem to be contrary to Muʿtazilī principles, al-Murtaḍā interprets them against their obvious meanings. By doing so, he admits the authenticity and legitimacy of such isolated traditions, so that they are considered among the true sayings of the Prophet or the Imams. He only rules out those traditions whose literal meanings support ideas like determinism, anthropomorphism and the like, or that contradict reason, for which there is no way to remove the contradiction without indulging in extreme hermeneutical choices that lead to arbitrary interpretations.

Al-Murtaḍā's approach to understanding traditions is based on the text proper rather than the *isnād*. In his view, a tradition is only considered authentic when it is *mutawātir* or the consensus of Imāmī scholars supports it. In other words, an isolated tradition is not acceptable if it is not supported by firm evidence, and the chain of transmitters is not regarded as firm evidence. Thus, there is no need to investigate its *isnād* and transmitters to determine its authenticity. When al-Murtaḍā interprets a tradition, he assumes that it is authentic; this may explain why he tries to remove any apparent contradiction between it and the Qur'an, the agreed-upon hadith, his theological principles or reason. In interpreting traditions, he applies a hermeneutical principle that any possible meaning may be suggested, provided there is evidence for it in Arabic literature. All semantic aspects of a statement should be considered, because the speaker may have intended any of those aspects, and we cannot be certain which one represents the original intention. Therefore, al-Murtaḍā mentions all the possible meanings of a given statement, even contradictory or conflicting meanings. In addition, he does not regard any of the various meanings of a tradition as incorrect, unless they contradict established knowledge and firm belief. At most he assesses and grades them relatively, considering some interpretations more likely than others.

For most traditions, al-Murtaḍā elaborates on their difficult vocabulary, thereby demonstrating his mastery of the Arabic language and literature. By referring to the Arabic lexicon, he sometimes suggests new meanings for obscure or rare words, and this leads to novel interpretations of the traditions. By mentioning various aspects of a tradition, he occasionally removes semantic ambiguities from it, to interpret its apparent contradiction with Qur'anic verses and other traditions. For al-Murtaḍā, reason and theological principles are essential criteria for understanding and interpreting hadiths. Indeed, this is the dominant approach of al-Murtaḍā's interpretations, and even when he defines words and presents the meanings of the traditions, the prominent role of his rational-theological presuppositions is evident in his argumentation.

Bibliography

Primary Sources

Abū ʿUbayd al-Qāsim b. Sallām. *Kitāb Gharīb al-ḥadīth*. Edited by Ḥusayn Muḥammad Muḥammad Sharaf. 6 vols. Cairo: al-Hayʾa al-ʿĀmma li-Shuʾūn al-Maṭābiʿ al-Amīriyya, 1404/1984.

al-ʿAskarī, Abū Aḥmad al-Ḥasan b. ʿAbdallāh. *Taṣḥīfāt al-muḥaddithīn*. Edited by Maḥmūd Aḥmad Mīra. 3 vols. Cairo: al-Maṭbaʿa al-ʿArabiyya al-Ḥadītha, 1402/1982.

al-Bukhārī, Abū ʿAbdallāh Muḥammad b. Ismāʿīl. *Ṣaḥīḥ al-Bukhārī*. 9 vols. Beirut: Dār al-Ṭawq al-Najāh, 1422/[2001]; repr. of Bulaq: al-Maṭbaʿa al-Kubrā al-Amīriyya, 1311–12/1894–95.

Ibn Abī al-Ḥadīd al-Muʿtazilī, ʿIzz al-Dīn Abū Ḥāmid ʿAbd al-Ḥamīd b. Hibatallāh. *Sharḥ Nahj al-balāgha*. Edited by Muḥammad Abū al-Faḍl Ibrāhīm. 20 vols. Cairo: Dār Iḥyāʾ al-Kutub al-ʿArabiyya, 1378/1959.

Ibn al-Anbārī, Abū Bakr Muḥammad b. al-Qāsim. *al-Zāhir fī maʿānī kalimāt al-nās*. Edited by Ḥātim Ṣāliḥ Ḍāmin. 2 vols. Baghdad: Dār al-Shuʾūn al-Thaqāfiyya al-ʿĀmma, 1987.

Ibn Bābūyah al-Ṣadūq, Abū Jaʿfar Muḥammad b. ʿAlī. *ʿIlal al-sharāʾiʿ*. Edited by Muḥammad Ṣādiq Baḥr al-ʿUlūm. 2 vols. Najaf: Manshūrāt al-Maktaba al-Ḥaydariyya, 1386/1966.

Ibn Bābūyah al-Ṣadūq, Abū Jaʿfar Muḥammad b. ʿAlī. *Kitāb al-Khiṣāl*. Edited by ʿAlī Akbar al-Ghaffārī. Qum: Manshūrāt Jāmiʿat al-Mudarrisīn fī al-Ḥawza al-ʿIlmiyya li-l-Kutub al-Islāmiyya, 1403/1983.

Ibn Bābūyah al-Ṣadūq, Abū Jaʿfar Muḥammad b. ʿAlī. *ʿUyūn akhbār al-Riḍā*. Edited by Sayyid Mahdī al-Husaynī al-Lājawardī. 2 vols. Qum: Dār al-ʿIlm, 1377–79/ [1958–59].

Ibn Fūrak al-Iṣbahānī, Abū Bakr Muḥammad b. al-Ḥasan. *Kitāb Mushkil al-ḥadīth aw taʾwīl al-akhbār al-mutashābiha*. Edited by Daniel Gimaret. Damascus: al-Maʿhad al-Faransī li-l-Dirāsāt al-ʿArabiyya, 2003.

Ibn Ḥanbal, Aḥmad b. Muḥammad. *Musnad al-imām Aḥmad ibn Ḥanbal*. 6 vols. Cairo: al-Maṭbaʿa al-Maymaniyya, 1313/1895.

Ibn Qutayba al-Dīnawarī, Abū Muḥammad ʿAbdallāh b. Muslim. *Iṣlāḥ ghalaṭ Abī ʿUbayd fī Gharīb al-ḥadīth*. Edited by ʿAbdallāh al-Jabūrī. Beirut: Dār al-Gharb al-Islāmī, 1403/1983.

Ibn Qutayba al-Dīnawarī, Abū Muḥammad ʿAbdallāh b. Muslim. *Taʾwīl mukhtalif al-ḥadīth*. Edited by Muḥammad Muḥyī al-Dīn al-Aṣfar. Beirut: al-Maktab al-Islāmī, 1419/1999.

Mālik b. Anas. *Muwaṭṭaʾ al-Imām Mālik*. Edited by Muḥammad Muṣṭafā al-Aʿẓamī. 8 vols. Abu Dhabi: Muʾassasat Zāyid b. Sulṭān Āl Nahyān, 1425/2004.

al-Iṣbahānī, Abū Muḥammad ʿAbdallāh b. Muḥammad. *Kitāb al-Amthāl fī al-ḥadīth al-nabawī*. Edited by ʿAbd al-ʿAlī ʿAbd al-Ḥamīd Ḥāmid. Bombay: al-Dār al-Salafiyya, 1408/1987.

al-Khaṭṭābī, Abū Sulaymān Ḥamd b. Muḥammad. *Gharīb al-ḥadīth*. Edited by ʿAbd al-Karīm Ibrāhīm al-Gharbāwī. 3 vols. Damascus: Dār al-Fikr, 1402/1982.

al-Kulaynī. *al-Kāfī*. Edited by ʿAlī Akbar al-Ghaffārī. 8 vols. Tehran: Dār al-Kutub al-Islāmiyya, 1388/1968.

al-Majlisī, Muḥammad Bāqir. *Biḥār al-anwār al-jāmiʿa li-durar akhbār al-aʾimma al-aṭhār*. 110 vols. Beirut: Dār Iḥyāʾ al-Turāth al-ʿArabī, 1403/1983.

al-Mufīd, Muḥammad b. Muḥammad b. Nuʿmān. *Awāʾil al-maqālāt*. Edited by Ibrāhīm al-Anṣārī. Qum: al-Muʾtamar al-ʿĀlamī li-Alfiyyat al-Shaykh al-Mufīd, 1413/1993.

al-Murtaḍā, al-Sharīf Abū al-Qāsim ʿAlī b. al-Ḥusayn al-Mūsawī. *Amālī al-Murtaḍā: Ghurar al-fawāʾid wa-durar al-qalāʾid*. Edited by Muḥammad Abū al-Faḍl Ibrāhīm. 2 vols. Cairo: Dār Iḥyāʾ al-Kutub al-ʿArabiyya, 1954.

al-Murtaḍā, al-Sharīf Abū al-Qāsim ʿAlī b. al-Ḥusayn al-Mūsawī. *al-Dhakhīra fī ʿilm al-kalām*. Edited by Sayyid Aḥmad Ḥusaynī. Qum: Muʾassasat al-Nashr al-Islāmī, 1411/1990.

al-Murtaḍā, al-Sharīf Abū al-Qāsim ʿAlī b. al-Ḥusayn al-Mūsawī. *al-Dharīʿa ilā uṣūl al-sharīʿa*. Edited by Abū al-Qāsim Gurji. 2 vols. Tehran: Intishārāt-i Dānishgāh-i Tehran, 1348 Sh./1969–70.

al-Murtaḍā, al-Sharīf Abū al-Qāsim ʿAlī b. al-Ḥusayn al-Mūsawī. *al-Intiṣār*. Qum: Muʾassasat al-Nashr al-Islāmī, 1415/1995.

al-Murtaḍā, al-Sharīf Abū al-Qāsim ʿAlī b. al-Ḥusayn al-Mūsawī. *Rasāʾil al-Sharīf al-Murtaḍā*. Edited by Sayyid Aḥmad Ḥusaynī. 4 vols. Qum: Dār al-Qurʾān al-Karīm, 1405–10/1985–90.

al-Murtaḍā, al-Sharīf Abū al-Qāsim ʿAlī b. al-Ḥusayn al-Mūsawī. *al-Shāfī fī al-imāma*. Edited by ʿAbd al-Zahrāʾ al-Ḥusaynī al-Khaṭīb. 4 vols. Tehran: Muʾassasat al-Ṣādiq, 1407/1986.

Muslim b. al-Ḥajjāj al-Qushayrī. *al-Jāmiʿ al-ṣaḥīḥ*. 8 vols. [Istanbul]: al-Maṭbaʿa al-ʿĀmira, 1330–4/1912–16.

Nahj al-balāgha, wa-huwa majmūʿ mā ikhtārahū al-Sharīf al-Raḍī min kalām sayyidinā amīr al-muʾminīn ʿAlī b. Abī Ṭālib ʿalayhi al-salām. Edited by Muḥammad ʿAbduh. Beirut: Dār al-Maʿrifa, n.d.

al-Raḍī, al-Sharīf Abū al-Ḥasan Muḥammad b. Ḥusayn al-Mūsawī. *al-Majāzāt al-nabawiyya*. Edited by Ṭāhā Muḥammad al-Zaynī. Cairo: Muʾassasat al-Ḥalabī, 1387/1967.

al-Ṣaffār al-Qummī, Abū Jaʿfar Muḥammad b. al-Ḥasan. *Baṣāʾir al-darajāt al-kubrā fī faḍāʾil āl Muḥammad*. Edited by Mīrzā Muḥsin Kuchehbāghī. Tehran: Manshūrāt al-Aʿlamī, 1404/1984.

al-Shāfiʿī, Muḥammad b. Idrīs. *al-Umm – al-juzʾ al-ʿāshir: [vol. 10] ikhtilāf al-ḥadīth*. Edited by Rafʿat Fawzī ʿAbd al-Muṭṭalib. 11 vols. Mansoura: Dār al-Wafāʾ, 1422/2001.

al-Ṭabarānī, Abū al-Qāsim Sulaymān b. Aḥmad. *al-Muʿjam al-kabīr*. Edited by Ḥamdī b. ʿAbd al-Majīd al-Salafī. 20 vols. Cairo: al-Maktabat Ibn Taymiyya [1397/1977].

al-Ṭūsī, Abū Jaʿfar Muḥammad b. al-Ḥasan. *al-ʿUdda fī uṣūl al-fiqh*. Edited by Muḥammad Riḍā Anṣārī Qummī. 2 vols. Qum: al-Muḥaqqiq, 1997.

Secondary Sources

Abdulsater, Hussein Ali. 'The Climax of Speculative Theology in Buyid Shīʿism: The Contribution of al-Sharīf al-Murtaḍā.' PhD dissertation, Yale University, 2013.

Abdulsater, Hussein Ali. *Shiʿi Doctrine, Muʿtazili Theology: al-Sharīf al-Murtaḍā and Imami Discourse*. Edinburgh: Edinburgh University, 2017.

Blecher, Joel. 'Ḥadīth Commentary', in *EI³*. <http://dx.doi.org/10.1163/1573–3912_ei3_COM_32080>, accessed 20 February 2022.

Davies, Stephen. *Philosophical Perspectives on Art*. Oxford: Oxford University Press, 2007.

El-Omari, Racha. 'Accommodation and Resistance: Classical Muʿtazilites on Ḥadīth.' *Journal of Near Eastern Studies* 71, no. 2 (2012): 231–256.

Goldziher, Ignaz. *Schools of Koranic Commentators*. Edited and translated by W. H. Behn. Wiesbaden: Harrassowitz, 2006.

Hubballāh, Ḥaydar. *Naẓariyyat al-sunna fī al-fikr al-Imāmī al-Shīʿī: al-takawwun wa-l-ṣayrūra*. Beirut: Muʾassasat al-Intishār al-ʿArabī, 2006.

Juynboll, G. H. A. 'Khabar al-Wāḥid', in *EI²*, online: <http://dx.doi.org/10.1163/1573-3912_islam_SIM_4112>, accessed 19 April 2019.

Kohlberg, Etan. 'Introduction.' In F. Daftary and G. Miskinzoda (eds), *The Study of Shiʿi Islam*. London: I. B. Tauris Publishers in association with the Institute of Ismaili Studies, 2014.

Lane, Edward William. *An Arabic-English Lexicon*. 8 vols. London: Willams & Norgate, 1863ff.

McDermott, Martin J. *The Theology of al-Shaikh al-Mufīd (d. 413/1022)*. Beirut: Dār al-Mashriq, 1978.

Madelung, Wilferd. "Alam-al-Hodā', in *EIr*, I/8: 791–795; online: http://www.iranicaonline.org/articles/alam-al-hoda-abul-qasem-ali-b, accessed 17 May 2014.

Madelung, Wilferd. 'Imāmism and Muʿtazilite Theology.' In Toufic Fahd (ed.), *Le Shīʿisme Imâmite*, pp. 13–29. Paris: Presses Universitaires de France, 1970; reprinted in W. Madelung, *Religious Schools and Sects in Medieval Islam*, chapter 7. London: Variorum, 1985.

al-Matouq, Ahmad Muhammad. 'Al-Sharīf al-Murtaḍā's Contribution to the Theory of Plagiarism in Arabic Poetry.' PhD dissertation, University of Pennsylvania, 1987.

Melchert, Christopher. 'The Theory and Practice of Hadith Criticism in the Mid-Ninth Century.' In Petra M. Sijpesteijn and Camilla Adang (eds), *Islam at 250: Studies in Memory of G. H. A. Juynboll*, pp. 74–102 Leiden: Brill, 2020.

Mourad, Suleiman A. 'Why Do We Need Tafsīr? The Muʿtazila Perspective.' *Mélanges de l'Université Saint-Joseph* LXVI (2015–16): 121–133.

Pavlovitch, Pavel. 'Ḥadīth: 7.1.1. *Mutawātir/khabar al-wāḥid*', in *EI³*. <http://dx.doi.org/10.1163/1573–3912_ei3_COM_30163>, accessed 19 April 2019.

Robson, J. 'Ḥadīth: II. Collections of Ḥadīth', in *EI²*. <http://dx.doi.org/10.1163/1573–3912_islam_COM_0248>, accessed 13 April 2019.

Sourdel, D. 'Dār al-ʿIlm', in *EI²*. <http://dx.doi.org/10.1163/1573–3912_islam_SIM_1702>, accessed 19 April 2019.

Stewart, Devin J. *Islamic Legal Orthodoxy: Twelver Shiite Responses to the Sunni Legal System*. Salt Lake City: University of Utah Press, 1998.

Stewart, Devin J. 'al-Sharīf al-Murtaḍā (d. 436/1044).' In Oussama Arabi, David S. Powers, and Susan A. Spectorsky (eds), *Islamic Legal Thought: A Compendium of Muslim Jurists*, pp. 167–210. Studies in Islamic Law and Society 36. Leiden: Brill, 2013.

van Ess, Josef. 'al-Manzila Bayn al-Manzilatayn', in *EI²*. <http://dx.doi.org/10.1163/1573-3912_islam_SIM_4949>, accessed 13 April 2019.

Watt, W. Montgomery. 'Mu'ākhāt', in *EI²*. <http://dx.doi.org/10.1163/1573-3912_islam_SIM_5267>, accessed 13 June 2021.

Zysow, Aron. *The Economy of Certainty: An Introduction to the Typology of Islamic Legal Theory*. Atlanta: Lockwood Press, 2013.

CHAPTER 3

'Blessed are the Strangers (ghurabā')': An Apocalyptic Hadith on the Virtues of Loneliness, Sadness and Exile

Youshaa Patel

The end returns to the beginning.

Mullā ʿAlī al-Qārī (d. 1014/1605)[1]

By definition, we know little about strangers – their identity, character or where they come from.[2] Enveloped in a thick fog of mystery, strangers (*ghurabā'*, sing. *gharīb*), are often characterised as lonely, marginal figures who are perceived as alien, foreign, other – outcasts who stand apart from the mainstream. A sympathetic and moving portrayal of the stranger is found in the lone surviving handwritten manuscript of the literary genius, William Shakespeare:[3]

> Imagine that you see the wretched strangers,
> Their babies at their backs and their poor luggage,
> Plodding to the ports and coasts for transportation.[4]

In this scene of the once banned play, Shakespeare gives voice to the historical figure of Sir Thomas More, deputy sheriff of London, who urges a xenophobic mob fresh from a riot against immigrants to sympathise with the victims of their rage by seeing themselves as 'wretched strangers'. More presses the mob to imagine how they would feel if they immigrated

---

1 '*Inna al-nihāya hiya al-rujūʿ ilā l-bidāya.*' al-Harawī, *Mirqāt al-mafātīḥ*, 1:378–379.
2 Were we to know the stranger well, that person would no longer be a stranger.
3 Harley MS 7368, British Library. See https://www.bl.uk/collection-items/shakespeares-handwriting-in-the-book-of-sir-thomas-more (accessed 16 January 2021).
4 Shakespeare, *The Oxford Shakespeare*, 821.

to a foreign land – poor, vulnerable, alone – and were spurned 'like dogs'.[5] 'This is the stranger's case', declares More, 'and this your mountainish inhumanity.'[6] In restoring the stranger's humanity, More exposes the mob's inhumanity – a brilliant inversion that portrays the stranger as a 'borderline figure' who 'defines the limits of the human'.[7]

Premodern Muslim intellectuals also remarked on the stranger's misery and marginality. The 'Abbāsid litterateur, Abū Ḥayyān al-Tawḥīdī (d. 414/1023), portrayed the stranger as a solitary figure: 'Wherever you see him, you find him always without a friend. People have one another, but he has no one to help him.'[8]

Indeed, as al-Tawḥīdī points out, while most people are embedded in a social network of family and friends, the stranger stands alone. Weak and vulnerable, the stranger has no one to call on for help during difficult times. The stranger's fundamental dilemma is thus one of belonging: most people belong somewhere, but the stranger belongs nowhere. We can imagine how the stranger's social isolation may effect a constant state of anxiety that eventually spills over into despair. 'It is not from grief caused by the fear of separation that my tears flow,' continues al-Tawḥīdī, 'but the *gharīb* is a *gharīb*'.[9] Here, al-Tawḥīdī suggests that there is something inherently dismal about being a *gharīb* – that is, the *gharīb* is a tragic figure. This evaluation is not merely academic, detached and impersonal, but appears to reflect al-Tawḥīdī's own experiences of being a *gharīb* – experiences that etched an enduring melancholy into his disposition.

Al-Tawḥīdī nevertheless belonged to a much larger community of strangers who commented on their misery. The experience of being a *gharīb* thus became part of a broader episteme in the premodern Muslim social

5 More's plea to the mob for mercy is as follows:

> 'Why, you must needs be strangers: would you be pleased
> To find a nation of such barbarous temper,
> That, breaking out in hideous violence,
> Would not afford you an abode on earth,
> Whet their detested knives against your throats,
> Spurn you like dogs, and like as if that God
> Owed not nor made not you, nor that the claimants
> Were not all appropriate to your comforts,
> But chartered unto them, what would you think
> To be thus used?'

Shakespeare, *The Oxford Shakespeare*, 822.

6 Shakespeare, *The Oxford Shakespeare*, 822.
7 Fiedler, *The Stranger in Shakespeare*, 15.
8 Al-Tawḥīdī, *al-Baṣā'ir*, 8:155; trans. Rosenthal, 'The Stranger', 55.
9 Al-Tawḥīdī, *al-Baṣā'ir*, 8:155.

imagination.[10] In what is considered the oldest dictionary of the Arabic language, *Kitāb al-ʿAyn* of al-Farāhīdī (d. c. 175/791), *ghurba* is defined as 'being [physically] distant from one's homeland' (*ightirāb min al-waṭan*), or more simply, 'exile'.[11] In this way, the presence of the *gharīb* signals the intrusion of the other among us, blurring boundaries between insider and outsider, native and foreign. The *gharīb*, so commonly characterised by his disconnection, ironically becomes what Michael Pifer calls a 'connective figure'.[12]

Authored in the fourth/tenth century, the *Kitāb al-Ghurabā'* (The book of strangers) is a compilation of poetry and anecdotes from Arabic graffiti left behind by exiles across the Islamic Middle East who lamented their condition.[13] The anonymous author of this compilation explains that 'writing of their sufferings on the walls and disclosing their secrets ... has become the custom of strangers in every country and destination, and a distinguishing feature of theirs in every place and site'.[14] They did so 'in order to seek blessing in the prayer of (other) strangers, travellers and people bereft of kith and kin'.[15] Disconnected from their loved ones, strangers connected with other strangers by leaving inscriptions like this one:

I wish I knew when my hardship would be over
And my trials will come to an end
I am displaced, cast out, devoid of solace
Far away from my home and distanced from my native land.[16]

According to the *Kitāb al-Ghurabā'*, the misery of being a stranger is a universal human experience, found 'in every country and destination'.[17]

Reading these premodern descriptions of the stranger today, one is reminded of the moral panic in Europe and the United States over foreign refugees crossing national borders – panic that evokes an almost uniformly negative portrayal of strangers. According to the late Franz Rosenthal, the stranger, the *gharīb*, also carried a primarily negative valence in premodern Muslim literature: 'the positive side, the possible advantages of being a stranger ... cannot match the diversity of the reflections on the stranger's utter wretchedness.'[18] It was just easier (and more common) for strangers to release emotional outpourings of grief and sadness.

---

10 Pifer, 'The Stranger's Voice', 30.
11 Al-Farāhīdī, *Kitāb al-ʿAyn*, 3:271.
12 Pifer, 'The Stranger's Voice', 32.
13 Crone and Moreh, *The Book of Strangers*.
14 Crone and Moreh, *The Book of Strangers*, 21.
15 Crone and Moreh, *The Book of Strangers*, 21.
16 Crone and Moreh, *The Book of Strangers*, 63.
17 Crone and Moreh, *The Book of Strangers*, 21.
18 Rosenthal, 'The Stranger', 49.

Nevertheless, Muslim thinkers did not exclusively portray this liminal state as a disability; many saw it as a virtue as well. The Mamlūk scholar, Ibn Taymiyya (d. 728/1328), called *ghurabā'* 'the happiest of people' (*as'ad al-nās*).[19] There were in fact advantages to being a *gharīb*. But given the overwhelming misery of being a stranger, how did Ibn Taymiyya and other Muslim scholars construe it as a virtue? Answering this question is my main task in this chapter. In fact, I wish not only to illuminate this alternative point of view, but also to suggest that this outlook is more prevalent in premodern Muslim writings on the subject than previously assumed in Western scholarship – that in the Muslim social imaginary, being a stranger was not so grim.

We may credit the Prophet Muhammad for this optimism. According to a hadith collected by Muslim b. al-Ḥajjāj (d. 261/875), the Prophet told his Companions, 'Islam began strange, and will [one day] return to being strange – just as it began – so blessed are the strangers (*ṭūbā li-l-ghurabā'*)'.[20] Rosenthal credits the hadith with 'merging all the various strands of thought about the stranger into one overarching concept'.[21] Other hadiths – and the substantial body of commentary on them – enrich the apocalyptic mythology enveloping the hadith.[22] Perceiving that the end times may indeed be imminent, today, many followers of extremist groups such as ISIS and al-Qaida call themselves *ghurabā'*, or strangers, to signal their religious credentials and disavowal of mainstream cultural norms.[23] So potent is this badge of non-conformity that a *nashīd* titled 'Ghurabā', ghuraba" has become a global anthem for Muslim extremists.[24] And while I am tempted to let present concerns dictate my enquiry, nonetheless I have chosen to narrow my focus to the Islamic past: How did premodern religious authorities – Sufis, jurists, theologians and historians – understand the virtues of being a stranger in light of this hadith?

19 Ibn Taymiyya, *Majmū'a*, 18:292.

20 Muslim, *Ṣaḥīḥ*, 80 (*Kitāb al-īmān, bāb bayān anna al-Islām bada'a gharīb wa-sa-ya'ūdu gharīb*); al-Tirmidhī, *Sunan*, 744 (*Kitāb al-īmān, bāb mā jā'a anna al-Islām bada'a gharīb wa-sa-ya'ūdu gharīb*); Ibn Mājah, *Sunan*, 602–603 (*Kitāb al-fitan, bāb bada'a al-Islām gharīb*); Ibn Abī Shayba, *al-Muṣannaf*, 7:83; Abū Ya'lā, *Musnad*, 11:52, and other narrations, 8:388, 2:99; al-Ṭaḥāwī, *Sharḥ Mushkil al-āthār*, 2:171, and other narrations 2:169–171; al-Quḍā'ī, *Musnad*, 2:138, and other narrations, 2:137–139; al-Bazzār, *Musnad*, 8:332, 12:209; al-Ṭabarānī, *al-Mu'jam al-kabīr*, 10:99, and another narration, 6:164. See nn. 35–39 below for references to other narrations of the hadith.

21 Rosenthal, 'The Stranger', 59.

22 I mention some of these other apocalyptic hadiths below. Also see references in notes 33–34.

23 Al-Thaghrī, 'And as for the Blessing'; Wood, *The Way of the Strangers*; McCants, *The ISIS Apocalypse*, 100–103; Fishman, 'After Zarqawi'; Creswell and Haykel, 'Battle Lines', 102–108.

24 Husain, *The House of Islam*, 141–154.

There are historical obstacles that hinder a straightforward answer to this question. Rosenthal lamented, 'A knowledge of the context in which it [the hadith] originated and what it originally referred to would be extremely helpful, but, to all indications, it is not within our reach ...'[25] Although it may be impossible to ascribe the hadith to a single origin, we can uncover some information about when and where it circulated.[26] It is likely that the strangers mentioned in this tradition do not refer to a single group, but to many groups – as the variants, briefly discussed below, suggest.

In what follows, I first examine the text of the hadith – what I call the hadith of *al-ghurabā'* – together with its transmission history, in order to illuminate when and where it first circulated and how it may have been understood during the first centuries of Islam. I demonstrate how variants of the hadith blur conventional scholarly distinctions between 'text' and 'commentary' by offering explanations of the key term, *ghurabā'*, in the text itself. I also demonstrate that key narrations of the hadith can be linked to specific geographic locales. After examining the text and transmission of the hadith, I trace its reception in a wide range of Islamic literary genres, including manuals of ethics and spirituality, *fatwā* collections, Sufi treatises, historical chronicles and independent treatises on *ghurba*, from the fourth/tenth century until the ninth/fifteenth century. This conceptual history illuminates the meaning and value of non-conformity in Islamic thought.

It is important to keep in mind that the experience of being a stranger was not limited to elite literary or scholarly circles but was woven into the everyday lives of Muslims. Recently, Kristina Richardson has shown that an itinerant tribal group, the Banū Sāsān, who renamed themselves 'the *ghurabā'* in the seventh/thirteenth century, possessed their own distinct language: 'the language of strangers' (*lisān al-ghurabā'*).[27] Beyond the archive of Arabic graffiti of poems and laments left by *ghurabā'* on stones, walls and gates in taverns, shrines and mosques, cosmopolitan cities like Damascus may even have had a 'strangers' quarter' (*hārat al-ghurabā'*), inhabited by travellers, foreigner merchants and students, as well as refugees.[28] And throughout premodern *dār al-Islām* – east (*mashriq*) and west (*maghrib*) – hostelries, called *fundūqs* or *khāns*, served as lodges for travellers, residents, pilgrims and merchants alike, helping to establish a

---

25 Rosenthal, 'The Stranger', 60; 'Alī al-Riḍā, *Ṣaḥīfat al-Riḍā*.
26 On dating (and locating) prophetic traditions, see Motzki, 'Dating Muslim Traditions'; Motzki, 'The *Muṣannaf*'; Berg, 'Competing Paradigms'; Sadeghi, 'The Traveling Tradition Test'; Yarbrough, 'I'll Not Accept Aid'. Also see my study, '"Whoever Imitates a People"'.
27 Richardson, 'The Invisible Strangers', 188.
28 Rosenthal, 'The Stranger', 63; see also al-Ghazzī, *Lutf al-samar*, 1:39 n.1.

society and culture of hospitality in which strangers could find a place, if only for a while.[29]

'Who are the *Ghurabā*'?'

Gharīb (pl. *ghurabā*'), as Michael Pifer explains, is an Arabic term that 'encompassed a broad range of theological concepts, social categories, affective states and topics of literary production among medieval Jews, Christians, and Muslims alike'.[30] Neither the idea nor the term was exclusive to Muslims. Its Semitic root, *gh-r-b*, meaning 'to enter', Rosenthal argues, is entwined with the original meaning of the Arabic *gharīb* as a newcomer who enters or intrudes on a group.[31] Eventually, the term came to describe what was strange in two primary senses: (1) foreigners, travellers and outsiders; and (2) unusual, rare or marvellous things. After the emergence of Islam, the semantic field of *gharīb* not only continued to encompass strangers of various types, but also evolved into a lexicographical term that identified rare and unusual words in Islamic scripture, the *gharīb al-Qurʾān* and *gharīb al-ḥadīth*.[32] The robust semantic field of *gharīb*, in fact, encompasses a cluster of Arabic words derived from the root *gh-r-b* that enhances our understanding of the stranger as a relational figure who straddles the dialectic between inclusion and exclusion, connection and disconnection; these variations include *ightirāb* (estrangement), *tagharrub* (emigration), *taghrīb* (expulsion or banishment) and *ghurba* (exile, or the state of being a stranger). The term, like the physical bodies of the subjects it represents, was also mobile, migrating beyond the linguistic boundaries of Arabic, and crossing into New Persian, Anatolian Turkish and Middle Armenian, thus crossing geographic, cultural and religious boundaries as well.[33]

Muslim scholars – like Jewish and Christian sages – transmitted and compiled traditions that purported to reveal the secrets of God, and are, in other words, apocalyptic; they prophesy, often through symbol and allegory, what will take place at the end of the world – the last days, the day of judgement, heaven and hell.[34] While some traditions detail future events that correspond to crises and catastrophes that preceded or were

29 Constable, *Housing the Stranger.*
30 Pifer, 'The Age of the *Gharīb*', 15.
31 Rosenthal, 'The Stranger', 38.
32 See, for example, al-Iṣfahānī, *Mufradāt* and Ibn al-Athīr, *al-Nihāya.*
33 Pifer, 'The Age of the *Gharīb*', 15.
34 On Muslim apocalyptic in premodern Islam, see Madelung, 'Apocalyptic Prophecies';
     M. Cook, 'Eschatology'; M. Cook, 'An Early Apocalyptic Chronicle'; D. Cook, *Studies in
     Muslim Apocalyptic*; Livne-Kafri, 'Some Notes'; Shoemaker, *The Apocalypse of Empire*;
     Velji, *An Apocalyptic History.* On Muslim apocalyptic in modern Islam, see D. Cook,
     Contemporary Muslim Apocalyptic Literature; D. Cook, 'Ḥadīth'; and Filiu, *Apocalypse.*

contemporary to the narrator, thus tantalising historians of early Islam with the possibility of determining their origin stories, others do not. By purporting to disclose a truth that has yet to come, the hadith of *al-ghurabā'* fits into a genre of Islamic apocalypticism. But due to the brevity and heterogeneity of the hadith's textual content, it defies easy placement into a specific historical context.[35]

The hadith of *al-ghurabā'* has been transmitted in multiple narrations, with variations in the text (*matn*) that range from minor to major. Although this textual heterogeneity further obscures an already enigmatic hadith, it is nonetheless productive; when taken together, the narrations provide an early semantic map of a tradition. In some narrations, the phrase 'blessed are the strangers' (*ṭūbā li-l-ghurabā'*) is absent. In other narrations, Islam is replaced with a related term such as *dīn* or *īmān*; and in yet others, the Prophet Muhammad is asked 'Who are they (i.e. strangers)?' and he replies with a variety of answers:

1. 'Those who have left their tribes.'[36]
2. 'Reformers at a time when the masses have become corrupt.'[37]
3. 'Those who love my Sunna and teach it to others.'[38]
4. 'A virtuous minority amidst a corrupt majority, who are disobeyed more often than obeyed,' or 'who are more loathed by the people than loved.'[39]
5. '[They are] fugitives of faith. They will gather with Jesus, the son of Mary, on the day of judgement.'[40]

In fact, most narrations include glosses on *al-ghurabā'*, the key term on which the meaning of the tradition hinges. In these narrations, the source

---

35 The hadith compiler, Ibn Mājah, categorises the hadith of *al-ghurabā'* under the heading 'The chapter on tribulations' (*kitāb al-fitan*): Ibn Mājah, *Sunan*, 602–603. The hadith is also found in the earliest complete work of apocalyptic to survive; this work dates to the early third/ninth century: al-Marwazī, *Kitāb al-Fitan*, 108; translated as al-Marwazī, 'The Book of Tribulations', 93. Later, Mamlūk-era religious scholars like Ibn Kathīr (d. 774/1373) continued to associate the hadith with the end times: Ibn Kathīr, *al-Nihāya*, 1:33–34.

36 'Al-nuzzāʿ min al-qabā'il.' Ibn Mājah, *Sunan*, 603 (*Kitāb al-fitan, bāb bada'a al-Islām gharīb*); al-Dārimī, *Sunan*, 3:1813 (*Kitāb al-riqāq, bāb inna al-Islām bada'a gharīb*); Ibn Ḥanbal, *Musnad*, 6:325; Ibn Abī Shayba, *al-Muṣannaf*, 7:83; Abū Yaʿla, *Musnad*, 8:388; al-Ṭaḥāwī, *Sharḥ Mushkil al-āthār*, 2:169.

37 'Alladhīna yuṣliḥūna idhā fasada al-nās', and similar statements. Al-Tirmidhī, *Sunan*, 744 (*Kitāb al-īmān, bāb mā jā'a anna al-Islām bada'a gharīb wa-sa-yaʿūdu gharīb*); al-Ṭabarānī, *al-Muʿjam al-awsaṭ*, 8:308; al-Ṭabarānī, *al-Muʿjam al-kabīr*, 6:164; Ibn Abī Shayba, *al-Muṣannaf*, 7:83; al-Ṭaḥāwī, *Sharḥ Mushkil al-āthār*, 2:170; al-Quḍāʿī, *Musnad*, 2:139.

38 Al-Quḍāʿī, *Musnad*, 2:138.

39 Ibn Ḥanbal, *Musnad*, 11:230–231.

40 Ibn Ḥanbal, *Kitāb al-Zuhd*, 187.

text cannot be neatly distinguished from its commentary since the text is itself a commentary on *al-ghurabā'*. The presence of these glosses suggests that some narrators exploited the ambiguity of the term *ghurabā'* to steer their interpretation of the hadith toward the meaning that aligned best with their subjective worldview, rhetorical objectives, emotional state and social circumstances.

Despite the diversity of the above glosses, these authors seem to agree that the *ghurabā'* are non-conformists; they are a minority who stand out from the crowd. But, the *ghurabā'* are also not a uniform category. Reflecting the heterogeneity of the texts that represent them, the *ghurabā'* are a diverse group. The plurality of narrations of the hadith indicate that there are numerous ways of being strange and different.

The strangers' difference is unique because it is not a deplorable or inferior kind of difference – as is often assumed of those who cannot, or refuse to, fit in. *Ṭūbā*, translated here as 'blessed', is the term that bestows a positive valence on the *ghurabā'*. Although *ṭūbā* is also a multivalent term, its semantic field is uniformly positive, encompassing the meanings of happiness, eternal salvation and a special tree in heaven.[41] Thus, in this context, the *ghurabā'* are spiritually and morally superior to the masses. They are an elite group whose members deserve God's favour; they have a noble status that, in both theory and practice, can be claimed by anyone who is viewed, or who views themselves, as strangers.

Transmission Network: Narrators as Interpreters

With the hadith's multivalence in mind, I offer a preliminary sketch of its transmission history. The hadith was widely circulated among Muslim traditionists, and is found in both early and late Sunnī collections of hadiths, including the *Ṣaḥīḥ* collection of Muslim, the *Sunans* of Ibn Mājah (d. 273/887), al-Tirmidhī (d. 279/892), and al-Dārimī (d. 255/869), and the *Musnad* of Aḥmad b. Ḥanbal (d. 241/855), among others.[42] The Companions most commonly credited with transmitting the tradition from the Prophet include 'Abdallāh b. Mas'ūd (d. c. 32–33/652–654) and Abū Hurayra (d. 58/678), although 'Abdallāh b. 'Umar (d. 73/692) and Anas b. Mālik (d. 91/709) are occasionally mentioned as well. Muslim and other hadith critics ranked its authenticity as sound (*ṣaḥīḥ*), although they deemed some narrations to be weak (*ḍaʿīf*), or very weak (*ḍaʿīf jiddan*).[43]

---

41 See the entry for *ṭ-y-b* in Lane and Lane-Pool, *An Arabic-English Lexicon*, 2: 1900–1904.

42 See n. 20, nn. 35–39 above for references.

43 See, for example, Nāṣir al-Dīn al-Albānī's grade of *ḍaʿīf jiddan* for one narration of the hadith of *al-ghurabā'* in al-Tirmidhī, *Sunan*, ed. al-Albānī, 593.

In my analysis, I focus on the two most widely circulated narrations. First, I examine what I refer to as the short narration, which does not include a gloss on the key term, *ghurabā*': 'Islam began strange, and will [one day] return to being strange – just as it began – so blessed are the strangers!' Next, I examine the specific narration that appends the gloss 'Those who shun their tribes'. The full text of this narration is '"Islam began strange, and will [one day] return to being strange – just as it began – so blessed are the strangers!" It was asked, "Who are the strangers, O' Messenger of God?" He replied, "Those who shun their tribes (*al-nuzzā' min al-qabā'il*)."' I draw on the recent studies of Behnam Sadeghi and Najam Haider who have explored how it is possible to link the circulation of some hadiths to specific geographic locales.[44]

Turning first to the short narration (see the *isnād* map in Figure 3.1), I examine the figure who circulated it most widely, Marwān b. Mu'āwiya b. al-Fazārī (d. 193/808–809) of Kufa.[45] Details from his biography and the presence of distinctive linguistic features from his narration reveal important details about its circulation. Al-Fazārī was born during the reign of the Umayyad caliph, Hishām b. 'Abd al-Mālik (r. 105–125/724–743), and died during the 'Abbāsid period. Al-Fazārī narrated the hadith on the authority of the Companion, Abū Hurayra, to many students during the second half of the second/eighth century. According to the *isnād*, al-Fazārī's teacher Yazīd b. Kaysān and his teacher Abū Ḥāzim al-Ashja'ī, who learned the hadith from Abū Hurayra, were Kufan as well.[46] Al-Fazārī eventually moved to Damascus – and the tradition travelled with him. All five students to whom he is said to have transmitted the tradition settled in cities outside Kufa: Ibn Abī 'Umar al-'Adanī, who was Yemeni, and Ya'qūb b. Ḥumayd b. Kāsib, who was Medinan, settled in Mecca; Suwayd b. Sa'īd of Herat settled in Anbar, Iraq; Muḥammad b. 'Abbād, who was Meccan, settled in Baghdad; and 'Abd al-Raḥmān b. Ibrāhīm (Duhaym) settled in Damascus.

The connection of this short narration to Kufa is strengthened by two other Kufan narrations: a *mursal* narration (in which the Companion it was transmitted from is missing) collected by the renowned Iraqi traditionist, Abū Bakr b. Abī Shayba (d. 235/849), and another narration transmitted by the Kufan judge, Ḥafṣ b. Ghiyāth (d. 194/809), on the authority of the Companion 'Abdallāh b. Mas'ūd, during the second half of the second/eighth

---

44 Haider, 'The Geography'; Sadeghi, 'The Traveling Tradition Test'.

45 Al-Dhahabī, *Siyar*, 9:51–53.

46 Abū Ḥāzim al-Ashja'ī (d. c. 100/718) was a companion of Abū Hurayra. See al-Dhahabī, *Siyar*, 5:7–8. For Yazīd b. Kaysān Abū Ismā'īl al-Yashkurī al-Kūfī, see Ibn Ḥajar, *Taqrīb al-tahdhīb*, 1:604.

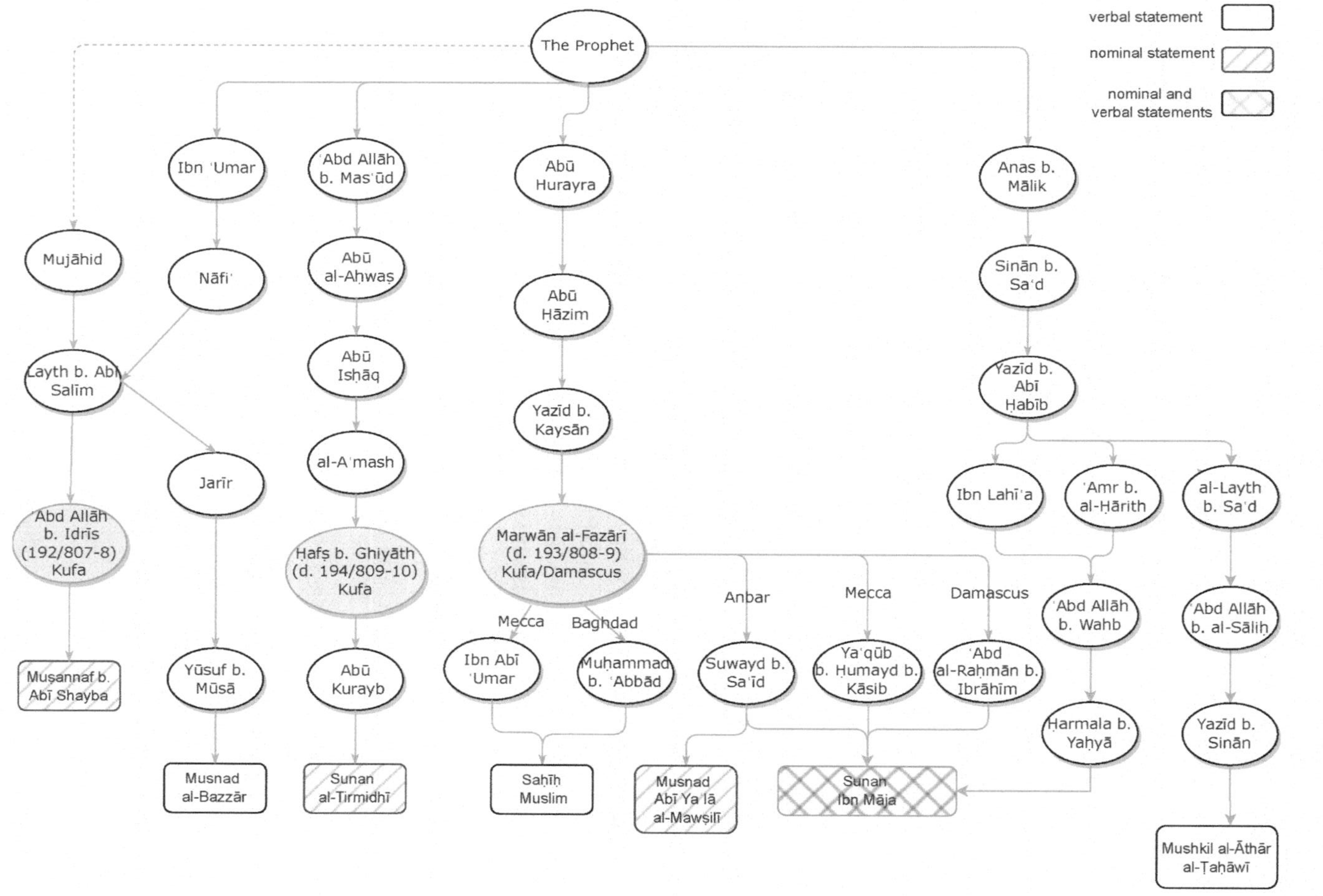

Figure 3.1 Isnād map of the short narration of the 'Blessed are the strangers' hadith.

century.[47] Although these two narrations are solitary transmissions, when combined with al-Fazārī's widely circulated narration, they strengthen our confidence that the short narration was circulated in Kufa no later than the second half of the second/eighth century.[48]

The second narration we examine, the one with the gloss 'Those who shun their tribes', links this hadith to Kufa more closely. It appears that Ḥafṣ b. Ghiyāth was mainly responsible for circulating this version during the second half of the second/eighth century (see Figure 3.2).[49] Like the narrators of the short version, the narrators preceding Ibn Ghiyāth (i.e. al-A'mash, Abū Isḥāq al-Sabī'ī, Abū al-Aḥwaṣ al-Ashja'ī) are all Kufan. Unlike al-Fazārī, however, Ibn Ghiyāth primarily transmitted the hadith to other Kufans, who then transmitted it to compilers of hadith. We can confidently conclude that the gloss 'those who shun their tribes' is distinctively Kufan.

What might explain the interest among Kufans in circulating hadiths that extol the *ghurabā*? As mentioned by subsequent commentators on the hadith, the phrase 'Those who shun their tribes' immediately evokes memories of the first Muslim converts who left their tribes and became exiles, emigrating from Mecca to Abyssinia, then to Medina. The turbulent social and political climate of Kufa during the first/seventh and second/eighth centuries fuelled apocalyptic imagination and may have resonated with the first generations of Kufans who perceived the Arab nobility (*ashrāf*) who immigrated to the city as usurpers who had seized power through the influence of tribal relations, not through piety and upright conduct. The Kufans who found themselves at the margins of political power loathed this reversal of fortune, which resulted in political crises

---

47 A Schachtian view would likely propose that the *mursal* narration is chronologically the oldest narration. It is also worth noting that there is a minor variation in the linguistic form of al-Fazārī's narration. Unlike the other two Kufan narrations, which take the form of a nominal statement (*inna al-Islām bada'a gharīb …*) in which the noun precedes the verb (*jumla ismiyya*), al-Fazārī's narration is a verbal statement (*bada'a al-Islām gharīb …*) in which the verb precedes the noun (*jumla fi'liyya*). All five of his students transmit the narration as verbal statements as well (see references in n. 20 to *Ṣaḥīḥ Muslim* and *Sunan Ibn Mājah*). Although Abū Ya'lā al-Mawṣīlī transmits one tradition from al-Fazārī in his *Musnad*, in the form of a *jumla ismiyya*, it is via Suwayd b. Sa'īd, who is also mentioned as a transmitter in Ibn Mājah's collection where it is transmitted as a *jumla fi'liyya*. Abū Ya'lā's transmission does not provide a strong basis to reject the much stronger evidence of Muslim and Ibn Mājah that al-Fazārī transmitted the narration as a *jumla fi'liyya*. Although the meanings of both forms are identical (with slight differences in rhetorical emphasis), the wide circulation of al-Fazārī's narration as a verbal statement is a distinctive feature of his narration in Kufa.

48 To be clear, this conclusion is not meant to imply that al-Fazārī invented the tradition, or that he was the first to transmit this specific narration.

49 On Ḥafṣ b. Ghiyāth, see al-Dhahabī, *Siyar*, 9:22–34; on his relationship to the Ḥanafī school, see Tsafrir, *The History*, 1–27.

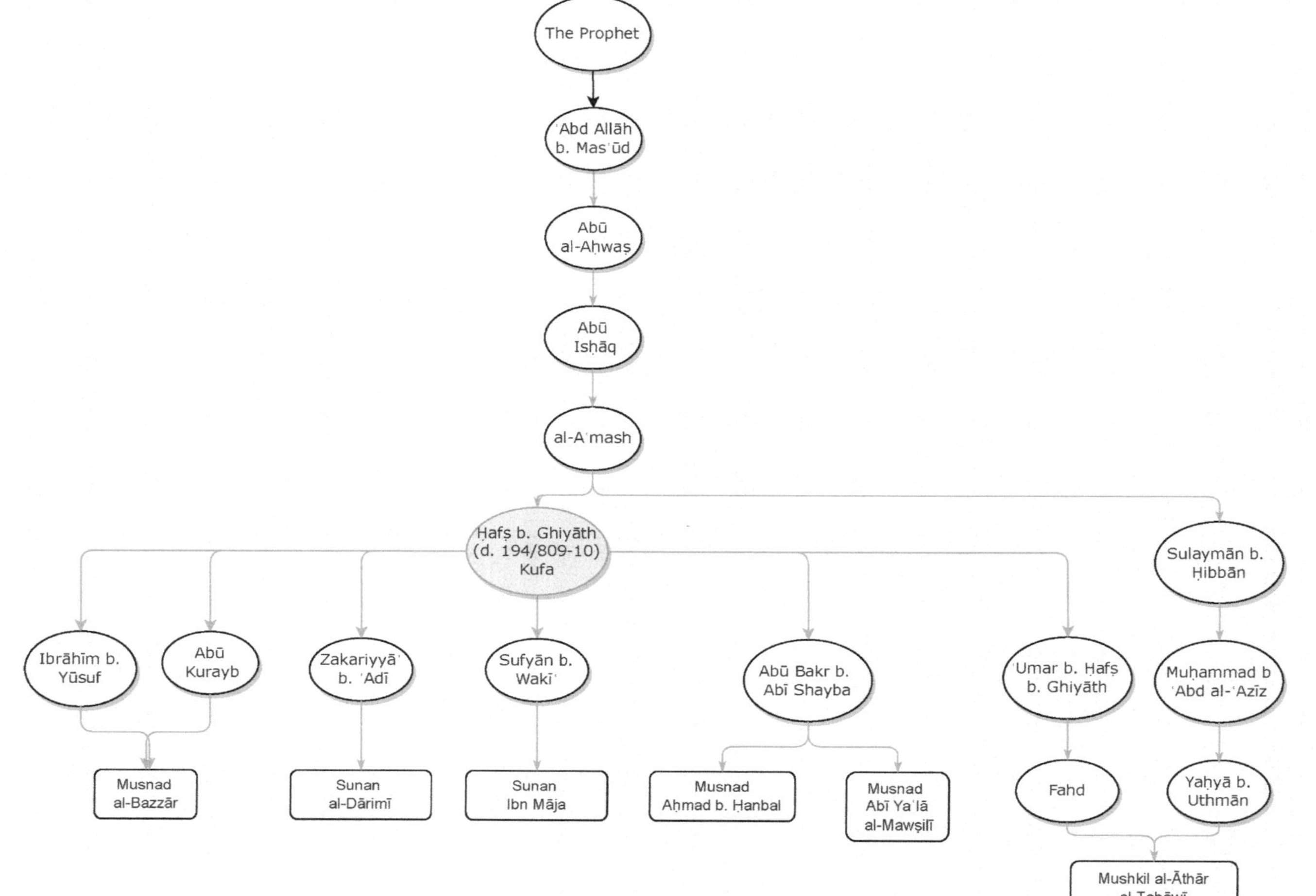

Figure 3.2 Isnād map of the 'Those who shun their tribes' narration.

and even revolution. Coming of age during the 'Abbāsid period, however, Ḥafṣ b. Ghiyāth, did not share this discontent. As a judge situated in the emerging Ḥanafī legal school and as a traditionist, he served as *qāḍī* of Kufa under the 'Abbāsids until 194/809 and argued that Muslim subjects should not rebel against the caliph. Although some Kufans believed that 'accursed Baghdād will be destroyed and Kufa will be queen of the world, after having been a dwelling of exile and waiting for true believers', Ibn Ghiyāth was likely not among them.[50] In summary, although we know that Kufa plays a central role in Imāmī Shīʿī apocalyptic lore (as the capital of the messianic figure of the Mahdī),[51] and a peripheral role in Sunnī apocalyptic, where Iraq is the setting for a climactic battle against Byzantine Christians,[52] it is difficult to assign a single sectarian or polemical motive to Kufans who transmitted this specific narration because they themselves were so diverse.

Imāmī Shīʿīs also transmitted the hadith of the *ghurabāʾ*, but less widely than their Sunnī counterparts. This is surprising given their self-perception as a righteous group on the margins of power. The hadith, however, can be found in a fourth-/tenth-century collection of apocalyptic hadiths about the great occultation of the twelfth imam and Mahdī (*Kamāl al-dīn wa-tamām al-niʿma*) compiled by the Persian Imāmī authority, al-Shaykh al-Ṣadūq Ibn Bābawayh al-Qummī (d. 381/991–992), who was born in Qum but also resided in Baghdad and Rayy.[53] I touch upon Imāmī Shīʿī interpretations of the hadith below.

Reception

The textual content (*mutūn*) of these hadith narrations presaged subsequent commentaries (*shurūḥ*) of it. After the third-/ninth-century canonical hadith compilations, the first commentaries on the hadith of the *ghurabāʾ* emerged, including *Kitāb al-Ghurabāʾ* (The book of strangers), a treatise by the Baghdadi-Meccan Shāfiʿī scholar Abū Bakr al-Ājurrī (d. 360/970), in which he explains the hadith. This should not be confused with the *Kitāb al-Ghurabāʾ* mentioned above, composed anonymously during the same century.[54] Neither that treatise nor *Tārīkh al-Ghurabāʾ*, a

---

50 Djait, 'al-Kūfa', *EI²*.

51 The Mahdī triumphs over the Antichrist figure of Sufyānī, a descendent of his nemesis, Muʿāwiya b. Abī Sufyān. See Madelung, 'The Sufyānī', 5–48; al-Marwazī, '*The Book of Tribulations*', 196–203; D. Cook, *Studies in Muslim Apocalyptic*, 122–136, 319–321.

52 In the Sunnī narrative of the end times, Jerusalem, not Kufa, becomes the capital of the Mahdī's reign. Al-Marwazī, '*The Book of Tribulations*', 207–208; D. Cook, *Studies in Muslim Apocalyptic*, 172–182.

53 Al-Qummī, *Kamāl al-dīn*, 72, 193–194.

54 Al-Ājurrī, *Kitāb al-Ghurabāʾ*.

compilation of the narratives of foreigners who immigrated to Egypt, even mention the hadith.[55]

Al-Ājurrī's *Kitāb al-Ghurabā'* is the most significant premodern treatise written on the hadith, not only because it is the earliest surviving treatise of its kind, but also because of the literary and intellectual value of its content. Although Iḥsān ʿAbbās examined the treatise in a brief chapter composed in Arabic, Rosenthal did not have access to the treatise and therefore did not include it in his study.[56] I begin with a summary and analysis of al-Ājurrī's *Kitāb al-Ghurabā'* to set the stage for my analysis of the commentaries that follow.

Having immigrated to Mecca from his native Baghdad, al-Ājurrī experienced being a *gharīb* first-hand. In *Kitāb al-Tafarrud wa-l-ʿuzla*, now lost, al-Ājurrī also explores the virtues of solitude and indicates his interest in the subject of non-conformity.[57] He enjoyed compiling traditions – prophetic and non-prophetic – on topics of spirituality and piety, as is apparent in the organisation of *Kitāb al-Ghurabā'*. Individual chapters begin with traditions that address the following topics: what is meant by the term *ghurabā'*, why it is desirable to become a *gharīb*, how a *gharīb*'s divine oaths attract spiritual power, why a *gharīb* should be loved and how a *gharīb* dies.

Al-Ājurrī introduces the treatise with a cluster of variations on the hadith of the *ghurabā'*, all of which stress the minority status of the *ghurabā'*. He begins with a narration that identifies them as 'reformers at a time when the masses have become corrupt'.[58] Having introduced the reader to this tradition, al-Ājurrī adds his own explanation on how 'Islam began strange':

Before the Prophet Muḥammad was sent by God, people followed different religions; there were Jews, Christians, Magians, and idolaters. So, when the Prophet came, converts to Islam became strangers in their neighbourhoods and among their people. Forced to disguise their faith, they were shunned by their families, disgraced and despised, but they nonetheless patiently endured the suffering until God empowered Islam; its supporters grew so that the defenders of truth became supreme while the defenders of falsehood were subdued.[59]

---

55 See al-Ṣadafī, *Tārīkh*, vol. 2, *Tārīkh al-Ghurabā'*.

56 'Although the work is said to be published, its full text has not been available.' Rosenthal, 'The Stranger', 60. ʿAbbās, '*Kitāb al-Ghurabā'*'.

57 See the list of lost works in the editor's introduction to al-Ājurrī, *Kitāb al-Ghurabā'*, 12.

58 Al-Ājurrī, *Kitāb al-Ghurabā'*, 23–30. See n. 37 for references to collections that contain narrations with the phrase *alladhīna yuṣliḥūna idhā fasada al-nās*, or similar renderings.

59 Al-Ājurrī, *Kitāb al-Ghurabā'*, 31.

Al-Ājurrī then speculates on the more mysterious question of why Islam 'will [one day] return to being strange'. He surmises that the masses will be misled by their passions (*al-ahwā*), so that the minority who adhere to the *sharī'a* will become *ghurabā'* once again. To support this interpretation, he cites the famous hadith in which Muhammad prophesies that Islam will fracture into seventy-three sects, but only one will prevail.[60] Like the text of the hadith, al-Ājurrī's gloss follows a simple rise-and-fall narrative, in which Islam's transformation into a flourishing civilisation removes it from obscurity only for Muslims to lose their way and return to obscurity.

Based on this interpretation, al-Ājurrī describes the *ghurabā'* as true adherents to the Qur'an and Sunna of Muhammad; they are people who courageously resist the social pressure of family and friends to leave the straight path. Unfortunately, al-Ājurrī warns, their perseverance leads them to isolation and misery:

> He [the stranger] is sad all the time – he is sad when he awakens and he is sad when he falls asleep. He is overwhelmed with grief and deprived of joy – as if condemned to [life in] prison. He is given to weeping, like an exile in a foreign land who has no friends ... if you were to behold him in his solitude, he would be crying from the burning pain in his heart, moaning and sighing, tears streaming down his cheeks. If you saw him – not knowing who he was – you would think him a parent who has just lost his child ...[61]

Al-Ājurrī reassures the reader that this misery stems not from the fear of material loss but from deep concern over his spiritual life. He closes the section with poems that vividly depict the stranger's noble suffering – the misery, loneliness and sadness endured by the spiritual outcast who refuses to follow the crowd.

In the following section, al-Ājurrī elevates the stranger's virtue into a distinct spiritual rank that ordinary believers should strive to attain. Intertwining the apocalyptic with the ascetic, he cites another famous hadith, in which the Prophet Muhammad urged Ibn 'Umar, 'Be in this world as if you were a stranger (*gharīb*), or a traveller, and count yourself among the dead'.[62] This hadith is included in canonical collections of hadith, and also in early Islamic treatises on asceticism.[63] Like the hadith of *al-ghurabā'*, this hadith ascribes a positive value to the *gharīb*, although the meaning of the hadith differs; that is, being a *gharīb* not only signifies physical exile

---

60 Al-Ājurrī, *Kitāb al-Ghurabā'*, 31.
61 Al-Ājurrī, *Kitāb al-Ghurabā'*, 33–34.
62 Al-Ājurrī, *Kitāb al-Ghurabā'*, 36–37.
63 See, for example, Ibn Ḥanbal, *Kitāb al-Zuhd*, 14–15.

to a foreign land, but also spiritual exile from this world to the world to come. Wandering from place to place, the exile has no permanent home, just as the true believer has no permanent home in this world; he already counts himself among the dead. The *gharīb*'s nomadic lifestyle embodies this spiritual ideal, reminding the believer that because nothing in this world lasts, he should reign in his passions and remain detached. Al-Ājurrī elaborates on the apparent meaning of the hadith by portraying a hypothetical scenario in which a man has been blessed with 'wealth and children … a beautiful wife and a large house, fine clothes and good food', but is compelled to depart on a journey.[64] The journey takes him far away, until he eventually loses everything, and becomes a stranger in a strange land. He wants nothing more than to return home to his family, and so he resolves to return. During his exile, despite suffering from the pain of isolation and sadness, his perspective on life evolves: 'everything in the world becomes unimportant to him until his journey ends and he returns home'.[65] This single-minded focus on his destination enables the *gharīb* to observe exemplary self-discipline and avoid distractions like petty interpersonal conflicts: 'he is gentle with the one who is rude to him; he refrains from harming one who harms him; and he ignores one who acts ignorantly toward him'.[66] Like a modern-day self-help manual, al-Ājurrī then directs his attention to the reader, turning the commentary into a homily: 'If you behave in this way, you will become a *gharīb*, a traveller who remains inconspicuous in this world and pursues the world to come.'[67] In this vein, *Kitāb al-Ghurabā'* comes to resemble early Islamic treatises on asceticism (*zuhd*) that portray ideal Muslim piety.[68]

The third and fourth sections of al-Ājurrī's treatise deepen its ascetic orientation; the third illustrates that people who appear lowly to others may in fact be exalted before God: 'Blessed (*ṭūbā*) is the servant (*'abd*), whose feet become covered in dust [fighting] in the path of God, his hair disheveled.'[69] Though not labelled a *gharīb* in this hadith cited by al-Ājurrī, the poor and dishevelled 'servant' nonetheless resembles a *gharīb*, his filthy appearance a stark contrast to his inner piety. The fourth section on loving the *gharīb* is comprised of hagiographical anecdotes of well-known early ascetics such as Mālik b. Dīnār (d. 130/747–748), Sufyān al-Thawrī

---

64 Al-Ājurrī, *Kitāb al-Ghurabā'*, 40–41.

65 Al-Ājurrī, *Kitāb al-Ghurabā'*, 41.

66 Al-Ājurrī, *Kitāb al-Ghurabā'*, 41.

67 Al-Ājurrī, *Kitāb al-Ghurabā'*, 41.

68 Christopher Melchert has published many excellent studies on early Muslim ascetics (renunciants) and their treatises: 'Aḥmad Ibn Ḥanbal's Book of Renunciation'; 'Early Renunciants'; 'Before *Ṣūfiyyāt*'; 'Renunciation'; 'Ibn al-Mubārak's *Kitāb al-Jihād*'.

69 Al-Ājurrī, *Kitāb al-Ghurabā'*, 46. Also see al-Bukhārī, *Ṣaḥīḥ*, 518 (*Kitāb al-jihād, bāb al-ḥirāsa fī al-ghazwi fī sabīl Allāh*).

(d. 161/777–778) and Dhū al-Nūn al-Miṣrī (d. 245–246/860–861). In one anecdote, Dhū al-Nūn introduces himself to a woman, saying "'I am a stranger." She replies, "Stranger! When one is [always] with God, how is it possible to experience the sorrow of *ghurba*? He is the friend of strangers and the helper of the helpless.'" Dhū al-Nūn then begins to cry.[70] He realises that a *gharīb* in permanent exile with God is a *gharīb* in name only. True strangers never experience the sadness and isolation that al-Ājurrī argues comes to define the experience of *ghurba* because true strangers remain with God wherever they go.

But what is the consolation for strangers who die alone with no one to mourn them? In the final section of his treatise, al-Ājurrī describes the value of their death – in contrast to their apparent lack of value when alive – by citing hadiths that destine strangers for martyrdom (and paradise).[71] Only *ghurabā'* who become estranged because of their sincere faith, not as a result of their impiety, qualify for this elite status. Legitimate reasons to become an exile include making the pilgrimage to Mecca for hajj or *'umra*; seeking religious knowledge; visiting friends or family to maintain kinship ties; leaving one's homeland to escape tribulations that may harm one's faith or to earn a *sharī'a*-compliant livelihood; and, finally, chasing after one's runaway slave. At the conclusion of this section, al-Ājurrī applauds the true *gharīb*, exclaiming, 'Blessed is he (*ṭūbā la-hu*)! Blessed is he (*ṭūbā*)!' – leaving the reader with echoes of the hadith of *al-ghurabā'*.[72]

With al-Ājurrī's commentary on the hadith in mind, I now turn to commentaries written after the fourth/tenth century; these reveal both continuity and change in the discourse on estrangement. During the fifth/eleventh and sixth/twelfth centuries, Muslim thinkers across *dār al-Islām* from Ibn 'Abd al-Barr (d. 463/1071) and Qāḍī 'Iyāḍ al-Yaḥṣubī (d. 544/1149) in the west (*maghrib*) to Abū Ḥāmid al-Ghazālī (d. 505/1111) in the east (*mashriq*) cited and commented on the hadith, laying the epistemic foundations for later commentaries authored by scholars during seventh/thirteenth to eighth/fourteenth centuries.[73] These later commentators include the Andalusī Mālikī jurist Abū Isḥāq al-Shāṭibī (d. 790/1388), the Persian poet, Jalāl al-Dīn Rūmī (d. 672/1273), and a group of interconnected scholars from the Mamlūk dynasty: Ibn Taymiyya and his student, Ibn Qayyim al-Jawziyya (d. 751/1350), and his student, Ibn Rajab al-Ḥanbalī (d. 795/1393), as well as the Cairene Mālikī jurist, Ibn al-Ḥājj al-'Abdarī (d. 737/1336), and the Alexandrian Shādhilī Sufi, Ibn 'Aṭā' Allāh al-Iskandarī

---

70 Al-Ājurrī, *Kitāb al-Ghurabā'*, 64–65.

71 Al-Ājurrī, *Kitāb al-Ghurabā'*, 76–91.

72 Al-Ājurrī, *Kitāb al-Ghurabā'*, 91.

73 Qāḍī 'Iyāḍ's brief gloss on the hadith is included in al-Nawawī's commentary on Muslim. See al-Nawawī, *al-Minhāj*, 1:354.

(d. 709/1309). Of these later commentators, only Ibn Rajab al-Ḥanbalī composed an independent treatise on the subject, *Kashf al-kurba bi-waṣf ḥāl ahl al-ghurba*. The others composed glosses in relevant sections of treatises on other topics.

In general, I found that these thinkers concentrate far less on the emotional trauma of estrangement than those who composed the treatises in the fourth/tenth century discussed above. They appear less concerned with the suffering of strangers and more preoccupied with defining their identity and its relevance to Islamic orthodoxy and history. Although most narrations of the hadith pose the question of 'who are the *ghurabāʾ*', the responses generally identify them through their behaviour (i.e. 'those who depart from their tribes' or 'those who revive the Sunna'). They do not name a specific group. Later commentators, however, commonly invoke the *ghurabāʾ* as a distinctive label linked to a specific community of Muslims. In a seventh-/thirteenth-century commentary on *Nahj al-balāgha*, the Muʿtazalī, Ibn Abī al-Ḥadīd (d. 656/1258), explains that Muslims in his era saw the *gharīb* through their own distinctive ideological lens:

> The Imāmī Shīʿa claim the intended meaning is the Mahdī … the Sufis claim it means the friend of God … our companions [the Muʿtazalīs] claim that God will not leave the Muslim community without a group of true believers, *ʿulamāʾ* who uphold justice and divine unity [i.e. Muʿtazalīs] … the philosophers claim that what is intended is the gnostic (*ʿārif*).[74]

Thus, it should not be surprising that nearly all the commentators discussed below were considered, or considered themselves, *ghurabāʾ*; that is, outcasts whose true virtue was unknown to the ignorant masses. 'When I desired to walk upright upon the path,' writes al-Shāṭibī, 'I found myself a stranger among the majority of people in my era.'[75]

To trace the evolving Muslim politics of estrangement, I organise my analysis of classical commentaries on the hadith around three broad themes: piety, apocalypse, and orthodoxy.

The Truest Stranger

While al-Ājurrī portrayed the stranger as a religious model to follow, the adulation of later commentators went even further, transforming the figure from the ideal Muslim to the spiritual master. This conceptual development illustrates how the figure of the *gharīb* became incorporated in

74 Ibn Abī al-Ḥadīd, *Sharḥ*, 10:56–57.
75 Al-Shāṭibī, *al-Iʿtiṣām*, 1:15.

the distinctive nomenclature of the Sufis. In *Madārij al-sālikīn* (Spiritual ranks of the seekers), a multi-volume commentary on the fifth-/eleventh-century Sufi treatise of Shaykh al-Anṣārī al-Harawī (d. 481/1088), entitled *Manāzil al-sā'irīn*, Ibn al-Qayyim al-Jawziyya comments on the hadith of *al-ghurabā*.[76] According to Ibn al-Qayyim, the most essential characteristic of strangers is that they are a minority. By the grace of God, they possess a set of distinctive traits that few possess. To be a stranger is thus relative: Muslims are strangers among unbelievers; Sunnī Muslims (*ahl al-sunna*) are strangers among deviant sects; true believers (*mu'minūn*) are strangers among Muslims; and religious scholars are strangers among the true believers.[77] These groups and subgroups are all strangers in some way, depending on the comparison drawn. We may thus view the experience of being a stranger along a spectrum. As the strangers' degree of estrangement from society increases their spiritual rank also increases, as they turn away from other people and toward God.

Ibn al-Qayyim categorises strangers into three types, each possessing a distinct moral valence. The first and most praiseworthy category is comprised of the people of God, who are fervent supporters of the Sunna. They are never truly alone. Though poor, unknown and unloved, these strangers are at home with God. The second and most blameworthy category is comprised of those who oppose the Sunna. This kind of stranger is truly alone and truly strange. The final category, who inhabit a morally ambiguous space that is neither praiseworthy nor blameworthy, encompass all humanity. They must endure the existential condition of being spiritually homesick. Ibn al-Qayyim encourages these strangers to 'Be in this world as if you were a stranger, or traveller'.[78] Unlike al-Ājurrī who reads this well-known hadith as a sign of the *gharīb*'s elite spiritual status, Ibn al-Qayyim reads it as a general commentary on the human condition – the condition of being estranged from God.

Ibn Rajab al-Ḥanbalī shared his teacher's stratified view of spiritual estrangement. In *Kashf al-kurba*, Ibn Rajab classifies strangers into the *ghurabā* of the outward realm (*ẓāhir*) and the *ghurabā* of the inward realm (*bāṭin*). Drawing from a statement attributed to the Persian mystic, Yaḥyā b. Mu'ādh (d. 258/872), 'the ascetic (*zāhid*) is a stranger to the *dunyā* and the gnostic (*'ārif*) is a stranger to the *ākhira*', Ibn Rajab defines the *ghurabā* of the *ẓāhir* as the ascetic and the *ghurabā* of the *bāṭin* as the gnostic.[79]

The Shādhilī Sufi master, Abū al-'Abbās al-Mursī (d. 686/1287), appears to have also glossed the aphorism attributed to Yaḥyā b. Mu'ādh:

<hr>

76 Ibn al-Qayyim al-Jawziyya, *Madārij al-sālikīn*, 3:184–195.
77 Ibn al-Qayyim al-Jawziyya, *Madārij al-sālikīn*, 3:186.
78 Ibn al-Qayyim al-Jawziyya, *Madārij al-sālikīn*, 3:190.
79 Ibn Rajab, *'Kashf al-kurba'*, 329.

'An ascetic (*zāhid*) is a stranger to the *dunyā* because the *ākhira* is his true home, while a gnostic (*'ārif*) is a stranger to the *ākhira* because he is with God.'[80] A student of al-Mursī, Ibn 'Aṭā' Allāh al-Iskandarī later wrote a gloss on his teacher's gloss. Citing the hadith of *al-ghurabā'*, he explains that the sincere ascetic becomes estranged from this world, but is at home in the next. The gnostic, however, is truly rarified, elevated through his sincerity and devotion to another spiritual level altogether. He feels estranged not only from the *dunyā*, but also from the *ākhira* because he feels at home only with God. No one, besides the prophets themselves, is more estranged from material reality than an *'ārif*.

The celebrated Persian Sufi, Jalāl al-Dīn Rūmī, as well as those in his entourage, also viewed the *gharīb* as the supreme spiritual master. Rūmī's spiritual teacher, Shams al-Dīn of Tabrīz (d. 645/1247), once told Rūmī's son: 'The secret of [Rūmī] is veiled as is the secret of Islam. Like Islam, he has come as a *gharīb*. See how his secret shall be as "Islam began as a *gharīb* and will return as a *gharīb*. Blessed are the strangers!"'[81] Here, Shams al-Dīn compares Rūmī to the religion of Islam itself, drawing an analogy to the obscure manner in which they each entered the world through the hadith of *al-ghurabā'*. As the Persian Sufi, Fakhr al-Dīn 'Irāqī (d. 688/1289), explains, 'No one understood Mowlānā [Rūmī] as he ought to be [understood]. He came into this world a *gharīb* and departed from it a *gharīb*.'[82] Because the spiritual limitations of the masses prevented them from perceiving Rūmī's true spiritual greatness, they could not truly know or understand Rūmī, and, in this sense, he entered and departed the world as a stranger. The *gharīb* also appears in Rūmī's grand collection of Persian poetry, the *Masnavi*, as figures who realised their full spiritual potential, such as a physician who assists a handmaiden in cutting her ties with the material world, and as a gazelle whose spiritual condition is misjudged by a myopic donkey consumed by its carnal passions.[83]

Apocalypse Now?

Iḥsān 'Abbās considered the question of how 'Islam began strange' as the 'simplest' (*absaṭ*) question implicitly posed by the hadith of *al-ghurabā'* because it could be answered using available historical data and without much speculation.[84] Al-Ājurrī, for example, described the first Muslim converts as 'disgraced and despised'.[85] Later commentators conformed to this reading, but added more detail. Ibn al-Qayyim believed that the *ghurabā'*

---

80 Al-Iskandarī, *Laṭā'if al-minan*, 149–150.
81 Aflākī, *Manāqeb al-'ārefīn*, 1:308–309; translation from Pifer, 'The Stranger's Voice', 57.
82 Aflākī, *Manāqeb al-'ārefīn*, 1:400. Translation from Pifer, 'The Stranger's Voice', 57.
83 Rūmī, *Masnavī-yi Ma'navī*, 1:48–50, 3:54–9. See also, Pifer, 'The Stranger's Voice', 70–79.
84 'Abbās, '*Kitāb al-Ghurabā'*', 94.
85 Al-Ājurrī, *Kitāb al-Ghurabā'*, 31.

in the early years of Islam are best described as 'those who left their tribes'. After all, the first Arab Muslim converts fled from Mecca to Abyssinia, and later to Medina, as refugees.[86] Nor was the extent of their *ghurba* limited to their small number; as foreigners in a foreign land they were weak and poor, estranged from their families and their homeland. They – and therefore Islam – were *gharīb* in nearly every sense of the term. Al-Shāṭibī describes how the Prophet Muhammad overcame many obstacles, including wars, economic boycotts and persecution from his own tribe and relatives.[87] In exceptional situations, even 'verbally denying God (*kufr*) under duress' was permitted as 'a clear', and perhaps ultimate, 'form of strangeness'.[88]

But, as we know, the hadith's content is not limited to the historical origins of Islam. It includes the more enigmatic prophecy that Islam 'will [one day] become strange just as it began'. This prophecy also assumes that Islam will enter a period in which it is not strange. It is now common knowledge that Islam became ascendant and Muslims became a powerful majority in *dār al-Islām*. However, the hadith forecasts that history will come full circle. Islam will become strange once again and Muslims will again become a besieged minority. But it remains a mystery when this glory will begin to fade, and what will cause it. Has the process of decline already begun or is it still yet to come?

Commentators had different opinions. As already mentioned, al-Ājurrī predicted that Muslims would be overtaken by their passions and begin to follow their own opinions over the Sunna, but he refrained from declaring when and where this will take place. During a pilgrimage to Mecca in 353/964, al-Tawḥīdī transmits a grim commentary on the hadith of the *ghurabā'* he has heard from one of his companions:

> [The *gharīb*] is the one who flees from city to city, from mountaintop to mountaintop, from country to country, from sea to land, until he finds safety. But how can he find safety as these fires engulf east and west and scorch crops and cattle, which [encircle humanity] and seal every mouth, silence every voice, perplex every genius, choke the one drinking, and embitter the taste of the one eating? Dwelling upon this matter takes hold of the mind, distresses the soul, and burns the heart in anguish.[89]

Are the stranger's futile attempts to escape these 'fires' a metaphor for the tribulations (*fitan*) taking place before them or an ominous prophecy of the end times?

86 Ibn al-Qayyim al-Jawziyya, *Madārij al-sālikīn*, 3:188–189.
87 Al-Shāṭibī, *al-Iʿtiṣām*, 1:7.
88 Al-Shāṭibī, *al-Iʿtiṣām*, 1:9.
89 Al-Tawḥīdī, *al-Imtāʿ wa-l-muʾānasa*, 208.

In Ibn Rajab al-Ḥanbalī's reading, the historical arc of Islam began to descend soon after the Prophet's death. After the reigns of the first two caliphs, Abū Bakr and ʿUmar, 'Satan worked his machinations on the Muslim community, inciting distrust and division between them . . . until, slowly but surely, the majority succumbed to it'.[90] Al-Shāṭibī, whose view I discuss in more detail below, agreed, stating that this decline began 'as the era of the Companions came to an end'.[91] Ibn al-Qayyim al-Jawziyya, on the other hand, believed that this prophecy had already come to pass: 'Today, true Islam has become stranger than it was when it first appeared – even though its external signs and forms are now widespread! True Islam has become very strange; and its people are the strangest of people.'[92] Belonging to the vanguard of true Islam, Ibn al-Qayyim appears to consider himself among the *ghurabāʾ* of his era.

In the relatively early Imāmī Shīʿī compilation of apocalyptic narratives, *Kamāl al-dīn wa-tamām al-niʿma*, al-Shaykh al-Ṣadūq cites the hadith of *al-ghurabāʾ* on the authority of ʿAlī b. Abī Ṭālib as scriptural evidence for the return of the hidden imam during the end times.[93] In one instance, it is used to refute the theological objections of Zaydī Shīʿīs, and in another, it refers to Zayd b. ʿAmr b. Nawfal, a pre-Islamic monotheist (*ḥanīf*) who died while awaiting the advent of a new prophet. In both contexts, al-Shaykh al-Ṣadūq mobilises the hadith to connect the Islamic past to the present: 'If we take a moment to reflect, we find that the condition of prophets and nations in the past resembles the condition of our nation [today].'[94] Recalling that in its early days, Islam was scorned by sceptics, he remarks, 'It is just as the ignoramuses question us today: "When will this Mahdī, whom you claim will appear, actually appear?" One community denies him while another believes in him.'[95] But looking toward the future, he reassures the reader that just as the emergence of prophets silenced the sceptics, so will the reemergence of the hidden imam silence them.

In the *Majmūʿat al-fatāwa* which, despite its name, encompasses numerous subjects beyond law (for example, hadith commentary), Ibn Taymiyya reminds readers that whenever Islam becomes strange, a renewer (*mujaddid*) arises who makes Islam familiar again.[96] One such renewer was ʿUmar b. ʿAbd al-ʿAzīz (r. 99–101/717–720), who reigned as Umayyad caliph at the end of the first/seventh century. Islamic history is thus seasonal. It has its ups and downs. According to Ibn Taymiyya, Islam's *ghurba* is

90 Ibn Rajab, '*Kashf al-kurba*', 317.
91 Al-Shāṭibī, *al-Iʿtiṣām*, 1:10.
92 Ibn al-Qayyim al-Jawziyya, *Madārij al-sālikīn*, 3:188.
93 Al-Qummī, *Kamāl al-dīn*, 72, 193–194.
94 Al-Qummī, *Kamāl al-dīn*, 71.
95 Al-Qummī, *Kamāl al-dīn*, 193.
96 Ibn Taymiyya, *Majmūʿa*, 18:292–305.

never absolute. At any historical moment, some dimensions of Islam may be strange in some places and not others. In places where Islam becomes strange, true adherents of the *sharīʿa* are *ghurabāʾ*, and therefore blessed. However, Muslims who refuse to exert effort and fail to prevent the masses from committing vices are sinful and lacking in faith.

It is reasonable to wonder if this cyclical view of history undermines the famous hadith, which declares that the first generations of Muslims are the best generations of humanity. Ibn Taymiyya reassures the reader that this hadith still holds true, although it may not apply to every single Muslim from the first generation: 'Perhaps this statement only applies to a limited number of people in a generation just as it applies to a limited number of Muslims in some respects, as is customary in every era.'[97] That is, some Muslims in later generations are in fact spiritually superior to some Muslims from the first generation. In this moderately progressive view of human history, the *ghurabāʾ* represent the best Muslims of every generation until the day of judgement.

Orthodoxy

As implied in the discourses above, an underlying concern of Muslim commentators on the hadith of *al-ghurabāʾ* is the fragility of orthodoxy, or correct belief. Prophesying the demise of Islam, this hadith alerted the *ʿulamāʾ* to vigilantly guard orthodoxy against the looming threat of reprehensible innovations and sectarianism. And given that multiple narrations of this hadith define the *ghurabāʾ* as those who cling to the Sunna, as guardians of the Islamic tradition and 'inheritors of the Prophet', the *ʿulamāʾ* were charged with defending orthodoxy.[98] As Ibn al-Qayyim declared, *ʿulamāʾ* are *ghurabāʾ* among the masses. But this self-perception had set in centuries earlier with the rise of *ʿulamāʾ* as a distinct class. In the fifth/eleventh century, the Andalusī Mālikī judge Ibn ʿAbd al-Barr cited a tradition stating that 'the *ʿulamāʾ* are strangers due to the ignorance of the masses'.[99] In his great summa of Islamic spirituality, the *Iḥyāʾ ʿulūm al-dīn*, Abū Ḥāmid al-Ghazālī drew on Abū Ṭālib al-Makkī's (d. 386/996) commentary on the hadith of *al-ghurabāʾ* and lamented that true *ʿulamāʾ* are strangers in his era. He claimed that the masses had succumbed to reprehensible innovations, while the original religious wisdom of the first Muslims had been forgotten.[100] 'Those who even mention them are scorned.'[101]

---

97 Ibn Taymiyya, *Majmūʿa*, 18:303.

98 Gilliot, "Ulamā", in *EI²*.

99 Ibn ʿAbd al-Barr, *Jamiʿ bayān*, 120.

100 Al-Makkī, *Qūt al-qulūb*, 1:259; al-Ghazālī, *Iḥyāʾ ʿulūm al-dīn*, 1:110; al-Ghazālī, *Kitāb al-ʿIlm*, 105.

101 Al-Ghazālī, *Iḥyāʾ ʿulūm al-dīn*, 1:110.

Ibn Taymiyya's commentary on the hadith begins with a defence of orthodoxy. He refutes the reading that it is permissible for strangers to leave Islam by citing several Qur'anic verses that, at face value, claim that Islam is the sole path to salvation: 'Anyone who seeks to follow a *dīn* other than Islam will not find it accepted [by God], and in the afterlife, he will be among the losers' (Q. 3:85). 'When Islam arrived as an obscure entity,' Ibn Taymiyya elaborates, 'other *dīn*s became unacceptable [as paths to salvation].'[102]

Ibn Rajab al-Ḥanbalī also worried about the fragility of orthodoxy. Quoting the early Muslim authority, Sufyān al-Thawrī, 'Treat the adherents of the Sunna well for they are the [true] strangers', Ibn Rajab argues that following the Sunna requires that correct belief be safeguarded from any doubt in God, scriptures, prophets, angels, the day of judgement and divine predestination.[103] Unfortunately, for Ibn Rajab, the number of true adherents of the Sunna dwindles with the passage of time.

But the most compelling defence of orthodoxy as strangeness came from Abū Isḥāq al-Shāṭibī in his treatise against innovations, *al-Iʿtiṣām* (Holding on), in which he frames himself at the outset as a minority of one:

> When I resolved to walk straight upon the path [of Truth], I found myself a stranger among the majority of people in my era because their everyday behaviours were dominated by customs and their original traditions were polluted by unnecessary innovations that did not even exist in earlier times, let alone our time![104]

He explains that he was removed from his post of imam because he refused to supplicate for the rightly guided caliphs or for the rulers during the Friday sermon. According to al-Shāṭibī, he was forced to choose between following the Sunna and opposing the practices of the masses or opposing the Sunna and following the practices of the masses. Having opted for the former, he says, 'they smeared me with labels linking me to sects that are outside the Sunna'.[105]

Al-Shāṭibī, in fact, centres his narrative of how 'Islam will [one day] return to being strange' on the rise of sectarianism, which frames how he positions himself in the treatise:

> The [power and influence] of Islam continued to expand and [its adherents] followed the straight path during the lifetime of the

---

102 Ibn Taymiyya, *Majmūʿa*, 18:292.
103 Ibn Rajab, '*Kashf al-kurba*', 319.
104 Al-Shāṭibī, *al-Iʿtiṣām*, 1:15.
105 Al-Shāṭibī, *al-Iʿtiṣām*, 1:19.

Prophet and during the lifetimes of most of the Companions – until there arose heretics who deviated from the Prophet's way (Sunna) and inclined toward misleading innovations, like the Qadariyya and the Khawārij … and this all took place as the era of the Companions came to an end.

The number of sects continued to increase, as prophesied by the Truthful One [the Prophet] who said, 'Jews and Christians will split into seventy-one sects, but my community will split into seventy-three.' In another hadith, he [the Prophet] said, '"You will follow the ways of those nations who preceded you, span by span, cubit by cubit, so that if they entered a lizard's hole you would follow them." We asked, "O Messenger of God, do you mean the Jews and Christians?" He replied, "Who else?"'[106]

Al-Shāṭibī, like al-Ājurrī and Ibn al-Qayyim al-Jawziyya before him, cites the famous hadith prophesying that Islam will splinter into seventy-three sects, and only one will prevail. He adds another well-known hadith prophesying that Muslims will follow Jews and Christians down a 'lizard's hole', meaning that they will succumb to the same fate of fracturing into warring sectarian factions. He continues:

God fulfilled His promise to the Prophet that Islam would become strange once again, because strangeness happens only if its devotees are few, or have become extinct. When that happens, right becomes wrong and wrong becomes right; Sunna becomes innovation and innovation becomes Sunna. Meanwhile, the true devotees of the Sunna are subject to denunciation and criticism from heretics who are eager for the voices of misguidance to come together [and prevail].

But God prevents these voices from coming together until the day of judgement. So these heretical sects will not join forces against the Sunna, either in theory or in practice. Rather, the true devotees of the Sunna will remain firm [on the path of Truth] until God's decree comes to pass. Nevertheless, deviant sects will relentlessly attack the adherents of the Sunna, inciting hostility and hatred in the process, hoping they will eventually succumb to the pressure and conform. As a result, the true devotees of the Sunna will remain engaged in struggle and conflict, defending [the truth] day and night. By means of this trial, God will augment their bounty and repay them with an immense reward.[107]

106 Al-Shāṭibī, *al-Iʿtiṣām*, 1:10–11.
107 Al-Shāṭibī, *al-Iʿtiṣām*, 1:12–13.

A complete reversal of fortunes, as prophesied by the hadith of *al-ghurabāʾ* in which right becomes wrong and wrong becomes right and Sunna becomes innovation and innovation becomes Sunna, will not occur until the end days. In the meanwhile, however, 'devotees of the Sunna' – true *ghurabāʾ* – 'will remain engaged in struggle and conflict, defending [the truth] day and night'.[108]

In fighting for orthodoxy and against reprehensible innovations, then, these 'connective figures' – Ibn ʿAbd al-Barr, al-Ghazālī, Ibn al-Qayyim al-Jawziyya, Ibn Rajab al-Ḥanbalī, Ibn Taymiyya and al-Shāṭibī – viewed themselves as *ghurabāʾ*, defined mainly by their role as Sunnī *ʿulamāʾ*, which entailed their intellectual distance from the Muslim majority. What is more, for many of them, their intellectual exile was enhanced by physical exile as well. For several years, al-Ghazālī voluntarily left his family, friends and illustrious scholarly career in Baghdad to venture alone in search of himself; during this journey he wrote his most spiritually potent works.[109] Ibn Taymiyya spent his final years in prison, alone.[110] And al-Shāṭibī was exiled from his own mosque. There can be little doubt that exile expanded their imaginations of *ghurba* beyond the zone of scholarship; it taught them to see themselves, the world and God anew.

The Stranger's Jihad

Modern-day extremists, self-proclaimed *ghurabāʾ*, have likened 'fighting in the path of God' (Q. 2:190) to an exilic journey. But in my study of fifteen classical manuals on jihad, I could not find a complete narration of the hadith of *al-ghurabāʾ* in any of them.[111] I found only one narration

108 Al-Shāṭibī, *al-Iʿtiṣām*, 1:13.

109 For al-Ghazālī's autobiographical account of his spiritual and intellectual journey, see al-Ghazālī, *al-Ghazali's Path to Sufism*. For an illuminating discussion on the relationship of exile (*ghurba*) to creativity and imagination in al-Ghazālī's life and works, see Moosa, *Ghazālī and the Poetics of Imagination*, 119–138, 275–280.

110 Little, 'The Historical'; Bori, 'A New Source'. Also see Ibn Taymiyya's alleged letters from prison: Ibn Taymiyya, *Rasāʾil min al-sijn*.

111 I surveyed the following treatises on jihad: Ibn al-Mubārak (d. 181/797), *Kitāb al-Jihād*; Ibn Jamāʿa (d. 733/1333), *Mustanad* and *Mukhtaṣar fī faḍl al-jihād*; Abū Yaʿqūb Ishāq b. Ibrāhīm al-Harawī al-Qarrāb (d. 429/1037), *Faḍāʾil al-ramī fī sabīl Allāh*; ʿAlī b. Ṭāhir b. Jaʿfar al-Sulamī (d. 500/1107), *Kitāb al-Jihād*; al-Qāḍī Abū al-Maḥāsin Yūsuf b. Shaddād (d. 632/1235), *Kitāb Faḍāʾil al-jihād*; Ibn Kathīr (d. 774/1373), *Kitāb Ijtihād fī ṭalab al-jihād*; Ibn ʿAbd al-Salām (d. 660/1262–63), *Aḥkām al-jihād*; Ibn Asākir (d. 571/1176), *al-Arbaʿūn fī ḥathth*; Ibn Baṭṭa al-ʿUkbarī al-Ḥanbalī (d. 387/997), *Sabʿūn ḥadīth*; al-Wāsiṭī (d. 618/1221), *Kitāb al-Arbaʿīn fī al-jihād*; al-ʿIrāqī (d. 804/1404), *Kitāb al-Arbaʿīn al-ʿishāriyya*; al-Ḍaḥḥāk (d. 287/900), *Kitāb al-Jihād*; Ibn al-Naḥḥās (d. 814/1411), *Mashāriʿ al-ashwāq*; and Ibn Aṣbagh (d. 620/1223–4), *Kitāb al-Injād*. The treatises of al-Sulamī, Ibn Shaddād, and Ibn Kathīr have also been collected and published by Suhayl Zakkār in the edited volume, *Arbaʿat kutub fī al-jihād min aṣr al-ḥurūb al-Ṣalībiyya*.

in which the Companion Ibn 'Umar (not the Prophet Muhammad), proclaims, 'Blessed are the strangers who are righteous despite [widespread] corruption among the masses', without the key prefatory statement that 'Islam began strange ...' This is cited in *Kitāb al-Jihād* of 'Abdallāh b. al-Mubārak (d. 181/797), the first such compilation ever written.[112] In fact, the earliest complete apocalyptic treatise to survive, *Kitāb al-Fitan* (Book of tribulations) of Nu'aym b. Ḥammād al-Marwazī (d. 228/843–4), includes the hadith of *al-ghurabā'* in a chapter entitled *I'tizāl* (On retreat and seclusion) in the face of widespread tribulations. In this context, however, the hadith is an exhortation to stay home, not fight in war.[113]

Although this finding does not mean that modern-day extremists lack any grounds on which to view themselves as strangers, or that premodern Muslim soldiers never viewed themselves as strangers, the absence of the hadith of *al-ghurabā'* from classical manuals on jihad does suggest that the label of *ghurabā'* did not signal jihad as prominently as it does today.[114] Although the premodern *ghurabā'* and modern-day extremist *ghurabā'* both embrace their strangeness and share a common aspiration to find belonging in exile, their means of doing so nonetheless diverge. None of the premodern commentaries on the hadith of *al-ghurabā'* that I studied address the topic of jihad prominently. Again, this does not mean that those who perceived themselves as *ghurabā'* never fought in jihad (or that such commentaries cannot be found), but that in the most widely read premodern commentaries on the hadith of *al-ghurabā'*, fighting in jihad did not define who belonged to the *ghurabā'*.

What does appear to be an important factor, however, is the struggle against oneself – what the Prophet allegedly called 'the greater jihad' (*al-jihād al-akbar*). This is described as an interior battle within an individual, not an exterior battle against others.[115] Although the commentators I surveyed did not use this phrase, they nonetheless spoke of being a *gharīb* as an emotional, intellectual and spiritual struggle that may appropriately be described as a jihad against oneself. Given that so many of

---

112 Ibn al-Mubārak, *Kitāb al-Jihād*, 181.

113 Al-Marwazī, *Kitāb al-Fitan*, 108.

114 I would suggest that imagining oneself as a *gharīb* opens up the potential to lapse into a self-righteous delusion in which 'I am right and everyone else is wrong'. If this hubris festers into bitterness and anger, and becomes inflamed with the doctrine of jihad, it may mutate into vilification of and violence toward the Other, Muslim or non-Muslim.

115 According to the well-known hadith, whose chain of transmission is nonetheless graded as weak or fabricated by critics, the Prophet said, 'You have come for the best. You have come from the smaller jihad to the greater jihad.' They said, 'What is the greater jihad, Messenger of God?' He said: 'The servant's struggle against his desires.' See D. Cook, *Understanding Jihad*, 32–48.

these commentaries were shaped by the discourses of Muslim ascetics and Sufis, this should not come as a surprise. Unlike modern-day extremists, they did not rush to realise an Islamic utopia here and now, in this world; rather, their primary objective was to remind believers that, while they are called to resist blind social conformity and become *ghurabā'*, their true home is not here in this world, but with God in the world to come.

In this sense, then, classical Muslim thinkers construed being strange (*gharīb*) as a virtue. It is, of course, much easier to follow the crowd than to patiently endure the pain of being an outcast. The *ghurabā's* courage to suffer through the misery of loneliness and exile in this world in pursuit of the world to come reflects their sincerity and authenticity. The hadith and its commentators impress on the reader that the elect who possess these noble attributes in abundance are not to be pitied, but envied. The portrayal of non-conformity as a badge of prestige instead of abasement, as a virtue instead of a vice, is an inversion of conventional social logic and positions the stranger as a model of piety in normative Islam.

In this chapter, I have contended that the figure of the stranger is ironic – that the *gharīb*, defined by his separation from others, is a connective figure. Most apparently, the stranger's physical movement across geographic boundaries connects people and places. But the stranger's connectivity is also apparent at the level of discourse, where textual representations frequently mirror social reality. The heterogeneity of the strangers as a category, as we have seen, is reflected in the multiplicity of narrations of the hadith of *al-ghurabā'*. And as demonstrated above, classical commentators connected the discourse and experience of estrangement to key Islamic discourses on the apocalypse, orthodoxy and piety. But perhaps most importantly, the figure of the stranger connects believers across time, linking the Islamic past to its present and future. Indeed, as the Prophet foretold, the end returns to the beginning: 'Islam began strange, and will [one day] return to being strange – just as it began – so blessed are the strangers!'

Bibliography

'Abbās, Iḥsān. '*Kitāb al-Ghurabā' li'l-Ājurrī*', *Mélanges de l'Université Saint-Joseph* 50, no. 1 (1984): 91–101.

Abū Yaʿlā al-Mawṣilī. *Musnad Abī Yaʿlā*. Damascus: Dār al-Ma'mūn li-l-Turāth, 1984.

Aflākī, Shams al-Dīn Aḥmad. *Manāqeb al-ʿārefīn*. Edited by T. Yazıcı. 2 vols. Ankara: Türk Tarih Kurumu Basımevi, 1959–61.

al-Ājurrī, Abū Bakr. *Kitāb al-Ghurabā' min al-mu'minīn*. Damascus: Dār al-Bashā'ir, 1992.

al-Bazzār, Abū Bakr Aḥmad b. 'Amr. *Musnad al-Bazzār*. 18 vols. Medina: Maktabat al-'Ulūm wa-l-Ḥikam, 1988–2009.

Berg, Herbert. 'Competing Paradigms in the Study of Islamic Origins: Qurʾān 15:89–91 and the Value of *Isnāds*.' In H. Berg (ed.), *Method and Theory in the Study of Islamic Origin*, pp. 259–290. Leiden: Brill, 2003.

Bori, Caterina. 'A New Source for the Biography of Ibn Taymiyya.' *Bulletin for the School of Oriental and African Studies* 67, no. 3 (2004): 321–348.

al-Bukhārī, Muḥammad b. Ismāʿīl. *Ṣaḥīḥ al-Bukhārī*. Beirut: Dār Ibn Ḥazm, 2002.

Constable, Olivia Remie. *Housing the Stranger in the Mediterranean World: Lodging, Trade, and Travel in Late Antiquity and the Middle Ages*. Cambridge: Cambridge University Press, 2009.

Cook, David. *Contemporary Muslim Apocalyptic Literature*. Syracuse: Syracuse University Press, 2005.

Cook, David. 'Ḥadīth, Authority and the End of the World: Traditions in Modern Muslim Apocalyptic Literature.' *Oriente Moderno* 82, no. 1 (2002): 31–53.

Cook, David. *Studies in Muslim Apocalyptic*. Princeton, NJ: Darwin Press, 2002

Cook, David. *Understanding Jihad*. Berkeley: University of California Press, 2005.

Cook, Michael. 'An Early Apocalyptic Chronicle.' *Journal of Near Eastern Studies* 52, no. 1 (1993): 25–29.

Cook, Michael. 'Eschatology and the Dating of Traditions.' *Princeton Papers in Near Eastern Studies* 1 (1992): 23–47.

Creswell, Robyn and Bernard Haykel. 'Battle Lines: Want to Understand the jihadis? Read Their Poetry.' *New Yorker*, June 8 and June 15, 2015.

Crone, Patricia and Shmuel Moreh. *The Book of Strangers: Medieval Arabic Graffiti on the Theme of Nostalgia*. Princeton, NJ: Markus Weiner, 2000.

al-Ḍaḥḥāk, Ibn Abī ʿĀṣim. *Kitāb al-Jihād*. Damascus: Dār al-Qalam, 1989.

al-Dārimī, Abū Muḥammad. *Sunan al-Dārimī*. 4 vols. Riyadh: Dār al-Mughnī li-l-Nashr wa-l-Tawzīʿ, 2000.

al-Dhahabī, Shams al-Dīn. *Siyar aʿlām al-nubalāʾ*. Edited by Shuʿayb al-Arnāʾūṭ. 25 vols. Beirut: Muʾassasat al-Risāla, 1982.

al-Farāhīdī, Khalīl b. Aḥmad. *Kitāb al-ʿAyn*. 5 vols. Beirut: Dār al-Kutub al-ʿIlmiyya, 2003.

Fiedler, Leslie A. *The Stranger in Shakespeare*. London: Paladin, 1974.

Filiu, Jean-Pierre. *Apocalypse in Islam*. Berkeley: University of California Press, 2012.

Fishman, Brian. 'After Zarqawi: The Dilemmas and Future of Al Qaeda in Iraq.' *Washington Quarterly* 29, no. 4 (2006): 21–23.

al-Ghazālī, Abū Ḥāmid. *Iḥyāʾ ʿulūm al-dīn*. Edited by Muḥammad Wahbī Sulaymān and Usāma ʿUmūra. 5 vols. Damascus: Dār al-Fikr, 2006.

al-Ghazālī, Abū Ḥāmid. *Kitāb al-ʿIlm, The Book of Knowledge: Book 1 of the Iḥyāʾ ʿulūm al-dīn. The Revival of the Religious Sciences*. Translated by Kenneth Honerkamp. Louisville, KY: Fons Vitae, 2015.

al-Ghazālī, Abū Ḥāmid. *al-Ghazali's Path to Sufism and His Deliverance from Error: An Annotated Translation of al-Ghazali's al-Munqidh Min al-Dalal*. Translated by Richard Joseph McCarthy. Louisville, KY: Fons Vitae Publishing, 2000.

al-Ghazzī, Najm al-Dīn. *Lutf al-samar qatf al-thaman*. Edited by Maḥmūd al-Shaykh. 2 vols. Damascus: Wizārat al-Thaqāfa wa-l-Irshād al-Qawmī, 1981.

Haider, Najam. 'The Geography of the *Isnād*: Possibilities for the Reconstruction of Local Ritual Practice in the 2nd/8th Century.' *Der Islam* 90, no. 2 (2013): 306–346.

al-Ḥanbalī, Ibn Baṭṭa al-ʿUkbarī. *Sabʿūn ḥadīth fī al-jihād.* Cairo: Maktabat al-Qurʾān, 1989[?].

al-Harawī, Mullā ʿAlī al-Qārī. *Mirqāt al-mafātīḥ: Sharḥ Mishkāt al-Maṣābīḥ.* 11 vols. Beirut: Dār al-Kutub al-ʿIlmiyya, 2001.

Husain, Ed. *The House of Islam: A Global History.* New York: Bloomsbury, 2018.

Ibn ʿAbd al-Barr, Yūsuf. *Jamiʿ bayān al-ʿilm wa-faḍlihi.* Cairo, Idārat al-Ṭibāʿa al-Munīriyya, n.d.

Ibn ʿAbd al-Salām, ʿIzz al-Dīn. *Aḥkām al-jihād wa-faḍāʾiluh.* Jedda: Maktabat Dār al-Wafāʾ, 1986.

Ibn Abī al-Ḥadīd, ʿAbd al-Ḥamīd. *Sharḥ Nahj al-balāgha.* 18 vols. Beirut: Dār al-Kutub al-ʿIlmiyya, 2009.

Ibn Abī Shayba, Abū Bakr. *al-Muṣannaf.* Edited by Ḥamad al-Jumʿa and Muḥammad al-Laḥīdān. 16 vols. Riyadh: Maktabat al-Rushd, 2004.

Ibn Asākir. *al-Arbaʿūn fī ḥathth ʿalā al-jihād.* Kuwait: Dār al-Khulafāʾ li-l-Kitāb al-Islāmī, 1984.

Ibn Aṣbagh, Muḥammad b. ʿIsā. *Kitāb al-Injād fī abwāb al-jihād.* Abu Dhabi: Dār al-Imām Mālik. Beirut: Muʾassasat al-Rayyān, 2005.

Ibn al-Athīr, Majd al-Dīn al-Mubārak b. Muḥammad. *al-Nihāya fī gharīb al-ḥadīth wa-l-athar.* Beirut: Dār al-Maʿrifa, 2011.

Ibn Ḥajar al-ʿAsqalānī. *Taqrīb al-tahdhīb.* Edited by Muḥammad ʿAwwāma. 1 vol. Aleppo: Dār al-Rashīd, 1991.

Ibn Ḥanbal, Aḥmad. *Kitāb al-Zuhd.* Beirut: Dār al-Kutub al-ʿIlmiyya, 1983.

Ibn Ḥanbal, Aḥmad. *Musnad.* Edited by Shuʿayb al-Arnaʾūṭ et al. 50 vols. Beirut: Muʾassasat al-Risāla, 1995–2001.

Ibn Jamāʿa, Muḥammad b. Ibrāhīm and Abū Yaʿqūb Isḥāq b. Ibrāhīm al-Harawī al-Qarrāb. *Mustanad al-ajnād fī ālāt al-jihād wa-mukhtaṣar fī faḍl al-jihād.* Edited by Usāma Nāṣir al-Naqshabandī. Damascus: Dār al-Wathāʾiq, 2008.

Ibn Kathīr. *al-Nihāya fī al-fitan wa-l-malāḥim.* 2 vols. Beirut: Dār al-Jīl, 1988.

Ibn Mājah, Abū ʿAbdallāh al-Qazwīnī. *Sunan Ibn Mājah.* Beirut: Dār Ibn Ḥazm, 2002.

Ibn al-Mubārak, ʿAbdallāh. *Kitāb al-Jihād.* Edited by Nazīh Ḥammād. Jedda: Dār al-Maṭbūʿāt al-Ḥadītha, n.d.

Ibn al-Naḥḥās, Aḥmad b. Ibrāhīm. *Mashāriʿ al-ashwāq ilā mashāriʿ al-ʿushshāq wa-muthīr al-gharām ilā Dār al-Salām: fī faḍāʾil al-jihād.* Beirut: Dār al-Bashāʾir al-Islāmiyya, 2002.

Ibn al-Qayyim al-Jawziyya. *Madārij al-sālikīn.* Beirut: Dār al-Kitāb al-ʿArabī, 2003.

Ibn Rajab al-Ḥanbalī. 'Kashf al-kurba bi-waṣf ḥāl ahl al-ghurba.' In *Majmūʿ rasāʾil al-Ḥāfiẓ ibn Rajab al-Ḥanbalī.* Cairo: al-Fārūq al-Ḥadītha li-l-Ṭibāʿa wa-l-Nashr, 2003.

Ibn Taymiyya, Taqī al-Dīn. *Majmūʿat al-fatāwa.* Edited by ʿĀmir Jazzār and Anwar al-Bāz. 37 vols. Mansoura: Dār al-Wafāʾ, 2005.

Ibn Taymiyya, Taqī al-Dīn. *Rasāʾil min al-sijn.* Riyadh: Dār Ṭība, 1987.

al-Iṣfahānī, al-Rāghib. *Mufradāt alfāẓ al-Qurʾān*. Edited by Ṣafwān ʿAdnān Dāwūdī. Damascus: Dār al-Qalam, 2009.

al-Iskandarī, Aḥmad b. Muḥammad b. ʿAṭāʾ Allāh. *Laṭāʾif al-minan fī manāqib sayyadī al-Shaykh Abī al-ʿAbbās al-Mursī wa-shaykhihi al-Shaykh Abī al-Ḥasan*. Beirut: Dār al-Kutub al-ʿIlmiyya, 2017.

Lane, E. W. and Stanley Lane-Poole. *An Arabic-English Lexicon*. 2 vols. Beirut: Librairie du Liban, 1968.

Little, D. P. 'The Historical and Historiographical Significance of the Detention of Ibn Taymiyya.' *International Journal of Middle Eastern Studies* 4, no. 3 (1973): 311–327.

Livne-Kafri, Ofer. 'Some Notes on the Muslim Apocalyptic Tradition.' *Quaderni di Studi Arabi* 17 (1999): 71–94.

Madelung, Wilferd. 'Apocalyptic Prophecies in Ḥimṣ in the Umayyad Age.' *Journal of Semitic Studies* 31, no. 2 (1986): 141–185.

Madelung, Wilferd. 'The Sufyānī between Tradition and History.' *Studia Islamica* 63 (1986): 5–48.

al-Makkī, Abū Ṭālib. *Qūt al-qulūb fī muʿāmalat al-maḥbūb wa-waṣf ṭarīq al-murīd ilā maqām al-tawḥīd*. Edited by Bāsil ʿUyūn al-Sūd. 2 vols. Beirut: Dār al-Kutub al-ʿIlmiyya, 1997.

al-Marwazī, Nuʿaym b. Ḥammād. *'The Book of Tribulations': The Syrian Muslim Apocalyptic Tradition: An Annotated Translation*. Translated by David Cook. Edinburgh: Edinburgh University Press, 2019.

al-Marwazī, Nuʿaym b. Ḥammād. *Kitāb al-Fitan*. Beirut: Dār al-Fikr, 2003.

McCants, William F. *The ISIS Apocalypse: The History, Strategy, and Doomsday Vision of the Islamic State*. New York: Palgrave Macmillan, 2015.

Melchert, Christopher. 'Aḥmad Ibn Ḥanbal's Book of Renunciation.' *Der Islam* 85 (2008): 345–359.

Melchert, Christopher. 'Before *Ṣūfiyyāt*: Female Muslim Renunciants in the 8th and 9th Centuries CE.' *Journal of Sufi Studies* 5 (2016): 115–139.

Melchert, Christopher. 'Early Renunciants as *Ḥadīth* Transmitters.' *Muslim World* 92 (2002): 407–418.

Melchert, Christopher. 'Ibn al-Mubārak's *Kitāb al-Jihād* and Early Renunciant Literature.' In Robert Gleave and István Kristó-Nagy (eds), *Violence in Islamic Thought from the Qurʾān to the Mongols*, pp. 49–69. Edinburgh: Edinburgh University Press, 2015.

Melchert, Christopher. 'Renunciation (*Zuhd*) in the Early Shiʿi Tradition.' In Farhad Daftary and Gurdofarid Miskinzoda (eds), *The Study of Shiʿi Islam: History, Theology and Law*, pp. 271–294. London: I. B. Tauris, 2014.

Moosa, Ebrahim. *Ghazālī and the Poetics of Imagination*. Chapel Hill: University of North Carolina Press, 2006.

Motzki, Harald. 'Dating Muslim Traditions: A Survey.' *Arabica* 52 (2005): 204–253.

Motzki, Harald. 'The *Muṣannaf* of ʿAbd al-Razzāq al-Ṣanʿānī as a Source of Authentic *Aḥādīth* of the First Century AH.' *Journal of Near Eastern Studies* 50 (1991): 1–21.

Muslim b. Ḥajjāj. *Ṣaḥīḥ Muslim*. Beirut: Dār Ibn Ḥazm, 2002.

al-Nawawī, Sharaf al-Dīn. *al-Minhāj fī sharḥ Ṣaḥīḥ Muslim b. al-Ḥajjāj*, 10 vols. Beirut: Dār al-Maʿrifa, 2001.

Patel, Youshaa. '"Whoever Imitates a People Becomes One of Them": A Hadith and Its Interpreters.' *Islamic Law and Society* 25, no. 4 (2018): 359–426.

Pifer, Michael. 'The Age of the *Gharīb*: Strangers in the Medieval Mediterranean.' In Kathryn Babayan, and Michael Pifer (eds), *Armenian Mediterranean: Words and Worlds in Motion*, pp. 13–37. Cham, Switzerland: Palgrave Macmillan, 2018.

Pifer, Michael. 'The Stranger's Voice: Integrated Literary Cultures in Anatolia and the Premodern World.' PhD dissertation, University of Michigan–Ann Arbor, 2014.

al-Quḍāʿī, Abū ʿAbdallāh Muḥammad b. Salāma. *Musnad al-Shihāb*. 2 vols. Beirut: Muʾassasat al-Risāla, 1985.

al-Qummī, al-Shaykh al-Ṣadūq Ibn Bābawayh. *Kamāl al-dīn wa-tamām al-niʿma*. Beirut: Muʾassasat al-Aʿlamī li-l-Maṭbūʿāt, 1991.

Richardson, Kristina. 'The Invisible Strangers, or Romani History Reconsidered.' *History of the Present* 10, no. 2 (October 2020): 187–207.

Rosenthal, Franz. 'The Stranger in Medieval Islam.' *Arabica* 44 (1997): 35–75.

Rūmī, Jalāl al-Dīn. *Masnavi-yi Maʿnavī*. Edited by R. A. Nicholson. 8 vols. Tehran: Amīr Kabīr, 1984.

al-Ṣadafī, Abū Saʿīd b. Yūnus. *Tārīkh Ibn Yūnus al-Ṣadafī*. 2 vols. Beirut: Dār al-Kutub al-ʿIlmiyya, 2000.

Sadeghi, Behnam. 'The Traveling Tradition Test: A Method for Dating Traditions.' *Der Islam* 85, no. 1 (2008): 203–242.

Shakespeare, William. *The Oxford Shakespeare: The Complete Works*. Edited by Stanley Wells et al. Oxford: Oxford University Press, 2005.

al-Shāṭibī, Abū Isḥāq. *al-Iʿtiṣām*. 4 vols. Manama: Maktabat al-Tawḥīd, 2009.

Shoemaker, Stephen J. *The Apocalypse of Empire: Imperial Eschatology in Late Antiquity and Early Islam*. Philadelphia: University of Pennsylvania Press, 2018.

al-Ṭabarānī, Abū al-Qāsim Sulaymān. *al-Muʿjam al-awsaṭ*. 10 vols. Cairo: Dār al-Ḥaramayn, 1995.

al-Ṭabarānī, Abū al-Qāsim Sulaymān. *al-Muʿjam al-kabīr*. 25 vols. Cairo: Maktabat Ibn Taymiyya, 1983.

al-Ṭaḥāwī, Abū Jaʿfar Aḥmad. *Sharḥ Mushkil al-āthār*. Edited by Shuʿayb Arnāʾūṭ. 16 vols. Beirut: Muʾassasat al-Risāla, 1415/1994.

al-Tawḥīdī, Abū Ḥayyān. *al-Baṣāʾir wa-l-dhakhāʾir*. Edited by Wadād al-Qāḍī. Beirut: Dār Ṣādir, 1988.

al-Tawḥīdī, Abū Ḥayyān. *al-Imtāʿ wa-l-muʾānasa*. Beirut: Maktabat al-ʿAṣriyya, 2004.

al-Thaghrī, Abū al-Harith. 'And as for the Blessing of Your Lord Then Mention It.' *Dabiq* 12 (2015): 29–32.

al-Tirmidhī, Abū ʿĪsa, *Sunan al-Tirmidhī*. Beirut: Dār Ibn Ḥazm, 2002.

al-Tirmidhī, Abū ʿĪsa. *Sunan al-Tirmidhī*. Edited by Nāṣir al-Dīn al-Albānī. Riyadh: Maktabat al-Maʿārif, n.d.

Tsafrir, Nurit. *The History of an Islamic School of Law: The Early Spread of Hanafism*. Cambridge, MA: Harvard University Press, 2004.

Velji, Jamel. *An Apocalyptic History of the Early Fatimid Empire*. Edinburgh: Edinburgh University Press, 2016.

al-Wāsiṭī, Abū al-Faraj al-Muqri' and Zayn al-Dīn al-'Irāqī. *Kitāb al-Arba'īn fī al-jihād wa-l-mujāhidīn wa-yalīhi Kitāb al-Arba'īn al-'ishāriyya*. Beirut: Dār Ibn Ḥazm, 1995.

Wood, Graeme. *The Way of the Strangers: Encounters with the Islamic State*. New York: Random House, 2017.

Yarbrough, Luke. 'I'll Not Accept Aid from a *Mushrik*.' In A. Delattre, M. Legendre and P. M. Sijpesteijn (eds), *Authority and Control in the Countryside: Late Antiquity and Early Islam, Continuity and Change in the Mediterranean 6th-10th century*. Leiden: Brill, 2018.

Zakkār, Suhayl, ed. *Arba'at kutub fī al-jihād min aṣr al-ḥurūb al-Ṣalībiyya*. Damascus: al-Takwīn, 2007.

CHAPTER 4

Sufi Contributions to Hadith Commentary

Samer Dajani

Several studies examine Sufi contributions to Qur'anic exegesis and the genre of Sufi Qur'an commentaries, but there is a dearth of studies on Sufi contributions to the genre of hadith commentaries. In this chapter I highlight some of the most important contributions to the field of hadith commentaries by Sufis in order to show the different qualities of these commentaries.[1] Of course, many if not most of Sunnī Islam's greatest hadith commentators were themselves initiated into Sufi *ṭarīqa*s and were influenced by Sufi thought, but not all of them were seen primarily as Sufis, and their commentaries did not necessarily contain many Sufi themes. In this chapter, I look at major works by those who are strongly identified as Sufis, and whose works show Sufi themes as present if not dominant. In addition, in response to Jamal Elias's questioning of the existence of Sufi Qur'an commentaries as a separate genre,[2] my survey and analysis leads to the question of whether these hadith commentaries can be classified as a separate genre or if there is a more meaningful way to distinguish these works. I use two stories about a meeting – or perhaps two meetings – between the major hadith transmitter, Abū Dāwūd al-Sijistānī (d. 275/889), and the prominent Sufi figure, Sahl al-Tustarī (d. 283/896), to frame and direct this enquiry.

---

1 A more comprehensive survey, with understandable inaccuracies due to its preliminary nature and large scope, was undertaken by Hasan Kamil Yilmaz in the introduction to his edition and Turkish translation of Qūnawī's *Sharḥ al-arbaʿīna ḥadīthan*; see Yilmaz, *Tasavvufî Hadîs Şerhleri*. There is also a study by Zayn b. Muḥammad b. Ḥusayn al-ʿAydarūs providing examples of *ishārī* (metaphorical/allusory) explanations of hadith from the beginnings of Islam until the present; this study does not make the mistake of assuming that *ishārī* explanations are an exclusively Sufi practice and notes that other scholars have also used them. See al-ʿAydarūs, *al-Maʿānī al-ishāriyya*, 46.

2 Elias, 'Ṣūfī *tafsīr* Reconsidered'.

The well-known traditionist, Abū Ṭāhir al-Silafī (d. 576/1180), narrates two stories about the meeting between Abū Dāwūd and al-Tustarī.[3] According to one, when al-Tustarī first met Abū Dāwūd, he asked Abū Dāwūd to put out his tongue, which he used to teach the words of Muḥammad, and al-Tustarī proceeded to kiss it, either to honour it or to receive the blessings and light of the hadith. According to the second story of their meeting, a man seeking to receive Abū Dāwūd's great work, the *Sunan*, thought to first take the opportunity to visit the famed al-Tustarī, who was on the way.[4] Al-Tustarī advised him that even if he received Abū Dāwūd's hadith, in fact even if he became Abū Dāwūd himself, that it would not benefit him unless he acted on his knowledge. The man was hurt by what he thought was a criticism of the life of hadith transmitters, and so he conveyed al-Tustarī's words to Abū Dāwūd when he saw him. Abū Dāwūd asked the man to take him to al-Tustarī, who only showed him the greatest respect. During their conversation, Abū Dāwūd asked al-Tustarī about a hadith that was troubling him because unorthodox sects were using it to defend their doctrine against proto-Sunnī orthodoxy. Al-Tustarī was able to explain the hadith to Abū Dāwūd in a way that removed his concerns and Abū Dāwūd was so grateful that he kissed al-Tustarī's feet out of respect. These stories bring out two important points: (1) that the early Sufis were very closely connected to the hadith transmitters and the proto-Sunnī Ahl al-Ḥadīth movement, and yet remained in some way separate, having identifiably different concerns, and (2) that these Sufis contributed to the explication of hadiths and were respected in this field. I begin with the first point.

Sufis and the Ahl al-Ḥadīth

It is now well known that the early Sufis were closely connected to, and in many cases part of, the proto-Sunnī Ahl al-Ḥadīth movement.[5] However, not much has been said about the contribution of Sufis to the various fields of hadith sciences and transmission. Many early Sufis were important hadith scholars in the emerging Ahl al-Ḥadīth environment. Among the first was Ibn Abī ʿĀsim (d. 287/900), the *ẓāhirī* (i.e. textualist and antirationalist) judge of Isfahan. He came from the earliest group identified as 'Sufis'; namely, the school of Abū Ḥātim al-ʿAṭṭār, which was based in the

---

3 Al-Silafī, *Faḍāʾil Sunan Abī Dāwūd*, 33–36; al-Dhahabī, *Siyar*, 15:213–221.

4 This illustrates the close connections and mutual respect between those in hadith circles and Sufis. Among those figures from the Ahl al-Ḥadīth movement who went to study with Sahl al-Tustarī, the most prominent is the early leader of the Ḥanbalī school, Abū Muḥammad al-Barbahārī (d. 329/941), who spent some years as Sahl al-Tustarī's disciple (see Böwering, *The Mystical Vision*, 82).

5 Karamustafa, *Sufism*; Dajani, *Sufis and Sharīʿa*, 47–61.

grand mosque of Basra, and in which many of the founders of the Baghdadi school of Sufism were educated.[6] Ibn Abī ʿĀṣim wrote more than 300 works of hadith, including a *musnad* of 40,000 hadith, and the very influential *Kitāb al-Sunna*.[7] Al-Ḥākim al-Nīsābūrī (d. 405/1014), the author of the *Mustadrak*, which is one of the most important sources of hadith after the six canonical collections, was known to have been a disciple of at least four major Sufis. These included Jaʿfar al-Khuldī, al-Junayd's successor as head of the Baghdad circle of Sufis, and al-Kharkūshī (d. 407/1016) the author of *Tahdhīb al-asrār*, one of the earliest extant Sufi works.[8] Abū Nuʿaym al-Iṣfahānī (d. 438/1040) wrote *Ḥilyat al-awliyāʾ*, *Dalāʾil al-nubuwwa* and a *mustakhraj*[9] on *Ṣaḥīḥ Muslim* among other hadith collections, and for fourteen years he held the distinction of having the world's shortest chains of hadith and the largest number of narrations, such that traditionists travelled to him from every corner of the Muslim world.[10] Other Sufis became central figures in the transmission of canonical hadith works, among them, Abū Saʿīd b. al-Aʿrābī (d. 340/951), who has a key transmission of Abū Dāwūd's *Sunan* named after him, while Abū al-Waqt al-Sijzī al-Ṣūfī (d. 553/1158) has a key transmission of al-Bukhārī's *Ṣaḥīḥ* named after him and is also a central figure in the reception of *Sunan al-Dārimī*.[11]

Regarding works on hadith science and terminology, al-Ḥākim al-Nīsābūrī wrote *Maʿrifat ʿulūm al-ḥadīth*, the earliest known comprehensive work on hadith sciences and terminology; this was followed by multiple works by al-Khaṭīb al-Baghdādī (d. 463/1071) on the subject.[12] Al-Khaṭīb's biographical entries on Sufis reveal the extent to which he revered them, learned from them, sought their blessings, defended them and even visited their graves; among those he was closest to were his teacher Abū Nuʿaym and his friend al-Qushayrī (d. 465/1079), author of the Sufi classic *al-Risāla*.[13] Abū Nuʿaym wrote early books on hadith transmitters; namely, *Muʿjam al-ṣaḥāba* and *Tārīkh Iṣfahān*. Abū ʿAbd al-Raḥmān al-Sulamī (d. 412/1021) travelled extensively to learn hadith and studied with al-Dāraquṭnī (d. 385/995), who was seen as the last true master

---

6 See Melchert, 'Baṣran Origins'.

7 See Melchert, 'Baṣran Origins', 234–240; al-Dhahabī, *Tārīkh al-islām*, 6:461.

8 Al-Dhahabī, *Siyar*, 17: 163–178, 256–258.

9 A *mustakhraj* is an extract or excerpt from a work in which the author seeks alternate chains of narration for the same hadith.

10 Al-Dhahabī, *Tadhkirat*, 3:1094.

11 This work was written by Abū Muḥammad al-Dārimī (d. 255/869), an important teacher of al-Bukhārī and Abū ʿĪsā al-Tirmidhī. Some scholars considered his work as more deserving of inclusion in the hadith canon than the *Sunan* of Ibn Mājah, because Ibn Mājah's collection was known to contain a large number of problematic traditions.

12 On these two authors see Brown, 'A Segment of the Genealogy'.

13 For a survey of al-Khaṭīb's entries on Sufi figures and his relationships with Sufis, see Jamil, 'Traditional Sunnī Epistemology', 262–279.

of hadith criticism. Al-Sulamī left a valuable work of *su'ālāt* (questions) recording his questions to al-Dāraquṭnī on hadith transmitters; according to al-Dhahabī, this reveals al-Sulamī's mastery of the subject. Al-Sulamī authored works on Sufism and hadith, and acted as a Sufi guide while also teaching hadith for forty years.[14]

The story of Sahl al-Tustarī's warning to the student seeking to receive Abū Dāwūd's *Sunan* from its author serves to remind us that for Sufis, the defining quality was to prioritise worship and internal matters like the purification of the heart over hadith transmission and other outward sciences. However, this did not mean that they did not consider these sciences important. While it is true that some Sufis and ascetics came to see hadith transmission with suspicion for the worldly prestige that it came to signify and for the competitiveness of hadith transmitters over the shortest chains of transmission, many of them, like Ibn Abī 'Āṣim, Abū Nu'aym, Ibn al-A'rābī, al-Sulamī, and al-Ḥakim were able to strike a balance between their dedication to Sufism and their dedication to hadith.[15]

Sufis and Hadith Commentary

The first author to write a commentary on a canonical hadith collection was Abū Sulaymān al-Khaṭṭābī, who wrote commentaries on al-Bukhārī's *Ṣaḥīḥ* and Abū Dāwūd's *Sunan*. Prior to his contributions, there were only a handful of works that clarified the meanings of the vocabulary of Mālik b. 'Anas's *Muwaṭṭa'*. Al-Khaṭṭābī's most important teacher of hadith was the Sufi hadith transmitter mentioned above, Abū Sa'īd b. al-A'rābī, author of *Ṭabaqāt al-nussāk*; al-Khaṭṭābī also studied with Ja'far al-Khuldī, head of the Baghdadi circle of Sufis in his time.[16] Al-Khaṭṭābī was not the first to write a full-fledged book of hadith commentary; rather, the first full hadith commentary was written by the mystic al-Ḥakīm al-Tirmidhī (d. c. 298/910) who wrote *Nawādir al-uṣūl*, a commentary on roughly three hundred hadiths he chose himself.[17]

Al-Tirmidhī was the first mystic to provide a 'theory or complete system of thought' regarding sainthood, and this is what later Sufis recognised

14 Al-Dhahabī, *Siyar*, 17:247–255. See also al-Sulamī, *Su'ālāt al-Sulamī li-l-Dāraquṭnī*.

15 Melchert's 'Early Renunciants' gives a portrait of how ascetics and Sufis withdrew, over time, from the field of hadith transmission, but this picture is incomplete and neglects to consider many major Sufis, such as those mentioned above, who remained dedicated to the transmission and teaching of hadith.

16 Al-Dhahabī, *Siyar*, 17:23–29.

17 See al-Ḥakīm al-Tirmidhī, *Nawādir al-uṣūl*; the best edition is in 5-volumes, published in Jedda. The 4-volume edition (Beirut: Dār al-Jīl, 1992) appears to be an abridgement by the author himself.

him for.[18] In fact, no one before or after him, until Ibn ʿArabī, described such a comprehensive worldview, one that encompassed and synthesised metaphysics, cosmology, theology, anthropology, sainthood, mystical experiences, jurisprudence and language.[19] Al-Tirmidhī's *Nawādir al-uṣūl* cleverly employs around three hundred hadith as doors of entry to various aspects of his worldview. Using the commentary on each hadith, and the supplementary hadiths he narrated in the commentary, he explains his views to the reader. Though he does not use the word Sufi in this work, his hadith commentary was primarily concerned with Sufi themes such as sainthood and inspired knowledge, knowledge of God and metaphysics.[20] This book was the first in several ways: it was the first full book of hadith commentary, the first work of hadith commentary on an original collection of hadith (the author's own – earlier partial commentaries and most commentaries focused on the collections of previous authors), and it was also the first hadith commentary with a specific focus on Sufi matters.[21] Al-Tirmidhī also wrote *al-Manhiyyāt*, a much shorter work in which he briefly comments on the wisdom behind eight hundred prohibitions in hadith, and explains that not all of these were meant to signify that these actions are forbidden, and therefore destructive to the self, but that many if not most prohibitions were to teach *adab* (propriety), and were intended to prevent people from descending to a lower level than they deserve. While propriety was very important to Sufis, the writings and teachings of al-Shāfiʿī and Ibn Ḥanbal clearly differentiate between what the *sharīʿa* prohibited in order to teach *adab* and what was prohibited because it was sinful.[22]

Abū Bakr al-Kalābādhī (d. 384/994) was famous for *al-Taʿarruf li-mad-hhab ahl al-taṣawwuf*, his early introduction to Sufism and Sufis. His lesser-known work is a substantial book of hadith commentary, *Baḥr al-fawāʾid*, in which he followed al-Tirmidhī's example and chose his own collection of 222 hadiths to comment on. In this collection, al-Kalābādhī's primary interest in Sufi themes like love and nearness to God is apparent, and in some cases, he interprets hadiths metaphorically, such that the outward meanings of hadiths refer to inward realities of the soul.[23] The Ḥanbalī Sufi

---

18 Radtke and O'Kane, *The Concept of Sainthood*, 8.

19 Radtke and O'Kane, *The Concept of Sainthood*, 6.

20 In al-Tirmidhī's time, the word 'Sufi' had not yet gained currency throughout the Muslim world; it referred to particular schools in Basra and then in Baghdad; see Sviri, 'Ḥakīm Tirmidhī'. Later authors on Sufism, however, rightly considered al-Ḥakīm al-Tirmidhī one of the most influential founders of Sufism in its broader sense.

21 Al-Tirmidhī is also the author of the first known autobiography in Islam, *Budū shaʾn al-Ḥakīm al-Tirmidhī*.

22 See Dajani, *Sufis and Sharīʿa*, 218.

23 Al-Kalābādhī, *Baḥr al-fawāʾid*.

Abū Manṣūr Maʿmar al-Iṣfahānī (d. 418/1027) has a similar early commentary. He contributed to the by-then popular genre of forty hadiths and wrote a commentary on his own collection. Before him, al-Sulamī and al-Qushayrī had written works on forty hadiths; theirs were intended for Sufi aspirants, with the commentaries appearing only as headings for each hadith. These headings show how the hadiths demonstrated important principles on the Sufi path. Of course, even a short heading serves an important commentarial purpose and should be understood as a commentary, despite its brevity, and al-Bukhārī himself had pioneered the use of section headings to draw out the legal or theological meanings of hadith.[24] A final prominent example is Aḥmad al-Rifāʿī's (d. 578/1182) *Ḥālat ahl al-ḥaqīqa maʿ Allāh*, which is a compilation, made by a student, of forty lessons given by al-Rifāʿī, each of which began with a hadith he narrated with his own chain back to the Prophet Muhammad.[25] Though this work may appear at first to be a commentary on forty hadith, it is in fact a compilation of exhortations and lessons on the Sufi path, taking hadiths as their starting point. While many of these lessons focus on explaining the hadith, some do not interpret the hadith at all.

The above-mentioned examples – apart from al-Tirmidhī's *al-Manhiyyāt* – should be understood for what they really were: books on Sufism. Some were written in the form of short hadith collections with headings, while others took the form of long commentaries, but here hadith commentaries – whether in section headings or long discussions – served as a medium to discuss Sufi ideas.[26] *Al-Manhiyyāt* is more a work on the wisdom of the *sharīʿa* than it is a Sufi work or a work of hadith commentary per se, though it may rely on al-Tirmidhī's Sufi concept of spiritual insight to explain the wisdom behind the hadiths. Jamal Elias pointed out that the structure of a Qur'an commentary, with its line-by-line format and the Qur'an's changing topics and themes, was not the best way for a Sufi to give a detailed presentation of their ideas; rather a Sufi would find it much easier to set out their mystical views in a treatise where their ideas could be treated fully and coherently in an organised fashion without having to follow the Qur'an's content and structure.[27] This problem does not arise in hadith commentaries, in which authors could choose which hadiths they thought would be beneficial to their project and use them as doors to explain their ideas, while at the same time legitimising their teachings by linking them to the hadith.

24 On this topic see Blecher, *Said the Prophet of God*, 111–128.
25 Al-Rifāʿī, *Ḥālat ahl al-ḥaqīqa*.
26 For a more recent example of a book on the Sufi path that employs the medium of a forty-hadith commentary, see Ṣāliḥ al-Jaʿfarī's *al-Fawāʾid al-Jaʿfariyya*, which I translated in Dajani, *Reassurance for the Seeker*.
27 Elias, 'Ṣūfī *tafsīr* Reconsidered', 47.

Sunnī scholars long held that the hadiths were inspired to the Prophet Muhammad and constituted a sort of inspiration that complemented the Qur'anic revelation, thus they were almost a second revelation.[28] Both the Qur'an and hadith employ many parables, similes and metaphors in their teachings, and so it was only natural for Sunnīs to take some of the Prophet Muhammad's words beyond their literal meanings and give them meta-phorical interpretations.[29] Al-Kalābādhī, for example, took Muhammad's supplication for health and chastity to also refer to the health of the heart and the importance of avoiding what God forbade. He took the hadith that 'only a believer remains in a state of purity' to refer to outward purity, but also to refer to the purity of the heart; this, he said, is achieved by not look-ing at anything but God.[30] Abū Ḥāmid al-Ghazālī (d. 505/1111) famously argued that when Muhammad stated that angels do not enter houses in which dogs live, he wanted his Companions to understand that the light of God will not enter hearts that are filled with bad traits such as rancour, anger, envy and the like; and he explained this without nullifying the outward understanding of the statement.[31]

Some Sufis went beyond metaphorical understandings and treated the hadith in the same way that they treated the Qur'an – by holding that it contained within it layers of meaning that were all intended at the same time, and were accessible to those given success by God. This is not neces-sarily a Sufi concept, as many non-Sufis also viewed the Qur'an and had-ith as containing immense wisdom behind their more immediate outward meanings. The earliest example of such a treatment of the hadith that I have located is that of the Ḥanbalī 'Abdallāh al-Anṣārī's (d. 481/1089) dis-cussion of the 'Hadith of Gabriel', in which the Prophet Muhammad stated that 'excellence (*iḥsān*) is to worship God as if you saw Him **for if you do not see Him, verily He sees you** (*fa in lam takun tarāh fa-innahu yarāk*)'. In the beginning of *Manāzil al-sā'irīn*, al-Anṣārī hinted that if this hadith was read in a certain way it would reveal the basis for the Sufi doctrine of spiritual witnessing of God in the heart, a state that could be attained only through the annihilation of the self. Here al-Anṣārī wants the reader to reread the sentence (specifically that in bold above) with different punctua-tion than usual: 'if you cease to be, then you will see Him. And verily He sees you' (*fa in lam takun, tarah, fa-innahu yarāk*)![32] This interpretation was a favourite of Muḥyī al-Dīn Ibn 'Arabī and formed the basis of his

---

28 On this, see the excellent study of Graham, *Divine Word*.

29 Al-Ḥakīm al-Tirmidhī wrote a work on the similes in the Qur'an and hadith: *al-Amthāl min al-Qur'ān wa-l-Sunna*.

30 Al-Kalābādhī, *Baḥr al-fawā'id*, 1:123–124.

31 Al-Ghazālī, *Iḥyā' 'ulūm al-dīn*, 1:181.

32 Several editions of the work and commentaries on it have been published. Al-Kūrānī quotes the opening section of the book in al-Kūrānī, *al-Amam li-īqāẓ al-himam*, 113–118.

Kitāb al-Fānā' fī al-mushāhada. It was also favoured by a follower of Ibn 'Arabī named al-Kūrānī who, in his work *al-Amam*, defended this interpretation against Ibn Ḥajar's criticism of Ibn 'Arabī's treatise.[33]

This type of interpretation of the hadith assumes that the Prophet intended his words to have a variety of meanings to diverse audiences at the same time, and that he carefully fashioned his words (or God inspired them) in a way that they could carry multiple meanings. This view was taken up and advanced by Ibn 'Arabī and his student al-Qūnawī (d. 673/1274). In fact, al-Qūnawī wrote a 'forty-hadith commentary' that contained twenty-nine hadiths, to prove that hadiths carry within them allusions to metaphysical and spiritual realities and secrets that could only be accessed by the Sufis. Unlike the works of al-Tirmidhī, al-Kalābādhī, and al-Rifā'ī, this was not a work of Sufism through the medium of hadith commentary, but was first and foremost a commentary on hadith, designed to show that they contain more depth than meets the eye.[34] The motivation for such a treatment of the hadith appears to fall in line with Jamal Elias's discussion behind the motives for 'Alā' al-Dawla al-Simnānī's (d. 736/1336) commentary on the Qur'an. Elias notes that al-Simnānī's first intention was the elucidation of scripture, as he and Sufis like him genuinely believed that the Qur'an (and in our case the hadith) used metaphorical language to refer to a vast (in the case of the Qur'an, infinite) underlying body of knowledge. Elias remarks,

> To comment on it, therefore, is not just to explain its subject but to publicly recognise its rhetorical excellence and therefore its beauty. The relationship between beauty and virtue was well established in Islamic aesthetics some centuries before Simnānī was born. As such, one can see that the writing of *tafsīr* for Simnānī would have been an act of piety as much as anything else.[35]

33 Though al-Anṣārī never spelled out this interpretation, Ibn 'Arabī and al-Kūrānī must be correct in attributing this understanding to him because nowhere does the hadith contain any mention of annihilation or of witnessing God except if read this way. Strangely, Basheer Nafi based his appraisal of al-Kūrānī as a reformer largely on the claim that he rejected this interpretation (see Nafi, 'Taṣawwuf and Reform'). The charitable interpretation of Nafi's claim is to assume he only read the first two sentences of the entire discussion, stopped at al-Kūrānī's quotation of Ibn Ḥajar's criticism, and failed to see that the remainder of the discussion was a rejoinder to Ibn Ḥajar and a defence of Ibn 'Arabī. For a study of how Ibn 'Arabī interpreted the hadith the same way he did the Qur'an see Gril, 'Ḥadīth in the Work of Ibn 'Arabī', 56.

34 For this commentary see Yilmaz, *Sharḥ al-arba'īna hadīthan*, published in his *Tasavvufi Hadîs Şerhleri*. A more recent edition is al-Qūnawī, *Kirk Hadis Şerhi: Sharḥ al-aḥādīth al-arba'īn*. A study of some of al-Qūnawī's commentaries in this work can be found in Hirtenstein, 'The Image of Guidance'.

35 Elias, 'Ṣūfī *tafsīr* Reconsidered', 52.

Elias gives a second intention for al-Simnānī's work: it was an act of respect for his predecessors; al-Simnānī's work was the completion of an unfinished work by previous shaykhs from his *ṭarīqa*. While al-Qūnawī's commentary was not a completion of a predecessor's work, it was still an act of respect for his teachers, in that it was meant to elevate the status of the Sufis by showing that their piety and spiritual insight gave them a privileged position from which to understand the hidden depth of the Prophet Muhammad's words which non-Sufis could not access. Ultimately, it was his intention to elevate, honour and show particularly the prestige of Sufi shaykhs. Al-Qūnawī was also able, through his commentary, to link the words of Muhammad to the metaphysical doctrines of the Akbarian school of his main teacher Ibn 'Arabī; thus through his commentary he was serving that school.

A prime and influential example of this type of commentary is that of Ibn Abī Jamra (d. 699/1300) who first compiled a popular selection of 297 hadiths from *Ṣaḥīḥ al-Bukhārī* and later wrote a commentary on them.[36] In this commentary, Ibn Abī Jamra sought to reveal the immense wisdom in the Prophet Muhammad's words and actions, drawing out as many points of etiquette, wisdom, intelligence and meaning as he could from each choice of word, every omission and every action, all of which filled the hadith with meaning. In the introduction to his work, he stated that the sayings of Muhammad were so perfect that one needed to attribute to them every possible inference of meaning. Clearly, this was a pious endeavour in the service of the Prophet Muhammad, an effort to explain the perfection and beauty in his words. The difference between this work and al-Qūnawī's is that in this work there are no metaphysical Akbarian interpretations. In fact, there are no particularly Sufi interpretations in this work, except his emphasis on *adab*, which Sufis had long seen as a cornerstone of their teaching. The centrality of *adab* was expressed in the saying 'Sufism is all about propriety (*ādāb*); for every time there is an etiquette and for every station there is an etiquette'.[37] The one distinctly Sufi aspect to his work can be seen in the connections that Ibn Abī Jamra identified between each hadith and a Sufi practice or belief; almost all his three hundred commentaries contain one or more points beginning with 'In this hadith there is evidence for the people of Sufism in that ...'

Ibn Abī Jamra's work comes with an appendix of seventy dreams or visions that he or his disciples saw of the Prophet Muhammad praising his commentaries.[38] The content of these visions demonstrates what Ibn

---

36 For the original selection, see Ibn Abī Jamra, *Mukhtaṣar Ṣaḥīḥ al-Bukhārī*; for the commentary, see Ibn Abī Jamra: *Bahjat al-nufūs*.
37 Al-Sulamī, *Ṭabaqāt al-ṣūfiyya*, 106.
38 These visions have been published independently as Ibn Abī Jamra, *al-Marāʾī al-ḥisān*.

Abī Jamra and his disciples saw as the most important contributions of his commentaries; according to their view, these contributions were his commentaries on

1. the hadith regarding the slander against 'Ā'isha, which served to protect her honour and therefore serves Sunnī Islam as a whole;
2. the 'Hadith of Ibn al-Ṣāmit', which the author used to defend the Ash'arī creed against literalist understandings of God's attributes, and was described as outweighing all the books of the *fuqahā*';
3. the 'Hadith of the Nightly Journey and Ascension', which was praised for its explanation of the benefits of the daily prayer and was described as outweighing all the books of the Sufis;
4. the hadith that 'this religion is an easy one', which was seen as a service to the *sharīʿa*; and
5. the hadith on the beginning of revelation, which is concerned with the greatness of the Prophet Muhammad himself.

This list shows that Ibn Abī Jamra's work was not oriented toward Sufis in particular, but rather that it aimed to cover the entire gamut of Sunnī teachings from creed to jurisprudence to Sufism. Furthermore, these visions reveal that Ibn Abī Jamra's claim to excellence was not necessarily tied to inspiration or insight, as might be assumed of a Sufi, but sometimes related to his mastery of the Arabic language in all its pre-Islamic tribal dialects and variations (such as the dialects of Tamīm, Thaqīf, Ṭaī, and Quraysh), coupled with success (*tawfīq*) from God.

Al-Ḥusayn al-Ṭībī (d. 743/1342) was a direct student of the great Sufi master Abū Ḥafs 'Umar al-Suhrawardī (d. 632/1234), and was one of his successors and a Sufi master himself. He wrote the first commentary on *Mishkāt al-maṣābīḥ* that was compiled by al-Ṭībī's own disciple al-Khaṭīb al-Tabrīzī, at al-Ṭībī's behest.[39] After the student finished the work under al-Ṭībī's direction, the master, al-Ṭībī, wrote the commentary. Al-Ṭībī was known as a Sufi, but also as a traditionist, jurist and one of the Muslim world's foremost grammarians; his *ḥāshiya* on al-Zamakhsharī's Qur'an commentary *al-Kashshāf* was praised by 'Abd al-Wahhāb al-Sha'rānī (d. 973/1565) as the finest *ḥāshiya* on that exegesis (which focuses on grammar), and is still prized as such by Muslim grammarians today. Al-Sha'rānī noted that al-Ṭībī was unique for mastering several fields. He wrote: 'He [al-Ṭībī] was a traditionist, Sufi, grammarian, *faqīh* [jurist], and *uṣūlī*. It is rare for all these attributes to be combined in one scholar.'[40] The *Mishkāt al-maṣābīḥ* soon became the most important hadith collection in the Indian

39 Al-Ṭībī, *Sharḥ al-Ṭībī*.
40 Al-Sha'rānī, *Laṭā'if al-minan*, 85.

subcontinent and al-Ṭībī's commentary was the basis for its many subsequent commentaries. His work was also heavily used by those who commented on other collections, especially Ibn Ḥajar's commentary on *Ṣaḥīḥ al-Bukhārī*. Sufi perspectives are apparent, but not prominent, throughout his interpretations of hadith. Nonetheless, in the next section we see the significance of this Sufi content. Another such commentary is that of the Sufi traditionist ʿAbd al-Raʾūf al-Munāwī (d. 1031/1622), the student of the great Sufi ʿAbd al-Wahhāb al-Shaʿrānī, and the author of two biographical compendia of Sufis. Al-Munāwī commented on al-Suyūṭī's hadith compendium *al-Jāmiʿ al-ṣaghīr*, and often quoted Sufis like Ibn ʿArabī and al-Qūnawī in his commentary.

The hadith commentary *al-Maknūn fī ḥaqāʾiq al-kalim al-nabawiyya* by Rūzbihān Baqlī (d. 606/1209) stands out from the others in that he conceived his work specifically as a Sufi commentary. He stated that just as there were works like those of al-Khaṭṭābī that explain the exterior (*ẓāhir*) meanings of the hadith, he felt a need for a work that explained its secrets and inner realities (*ḥaqāʾiq*). He wanted it to become a reference and guide for Sufis, to link the vocabulary in the hadith with the spiritual truths or realities accessed by the Knowers of God. He stated that his explanations were written in the language and terminology of Sufi shaykhs in order to point out Muhammad's allusions to the divine realities they speak of. He further stated that the ability to draw these meanings from the hadith was possible in direct proportion to the spiritual openings that God gave His saints (*awliyāʾ*) onto the world of the unseen.[41]

Is There Such a Thing as a 'Sufi' Commentary?

In his article 'Ṣūfī *tafsīr* Reconsidered', Jamal Elias questions the accuracy of conceiving of Qurʾan commentaries written by Sufis as constituting a separate genre of Sufi commentaries. He argues that these works cannot be conceived of as a genre of their own, because commentaries written by Sufis 'lack a shared structure or identifiable set of concerns that distinguish them from the wider category of *tafsīr* literature'.[42] Second, he states that the fact that Sufis often resort to allegorical/allusory (*ishārī*) interpretations of the Qurʾan does not make their commentaries distinct, because allegorical interpretations are normal in Qurʾanic commentary and are not only employed by Sufis. The allegorical interpretations by Sufis are often described as 'esoteric', which is not always accurate, and furthermore, the term esoteric could also be applied to commentaries written by philosophers. Elias did note, however, that 'there is no doubt that identifiable Sufi

41 Baqlī, *al-Maknūn*.
42 Elias, 'Ṣūfī *tafsīr* Reconsidered', 45.

commentaries on the Qur'an exist, both in the sense that there are Sufi themes apparent (even dominant) within them and they are also written by figures strongly and self-consciously identified as Sufis'.[43]

We should also add that it is expected for an author's background to influence their perspective and limit, expand or shift the scope of interpretations they give to any text. Therefore, the range of interpretations from a scholar with mainly Sufi interests might differ from those of a linguist. For example, with regard to a hadith transmitted by al-Bukhārī, that after a Muslim is buried he will be asked about which God he worshipped, which religion he followed and 'what did you use to say about *this* man [i.e. Muḥammad]',[44] al-Kirmānī (d. 786/1384) sees this as evidence that Muhammad's spirit will accompany every Muslim during the questioning; by contrast, this explanation does not even appear as a possible interpretation in commentaries that benefited from al-Kirmānī's text but were written by scholars who, like Ibn Ḥajar, were not as strongly influenced by Sufi thought.[45]

In terms of the commentaries described above, we could question the validity of calling these works 'Sufi hadith commentaries' because the exegetical techniques they used were not necessarily exclusive to Sufism. An exception to this would be Baqlī's *al-Maknūn* because it was specifically written to explain every hadith using terms and concepts found only among Sufis. We could also refer to several passages in al-Qūnawī's commentary as Akbarian because they relate the hadith to the doctrines of the school of his teacher Ibn 'Arabī. Similarly, we could say that Ibn Abī

---

43 Elias, 'Ṣūfī *tafsīr* Reconsidered', 45.

44 Al-Bukhārī, *Ṣaḥīḥ*, Kitāb al-Janā'iz, Bāb al-mayyit yasma' khafq al-ni'āl.

45 Al-Kirmānī's commentary is the earliest of the four most well-known and influential commentaries on al-Bukhārī, and was regularly quoted by Ibn Ḥajar. Al-Kirmānī's commentary on the Qur'an, *Ḍamā'ir al-Qur'ān*, has been described as a 'Sufi commentary'. While his commentary on *Ṣaḥīḥ al-Bukhārī* does not show an overwhelmingly Sufi influence, this is just a small example of how a scholar's range of interpretations are influenced by their backgrounds and perspectives. A conversation between the Sufi scholar Yūsuf al-Dijwī (d. 1946), whose world-renowned *fatwās* made him the most prominent voice of the Sunnī Traditionalism of al-Azhar in the first half the twentieth century, and his disciple Ṣāliḥ al-Ja'farī (d. 1979), who became the Imam of al-Azhar and the founder of a Sufi *ṭarīqa* that carries his name, points to the unique nature of al-Kirmānī's explanation and its appeal to Sufis. Al-Ja'farī relates that when he was studying at al-Azhar he attended al-Dijwī's lessons of commentary on *Ṣaḥīḥ al-Bukhārī*. In one lesson, al-Dijwī commented on this same hadith – that after a Muslim is buried, he will be asked about which God he worshipped – and when the lesson finished, al-Ja'farī, who had been reading al-Kirmānī's commentary on his own, approached his teacher and mentioned to him al-Kirmānī's interpretation. Al-Dijwī said, 'I had studied the commentary of al-Kirmānī and read that matter in it. Why did you not remind me of it during the lesson so that the people would hear it from me?' (see Dajani, *Reassurance for the Seeker*, 26).

Jamra's commentary is only a 'Sufi commentary' in those passages in which he attempts to prove a Sufi doctrine or practice, while otherwise it is a standard commentary. Al-Ṭībī's tendency to explain the words and actions of Muhammad as based largely on his intense love and longing for God does not itself make it a 'Sufi commentary' even if al-Ṭībī's *taṣawwuf* most probably motivated it.

This brings us to another important consideration, namely, the idea of Sufi concerns and themes. While certain ideas and their associated terms, such as separation (*farq*) and its counterpart bringing together (*jamʿ*), and the related annihilation (*fanāʾ*) and subsistence (*baqāʾ*), are specifically Sufi, other themes that are strongly associated with Sufism, or are expected to be found in Sufi texts, such as experiential knowledge of God (*maʿrifa*), inspiration (*ilhām*), love (*maḥabba*), nearness to God/saintliness (*walāya/wilāya*), purification of the heart (*tazkiya*) and even spiritual upbringing (*tarbiya*), are not exclusively the concern of Sufis. We should not be surprised to find these ideas mentioned by other Muslim authors, though we are more likely to find them in the works of Sufis. Furthermore, given the place of Sufism in Islamic societies, it was natural for Sunnī Muslims in general to view Sufis as experts in these fields. In fact, if one thing distinguished Sufis from others, it was their prioritisation of these concerns, so it was only natural for them to be seen as experts in these internal matters. This specialisation appears very early in Islam. One particularly illustrative example is the report about the great traditionist and jurist Sufyān al-Thawrī (d. 161/778). It was said that when he finished the lessons he gave when visiting Mecca, he said to his students, 'Now let us get up and go to the doctor [of hearts]',[46] meaning the Meccan devotee Wuhayb b. al-Ward (d. 153/773). Wuhayb's teachings centred on the importance of achieving knowledge of God and certainty in the heart and on the miraculous power of this knowledge and certainty.[47]

Al-Zamakhsharī's Qurʾan commentary *al-Kashshāf* is not labelled a 'grammatical commentary on the Qurʾan', because grammatical discussions are not its only characteristic, and grammatical analysis is present in almost every Qurʾan commentary. But those looking for authoritative grammatical analysis of Qurʾanic passages might see *al-Kashshāf* as the primary reference because it devotes particular attention to grammatical discussions and its author was seen as an authority in the field. Al-Bayḍāwī's commentary on the Qurʾan is not labelled simply a 'theological/Ashʿarī' commentary on the Qurʾan, but those wishing for authoritative theological-Ashʿarī explanations of certain verses might see it as the primary reference point on the subject. The same could be said about al-Rāzī's commentary regarding Islamic philosophy and al-Qurṭubī's commentary regarding jurisprudence. In the same

46 Abū Nuʿaym, *Ḥilyat al-awliyāʾ*, 8:140.
47 Al-Dhahabī, *Siyar*, 7:198–199; Abū Nuʿaym, *Ḥilyat al-awliyāʾ*, 8:140–161.

way, we could describe many of the hadith commentaries written by Sufis as being focused on metaphorical or allusory interpretations, or as emphasising spiritual matters more than legal or theological ones, rather than claiming that they employed specifically Sufi techniques of exegesis or that the themes they discuss are particular only to Sufis. For Muslim scholars in the tradition itself, the writings of Sufis were often deemed to be particularly helpful regarding certain topics in which they were seen to be authorities; the same could be said of hadith commentaries written by Sufis. I illustrate this point by briefly examining how the hadith commentaries of Sufis were employed and referred to in Ibn Ḥajar's *Fatḥ al-Bārī* and in other important classics.

Ibn Ḥajar's *Fatḥ al-Bārī* contains roughly twenty references to al-Ḥakīm al-Tirmidhī's *Nawādir al-uṣūl*. As al-Tirmidhī was an early hadith transmitter, a contemporary of the authors of the canonical collections, he was used as a source of unique hadith transmissions that did not exist in the canon. However, beside his role as hadith transmitter, al-Tirmidhī's own views were quoted, most often in relation to discussions of spiritual topics seen as the specialty of Sufis. To give some examples, Ibn Ḥajar quotes al-Tirmidhī's discussion of the difference between two words given for the human heart (*qalb* and *fuʾād*); in it al-Tirmidhī states that only people of spiritual insight are capable of knowing this difference and of assigning each name to the proper spiritual faculty associated with the heart. Ibn Ḥajar also quoted al-Tirmidhī on topics such as dreams and issues relating to what the spirit experiences after death.[48]

Regarding al-Kalābādhī, Ibn Ḥajar quoted him roughly eleven times, and benefited from him more as a hadith transmitter and general scholar. Some of al-Kalābādhī's hadith narrations included important details that were not preserved in the versions narrated in more famous collections and that Ibn Ḥajar found helpful in clarifying the context and legal implications of the hadiths.[49] In two cases Ibn Ḥajar relied on al-Kalābādhī's brilliant

---

48 Al-Qurṭubī's commentary on the Qurʾan shows far greater influence from *Nawādir al-uṣūl* than from *Fatḥ al-Bārī*. Al-Qurṭubī quotes al-Tirmidhī more than eighty times, sometimes even quoting lengthy passages or entire hadith commentaries without attribution (such as al-Tirmidhī's 227th chapter in Nawādir *al-uṣūl*, 3:588). Ibn Qayyim al-Jawziyya not only quoted al-Tirmidhī more than once in *Kitāb al-Rūḥ* in discussions on the life of the spirit after death, but also copied, in an edited format, several chapters from al-Tirmidhī's *al-Furūq* at the end of *Kitāb al-Rūḥ*, and added some of his own chapters following al-Tirmidhī's model.

49 Note that regarding the famous hadith claiming that Muhammad was made to love prayer, women and perfume, the wording of the hadith that was popularised by the theologian Ibn Fūrak, and even more so by Ibn ʿArabī in his *Fuṣūṣ*, is not found in the canonical version in al-Nasāʾī's *Sunan*. Both scholars, but especially Ibn ʿArabī, made much of the hadith's use of the term 'three things', even though this term does not exist in al-Nasāʾī's version and scholars have struggled to find a source for it. However, I have found that this is the wording that al-Kalābādhī has in his *Baḥr al-fawāʾid*, 1:113 (third hadith).

ability to reconcile seemingly contradictory hadith reports; this shows that al-Kalābādhī's influence was not as a Sufi but as a scholar. However, in one case Ibn Ḥajar quotes al-Kalābādhī for a Sufi-influenced explanation of how spirits will be able to know or recognise God on the day of judgement. Here, like al-Tirmidhī, we see that Ibn Ḥajar found al-Kalābādhī helpful for his expertise in the fields of hadith and spirituality, the latter of course strongly associated with Sufism.

Ibn Abī Jamra wrote his commentary on a selection from *Ṣaḥīḥ al-Bukhārī*, and so it would be natural for Ibn Ḥajar to reference it, and he does so, more than 160 times. However, Ibn Ḥajar's treatment of Ibn Abī Jamra shows very clearly that he treats him differently than he treats other scholars, because of the saintliness Ibn Ḥajar believed that Ibn Abī Jamra possessed. Whereas Ibn Ḥajar's sources were introduced simply by their names, Ibn Ḥajar twice described Ibn Abī Jamra as *al-qudwa* (the exemplar) or *al-imām al-qudwa*, a distinction he only gave to Ibn Abī Jamra.[50] Ibn Ḥajar once followed Ibn Abī Jamra's name with the words 'may God allow us to benefit from his *baraka* (spiritual blessing)'; certainly it is notable that Ibn Ḥajar only used this honorific one other time, after the name of al-Junayd, another Sufi.[51] In ten instances, after writing Ibn Abī Jamra's name, Ibn Ḥajar wrote the words 'may God benefit us through him'; by contrast, he only used this expression once for one other person, the saintly scholar al-Nawawī.[52] Thus, in a markedly clear way, Ibn Ḥajar treated Ibn Abī Jamra differently from his other sources *because* of his Sufism. Ibn Ḥajar's special admiration may have been enhanced by Ibn Abī Jamra's reputation for closely following the Sunna, for his prestige at having a disciple like the esteemed Ibn al-Ḥājj al-Mālikī (the author of *al-Madkhal*, an acclaimed work against religious innovation), and for Ibn Abī Jamra's burial in Ibn Ḥajar's city of Cairo and the love exhibited for the author and his grave by the city's inhabitants. Quite often Ibn Ḥajar described Ibn Abī Jamra's unique ability to extract subtle meanings from the hadith; Ibn Ḥajar used words such as *istinbāṭ* (deduction/drawing out), *ʿilla* (ratio), *ḥikma* (wisdom) and *ishāra* (allusion), some of which could be directly linked to his perceived status as a man of spiritual insight. Ibn Ḥajar quoted Ibn Abī Jamra on matters such as spiritual experiences and the realities of *taqwā* and *īmān* – Ibn Abī Jamra stated that the *fuqahāʾ* interpret Muhammad's description of 'faith's sweetness' in an allegorical sense because they had not experienced it, whereas Sufis knew from experience that faith literally had a sweetness that could be tasted. Ibn Ḥajar also quoted Ibn Abī

---

50 Ibn Ḥajar, *Fatḥ al-Bārī*, 1:13, 71.
51 Ibn Ḥajar, *Fatḥ al-Bārī*, 2:87; 11:331.
52 For Ibn Abī Jamra, see the following three examples: Ibn Ḥajar, *Fatḥ al-Bārī*, 2:507; 8:480; 9:340; and Ibn Ḥajar mentions al-Nawawī in *Fatḥ al-Bārī*, 1:8.

Jamra on other issues strongly associated with Sufism, issues such as *zuhd* (asceticism), *adab* (propriety), etiquette and good character. These were not the only elements Ibn Ḥajar quoted Ibn Abī Jamra about; on occasion he also benefited from his legal discussions.[53]

Ibn Ḥajar quotes al-Ḥusayn al-Ṭībī more than 335 times. This large number can be explained by the fact that al-Ṭībī commented on the entire *Mishkāt al-maṣābīḥ*, which covered the same topics as al-Bukhārī's *Ṣaḥīḥ*, whereas previously mentioned Sufis commented on a far smaller number of traditions, ones they themselves selected as a basis for their own Sufi works. In the case of Ibn Abī Jamra, he commented on his own small selection of hadiths from *Ṣaḥīḥ al-Bukhārī* and wrote them for the layperson. Al-Ṭībī, as we have also seen, was considered a master in many fields, including grammar, rhetoric (*balāgha*), jurisprudence and hadith sciences, and Ibn Ḥajar made use of his expertise in all these fields. Ibn Ḥajar also relied on al-Ṭībī's ability to extract 'subtleties' and wisdom (*ḥikma*) from the hadith. Al-Ṭībī's interpretations of Muhammad's words and actions often related them to Muhammad's intense love for God, giving many of the passages that Ibn Ḥajar quotes from al-Ṭībī a distinct and easily recognisable nature. Therefore, although al-Ṭībī's commentary is considered the least 'Sufi' commentary – in that it is not an *ishārī* commentary, nor does it employ specifically Sufi terms, or deal with topics unique to the Sufis – al-Ṭībī's quotes in *Fatḥ al-Bārī* are often those that we most immediately attribute to a Sufi.

The discussion above leads us back to the story of the meeting between Abū Dāwūd al-Sijistānī and Sahl al-Tustarī. In this story, Abū Dāwūd was troubled by how the Qadariyya sect employed an authentic hadith to support their position of complete free will. The hadith in question states that 'Every newborn is born on the *fiṭra* (natural state), and it is his parents who make him a Christian or a Jew'.[54] Abū Dāwūd expressed his concern and was troubled that the Qadariyya used this hadith as evidence that disbelief and disobedience to God were not predestined, but were brought about by humans.[55] Al-Tustarī gave his own explanation of the hadith; namely, that children's parents were not able to actually change

---

53 Muḥammad al-Shinwānī (d. 1233/1817), who held the post of Grand Shaykh of al-Azhar, wrote a *ḥāshiya* on Ibn Abī Jamra's commentary that is often used to teach it. Contemporary neo-traditionalist Sufi institutions of knowledge serving Western Muslims, such as SunniPath (now known as Qibla) and SeekersHub, regularly offer courses based on Ibn Abī Jamra's commentary and al-Shinwānī's *ḥāshiya*.

54 Abū Dāwūd, *al-Sunan*.

55 That this hadith troubled Abū Dāwūd is borne out by his treatment of it in his *Sunan*, 870. There, he chose a longer version, via Mālik b. Anas's *Muwaṭṭa'*, that has the following addition: 'The Prophet was asked what happened to those who died when still young, and the Prophet replied, "God knows best what they would have done if they

their children's original state of *fiṭra*, rather they invited them to their own beliefs through instruction. Ultimately, however, guidance was in the hands of God alone, for the Qur'an told Muhammad that he could not guide whomever he wishes, that only God could do that, and the hadith literature showed that Iblīs (Satan) was not able to misguide anyone, rather he could only entice people to his way. When he heard this explanation, Abū Dāwūd bent down and kissed al-Tustarī's feet. Perhaps this story conveys more than Abū Dāwūd's simple gratitude and respect for al-Tustarī's convincing answer: perhaps it is founded on the belief that al-Tustarī, the famed spiritual guide whose teachings and writings deal with the nature of the human spirit, was seen as especially authoritative in this subject relating to spiritual guidance.

In Sunnī Islam, a division of expertise can be seen very early on; in this division, the explanations of Sufis can be seen as not necessarily having a unique method, but as having a unique authority tied to their perceived specialisation in certain fields related to the heart and spirit, and to the belief that they possessed spiritual insight. Likewise, viewing the tradition from outside it, we could say that it is not accurate to categorise the hadith commentaries of the Sufis as falling within one particular genre, or we could mistakenly assume that there is something inherently unique to their interpretive methods. We could say, however, that just as certain commentaries on the Qur'an and hadith reveal the interests and strengths of various scholars, likewise the Qur'an and hadith commentaries of Sufis reveal the interests and perspectives of each Sufi, and these shaped the range of their interpretations and their choices in commentaries that were often otherwise very different from each other in style and method.

had grown up".' Abū Dāwūd then followed the hadith with a narration about Mālik b. Anas being confronted with the same problem of the Qadariyya's use of this hadith; according to this narration, Mālik replied that this additional phrase at the end of the hadith provided the response to the Qadariyya: that God knows people's destinies. It is interesting that this addition was treated as suspicious by al-Bukhārī. In his *Ṣaḥīḥ*, al-Bukhārī's custom was to always give preference to Mālik b. Anas's narrations over all others, and to quote them first on any topic. However, for this hadith, Mālik's narration is completely absent, and is replaced by five others that do not include the addition. This shows that al-Bukhārī treated this addition as a mistake. Muslim also treated this addition with suspicion in his own *Ṣaḥīḥ*; this can be inferred from his ordering of narrations, where he always began with the most authentic narration of a hadith and then followed it with supplementary narrations that may contain anomalous additions or mistakes. While al-Bukhārī and Muslim chose the version of the hadith they thought was more authentic, it is possible that Abū Dāwūd chose this version, despite knowing that it was suspect, because he thought it gave some sort of response, even if not a completely convincing one, to the argument of the Qadariyya.

Bibliography

Abū Dāwūd al-Sijistānī. *al-Sunan*. Cairo: Dār al-Ta'ṣīl, 2018.

Abū Nuʿaym al-Iṣfahānī. *Ḥilyat al-awliyā' wa-ṭabaqāt al-aṣfiyā'*. 10 vols. Cairo: Maṭba'at al-Sa'āda, 1974.

al-'Aydarūs, Zayn b. Muḥammad b. Ḥusayn. *al-Ma'ānī al-ishāriyya fī al-sunna al-nabawiyya*. Cairo: Dār al-Ṣāliḥ, 2015.

Baqlī, Rūzbihān. *al-Maknūn fī ḥaqā'iq al-kalim al-nabawiyya*. Edited by 'Alī Ṣadrā'ī Khu'. In Mahdī Mihrīzī and 'Alī Ṣadrā'ī Khu'ī (eds), *Mīrāth-i ḥadīth-i shī'a*, vol. 8, pp. 255–363. Qum: Mu'assasa-yi Farhang-i Dār al-Ḥadīth, 1381/2002.

Blecher, Joel. *Said the Prophet of God: Hadith Commentary Across a Millenium*. Oakland: University of California Press, 2018.

Böwering, Gerhard. *The Mystical Vision of Existence in Early Islam*. Berlin: Walter de Gruyter, 1980.

Brown, Jonathan. 'A Segment of the Genealogy of Sunni Ḥadīth Criticism: The Mysterious Relationship Between al-Khaṭīb al-Baghdādī and al-Ḥākim al-Naysābūrī.' In Maurice A. Pomerantz and Aram A. Shahin (eds), *The Heritage of Islamo-Arab Learning: Studies in Honour of Wadad Kadi*, pp. 227–235. Leiden: Brill, 2016.

Dajani, Samer. *Sufis and Sharī'a: The Forgotten School of Mercy*. Edinburgh: Edinburgh University Press, 2023.

Dajani, Samer. *Reassurance for the Seeker: A Biography and Translation of Ṣāliḥ al-Ja'farī's al-Fawā'id al-Ja'fariyya, a Commentary on Forty Prophetic Traditions*. Louisville, KY: Fons Vitae, 2013.

al-Dhahabī, Muḥammad. *Siyar a'lām al-nubalā'*. 25 vols. Beirut: Mu'assassat al-Risāla, 1985.

al-Dhahabī, Muḥammad. *Tadhkirat al-ḥuffāẓ*. 4 vols. Beirut: Dār al-Kutub al-'Ilmiyya, 1998.

al-Dhahabī, Muḥammad. *Tārīkh al-islām wa-wafayāt al-mashāhīr wa-l-a'lām*. 52 vols. Beirut: Dār al-Kutub al-'Ilmiyya, 1993.

Elias, Jamal. 'Ṣūfī *tafsīr* Reconsidered: Exploring the Development of a Genre.' *Journal of Qur'anic Studies* 12 (2010): 41–55.

Graham, William A. *Divine Word and Prophetic Word in Early Islam: A Reconsideration of the Sources with Special Reference to the Divine Saying or Ḥadīth Qudsī*. The Hague: Mouton, 1977.

al-Ghazālī, Abū Ḥāmid. *Iḥyā' 'ulūm al-dīn*. 10 vols. Jedda: Dār al-Minhāj, 2011.

Gril, Denis. 'Ḥadīth in the Work of Ibn 'Arabī: The Uninterrupted Chain of Prophecy.' *Journal of the Muhyiddin Ibn 'Arabī Society* 50 (2011): 45–76.

al-Ḥakīm al-Tirmidhī, Muḥammad b. 'Alī. *Budū sha'n al-Ḥakīm al-Tirmidhī*. In al-Tirmidhī, *Kitāb khatm al-awliyā'*, edited by Othman Yaḥyā. Beirut: al-Maṭba'a al-Kāthūlīkiyya, n.d.

al-Ḥakīm al-Tirmidhī, Muḥammad b. 'Alī. *al-Furūq wa-man' al-tarāduf*. Cairo: al-Nahār, 1998.

al-Ḥakīm al-Tirmidhī, Muḥammad b. 'Alī. *Nawādir al-uṣūl fī ma'rifat akhbār al-rasūl*. 5 vols. Jedda: Dār al-Minhāj, 2015; 4 vols. Beirut: Dār al-Jīl, 1992.

Hirtenstein, Stephen. 'The Image of Guidance: Ṣadr al-Dīn al-Qūnawī as Ḥadīth Commentator.' *Journal of the Muhyiddin Ibn 'Arabī Society* 49 (2011): 69–82.

Ibn Abī Jamra, Abū Muḥammad. *Bahjat al-nufūs wa-taḥliyahā bi-maʿrifat mā lahā wa-mā ʿalayhā.* 4 vols. Beirut: Dār al-Jīl, 1355.

Ibn Abī Jamra, Abū Muḥammad. *al-Marāī al-ḥisān.* Cairo: Dār Jawāmiʿ al-Kalim, 2004.

Ibn Abī Jamra, Abū Muḥammad. *Mukhtaṣar Ṣaḥīḥ al-Bukhārī.* Jedda: Dār al-Minhāj, 2008.

Ibn Ḥajar al-ʿAsqalānī. *Fatḥ al-Bārī.* 13 vols. Beirut: Dār al-Maʿrifa, 1379.

Ibn Qayyim al-Jawziyya, Muḥammad. *Kitāb al-Rūḥ.* 2 vols. Beirut: Dār Ibn Ḥazm, 2019.

Jamil, Khairil Husaini Bin. 'Traditional Sunnī Epistemology in the Scholarship of al-Ḥāfiẓ al-Khaṭīb al-Baghdādī (463 AH/1071 CE).' PhD dissertation, University of London, School of Oriental and African Studies, 2017.

al-Kalābādhī, Abū Bakr. *Baḥr al-fawāʾid al-mashhūr bi-maʿānī al-akhbār.* 2 vols. Cairo: Dār al-Salām, 2008.

Karamustafa, Ahmet T. *Sufism: The Formative Period.* Edinburgh: Edinburgh University Press, 2007.

al-Kūrānī, Ibrāhīm. *al-Amam li-īqāẓ al-himam.* Hyderabad: Maṭbaʿat Majlis Dāʾirat al-Maʿārif al-Niẓāmiyya, 1328/1910.

Melchert, Christopher. 'Baṣran Origins of Classical Sufism.' *Der Islam* 82 (2005): 234–238.

Melchert, Christopher. 'Early Renunciants as Ḥadīth Transmitters.' *Muslim World* 92 (2002): 221–240.

Nafi, Basheer M. 'Taṣawwuf and Reform in Pre-Modern Islamic Culture: In Search of Ibrāhīm al-Kūrānī.' *Die Welt des Islams,* New Series, 42, no. 3 (2002): 307–355.

al-Qūnawī, Ṣadr al-Dīn. *Kirk Hadis Şerhi: Sharḥ al-aḥādīth al-arbaʿīn.* Edited and translated by Abdullah Aydinli. Istanbul: Marmara Üniversitesi Ilâhiyat Fakültesi Vakfi Yayinlari Nu. 327, 2015.

al-Qurṭubī, Abū ʿAbdallāh Muḥammad. *al-Jāmiʿ li-aḥkām al-Qurʾān.* 20 vols integrated in 10. Cairo: Dār al-Kutub al-Miṣriyya, 1964.

Radtke, Bernd and J. O'Kane. *The Concept of Sainthood in Early Islamic Mysticism: Two Works by al-Ḥakīm al-Tirmidhī; An Annotated Translation with Introduction.* Richmond: Curzon Press, 1996.

al-Rifāʿī, Aḥmad. *Ḥālat ahl al-ḥaqīqa maʿ Allāh.* Beirut: Dār Ṣādir, 2009.

al-Shaʿrānī, ʿAbd al-Wahhāb. *Laṭāʾif al-minan wa-l-akhlāq.* Damascus: Dār al-Taqwa, 2004.

al-Silafi, Abū Ṭāhir. *Faḍāʾil Sunan Abī Dāwūd.* Beirut: Dār al-Muqtabas, 2014.

al-Sulamī, Abū ʿAbd al-Raḥmān. *Suʾālāt al-Sulamī li-l-Dāraquṭnī.* Edited by Saʿd al-Ḥumayyid and Khālid al-Jurīsī. Riyadh: N.p., 1427.

al-Sulamī, Abū ʿAbd al-Raḥmān. *Ṭabaqāt al-ṣūfiyya.* Beirut: Dār al-Kutub al-ʿIlmiyya, 1998.

Sviri, Sara. 'Ḥakīm Tirmidhī and the Malāmatī Movement in Early Sufism.' In L. Lewisohn (ed.), *The Heritage of Sufism,* vol. 1, pp. 583–613. Oxford: Oneworld Publications, 1999.

al-Ṭībī, Ḥusayn. *Sharḥ al-Ṭ ībī ʿalā Mishkāt al-maṣābīḥ al-musammā bi: al-Kāshif ʿan ḥaqāʾiq al-sunan.* 7 vols. Karachi: Idārat al-Qurʾān wa-l-ʿUlūm al-Islāmiyya, 1435.

Yilmaz, Hasan Kamil. *Kirk Hadis Şerhi: Sharḥ al-aḥādīth al-arbaʿīn.* Edited and translated by Abdullah Aydinli. Istanbul: Marmara Üniversitesi Ilâhiyat Fakültesi Vakfi Yayinlari Nu. 327, 2015.

Yilmaz, Hasan Kamil. *Tasavvufî Hadîs Şerhleri ve Konevînin Kirk Hadîs Şerhi.* Istanbul: Marmara Üniversitesi Ilâhiyat Fakültesi Vakfi Yayinlari Nu. 38, 1990.

CHAPTER 5

Ibn Rajab's Commentary on al-Nawawī's Forty Hadith: Innovation and Audience in the Jāmiʿ al-ʿulūm wa-l-ḥikam

Mohammad Gharaibeh

Introduction

The 'forty hadith' genre is without doubt one of the most well-known and popular genres in Muslim scholarship, past and present. Hadith scholars, jurists, Sufis, historians and littérateurs alike produced such countless collections over the course of the history of Muslim societies. The total number of forty hadith collections might never be fully known, although some have tried to establish their precise number. The printed editions of collections as well as those that were produced in the modern period are already difficult to quantify; and this is in addition to the unknown number of unedited collections (availability aside) that are hidden in manuscript collections around the world.[1]

The fact that there are countless forty hadith collections on a wide array of topics from the second/eighth century onward in almost all parts of the Muslim world makes the genre much more than just one of the many kinds of hadith-related texts. We could even say that this genre is a transdisciplinary vehicle to express theological opinions on specific topics and relate them to, and therefore legitimise them, through prophetic traditions. The topics of the collections are almost as numerous as the number of compilations. Bartschat lists collections that seem to have no clear topic (these are

---

1 An attempt to count and list all known, available or not, was recently attempted by Swantje Bartschat, who drew information from manuscript catalogues and bio-bibliographical dictionaries. For her impressive chronologically arranged list of collections, see Swantje Bartschat, *Entstehung und Entwicklung*, 237–333. Alavi put together a list of forty collections up to the time of al-Nawawī (d. 676/1233); this list appears in comparison to Bartschat's study, as a 'brief survey'. See Alavi, 'A Brief Survey'. Sahl al-ʿŪd enumerated approximately five hundred such collections in published and unpublished volumes; see al-ʿŪd, *al-Muʿīn ʿalā maʿrifat kutub al-arbaʿīn*.

usually entitled *aḥādīth nabawiyya*) and collections on, for instance, mysticism (*taṣawwuf*), asceticism (*zuhd*), poverty and the poor (*faqr wa-fuqarā'*), the remembrance (*dhikr*) of God, moral life, law, societal issues, medicine, fear and hope, gratitude, theology and eschatology.[2]

Among the many collections of forty hadiths, the forty hadith collection of Abū Zakariyyā Yaḥyā al-Nawawī (d. 676/1277) is by far the most popular. As Jonathan Brown states, this collection is 'one of the most widely read books after the Quran among Sunni Muslims'.[3] Al-Nawawī compiled forty-two narrations on the principles of the religion, narrations that played and continue to play a significant role in the education of Muslims. Its significance is reflected in the many manuscript copies and the numerous contemporary editions.

But ordinary people were not the only ones who studied and memorised the prophetic traditions in this collection and acknowledged al-Nawawī's scholarly acumen in his selection of the hadith. Many scholars, past and present, were also interested in this collection. And although many of them could have compiled forty hadith collections of their own, a good number of scholars chose to author commentaries of al-Nawawī's compilation. With about twenty-five commentaries written during the Mamlūk period and many more afterward,[4] today's common assumption that commentaries are less innovative than 'original' works was clearly not shared by earlier scholars.

In the present chapter, I consider commentarial literature, such as on al-Nawawī's forty hadith collection, to be serious work, and as significant as an 'original' work. Commentaries should be regarded as unique and independent scholarly works; indeed, it is necessary to perceive them as more than 'just' supporting educational literature.[5]

Compiling an independent work poses several challenges for commentators. They must select a topic that awakens the interest of their readers, choose a style and structure that meet expectations, present a line of arguments that is convincing, and ultimately produce an innovative work worthy of a highly competitive scholarly discourse. Commentaries are a practical way to achieve these goals, as they relate to works that have already been accepted by the scholarly community.[6] Therefore, commentaries give

---

2 See Bartschat, *Entstehung und Entwicklung*, 334–412.

3 Brown, *Hadith*, 56.

4 For a comprehensive list of commentaries on al-Nawawī's collection, see Alavi, 'Arba'īn al-Nawawī', 350–353.

5 For the assumption that commentaries were mostly a result of the educational setting of the madrasa, see, for example, Schoeler, 'Text und Kommentar', 286; Smyth, 'Controversy in a Tradition of Commentary', 590; and Messick, *The Calligraphic State*, 30.

6 Commentaries usually result from the fact that the text that is commented on already holds a solid place in a scholarly community. For this argument, see Jan Assmann, 'Text und Kommentar', 11 and 30.

the author an advantage – the topic, style, structure and arguments of the original text have already convinced the readers, as is clear from their popularity. Hence, the most challenging aspect for commentators might be to design their commentary in a way that is perceived as innovative.

It is this aspect that I investigate further in the present chapter. The main case study involves the commentary of the Ḥanbalī scholar Zayn al-Dīn ʿAbd al-Raḥmān Ibn Rajab (d. 795/1393), who wrote a commentary on al-Nawawī's forty hadith collection. His *Jāmiʿ al-ʿulūm wa-l-ḥikam fī sharḥ khamsīn ḥadīthan min jawāmiʿ al-kalim* is one of the many commentaries from the Mamlūk period that left a recognisable trace in the scholarly discourse and was successfully perceived as an innovative text.[7]

In the following, I explore the key features of this commentary and consider how Ibn Rajab attracted an audience for it. To fully grasp the extent of the original character of Ibn Rajab's text I compare it to commentaries on al-Nawawī's forty hadith collection by other authors and to some of Ibn Rajab's other books.

Ibn Rajab: His Life and Work

Although Ibn Rajab can be counted among the more influential Ḥanbalī scholars in history, little biographical information has been preserved, and surprisingly we still lack a secondary study on him. His writings, especially his biographical dictionary of Ḥanbalī scholars (*al-Dhayl ʿalā Ṭabaqāt al-ḥanābila*) and his treatise on legal maxims (*al-Qawāʿid al-fiqhiyya*), were frequently quoted by later (Ḥanbalī) scholars.[8]

Ibn Rajab, whose full name was Zayn al-Dīn ʿAbd al-Raḥmān b. Aḥmad b. ʿAbd al-Raḥmān, was born in Baghdad in 736/1335–36.[9] His father, who educated Ibn Rajab in his youth, travelled with him from Baghdad to Damascus in 744/1343. At the age of eight, Ibn Rajab was introduced to many hadith scholars, first in Damascus and later, around 753/1352, in Cairo, too. He heard from Damascene scholars such as Sharaf al-Dīn b. Qāḍī al-Jabal (d. 771/1370),[10] Aḥmad b. ʿAbd al-Hādī, Ibn Qayyim al-Ḍiyāʾiyya,

---

7 Abdassamad Clarke's relatively recent 819-page English translation of the work also demonstrates the book's enduring readership for general audiences; see Ibn Rajab, *The Compendium of Knowledge and Wisdom*.

8 Besides the entries in the two latest editions of the *Encyclopaedia of Islam* written by Makdisi (*EI²*) and al-Matroudi (*EI³*), no secondary source has addressed his biography to a larger extent.

9 Al-Matroudi, 'Ibn Rajab', in *EI³*, online: http://dx.doi.org/10.1163/1573-3912_ei3_COM_32183 (accessed 20 February 2022).

10 His full name is Sharaf al-Dīn Abū al-ʿAbbās Aḥmad b. al-Ḥasan Ibn Qudāma al-Ḥanbalī, and he was known by Ibn Qāḍī al-Jabal. For his biography, see Ibn al-ʿImād, *Shadharāt al-dhahab*, 8:376–377.

'Ali b. al-Munajjā, Muḥammad b. Ismā'īl al-Khabbāz (d. 756/1354), and Cairene scholars such as al-Mīdūmī, Muḥammad b. Ismā'īl al-Ayyūbī, 'Abd al-'Azīz b. Jamā'a (d. 767/1365) and 'Abd al-Raḥīm b. al-Ḥusayn al-'Irāqī (d. 806/1403). During these years, Ibn Rajab also travelled back to Baghdad with his father; and in 748/1347 he studied for about a year, then performed the hajj in 749/1348, during which time he studied with scholars in Mecca and Medina.[11]

Al-Matroudi emphasises that '[t]he person who connected Ibn Rajab to the Damascene circle of Ḥanbalī *ḥadīth* jurists was Ibn al-Qayyim al-Jawziyya (d. 751/1350), the renowned scholar and student of Ibn Taymiyya (d. 728/1328)'.[12] Similarly, Anjum describes Ibn Rajab as Ibn al-Qayyim's student – which he probably was to a certain extent – and as his chief biographer.[13] Both seem to imply that Ibn al-Qayyim had a deep influence on Ibn Rajab. However, we might question whether this assumption or implication – provided this was meant – is true or how deep the influence could have been, given that Ibn Rajab was eight years old when he entered Damascus the first time and was clearly still under the care of his father, who died in 774/1372.[14] Both seemed to have travelled a great deal and since Ibn Rajab's teachers were the same as those of his father, it is more likely that his father introduced him to many scholars. When Ibn al-Qayyim died in 751/1350, Ibn Rajab was fifteen years old. Moreover, al-Matroudi writes that Ibn Rajab settled permanently in Damascus only after 763/1361.[15]

After Ibn Rajab settled in Damascus permanently, his recognition among the Ḥanbalī community is undeniable. When his teacher Ibn Qāḍī al-Jabal died in 771/1370, Ibn Rajab assumed several teaching posts previously occupied by Ḥanbalī luminaries. Besides the teaching positions at schools such as the Ḥanbaliyya al-Sharīfiyya (until 791/1389)[16] and al-Turba al-'Izziyya al-Badrāniyya al-Ḥamziyya,[17] Ibn Rajab began leading the 'Tuesday circle' in the Umayyad Mosque in Damascus, one of the most notable positions a Ḥanbalī scholar could hold.[18] Since he continued

---

11 Al-Ḥāfiẓ, *Dār al-Ḥadīth*, 85–86.

12 Al-Matroudi, 'Ibn Rajab'.

13 Anjum, 'Sufism without Mysticism?', 162.

14 See the biography provided by the editors of Ibn Rajab, *Jāmi' al-'ulūm*, 1:25–52, esp. 1:32.

15 One would have to conduct a thorough study of the writings of Ibn Rajab to evaluate the alleged influence of Ibn Qayyim. Unfortunately, this goes beyond the scope of the present chapter.

16 For the history of the school and for Ibn Rajab's appointment, see 'Abd al-Qādir al-Nu'aymī, *al-Dāris*, 2:50–62.

17 See al-Nu'aymī, *al-Dāris*, 2:201.

18 See al-Matroudi, 'Ibn Rajab'.

teaching there until his death in 795/1393, it is safe to assume that Ibn Rajab educated and influenced many Damascene Ḥanbalī scholars over the course of his career, as his biographer Ibn al-ʿImād (d. 1089/1679) reports on the authority of Ibn Ḥijjī.[19] Ibn Rajab also taught in the Dār al-Ḥadīth al-Sukriyya, where he lived until his death.[20]

Ibn Rajab authored and compiled many books, hadith collections, smaller treatises (rasāʾil) and one biographical dictionary. Most of his works fall within four major topics or disciplines.

The first field is Ḥanbalī law, in which Ibn Rajab had a recognisable influence. His book on legal principles entitled al-Qawāʿid, in which he evaluates the sometimes contradictory opinions of former Ḥanbalī authorities, was a basic text studied by many students.[21]

The second field is hadith studies. Here, Ibn Rajab compiled several small collections on various topics of devotional literature and commented on selected hadith, and on larger collections such as Ṣaḥīḥ al-Bukhārī, the ʿIlal of al-Tirmidhī and the forty hadith collection of al-Nawawī.[22] Notably, he chose to comment on collections that were predominantly authored, read and studied by Shāfiʿī scholars.[23]

The third field was that of devotional literature and exhortation. Ibn Rajab seems to have been influenced in this field particularly by the Ḥanbalī Baghdadi scholar Abū al-Faraj ʿAbd al-Raḥmān Ibn al-Jawzī (d. 597/1200).[24]

In addition to these three fields, Ibn Rajab compiled a biographical dictionary of the Ḥanbalī school; this work was an appendix (dhayl) to the Ṭabaqāt al-ḥanābil of the Baghdadi scholar Abū al-Ḥusayn Muḥammad b. Abī al-Yaʿlā (d. 526/1131).

Jāmiʿ Al-ʿulūm wa-l-ḥikam

Jāmiʿ al-ʿulūm wa-l-ḥikam fī sharḥ khamsīn ḥadīthan min jawāmiʿ al-kalim is often described as one of many commentaries on the forty hadith collection of al-Nawawī. Although, to a certain extent, this description is justified, and Ibn Rajab himself refers to al-Nawawī's collection in his introduction, *Jāmiʿ al-ʿulūm* can also be seen as an independent work, in which Ibn Rajab explains fifty prophetic traditions.

---

19 See Ibn al-ʿImād, *Shadharāt al-dhahab*, 8:580.
20 See also al-Nuʿaymī, *al-Dāris*, 2:60 (entry of Madrasat al-Ḥanbaliyya al-Sharīfa).
21 See al-Matroudi, 'Ibn Rajab'.
22 See al-Matroudi, 'Ibn Rajab'.
23 For an analysis of the ṣaḥīḥ movement, see the reception history of the Ṣaḥīḥayn and the process of their canonisation in Brown, *The Canonization*, 99–153. This is also true for most of the commentarial tradition of the Ṣaḥīḥayn.
24 See al-Matroudi, 'Ibn Rajab'.

When exactly Ibn Rajab authored his commentary is not clear. A manuscript copy of *Jāmiʿ al-ʿulūm* in the Khuda Baksh Oriental Public Library in Patna, India, bears certificates of transmission (*samāʿ*) notes and a remark by the copyist that reveals some details about when and where Ibn Rajab might have completed or at least read and taught his commentary. The manuscript was copied by ʿAbd al-Qādir b. Muḥammad al-Ḥajjār al-Ḥanbalī in 790/1388 and presented (*uriḍat*) to Ibn Rajab in several sessions. Ibn Rajab issued an *ijāza* for this copy on 12 Rajab 790 (17 July 1388) in Dār al-Ḥadīth al-Sukriyya in Damascus, where he lived and taught.[25] Even if we cannot be certain that Ibn Rajab finished his collection during this time – he might have finished it earlier – we can assume that Ibn Rajab had a primarily Ḥanbalī audience in mind. Dār al-Ḥadīth al-Sukriyya seems to have been built in 676/1277 after ʿUmar b. Muḥammad b. al-Sukrī (d. 671/1273) established an endowment for it. The sources mention only five scholars who had taught there previously: ʿAbd al-Ḥalīm b. Taymiyya (d. 682/1283), Taqī al-Dīn Aḥmad b. Taymiyya who also lived there, Shams al-Dīn al-Dhahabī (d. 748/1348) – though his appointment is not certain, Ṣadr al-Dīn Sulaymān b. ʿAbd al-Ḥakīm al-Bāridī al-Mālikī (d. 749/1348) and Ibn Rajab – presumably from the death of Ṣadr al-Dīn al-Mālikī till his own death.[26] This means that three of the five (or four) scholars were affiliated with the Ḥanbalī school, and that Ibn Rajab taught and lived there for a period of about forty-five years. During this long period under the influence of Ibn Rajab, chances are high that most of the students were adherents of the Ḥanbalī school. As I show below, *Jāmiʿ al-ʿulūm* seems to have been written for a mostly Ḥanbalī audience and the way it highlights the merits of the Ḥanbalī school supports this assumption.

To demonstrate the innovative and independent character of this work, I focus on a comparison with other commentaries of the forty hadith collection of al-Nawawī and other collections of Ibn Rajab, and I analyse some examples of his commentary.

Jāmiʿ al-ʿulūm and the Commentarial Tradition of the Forty Hadith of al-Nawawī

One way to identify the characteristics of Ibn Rajab's commentary is to compare it with other commentaries on al-Nawawī's collection. Among the twenty-five commentaries that were written during the Mamlūk period, about seventeen were authored by scholars who lived before Ibn Rajab or were his contemporaries, and some may have written commentaries that

25 Al-Ḥāfiẓ, *Dār al-ḥadīth*, 86.
26 See al-Ḥāfiẓ, *Dār al-ḥadīth*, 200–201; see also al-Nuʿaymī, *al-Dāris*, 1:56–60.

Ibn Rajab could have studied.[27] Of these seventeen works, I was able to consult eight for the comparison.[28] These are:

1. Shihāb al-Dīn Abū al-ʿAbbās Aḥmad b. Farḥ b. Aḥmad al-Ishbīlī (d. 699/1300), *Sharḥ al-Arbaʿīn al-Nawawiyya*.[29]
2. Muḥammad b. ʿAlī b. Qahb b. Daqīq al-ʿĪd (d. 702/1302), *Sharḥ al-Arbaʿīn ḥadīthan li-l-Nawawī*.[30]
3. Najm al-Dīn Sulaymān b. ʿAbd al-Qawī b. ʿAbd al-Marīn al-Ṭūfī al-Ḥanbalī (d. 716/1316), *al-Taʿyīn fī sharḥ al-arbaʿīn*.[31]
4. Al-Tāj ʿUmar b. ʿAlī b. Sālim b. Ṣadāqa al-Fākihānī al-Lakhmī (d. 731/1331), *al-Manhaj al-mubīn fī sharḥ al-Arbaʿīn*.[32]
5. Zayn al-Dīn Sarīja b. Muḥammad b. Sarīja b. Aḥmad al-Malṭī al-Shāfiʿī (d. 788/1386), *Nathr farāʾid al-murbiʿīn al-manwiyya fī nashr fawāʾid al-Arbaʿīn al-Nawawiyya* (manuscript incomplete, Chester Beatty, MS 3882).[33]
6. Saʿd al-Dīn Masʿūd ʿUmar al-Taftazānī (d. 793/1390), *Sharḥ al-Taftazānī ʿalā al-aḥādīth al-Arbaʿīn al-Nawawiyya*.[34]
7. Shams al-Dīn Muḥammad b. Aḥmad b. Shaykh al-Yusr al-Ḥanafī (d. 802/1399), *al-Durr al-raṣīn al-mustakhraja min baḥr al-Arbaʿīn*.[35]
8. Abū Ḥafṣ ʿAlī b. al-Mulaqqin al-Anṣārī (d. 804/1401), *al-Muʿīn ʿalā tafahhum al-arbaʿīn*.[36]

These works vary in length and the detail with which they explain the prophetic traditions, but they share the same structure. This is not surprising, since they follow the order of al-Nawawī's collection. Similarly, these works refer in their introductions – if applicable – to the collection of al-Nawawī as the original text. Most also refer to the forty hadith tradition, explain why this genre is important and cite the hadith 'Whoever preserves forty hadith for my *umma* . . .' in its various versions.[37] For example, al-Tāj ʿUmar al-Fākihānī (d. 731/1331) mentions in his introduction that he also wanted to collect forty hadith to achieve the promise made by the hadith,

---

27 For the list of commentaries on al-Nawawī's forty-hadith collection, see Alavi, ʿArbaʿīn al-Nawawī'.
28 The rest have either not survived or exist in manuscript form but could not be consulted for the present study.
29 Al-Mālikī, *Sharḥ al-Arbaʿīn al-nawawiyya*.
30 Ibn Daqīq al-ʿĪd, *Sharḥ al-Arbaʿīn ḥadīthan li-l-Nawawī*.
31 Al-Ṭūfī, *al-Taʿyīn fī sharḥ al-arbaʿīn*.
32 Al-Fākihānī, *al-Manhaj al-mubīn*.
33 Al-Shāfiʿī, *Nathr farāʾid al-murbiʿīn al-manwiyya*.
34 Al-Taftazānī, *Sharḥ al-Taftazānī*.
35 Al-Ḥanafī, *al-Durr al-raṣīn*.
36 Ibn al-Mulaqqin al-Anṣārī, *al-Muʿīn*.
37 For an example, see Ibn Daqīq al-ʿĪd, *Sharḥ al-arbaʿūn al-ḥadīthan*, 4–5.

but decided to author a commentary on al-Nawawī's collection since it was the best there is.[38]

The strongest and most distinctive features of Ibn Rajab's commentary are those that seem to be quite ordinary and self-evident. In his introduction, Ibn Rajab approaches al-Nawawī's collection not from the viewpoint of the forty hadith collection; rather he refers to the concept of *jawāmiʿ al-kalim* of the Prophet Muhammad. This concept describes the prophetic sayings as conveying the widest meanings despite their dense expressions. He begins his introduction with the opening statement: 'Indeed, God has sent Muḥammad with the shortest expression carrying the widest meanings (*jawāmiʿ al-kalim*)';[39] then he lists several prophetic traditions and Qurʾanic verses to support his statement. This difference is not just another way to start a commentary, or a collection of forty hadiths; in fact, it frees Ibn Rajab from the genre conventions of the forty hadith collections and opens several options for him to distinguish his commentary from others and to present his audience with a highly innovative work.

First, Ibn Rajab draws the reader's attention to the topic of *jawāmiʿ al-kalim*. With this, he sets his work apart from other commentaries and – most importantly – implies that the collection of al-Nawawī was originally intended to collect those narrations that can be subsumed under the category of *jawāmiʿ al-kalim*. Consequently, he interprets or extends al-Nawawī's intention to collect hadiths that each represent a principle of the religion (*qāʿida ʿaẓīma min qawāʿid al-dīn*).

Second, Ibn Rajab mentions some scholars who have written about this topic.[40] At this point, he introduces the most significant change of perspective on the forty hadith collection of al-Nawawī. Instead of placing his commentary among the many in the genre of the forty hadith collections, he places it in the context of collections and commentaries on *jawāmiʿ al-kalim*. In doing this, Ibn Rajab establishes al-Nawawī in a specific tradition of commentators and opens the door for others to continue in the same line. Ibn Rajab did not perceive of al-Nawawī's collection as originating from al-Nawawī's own effort. Rather, he states that Abū ʿAmr ʿUthmān b. al-Ṣalāḥ (d. 643/1245) had already started a reading session for universal hadith (*aḥādīth kulliyya*) including hadith that can be seen as the core of the religion (*madār al-islām ʿalayhā*). For Ibn Rajab these hadith belong to the category of *jawāmiʿ al-kalim*, such that Ibn al-Ṣalāḥ's twenty-six hadiths was a collection of *jawāmiʿ al-kalim*, too.[41]

<hr>

38 Al-Fākihānī, *al-Manhaj al-mubīn*, 30–31.
39 Ibn Rajab, *Jāmiʿ al-ʿulūm*, 1:53.
40 Ibn Rajab, *Jāmiʿ al-ʿulūm*, 1:55–56.
41 Ibn Rajab, *Jāmiʿ al-ʿulūm*, 1:56. Those twenty-six hadith are mentioned by al-Ishbīlī al-Mālikī in his commentary on al-Nawawī's collection of forty hadiths. See al-Ishbīlī al-Mālikī, *Sharḥ al-Arbaʿīn al-nawawiyya*, 4r–6r.

According to Ibn Rajab, al-Nawawī took those twenty-six hadith and added another sixteen to complete a collection of forty-two hadiths on *jawāmiʿ al-kalim*.[42] This change in perspective makes Ibn Rajab the latest commentator on the collections of hadith that are characterised as *jawāmiʿ al-kalim*. In the context of reshaping the forty hadith collection by choosing the *jawāmiʿ al-kalim*, Ibn Rajab chose a title that expressed this new perspective and draws the reader's attention to it: *Jāmiʿ al-ʿulūm wa-l-ḥikam fī sharḥ khamsīn ḥadīthan min jawāmiʿ al-kalim* (The collection of knowledge and wisdom: A commentary of fifty hadith of concise comprehensive words.)

Ibn Rajab affirms the independent character of his work in his introduction, in which he states that his intention is to occupy himself only with the prophetic words:

> Know that I only explain and comment on the words of the Prophet in these universal hadiths (*aḥādīth kulliyya*). Therefore, I do not deal with the shaykh's [al-Nawawī] remarks on the first narrator of the hadith, the Companions of the Prophet, nor do I address his [al-Nawawī's] explanations of which sources he drew his collection from. Occasionally, I briefly mention some aspects of that [his explanations], since I am, as I have already stated, only interested in explaining the meanings of the all-embracing words of the Prophet, their literary, ethical, moral and juridical aspects as well as the wisdom behind them.[43]

Third, this significant change in perspective frees Ibn Rajab from the restrictions of the forty hadith collections. One often-quoted criticism of al-Nawawī's collection was that he neglected some hadiths that were equally important as those he had selected; for example, the hadith 'Give the shares to those who are entitled to them …' (*alḥiqū al-farāʾiḍ bi-ahlihā …*), or the hadith 'The proof (*bayyina*) lies on the one who is making the claim …' (*al-bayyina ʿalā al-muddaʿī …*).[44] One could easily find other hadiths that al-Nawawī could or should have included that also fulfil the criterion of relating the principles of the religion. However, the challenge for al-Nawawī was to choose only forty hadiths – and in any case he already violated this by including forty-two hadiths. By turning the perspective away from a collection of forty hadiths to a collection of *jawāmiʿ al-kalim*, Ibn Rajab freed himself from this restriction; therefore,

---

42 Ibn Rajab, *Jāmiʿ al-ʿulūm*, 1:56.
43 See Ibn Rajab, *Jāmiʿ al-ʿulūm*, 1:58.
44 See Ibn Rajab, *Jāmiʿ al-ʿulūm*, 1:56–57.

it was easy for him to include more hadith without violating any genre conventions.

Hence, Ibn Rajab includes eight additional hadiths which, in his view, include the principles of the religion and were expressed by the Prophet in short expressions carrying universal meanings. The eight hadiths[45] that he added are the following:

Hadith no. 43:	'Give the shares to those who are entitled to them ...' (*alḥiqū al-farā'iḍ bi-ahlihā ...*).
Hadith no. 44:	'What is unlawful by reason of blood relationship is unlawful by reason of suckling relationship' (*yaḥrum min al-raḍā' mā yaḥrum min al-nasab*).
Hadith no. 45:	'When God declares something forbidden, He declares its price also forbidden' (*inna Allāh idhā ḥarrama shay'an ḥarrama thamanah*).
Hadith no. 46:	'Every intoxicant is unlawful' (*kull muskir ḥarām*).
Hadith no. 47:	'A human being fills no worse vessel than his stomach' (*mā mala'a ādamī wi'ā'an sharran min baṭn*).
Hadith no. 48:	'There are four qualities which, when found in a person, make him a hypocrite' (*arba' man kunna fīh kāna munāfiqan*).
Hadith no. 49:	'If you really put your trust in God, He will provide for you as He provides for the birds' (*law annakum tawakkalūn 'alā Allāh ḥaqq tawakkulih la-razaqakum kamā yarzuqu al-ṭayr*).
Hadith no. 50:	'Keep your tongue moist with the remembrance of God, most mighty and majestic' (*lā yazāl lisānuka raṭban min dhikr Allāh 'azza wa-jall*).

In comparison to the other commentarial works on al-Nawawī's collection of forty hadith, Ibn Rajab's commentary is clearly different; it is a highly innovative and even independent work. The main feature of his *Jāmi' al-'ulūm* is its focus on the concept of the *jawāmi' al-kalim*. This focus allows Ibn Rajab to relocate his commentary into another tradition of collections, and this changes the entire character of it. Ultimately, Ibn Rajab's work is a commentary of fifty traditions, rather than a commentary on al-Nawawī's collection. Thus, Ibn Rajab's book is an independent and original work that appears as the next step in the evolution of the text after Ibn al-Ṣalāḥ's collection of twenty-three hadiths and al-Nawawī's collection of forty-two hadiths.

---

45 These are listed by the hadith number, Ibn Rajab added those from 43 onward.

Jāmiʿ al-ʿulūm, its Commentarial Features, and its Relation to Ibn Rajab's Other Writings

I now turn to the formulation of Ibn Rajab's commentary. I have chosen to analyse his comments on three hadiths to demonstrate their commentarial features and the unique aspects of Ibn Rajab's text. Besides the comparison to the other commentaries on al-Nawawī's forty hadith collection, a comparison to Ibn Rajab's commentary entitled *Fatḥ al-Bārī* on *Ṣaḥīḥ al-Bukhārī* also reveals the independent character of Ibn Rajab's *Jāmiʿ al-ʿulūm*.

In his introduction, Ibn Rajab states that his main concern is the prophetic words and all their implications. In accordance with this statement, his commentaries are detailed and extensive, resulting in a two-volume print edition with more than one thousand pages.[46] Hence, the following examples give only a very brief and select impression of this voluminous work.

> Example 1: 'Actions are [judged] by intentions and [a man will] have [only] what he intended' (*innamā al-aʿmāl bi-l-niyyāt wa-li-kull imriʾ mā nawā*).

This hadith has a long tradition among Shāfiʿī scholars. For generations, throughout different eras and across the Muslim world, it was used as an introduction to a wide variety of hadith collections and other works. This tradition was probably initiated by Abū ʿAbdallāh Muḥammad b. Ismāʿīl al-Bukhārī (d. 256/870) who placed it at the beginning of his *Jāmiʿ al-ṣaḥīḥ*, instead of an introduction. Following him, many Shāfiʿī scholars chose to begin their collections with this hadith, among them, Abū Ṭāhir Aḥmad al-Silafī (d. 576/1180), Abū al-Qāsim ʿAlī b. ʿAsākir (d. 571/1175), and al-Nawawī.[47]

The other commentaries on the forty hadith collections address this hadith in relation to the following six topics.[48]

First, the transmission of the hadith is addressed. This hadith, despite its popularity, was only transmitted by one Companion of the Prophet, namely the second caliph ʿUmar b. al-Khaṭṭāb. After him only

---

46 See Ibn Rajab, *Jāmiʿ al-ʿulūm*.

47 For example, many Buldāniyyāt collections from the sixth/twelfth to the eighth/fourteenth centuries begin with this hadith. See Gharaibeh, 'The *Buldāniyyāt* of as-Saḥāwī', 81–105.

48 The following information is only an overview of a selection of the commentaries. The present work does not allow for a detailed presentation of the unique characteristics of each commentary. This overview is only meant to give an idea of what other commentators address, in order to compare them to Ibn Rajab.

one individual in each generation ('Alqama b. Waqqāṣ al-Laythī, then Muḥammad b. Ibrāhīm al-Taymī) transmitted this hadith until the fourth generation of transmitters (Yaḥyā b. Saʿīd al-Anṣārī), after which over 250 narrators studied and transmitted this hadith.

Second, the commentators stress the importance of this hadith and the fact that many scholars have stated that it should precede each action, speech and written work.

Third, Muḥammad b. Idrīs al-Shāfiʿī (d. 204/820), Aḥmad b. Ḥanbal (d. 241/855), and Abū Bakr al-Bayhaqī (d. 458/1066) are cited as having stated, in one form or another, that this hadith is perceived as a fundamental principle in the discipline of jurisprudence (*fiqh*).

Fourth, the terms of the hadith are explained linguistically and philologically (particularly the Arabic particle *innamā*).

Fifth, the commentators consider the explanation of what has been left out from the sentence. Grammatically, the Arabic sentence *innamā al-aʿmāl bi-l-niyyāt* is incomplete insofar as it is not clear what the Arabic preposition *bi-* (usually translated as 'by') refers to. Common interpretations include an implied addition of 'are valid', 'are being rewarded' or 'are judged' according to the intention, such that the hadith could be translated to 'actions are [valid/rewarded/judged] …'

Sixth, some commentators also address the issue of the 'intention' (*niyya*), and how it can be defined – is it a mental action or a decision taken in the heart, and does it require a physical expression (a pronunciation of the intention).[49]

Ibn Rajab includes all these aspects and more in his commentary. He does this in an extensive and detailed way (taking up approximately thirty-five pages in the print edition); he refers to the opinions of many scholars and gives examples.[50] In addition, Ibn Rajab includes a section (*faṣl*) of approximately seven pages in which he elaborates on all the hadith's legal implications. In this passage, his affiliation to the Ḥanbalī school becomes apparent. For example, he discusses several topics related to the prayer, fasting, ablution, and even contract and divorce law while citing Aḥmad b. Ḥanbal frequently, and more often than the other law schools. Clearly, Ibn Rajab is writing for a Ḥanbalī audience, or he intends to strengthen the image of the Ḥanbalī school among a more diverse audience.[51]

Ibn Rajab's affiliation to the Ḥanbalī school appears to be another significant characteristic of his commentary. While this might seem self-evident,

---

49 Al-Fākihānī, *al-Manhaj al-mubīn*, 77–95; Ibn Daqīq al-ʿĪd, *Sharḥ al-Arbaʿīn ḥadīthan*, 9–12; al-Taftazānī, *Sharḥ al-Taftazānī*, 53–61; al-Ishbīlī al-Mālikī, *Sharḥ al-Arbaʿīn al-nawawiyya*, 1v–4r; al-Ṭūfī, *al-Taʿyīn fī sharḥ al-Arbaʿīn*, 25–44.

50 Ibn Rajab, *Jāmiʿ al-ʿulūm*, 1:59–84.

51 Ibn Rajab, *Jāmiʿ al-ʿulūm*, 1:85–92.

even Najm al-Dīn al-Ṭūfī, another Ḥanbalī scholar, or Aḥmad al-Ishbīlī, a Mālikī scholar, do not include as many references to the authorities of their schools in their commentaries, nor do readers get the impression that they want to support their school's opinions.

> Example 2: 'No one becomes a true believer until he likes for his brother what he likes for himself' (*lā yu'minu aḥadukum ḥattā yuḥibbu li-akhīh mā yuḥibbu li-nafsih*).

While the first example demonstrates how Ibn Rajab's style differs in comparison to the other commentaries on al-Nawawī's collection, the second example explores whether his style in *Jāmiʿ al-ʿulūm* differs from that of his other writings. Ibn Rajab's *Fatḥ al-Bārī sharḥ Ṣaḥīḥ al-Bukhārī* is suitable for such a comparison. Like al-Nawawī's forty hadith collection, *Ṣaḥīḥ al-Bukhārī* was studied and commented on predominantly by Shāfiʿī scholars. It was during the Mamlūk period that scholars of other schools of law, such as Ibn Rajab, first wrote commentaries. Moreover, some of the hadiths that are included in the forty hadith collection are also included in *Ṣaḥīḥ al-Bukhārī*, so these hadiths enable us to compare whether Ibn Rajab employs different strategies and styles in these two works.

Among the fifty hadiths that Ibn Rajab included in his *Jāmiʿ al-ʿulūm*, only twenty-three were also included by al-Bukhārī.[52] Unfortunately, not all the hadiths that were included in both collections are found in Ibn Rajab's *Fatḥ al-Bārī*. This is because, first, Ibn Rajab died before he could complete his commentary. He only reached the chapter on prayer, and the subchapter on 'Mistakes in the prayer' (*abwāb al-sahw*). Therefore, any hadith after no. 1,236 (according to the order of *Ṣaḥīḥ al-Bukhārī*) is not included in *Fatḥ al-Bārī*.

Second, the chapters that Ibn Rajab commented on have not survived completely. For example, the entire chapter on the 'Beginning of the revelation' and the chapter entitled 'The book of knowledge' are missing; thus, the hadith 'Actions are [judged] by intentions . . .' and hadith no. 34 from the chapter called 'The book of belief' are not included in *Fatḥ al-Bārī*.[53]

This leaves us only able to compare hadith nos. 2, 3, 6, 12 and 13 (according to the order of hadiths in *Jāmiʿ al-ʿulūm*). Then, since hadith

---

52 In the following, the first number refers to the order of the hadith in Ibn Rajab, *Jāmiʿ al-ʿulūm* and the second to the order of the hadith in *Ṣaḥīḥ al-Bukhārī*: 1/1, 2/50, 3/8, 4/2969, 5/2697, 6/52, 8/25, 9/7288, 13/13, 14/6878, 15/6018, 16/6116, 20/3483, 26/2707, 33/4552, 37/6491, 38/6502.

53 For further information on which hadiths and chapters survived, see the introduction of the editors in Ibn Rajab, *Fatḥ al-Bārī*, 1:42–146. The editors compared eight manuscript copies for their edition; each manuscript omits certain parts, yet the editors put them together in such a way that they complement each other.

nos. 2 and 12 are not included in *Ṣaḥīḥ al-Bukhārī* with the same wording (they appear in different variations), we are left with hadith nos. 3, 6 and 13. In the following, I compare Ibn Rajab's comments on hadith no. 13 'No one of you becomes a true believer until he likes for his brother what he likes for himself' in *Fatḥ al-Bārī* versus *Jāmiʿ al-ʿulūm*.

In *Fatḥ al-Bārī*, Ibn Rajab is mainly concerned with four aspects of this hadith. First, he elaborates further on the wording of the Prophet. Since the Prophet negates the faith (*lā yuʾminu aḥadukum ḥattā . . .*) of someone who does not love for his brother what he loves for himself, Ibn Rajab questions the faith of this individual and explains that the Prophet meant that such a person's faith is incomplete.

Second, Ibn Rajab explores the reason that causes the state of the one described above. He explains that envy and arrogance prevent such an individual from loving for others what he loves for himself.

Third, Ibn Rajab states that knowledge is the best thing that one could love for others and himself. He cites Ibn ʿAbbās and al-Shāfiʿī who stated that they loved for everyone to study and understand the revelation as much as they could.

Fourth, Ibn Rajab cites another hadith that seems to contradict that hadith in question. In the second hadith, a man addresses the Prophet, saying that he loves beauty and that he does not love it if someone is more beautiful than him. The Prophet replies that this is not a result of arrogance. Obviously, the second hadith contradicts the hadith in question, since the man seems not to like for his brother what he likes for himself. However, the Prophet did not blame this man, but rather justified his words by confirming that it did not result from arrogance. Ibn Rajab explains that the man did not intend to be condescending toward others, or to be arrogant. He simply wanted to be the most beautiful man, but in all other respects equal to others. Therefore, this second hadith does not contradict the first one.

The entire commentary on this hadith occupies approximately two-and-a-half pages in the edition used for this article;[54] in it, Ibn Rajab addresses only aspects that lead to a better understanding of the hadith and related issues. Interestingly, he does not refer to or cite Aḥmad b. Ḥanbal in his explanations.

Ibn Rajab's commentary on this hadith in *Jāmiʿ al-ʿulūm* is similar; however, it is more extensive and includes more detail. It covers eight pages and frequently refers to Aḥmad b. Ḥanbal.[55]

At the beginning of his commentary in *Jāmiʿ al-ʿulūm*, Ibn Rajab cites a related hadith that was narrated by Ibn Ḥanbal and that should lead to the correct understanding. Ibn Ḥanbal narrates the following hadith:

54 Ibn Rajab, *Fatḥ al-Bārī*, 1:45–47.
55 Ibn Rajab, *Jāmiʿ al-ʿulūm*, 1:302–310.

'No servant reaches the true [or complete] faith till he likes for others the same good that he likes for himself.'[56] Ibn Rajab then elaborates on the meaning of the hadith while citing many other authorities, additional hadiths and some Qur'anic verses. In the process, he follows a similar pattern as that found in *Fatḥ al-Bārī*. Notably, Ibn Rajab returns to Aḥmad b. Ḥanbal, either to cite his opinion or to include a hadith that Ibn Ḥanbal narrated in his *Musnad*.

We might conclude that Ibn Rajab drew from his commentary in *Jāmiʿ al-ʿulūm* on this hadith for *Fatḥ al-Bārī*, but in an abridged way. This conclusion is supported by the fact that he authored *Jāmiʿ al-ʿulūm* much earlier than *Fatḥ al-Bārī*, which he began working on toward the end of his life. Ibn Rajab did not cite Ibn Ḥanbal in *Fatḥ al-Bārī*. It is true that, in general, Ibn Rajab cites many more authorities in *Jāmiʿ al-ʿulūm*, but we cannot help but notice the dominant position he grants Ibn Ḥanbal.

> Example 3: 'Keep your tongue moist with the remembrance of God, most mighty and majestic' (*lā yazālu lisānuka raṭban min dhikr Allāh ʿazz wa-jall*).

Hadith no. 50 was the last hadith of Ibn Rajab's completed commentary, the *Jāmiʿ*. Beyond including it because it works well as a final appeal to his audience, this hadith has another noteworthy characteristic. Aḥmad b. Ḥanbal alone narrated this hadith (with this wording) in his *Musnad*.[57] Al-Tirmidhī, Ibn Mājah, and Ibn Ḥibbān narrated a hadith with similar wording.[58] With at least three other options at his disposal, Ibn Rajab's decision to include the hadith with the wording of Ibn Ḥanbal must be seen as a continuation of his promotion of the Ḥanbalī school in this commentary. The fact that Ibn Ḥanbal is mentioned regularly in Ibn Rajab's extensive explanations (the comments on this hadith span twenty-five pages)[59] supports this conclusion. Even the last paragraph of his commentary is a quotation from the *Musnad* of Ibn Ḥanbal:

> In the *Musnad* on the authority of Ibn Masʿūd, who said: 'The Prophet was given the beginnings of all good and the entirety of it (*fawātiḥ*

56	Ibn Rajab, *Jāmiʿ al-ʿulūm*, 1:302 (*lā yablughu ʿabd ḥaqīqat al-īmān ḥattā yuḥibba li-l-nās mā yuḥibbu li-nafsih min al-khayr*).

57	The wording actually includes the entire hadith, which states: *atā al-nabī rajul fa-qāl yā rasūl Allāh inna sharāʾiʿ al-islām qad kathurat ʿalaynā fa-bāb natamassaku bih jāmiʿ qāl lā yazālu lisānuka raṭban min dhikr Allāh ʿazz wa-jall*. Ibn Rajab, *Jāmiʿ al-ʿulūm*, 2:510.

58	They differ most in the part *fa-bāb natamassaku bih jāmiʿ*. For example, other versions state *fa-akhbirnī bi-shayʾin atashabbathu bih* or something similar. See, for example, al-Tirmidhī, *al-Jāmiʿ al-kabīr*, 5:388.

59	Ibn Rajab, *Jāmiʿ al-ʿulūm*, 2:510–535.

al-khayr wa-jawāmiʻih), or the entirety of all good and its beginnings and endings (*jawāmiʻ al-khayr wa-fawātiḥih wa-khawātimih*). We did not know what to say in our prayer until he taught us. He said to us "Say greetings belong to God."[60]

This quotation can be seen as a summary of the main statement of the commentary, that is, that the Prophet was given *jawāmiʻ al-kalim*, and Aḥmad b. Ḥanbal stated this.

Conclusion

Ibn Rajab presents his *Jāmiʻ al-ʻulūm* as an innovative commentary designed as an original work. From the title of the work, he makes it clear that his commentary is not 'just' another of many commentaries on al-Nawawī's forty hadith collection. The cleverest aspect of Ibn Rajab's commentary is the way he was able to use an already established and accepted template – that of al-Nawawī's forty hadith collection – and present it as an independent, original and innovative work on its own terms. To accomplish this, Ibn Rajab chose a narrative framework that relocates his commentary from the abundant commentaries on the collections of forty hadiths to the tradition of *jawāmiʻ al-kalim* collections. Thus, Ibn Rajab compiled a commentary of the Prophet's shortest expressions that carry the widest meanings.

Moreover, Ibn Rajab's change in perspective also allows him to use al-Nawawī's collection not as a base text to comment on, but as a template that can be expanded. He achieves this goal by presenting a line of authors (Ibn al-Ṣalāḥ and al-Nawawī) who compiled collections of *jawāmiʻ al-kalim* in steps; first, he discusses a collection of twenty-six (the commentary of Ibn al-Ṣalāḥ), and second a collection of forty-two (that of al-Nawawī). Ibn Rajab appears as the completion of this line, making his work 'the next step' in this line of collections.

Thus, Ibn Rajab freed himself from the boundaries and limitations of the genre conventions of the forty hadith collections, the most characteristic one being the number forty. Ibn Rajab could easily have added eight other hadiths (in fact, the scholarly community was already calling for them to be integrated into the original collection).

Another striking characteristic of Ibn Rajab's commentary is the way he used a template that was popular among the Shāfiʻī scholarly community for his mainly Ḥanbalī collection (or a collection that was supported by Ḥanbalī scholars). In this feature, *Jāmiʻ al-ʻulūm* differs significantly from the commentarial tradition of the forty hadith collection of al-Nawawī, but it also differs from his other writings. His *Fatḥ al-Bārī*, a commentary on

60 Ibn Rajab, *Jāmiʻ al-ʻulūm*, 2:535.

Ṣaḥīḥ al-Bukhārī, the collection of a Shāfiʿī scholar, does not include as many references to Aḥmad b. Ḥanbal. Although we must emphasise that referring to many scholars and authorities is a characteristic feature of *Jāmiʿ al-ʿulūm*, Ibn Rajab's intention to highlight the qualities and merits of the Ḥanbalī school cannot be ignored.

This leads to the question of Ibn Rajab's audience. Evidence on one manuscript copy establishes that Ibn Rajab read his commentary in the Dār al-Ḥadīth al-Sukriyya, where mostly Ḥanbalī scholars taught, and although it does not exclude students from other schools of law, it might indicate that he wrote for mostly Ḥanbalī students. Even if this were not the case, there is no doubt that Ibn Rajab, who taught and lived there for approximately forty-five years, must have had a significant impact on the curriculum. Thus, his *Jāmiʿ al-ʿulūm* can be seen as an attempt to highlight the qualities of the Ḥanbalī school to students of other schools of law, or as an inter-disciplinary discourse among like-minded Ḥanbalī students. In any case, more studies are needed to investigate his hadith commentaries further and to gauge the extent of his impact.

Bibliography

Alavi, Khalid. 'Arbaʿīn al-Nawawī and its Commentaries. An Overview.' *Islamic Studies* 24, no. 3 (Autumn 1985): 349–356.

Alavi, Khalid. 'A Brief Survey of Arabʿin Literature (Up to the Time of al-Nawawi).' *Islamic Studies* 23 no. 2 (Summer 1984): 67–82.

Anjum, Ovamir. 'Sufism without Mysticism? Ibn Qayyim al-Ğawziyyah's Objectives in *Madāriğ al-Sālikīn*.' *Oriente Moderno* 90, no. 1 (2010): 161–188.

Assmann, Jan. 'Text und Kommentar. Einführung.' In Jan Assmann (ed.), *Text und Kommentar*, pp. 9–33. Munich: Wilhelm Fink Verlag, 1995.

Bartschat, Swantje. *'Wer meiner Gemeinde vierzig Hadithe bewahrt …' Entstehung und Entwicklung eines Sammlungstyps*. Baden-Baden: Ergon Verlag, 2019.

Brown, Jonathan. *The Canonization of al-Bukhārī and Muslim: The Formation and Function of the Sunnī Ḥadīth Canon*. Leiden: Brill, 2007.

Brown, Jonathan. *Hadith: Muhammad's Legacy in the Medieval and Modern World*. Oxford: Oneworld, 2009.

al-Fākihānī al-Lakhmī, al-Tāj ʿUmar b. ʿAlī b. Sālim b. Ṣadāqa. *al-Manhaj al-mubīn fī Sharḥ al-arbaʿīn*. Edited by Abū ʿAbd al-Raḥmān and Shawkat b. Rifqī b. Shawkat. Riyadh: Dār al-Ṣamīʿī, 2007.

Gharaibeh, Mohammad. 'The *Buldāniyyāt* of as-Saḥāwī (d. 902/1496): A Case Study on *Knowledge Specialization* and *Knowledge Brokerage* in the Field of *Ḥadīt* Collections.' In Stephan Conermann (ed.), *History and Society during the Mamluk Period (1250–1517): Studies of the Annemarie Schimmel Institute for Advanced Study II*, 81–105. Göttingen: V&R, 2016.

al-Ḥāfiẓ, Muḥammad Muṭīʿ. *Dār al-Ḥadīth al-Sukriyya: Suknā Shaykh al-Islām Taqī al-Dīn Aḥmad b. ʿAbd al-Ḥalīm Ibn Taymiyya*. Beirut: Dār al-Bashāʾir al-Islāmiyya, 2003.

al-Ḥanafī, Shams al-Dīn Muḥammad b. Aḥmad Ibn Shaykh al-Yusr. *al-Durr al-raṣīn al-mustakhraja min baḥr al-Arbaʿīn*. [Egypt]: al-Maktaba al-Azhariyya MS 5237 [600].

Ibn Daqīq al-ʿĪd, Muḥammad b. ʿAlī b. Qahb. *Sharḥ al-Arbaʿīn ḥadīthan li-l-Nawawī*. Mecca: al-Maktaba al-Fayṣaliyya, n.d.

Ibn al-ʿImād, ʿAbd al-Ḥayy b. Aḥmad. *Shadharāt al-dhahab fī akhbār man dhahab*. Edited by ʿAbd al-Qādir al-Arnaʾūṭ and Maḥmūd al-Arnaʾūṭ. 10 vols. Damascus and Beirut: Dār Ibn Kathīr, 1992.

Ibn al-Mulaqqin al-Anṣārī, Abū Ḥafṣ ʿAlī. *al-Muʿīn ʿalā tafahhum al-arbaʿīn*. Edited by Abī Islām ʿAbd al-ʿĀl Musʿad. Cairo: al-Fārūq al-Ḥadītha li-l-Ṭibāʿa, 2005.

Ibn Rajab, Zayn al-Dīn ʿAbd al-Raḥmān. *The Compendium of Knowledge and Wisdom*. Translated by Abdassamad Clarke. London: Turath Publishing, 2007.

Ibn Rajab, Zayn al-Dīn ʿAbd al-Raḥmān. *Fatḥ al-Bārī sharḥ Ṣaḥīḥ al-Bukhārī*. Edited by Maḥmūd b. Shaʿbān et al. 10 vols. Medina: Maktabat al-Ghurabāʾ al-Athariyya, 1996.

Ibn Rajab, Zayn al-Dīn ʿAbd al-Raḥmān. *Jāmiʿ al-ʿulūm wa-l-ḥikam fī sharḥ khamsīn ḥadīthan min jawāmiʿ al-kalim*. Edited by Shuʿayb al-Arnaʾūṭ and Ibrāhīm Bājus. 2 vols. Beirut: Muʾassasat al-Risāla, 2002.

al-Ishbīlī al-Mālikī, Aḥmad. *Sharḥ al-Arbaʿīn al-nawawiyya*. [Paris]: Bibliothèque nationale de France, MS Arabe 747.

Makdisi, George. 'Ibn Radjab', in *EI²*, 3:933–934.

al-Matroudi, Abdul-Hakim. 'Ibn Rajab,' in *EI³*. <http://dx.doi.org/10.1163/1573–3912_ei3_COM_32183>, accessed 5 July 2020.

Messick, Brinkley. *The Calligraphic State: Textual Domination and History in a Muslim Society*. Berkeley: University of California Press, 1993.

al-Nuʿaymī, ʿAbd al-Qādir. *al-Dāris fī tārīkh al-madāris*. Edited by Ibrāhīm Shams al-Dīn. 2 vols. Beirut: Dār al-Kutub al-ʿIlmiyya, 1990.

Schoeler, Gregor. 'Text und Kommentar in der klassisch-islamischen Tradition.' In Jan Assmann (ed.), *Text und Kommentar*, 279–292. Munich: Fink, 1995.

al-Shāfiʿī, Zayn al-Dīn Sarīja b. Muḥammad b. Sarīja b. Aḥmad al-Malṭī. *Nathr farāʾid al-murbiʿīn al-manwiyya fī nashr fawāʾid al-Arbaʿīn al-Nawawiyya*. [Dublin]: Chester Beatty MS 3882.

Smyth, William. 'Controversy in a Tradition of Commentary: The Academic Legacy of al-Sakkākī's *Miftāḥ al-ʿulūm*.' *Journal of the American Oriental Society* 112, no. 4 (1992): 589–597.

al-Taftazānī, Saʿd al-Dīn Masʿud ʿUmar. *Sharḥ al-Taftazānī ʿalā al-aḥādīth al-arbaʿīn al-Nawawiyya*. Edited by Muḥammad Ḥasan Muḥammad Ḥasan Ismāʿīl. Beirut: Dār al-Kutub al-ʿIlmiyya, 2004.

al-Tirmidhī, Abū ʿĪsā Muḥammad. *al-Jāmiʿ al-kabīr*. Edited by Bashshār ʿAwwād Maʿrūf. 6 vols. Beirut: Dār al-Gharb al-Islāmī, 1996.

al-Ṭūfī, Najm al-Dīn Sulaymān b. ʿAbd al-Qawī. *al-Taʿyīn fī sharḥ al-Arbaʿīn*. Edited by Aḥmad Ḥājj Muḥammad ʿUthmān. Beirut: Muʾassasa al-Rayyān, 1998.

al-ʿŪd, Sahl. *al-Muʿīn ʿalā maʿrifat kutub al-arbaʿīn min aḥādīth Sayyid al-Mursalīn*. Beirut: ʿĀlam al-Kutub, 2005.

CHAPTER 6

The Words of the Imam beyond Philosophy and Tradition: Shīʿī Hadith Commentaries in the Ṣafavid Period

Sajjad Rizvi

The neo-classicism of the Ṣafavid period (907–1135/1501–1722) emphasised the importance of the early hadith tradition. The intellectual context of Ṣafavid Isfahan encouraged the canonisation of texts and the production of new compilations by Muḥsin Fayḍ Kāshānī (d. 1090/1679), al-Ḥurr al-ʿĀmilī (d. 1104/1693) and Muḥammad Bāqir al-Majlisī (d. 1111/1699), each with their own instrumentalisation of the words of the Imams and a desire to recover 'lost' elements of the early tradition, and each, to an extent, acting as a commentary on the early 'four books'.[1] Along with the first commentators, who confronted each other over the very nature of the Shīʿī tradition, the Akhbārī commentaries, with their return to scripture, opposed legal and theological reasoning, while philosophers and mystics deployed hadith to confirm and corroborate their intellectual insights and investigated the possibility of considering exegesis *as* philosophy.

In the following study of hadith commentaries in the Ṣafavid period, I begin with an examination of Ṣafavid commentary traditions by analysing hadith compilations, 'recoveries', and commentaries in the period. In order to demonstrate the divergence and even plurality of the usage of hadith – usually a more important question than provenance and 'authenticity' – I then take one case study that analyses the various ways in which the notion of the *ʿaql* (intellect or reason) arising in hadith was collated in the first book of al-Kulaynī's *al-Kāfī*. I specifically analyse the way *ʿaql* is understood by four authors: Mullā Ṣadrā (d. 1045/1636), Muḥammad Ṣāliḥ Māzandarānī

---

1 The four books of the classical Shīʿī hadith tradition are *al-Kāfī* of Abū Jaʿfar al-Kulaynī (d. 329/941), *Man lā yaḥḍuruhu al-faqīh* of al-Shaykh al-Ṣadūq (d. 380/991), and *Tahdhīb al-aḥkām* and *al-Istibṣār fīmā ikhtulifa min al-akhbār* of al-Shaykh Abū Jaʿfar al-Ṭūsī (d. 460/1067). For a new comprehensive study on the emergence of the notion of four books, see Ehteshami, 'The Four Books of Shiʿi Hadith'.

(d. 1081/1670), Muḥammad Bāqir al-Majlisī (d. 1110/1699) and Qāḍī Saʿīd Qummī (d. 1107/1696). My central contention is that the philosophical exegesis of Mullā Ṣadrā acted as a provocation for the more exoterically inclined scholars who responded by trying to recover the tradition and preserve it from the 'eisegetical' gaze of the philosophers. In that sense, the process of writing hadith commentaries came, in part, as a response to the appropriation of the words of the Imams for the cause of *philosophia*.

Before discussing the commentaries, we should clarify what we mean by the Shīʿī hadith corpus and the canonisation of Shīʿī hadith and the redaction of the prophetic and imamic traditions (*tadwīn al-sunna*).[2] According to our earliest sources, texts of the sayings of the Imams were redacted, noted and disseminated from an early period. There was no rhetoric per se against the written redaction of these traditions; on the contrary, reports promoted the written transmission of texts from the Imams.[3] In the classical collection *al-Kāfī* of Abū Jaʿfar al-Kulaynī (d. 329/941), there is a chapter on *faḍl al-ʿilm* (the excellence of knowledge) on the importance of writing and recording hadiths in order to remember and disseminate them. One report from Imam Jaʿfar al-Ṣādiq states: 'Write, because you will not remember unless you write', and in another report: 'Preserve [knowledge] by writing it down because they [the people] will need it later.'[4] Based on early bibliographical lists, it seems that texts in the early period were, in fact, abundant.

The early confidants of the Imams compiled notebooks, sometimes called *uṣūl*, *kutub*, or *jawāmiʿ*, of sayings on particular issues. These cover the entire corpus transmitted by a particular individual or a chain, and these compilations led to the major compendia of the third/ninth to the fifth/eleventh century.[5] Whether the totality of these texts constituted the

---

2 For example, al-Jalālī, *Tadwīn al-sunna*, and Mahdawī-Rād, *Tadwīn al-ḥadīth*. For a brief survey article in English, see Ahmad, 'Twelver Šīʿī ḥadīt̲'.

3 On the prohibition of redacting hadith in the early proto-Sunnī tradition, see Cook, 'The Opponents of Writing of Tradition'; on reports on the prohibition of recording hadith not signifying that hadith were widely forged, see al-Aʿẓamī, *Studies in Early Hadith Literature*, 25–28.

4 Al-Kulaynī, *al-Kāfī*, *Kitāb faḍl al-ʿilm*, faṣl XVII, 1:129. The second hadith is found in the *aṣl* of ʿĀṣim b. Ḥumayd (fl. second/eighth century) from Muḥammad b. Muslim; see *al-Uṣūl al-sittat ʿashar*, 160.

5 On the problem of the so-called four hundred *uṣūl*, and there being only around seventeen extant, see Kohlberg, 'al-Uṣūl al-arbaʿumiʾa'. Al-Shaykh al-Mufīd (d. 413/1022) seems to be the first to have invoked the idea of the four hundred *uṣūl* as cited in Ibn Shahrāshūb (d. 588/1192), *Maʿālim al-ʿulamāʾ*, 3. The tradition considered the four books (or rather the larger compendia of the classical period) to be based on these early notebooks, a fact that is clear in the compilation of lists of extant works that were redacted in the *Risāla* of Abū Ghālib al-Zurārī (d. 368/978), *Kitāb al-Rijāl* of Ibn ʿUqda (d. 333/944), the *Fihrist* of Ibn Qūlawayh (d. 368/978), and the *Kitāb al-Rijāl* and the *Fihrist* of al-Ṭūsī (d. 460/1067).

classical compilations, starting with the homiletics of *Kitāb al-Maḥāsin* of Aḥmad b. Muḥammad al-Barqī (d. 274/888) and the theologically significant compilation of Imamology of *Baṣā'ir al-darajāt* of al-Ṣaffār al-Qummī (d. 290/903),[6] and later the four books – *al-Kāfī* of Abū Jaʿfar al-Kulaynī, *Man lā yaḥḍuruhu al-Faqīh* of Ibn Bābawayh al-Shaykh al-Ṣadūq (d. 381/991), and *Tahdhīb al-aḥkām fī sharḥ al-muqniʾa* and *al-Istibṣār fīmā ikhtulifa min al-akhbār* of Abū Jaʿfar al-Ṭūsī (d. 460/1067) in the fourth/ tenth and fifth/eleventh centuries – is a moot point.[7] Nevertheless, hadiths circulated and compilations were shared. But as we find in other Muslim confessions, the importance of hadith lay in their usage in legal and theological reasoning; the study of hadith was not an end in itself. While one might argue that a process of canonisation was completed with these four classical works, the question of why it took so long for a commentary tradition to develop around them was a feature very much of the Ṣafavid period. In that sense one might say that the Ṣafavids rediscovered hadith and initiated the Shīʿī hadith commentary tradition in order to reflect on tradition to explain philosophy, theology and law, not least in the polemical context of the early modern period and the desire to 'represent' it in contrast to the Ottoman Sunnī tradition.

While the manuscript traditions attest to the spread of the classical compilations, not least al-Kulaynī's *al-Kāfī*, the revival of tradition in the Ṣafavid period led to an increased interest in hadith and the various disciplines associated with it. This meant there was an increase in works of hadith criticism and method (*dirāya*) – not *ab initio*, since works had been written by al-Mufīd, al-Ṭūsī, Ibn Ṭāwūs and Ibn al-Muṭahhar al-Ḥillī – with the texts *al-Riʿāya fī ʿilm al-dirāya* of al-Shahīd al-Thānī (d. 965/1558) and his school, including 'al-Wajīza fī ʿilm al-dirāya'

6 Aḥmad al-Barqī. *Kitāb al-Maḥāsin*; for a study of al-Barqī, see Vilozny, *Constructing a Worldview*. On al-Ṣaffār al-Qummī, see Amir-Moezzi, *The Silent Qurʾan*, 97–123.

7 The 'canon' of the four books seems to be a Ṣafavid period construction. The earliest witness that mentions 'the four books of hadith' is an *ijāza* from al-Shahīd al-Thānī (II) dated 950/1543, 'Ijāzatuhu li-l-sayyid ʿAṭāʾ Allāh', in *Rasāʾil al-Shahīd al-thānī*, 4:413. In a work dating before 960/1553, a contemporary of a student of Shahīd II, al-Ḥusayn b. ʿAbd al-Ṣamad al-ʿĀmilī (d. 984/1576), talks of 'five works', the four that we are discussing plus the no-longer-extant *Madīnat al-ʿilm* of al-Shaykh al-Ṣadūq – see al-ʿĀmilī, *Wuṣūl al-akhyār*, 85. However, we do have an interesting witness in the case of Ibn Makkī al-Jizzinī (known as al-Shahīd al-Awwal [I] [d. 786/1385]), who mentions in his list of the 'traditions' the works of al-Ṣadūq, including *Madīnat al-ʿilm*, *al-Kāfī*, *al-Faqīh*, *al-Istibṣār* and *Tahdhīb*; while he stresses that *al-Kāfī* is more important than the six books of the Sunnīs – suggesting its canonical status – he does not mention the notion of four or five books. See al-Shahīd al-awwal (I), *Dhikrā al-shīʿa*, 1:59. I am grateful to colleagues on the Facebook group Shiʿi Studies: Medieval and Modern for discussions on this question of the canon of the four books.

of al-Shaykh Bahā' al-Dīn al-'Āmilī (d. 1030/1621) and *al-Rawāshiḥ al-samāwiyya* of his friend Mīr Dāmād (d. 1040/1631). In addition, works on the narrators of hadith and on compilations (*kutub*) appeared just as commentaries began to be written. These works included *Kitāb al-Rijāl* of Sayyid Ibrāhīm Āmulī (d. 1098/1688), *Jāmi' al-ruwāt* of Muḥammad Ardabīlī (d. 1110/1699) and *Kitāb al-Rijāl al-kabīr* or *Majma' al-rijāl* of 'Ināyatallāh Quhpā'ī Iṣfahānī (d. 1016/1606), which was itself a compilation of the classical works in the genre. By the middle of the Ṣafavid period the notion of the four classical books as constitutive of the Imāmī tradition was well-established, and was invoked by Sayyid Nūrallāh Shushtarī (d. 1019/1610) in his polemic *al-Ṣawārim al-muhriqa*, which was probably penned around 1000/1600.[8]

The Ṣafavid Commentary Tradition

The Ṣafavids undertook a major project of recovering texts and disseminating those compilations that they considered to be canonical; that is, the works of the Imams themselves, especially the collections of supplications entitled *al-Ṣaḥīfa al-sajjādiyya* by Imam Zayn al-'Ābidīn and the sermons and letters of 'Alī b. Abī Ṭālib in *Nahj al-balāgha*. In order to understand the commentary tradition on hadith in this period, I present four types of works in the context of how al-Majlisī understood the tradition. First, I discuss the works attributed to the Imams themselves that were disseminated in this period and comment briefly on the major commentaries on them. Second, I briefly mention the hadith element of al-Majlisī's conception of the Imāmī tradition. Third, I consider those works that were popularly glossed in the period. Finally, I look at the encyclopaedic works encompassing hadith that were produced during this period.

The Works Attributed to the Imams

Among the works attributed to the Imams as constituting the tradition, al-Majlisī mentions *Nahj al-balāgha*, the sermons, letters and sayings of 'Alī compiled by al-Sharīf al-Raḍī (d. 406/1015).[9] This work was widely attested in the pre-Ṣafavid period and cannot be considered a Ṣafavid 'recovery' or 'rediscovery'.[10] It is the only major text among the Ṣafavid

---

8 Shushtarī, *al-Ṣawārim al-muhriqa*, 213; al-'Āmilī, 'Wajīza fī 'ilm al-dirāya'; al-Ardabīlī, *Jāmi' al-ruwāt*.

9 Al-Majlisī, *Biḥār al-anwār*, 1:11.

10 For an indication of extant manuscript copies of various texts in this study, I refer to *Dinā*. In Iran, there are 377 extant copies of the *Nahj* of which over half are pre-Ṣafavid. See Dirāyatī (ed.), *Dinā*, 10:884–896.x

'canon' of hadith that had been commented on – the most famous ones being the narrative commentary of Ibn Abī al-Ḥadīd (d. 656/1258), and the three commentaries of Maytham al-Baḥrānī (d. c. 699/1300).[11] Codices of the *Nahj al-balāgha* proliferated in the Ṣafavid period. There were at least four known translations of it: two from the early Ṣafavid period by philosophers from Shiraz, Ḥusayn Ilāhī Ardabīlī (d. c. 950/1543) and Jamāl al-Dīn Maḥmūd Shīrāzī (d. c. 957/1550), and two from the later tenth/sixteenth century, *Tanbīh al-ghāfilīn wa-tadhkirat al-ʿārifīn* of Fatḥallāh Kāshānī (d. 977/1571), the famous Qur'anic exegete, and ʿAlī b. al-Ḥasan Zavārī Iṣfahānī, whose *Rawḍat al-abrār* is dated c. 956/1549.[12] The *Nahj al-balāgha* was popular, especially among philosophers of the period who demonstrated their understanding of scripture and the words of the Imam as the font of *ḥikma*. This already figured in the (pre-Ṣafavid) work of Ibn Abī Jumhūr al-Aḥsāʾī (d. after 906/1501) especially in his *Mujlī mirʾāt al-munjī*, in which he refers to ʿAlī as 'lord of the philosophers' (*raʾīs al-ḥukamāʾ*) and quotes from *Nahj al-balāgha*.[13] Commentaries on the text in the Ṣafavid period included short lexical glosses as well as philosophical summa, as in the case of *Anwār al-faṣāḥa wa-asrār al-barāʾa fī sharḥ Nahj al-balāgha* of Niẓām al-Dīn Gīlānī (d. after 1072/1662).[14]

Regarding the *Dīwān* attributed to ʿAlī, al-Majlisī says that most of the verses are well corroborated in other sources and that Ibn Shahrāshūb (d. 588/1192) was convinced of its attribution.[15] The *Dīwān* seems to have been a Ṣafavid rediscovery – although on the cusp of the tenth/sixteenth century, two figures cite it extensively: Ibn Abī Jumhūr and Mīr Ḥusayn Maybudī (d. 909/1504), the Tīmūrid philosopher who wrote an extensive commentary and considered it a font of wisdom. Maybudī's commentary on the *Dīwān* was completed in 890/1485.[16] Ibn Abī Jumhūr cites the famous verses on the human as a microcosm that seemed to be popular in Ṣafavid literature and beyond.[17] A popular old saying associated with this was attributed to ʿAlī: 'I am the dot under the *bāʾ*'; this was understood to

11 See the bibliography for information on printed editions of Ibn Abī al-Ḥadīd's *Sharḥ Nahj al-balāgha* and al-Baḥrānī's *Sharḥ Nahj al-balāgha* and *ʿAwālim al-ʿulūm wa-l-maʿārif*.
12 Dirāyatī (ed.), *Dinā*, 10:896–897; 3:355–356; 5:966 (*Rawḍat al-abrār* is extant in MS Marʿashī Qum 8838).
13 Ibn Abī Jumhūr, *Mujlī*, 2:545.
14 MS Malik (Tehran) 1343 – see the discussion in Bandy, 'Beyond a Mountain of Light', 376–408.
15 Al-Majlisī, *Biḥār al-anwār*, 1:22, 42.
16 All the extant codices in Iran are Ṣafavid – see Dirāyatī (ed.), *Dinā*, 5:49–50.
17 Ibn Abī Jumhūr, *Mujlī*, 1:439; 4:1505.

be part of an explanation of the role of the Imam as the 'perfect human' (*insān kāmil*).[18] Mullā Ṣadrā has an extensive discussion of the hadith of the dot in *al-Asfār al-arbaʿa* in the context of the meaning of God's attribute of speech.[19]

Next, we have works attributed to Imam Jaʿfar al-Ṣādiq, such as *al-Tawḥīd, Kanz al-ḥaqāʾiq wa-l-maʿārif, al-Ihlīlijā fī al-tawḥīd* (transmitted by al-Mufaḍḍal b. ʿUmar (d. 180/796)), *Miṣbāḥ al-sharīʿa wa-miftāḥ al-ḥaqīqa* and the *tafsīr* of Imam al-Ṣādiq narrated from ʿAlī.[20] For the authenticity of most of these texts al-Majlisī relies on the testimony of Sayyid Raḍī al-Dīn ʿAlī Ibn Ṭāwūs (d. 664/1266) – the exception is the *Miṣbāḥ*, which he thinks reads too much like a Sufi text.[21] The texts transmitted by al-Mufaḍḍal were certainly Ṣafavid rediscoveries, were well attested in the manuscript tradition of the period and are quoted in their entirety in the first volume on *tawḥīd* in *Biḥār al-anwār*.[22] The *Miṣbāḥ* is even better attested but circulated mainly among the more mystically inclined.[23] The *tafsīr* is only extant in South Asia, so al-Majlisī's comments on it are unusual.[24] *Al-Ihlīlijā* presents a teleological argument (an argument from design) for the existence of God and refutes naturalists and those who deny a creator.[25] *Al-Tawḥīd* purports to being a record of five sittings (*majālis*) during which Imam al-Ṣādiq responded to the doubts of the naturalist (or possibly dualist) Ibn Abī al-ʿAwjāʾ (d. 155/772) through arguments from design for the existence of God based on the order of the cosmos, the structure of human beings, and other elements of the natural world.

The works attributed to Imam al-Riḍā include *al-Ṣaḥīfa, al-Ṭibb* (or *al-Risāla al-dhahabiyya* written for al-Maʾmūn) and *Fiqh al-riḍā*.[26] Al-Majlisī was satisfied with the authenticity of these texts, and claimed

---

18 Ibn Abī Jumhūr, *Mujlī*, 4:1503. For a discussion of this 'hadith', see Dīmagār-Gurāb, 'Rivāyat-i *Anā al-nuqṭa*'.

19 Shīrāzī, *al-Ḥikma al-mutaʿāliya*, 7:43–46.

20 Al-Ṣādiq, *Kitāb al-Ihlīlijā*; Al-Ṣādiq, *Kitāb al-Tawḥīd*. Both texts are cited in their entirety in al-Majlisī, *Biḥār al-anwār*, 3:57–151, 152–198. On these texts, see Asatryan, *Controversies in Formative Shiʿi Islam*, 59–60.

21 Al-Majlisī, *Biḥār al-anwār*, 1:14–15, 32; Ibn Ṭāwūs, *Kashf al-muḥajja*, 50–51.

22 Dirāyatī (ed.), *Dīnā*, 2:291–292 (46 copies are all from the Ṣafavid period or later), 3:384–388 (125 copies start from the Ṣafavid period).

23 Dirāyatī (ed.), *Dīnā*, 9:656–663 (239 copies are from the Ṣafavid period, with only one attested before that).

24 The narrator of this commentary is Sayyid Abū al-Faḍl al-ʿAbbās b. Muḥammad b. al-Qāsim b. Ḥamza b. Mūsā b. Jaʿfar al-Ṣādiq, who is also the narrator of the famous *Tafsīr* of ʿAlī b. Ibrāhīm al-Qummī.

25 For a study of the complicated historical recensions of this text in the late antique context, see El-Shamsy, 'Al-Ghazālī's Teleology'.

26 Al-Majlisī, *Biḥār al-anwār*, 1:11; al-Riḍā, *Ṣaḥīfat al-Riḍā*.

that much of their content corresponds with what was narrated by al-Ṣadūq. These texts were rediscovered and popularised in the Ṣafavid period; barely a handful of manuscript witnesses before then are extant. The prophetic medical texts were linked to the revival of the genre in this period.[27] The *Fiqh* enjoyed a certain vogue as well, especially among more hadith-inclined jurists. It was first popularised and authenticated by the elder al-Majlisī.[28] The *Ṣaḥīfa* exemplified the revival of all classical hadith-related matters in the period.[29] *Al-Risāla al-dhahabiyya* was copied in its entirety by al-Majlisī as chapter 89 of volume 14 (*al-Samā' wa-l-ʿālam*) of the *Biḥār al-anwār*; the *Risāla* was based on a recension of ʿAlī al-Karakī (d. 940/1534) and its popularity owes much to al-Majlisī.[30]

The *tafsīr* attributed to Imam al-Ḥasan al-ʿAskarī, entitled *al-Tafsīr al-mansūb*, was fairly well attested in pre-Ṣafavid manuscripts, but was popularised in the Ṣafavid period.[31] Although the chain of transmission mentions al-Shaykh al-Ṣadūq, al-Majlisī transmits it from Abū al-Ḥusayn Muḥammad b. al-Qāsim, who was known as *al-mufassir* al-Astarābādī al-Jurjānī and was keen to deflect any suggestion that the text is Zaydī 'because most of the people of Astarābād are Zaydī'.[32] *Al-Tafsīr al-mansūb* became popular along with the works of al-Ṣadūq in the middle of the Ṣafavid period and was an important source for reports on the maximalist concept of the Imam. Al-Majlisī's trust in the reliability of the attribution seems to be based on the judgement of his father.[33]

The one text that al-Majlisī does not mention that was popularised in the Ṣafavid period is *al-Ṣaḥīfa al-sajjādiyya*, a collection of supplications narrated from Imam ʿAlī b. al-Ḥusayn Zayn al-ʿĀbidīn. He probably did not mention it because it was not, strictly speaking, a work of hadith. There were three recensions of the text in the Ṣafavid period: the first redaction was by Shaykh Bahāʾ al-Dīn al-ʿĀmilī (d. 1030/1621), the second by al-Ḥurr al-ʿĀmilī (d. 1104/1693) and the third by Mīrzā ʿAbdallāh Afandī

---

27 Dirāyatī (ed.), *Dinā*, 1:1079–1080 (58 copies), 5:791–795 (137 copies, of which only 3 are pre-Ṣafavid).

28 Dirāyatī (ed.), *Dinā*, 7:1079–1080 (26 copies, of which only one is pre-Ṣafavid). See Qāsimī, *Muḥaqqiq-i Majlisī*, 1:398–401.

29 Dirāyatī (ed.), *Dinā*, 7:59–63 (115 copies).

30 Al-Majlisī, *Biḥār al-anwār*, 59:306–356; for a study, see Newman, 'Bāqir al-Majlisī and Islamicate Medicine II'.

31 Dirāyatī (ed.), *Dinā*, 2:122–124 (94 copies, of which half are pre-Ṣafavid).

32 Al-Ḥasan al-ʿAskarī, *al-Tafsīr al-mansūb*, 23–24. For a study of the text and its dating to the fourth/tenth century, see Bar-Asher, 'The Qurʾān Commentary'; al-Ṣadūq cites the *tafsīr* in his works; see al-Ṣadūq, *ʿIlal al-sharāʾiʿ*, 1:298, and al-Ṣadūq, *Maʿānī al-akhbār*, 4 (on the *basmala*), 287–289 (on the meaning of death).

33 Qāsimī, *Muḥaqqiq-i Majlisī*, 1:401–403.

(d. c. 1130/1718).[34] There is an eleventh-/seventeenth-century Persian translation by a Muḥammad b. ʿAlī Daylamī attested in a *unicum*.[35] The earliest commentary, on the cusp of the Ṣafavid period, seems to be by the ʿĀmilī scholar Taqī al-Dīn Ibrāhīm al-Kafamī (d. 905/1499), extant in a *unicum*.[36] Apart from the many manuscript copies, there are a number of published commentaries on the text from the Ṣafavid period, such as a collection of eleventh-/seventeenth-century glosses by Muḥammad Taqī al-Majlisī (d. 1070/1659),[37] Shāh Muḥammad Dārābī Shīrāzī (d. 1130/1718),[38] Ibn Khātūn al-ʿĀmilī (d. 1059/1649), Ḥusayn Khwānsārī (d. 1098/1687)[39] and Mīr Dāmād. In addition, we know of *Nūr al-anwār fī sharḥ al-Ṣaḥīfa al-sajjādiyya* of Sayyid Niʿmatallāh al-Jazāʾirī (d. 1102/1701) and *Riyāḍ al-sālikīn fī sharḥ Ṣaḥīfat Sayyid al-Sājidīn* of Sayyid ʿAlī Khān Madanī Shīrāzī (d. 1119/1707).

The Imāmī Tradition According to al-Majlisī

The Ṣafavids also sought to recover early texts that exemplified their 'maximalist' notion of the Imams; they promoted the pre-Ṣafavid collection *ʿAwālī* (or *Ghawālī*) *al-laʾālī* of Ibn Abī Jumhūr al-Aḥsāʾī,[40] *Mashāriq anwār al-yaqīn* of Rajab al-Bursī,[41] *Muntakhab baṣāʾir al-darajāt* of al-Ḥasan al-Ḥillī[42] and other texts that became the core of the *Biḥār al-anwār* of al-Majlisī, such as *Baṣāʾir al-darajāt* of al-Ṣaffār al-Qummī[43] – in fact in his introduction to the *Biḥār*, he lists a series of noteworthy works that

34 The first is best attested in the manuscript collections – and in published versions. See Dirāyatī (ed.), *Dinā*, 7:70–101 (1,278 copies, including 14 valuable and early pre-Ṣafavid ones). For the second redaction, see Dirāyatī (ed.), *Dinā*, 7:63 (11 copies), and for the third, see Dirāyatī (ed.), *Dinā*, 7:63 (5 copies).
35 See Dirāyatī (ed.), *Dinā*, 7:63 citing MS Āstān-i quds-i Raḍawī (Mashhad) 8165.
36 MS Kitābkhāna-yi Millī (Tehran) 3027; see Dirāyatī (ed.), *Dinā*, 7:67.
37 Dārābī, *Riyāḍ al-ʿārifīn*; See Dirāyatī (ed.), *Dinā*, 7:63–64, which mentions a unicum and autograph: MS Malik (Tehran) 2987 dated 1 Rajab 1077/December 1666.
38 See Dirāyatī (ed.), *Dinā*, 7:63–64 which mentions a *unicum* and autograph: MS Malik (Tehran) 2987 dated 1 Rajab 1077/December 1666.
39 See Dirāyatī (ed.), *Dinā*, 7:65 (9 copies).
40 There are approximately 30 extant copies in Iranian collections – see Dirāyatī (ed.), *Dinā*, 7:814–815. An important commentary by Sayyid Niʿmatallāh al-Jazāʾirī was published recently. See al-Jazāʾirī, *Nūr al-anwār* and ʿAlī Khān Madanī Shīrāzī, *Riyāḍ al-sālikīn*.
41 Al-Bursī, *Mashāriq anwār al-yaqīn*; Dirāyatī (ed.), *Dinā*, 9:659–673 lists 108 manuscripts in Iran (of which only one is pre-Ṣafavid) and two Persian translations.
42 While written approximately a century before the Ṣafavid period, the extant manuscripts are Ṣafavid. See Dirāyatī (ed.), *Dinā*, 2:507–508 (19 copies).
43 The *Baṣāʾir* is a good example of a Ṣafavid rediscovery; it was discovered and popularised in that period, hence the proliferation of extant Ṣafavid manuscripts in Iran. See Dirāyatī (ed.), *Dinā*, 2:506–507 (53 copies).

define the tradition and are the foundations of his compilation.[44] The classical hadith texts that he cites include the works of al-Shaykh al-Ṣadūq,[45] *al-Maḥāsin* of Aḥmad al-Barqī[46] and *Kāmil al-ziyāra* of Ibn Qūlawayh, as well as classical hadith-based *tafsīr*. Interestingly, this list does not mention the four books as a particular canon, perhaps because al-Majlisī wrote commentaries on them, especially his voluminous commentary on *al-Kāfī*.

Key Texts that were Glossed

The following is a list of the key texts that were glossed; in most cases, these demonstrate that commentary was generally absent before the Ṣafavid period. These works can be broadly divided into works for jurists and those of theological and philosophical interest. For the jurists (and given the nature of those earlier compilations), the works of al-Ṭūsī and al-Ṣadūq were of paramount importance. On these, one finds manuscript evidence attesting to the following:

1. *Al-Istibṣār fī mā ikhtulifa min al-akhbār* of al-Ṭūsī is an attempt to reconcile contradictory reports.[47] As one expects, most of the commentaries on *al-Istibṣār* are by jurists such as Mīr Dāmād (d. 1040/1631).[48]
2. *Tahdhīb al-aḥkām* is a larger work by al-Ṭūsī. It is a commentary on al-Mufīd's fiqh manual entitled *al-Muqniʿa*, in which al-Ṭūsī asserts that contradictory hadith can lead to differences in substantive law (*ikhtilāf fī furuʿ al-fiqh*).[49] Glosses from the earlier Ṣafavid period were written by jurists.[50]

44 Al-Majlisī, *Biḥār al-anwār*, 2:6–25.

45 Andrew Newman suggests that the works of al-Ṣadūq are a good example of Ṣafavid recovery – see his 'The Recovery of the Past'.

46 The *Maḥāsin* on its own is not well attested though it was discovered and popularised in the Ṣafavid period, perhaps because much of the material was incorporated into other texts, including *al-Kāfī*. See Dirāyatī (ed.), *Dinā*, 9:147–149 (49 copies).

47 Dirāyatī (ed.), *Dinā*, 1:722–737 (491 copies, of which only 8 are pre-Ṣafavid).

48 Dirāyatī (ed.), *Dinā* 4:17; Muḥammad b. al-Ḥasan Shīrwānī (d. 1098/1687): MS Gulpāyigānī (Qum) 6305/2, *naskh* of Khalf b. Yūsuf Najafī dated 8 Jumāda II 1103/1692, 17ff.; Ḥusayn Khwānsārī (d. 1098/1687): MS Mahdawī (Tehran) 780 is an autograph; al-Jazāʾirī (d. 1112/1702): *Kashf al-asrār*.

49 Al-Ṭūsī, *Tahdhīb al-aḥkām*, 1:1; Dirāyatī (ed.), *Dinā*, 3:431–447 (991 copies, of which 13 are pre-Ṣafavid).

50 These glosses include the work of al-Ḥasan b. Zayn al-Dīn (Shahīd II) al-ʿĀmilī (d. 1011/ 1602): Dirāyatī (ed.), *Dinā* 4:82 mentions 8 copies; for the work of Shīrwānī, see Dirāyatī (ed.), *Dinā* 4:82; al-Majlisī: MS Sipahsālār (Madrasa-yi Muṭahharī, Tehran) 4512, dated to the twelfth/eighteenth century, and MS Āstān-i quds-i rażavī (Mashhad) 9268, 168ff., dated to the twelfth/eighteenth century; Muḥammad Jaʿfar b. Muḥammad Ṭāhir Khurāsānī (d. 1152/1739): Dirāyatī (ed.), *Dinā* 4:83 mentions one short codex: MS Majlis-i Shūrā-yi islāmī (Tehran) 795 tāʾ, *naskh* of the twelfth/eighteenth century, *kitāb al-ḥajj* only.

3. *Man lā yaḥḍuruhu al-faqīh* of al-Ṣadūq: this was mainly glossed by jurists such as Bahāʾ al-Dīn al-ʿĀmilī (d. 1030/1621).[51] The influential Persian commentary *Lawāmiʿ-yi ṣāḥibqirānī* and the Arabic commentary *Rawḍat al-muttaqīn*, both by Muḥammad Taqī al-Majlisī (d. 1070/1659) are also noteworthy because they were used as manuals by his many followers.[52] The legal selection *Arbaʿūnā ḥadīthan* of Bahāʾ al-Dīn al-ʿĀmilī, on which two important twelfth-/eighteenth-century commentaries are extant, can be seen as a related work.[53]

Theologically speaking, al-Kulaynī's work and al-Ṣadūq's theological masterpiece *al-Tawḥīd* were more relevant and influential than the other four books. The manuscript evidence – and now the extensive publication project of Dār al-Ḥadīth in Qum – suggests the following:

1. *Al-Tawḥīd of al-Shaykh al-Ṣadūq* was a popular text and one of the best examples of a Ṣafavid discovery;[54] of note is the commentary of the philosopher Qāḍī Saʿīd Qummī (d. 1107/1696) on *al-Tawḥīd*.[55]

2. *Al-Kāfī* of al-Kulaynī: In his introduction to the Shīʿī hadith tradition and to *al-Kāfī*, Mīr Dāmād says that despite the prominence of the text of al-Kulaynī, a learned and trustworthy scholar, no one (up to his time) – jurist, theologian or philosopher – has attempted to explain the complexities and gloss the text.[56] Given the central role of *al-Kāfī* as a purveyor of Shīʿī theology and Imamology, it is not surprising that there are large numbers of extant manuscripts of it from the Ṣafavid period. Importantly, al-Kulaynī suggests that those trained in philosophy are

---

51 See al-ʿĀmilī, *Arbaʿūna ḥadīthan*; two glosses of it were the *Ḥāshiya* of Sayyid ʿAbdallāh al-Jazāʾirī (d. 1173/1759), and the *Ḥāshiya* of Ismāʿīl Khājūʾī (d. 1173/1759). See Dirāyatī (ed.), *Dinā*, 4:13.

52 See the bibliography for printed editions of these two texts.

53 See al-ʿĀmilī, *Ḥāshiyat al-Faqīh*; two other glosses include the Akhbārī Muḥammad Amīn Astarābādī: MS Markaz-i Iḥyāʾ (Qum) 2352/2, eleventh-/seventeenth-century nastaʿlīq of Muḥammad b. Jābir al-Najafī, 35ff.; Niẓām al-Dīn Gīlānī (d. after 1072/1662): MS Sālār Jung (Hyderabad) Arabic Hadith Imāmiyya 38.

54 Dirāyatī (ed.), *Dinā*, 3:388–391 (218 copies, all from the Ṣafavid period).

55 Fāḍil-i Sarāb Muḥammad b. ʿAbd al-Fattāḥ Tunikābunī (d. 1124/1713): MS Majlis-i Shūrā-yi islāmī (Tehran) 14719/5, *nastaʿlīq* of Muḥammad b. Ḥabīb ʿAlī Gīlānī, dated Rabīʿ I, 1115/1703, 24ff.

56 Mīr Dāmād, *al-Rawāshiḥ al-samāwiyya*, 24. Mīr Dāmād never completed his commentary on the uṣūl of al-Kāfī and his rather limited set of glosses only reaches the beginning of *kitāb al-ḥujja* (incidentally this covers almost the same topics as Mullā Ṣadrā's commentary, but it is much more precise); see Mīr Dāmād, *al-Taʿlīqāt ʿalā kitāb al-Kāfī*. There are a huge number of extant manuscripts of *al-Kāfī* in Iran but only fifteen are pre-Ṣafavid – see Dirāyatī (ed.), *Dinā*, 8:375–432 (2,589 copies).

most suited to write such commentaries. The commentary that led to the flourishing of commentaries and glosses was that of Mullā Ṣadrā in the 1040s/1630s. Following Mullā Ṣadrā, major commentaries and glosses appeared. Among the commentaries, we must note the monumental work of Muḥammad Ṣāliḥ Māzandarānī (d. 1081/1670) (son-in-law of Muḥammad Taqī al-Majlisī, d. 1070/1659), and the voluminous *Mirʾāt al-ʿuqūl* of Muḥammad Bāqir al-Majlisī (d. 1110/1699). Only Māzandarānī and al-Majlisī cover the entirety of the text; others only gloss the *uṣūl*.[57] Among the glosses, we can include that of Mīr Dāmād and his students as well as some key figures like Muḥammad Amīn Astarābādī (d. 1036/1626).

Ṣafavid Encyclopaedia Works as Hadith Commentary

Notably, the hadith compilations and encyclopaedias of the Ṣafavid period also constitute a sort of commentary on the earlier hadith compilations. The *Biḥār al-anwār* of al-Majlisī, as we have seen, was based on a number of earlier hadith texts and transmissions and in some cases even revived interest in texts that seemed to have been forgotten, such as the works narrated by al-Mufaḍḍal b. ʿUmar from Imam al-Ṣādiq, and the hadith-based Qurʾanic exegesis narrated by Ibn Abī Zaynab ʿal-Kātib' al-Numʿānī (d. 360/971) from ʿAlī.[58] Another major compilation of that period was the *ʿAwālim al-ʿulūm* of Shaykh ʿAbdallāh al-Baḥrānī, a student and confidant of al-Majlisī; there is some evidence that this work was meant as a completion or continuation of the *Biḥār*. Although it was planned as a very large undertaking (over a hundred volumes – by contrast, the *Biḥār* was twenty-five volumes), it is unclear how much was completed; of what is now extant and published, there is one volume on the intellect, four volumes on the twelfth Imam, and two volumes on Fāṭima al-Zahrāʾ. It was conceived as fifty volumes on *uṣūl* and fifty on *furūʿ*. The first volume is on terminology, the second concerns the intellect, the third to the eighth are on the principles of faith and volumes 9 to 26 are biographies of the Prophet, Fāṭima and the Imams. The remaining volumes focus on ritual practices, social transactions and various elements of religious practice. It brings together texts from the four books but goes far beyond them. However, as a commentary, al-Baḥrānī's selection and corroboration of texts is more important than his exegetical or explanatory interventions.

---

57 *Al-Kāfī* is divided into three sections: theology (*uṣūl*), specific questions of law and social transactions (*furūʿ*) and miscellaneous issues (*rawḍa*).

58 Al-Majlisī, *Biḥār al-anwār*, 90:1–105.

The other two major hadith compilations of the period are also commentaries on earlier hadiths: *Wasāʾil al-shīʿa* of al-Ḥurr al-ʿĀmilī (d. 1104/1693) completed in 1087/1677 and *al-Wāfī* of Muḥsin Fayḍ Kāshānī (d. 1090/1679) completed in 1068/1658. The former work is a massive compendium divided into fifty books based on the order of the *fiqh* manual *Sharāʾiʿ al-islām fī masāʾil al-ḥalāl wa-l-ḥarām* of Najm al-Dīn, known as al-Muḥaqqiq al-Ḥillī (d. 676/1277).[59] As al-Ḥurr al-ʿĀmilī says in his introduction, the study of hadith as the ultimate science (not jurisprudence and legal theory based on the independence of reason, since he was an Akhbārī) is important because it comes from the Imams who are the infallible and inerrant source of knowledge; therefore, he sought to compile a work based on the earlier reliable sources of hadith that included all the issues of law.[60] Al-ʿĀmilī sifted through the various texts and reconciled them in order to base the law on the Imams alone, and no one else (this was likely a critique of the more rationally minded *uṣūlī* jurists).[61] In terms of his sources, he was clear that while he used the 'four famous books of hadith' (*kutub al-ḥadīth al-arbaʿa*), he was not restricted by them; he also quoted from other works and was careful to cite the proper references, as long as the work and the report were trustworthy and reputable.[62] In this sense, one could say that in matters of ritual and transactional law, the compilation is a critical commentary and evaluation of the hadith in the four books, drawing upon other works as well. He indicates his method by citing the texts he used: along with the four books, he used works of al-Ṣadūq such as *al-Tawḥīd, Madīnat al-ʿilm* (now lost) and *ʿIlal al-sharāʾiʿ, al-Iḥtijāj* of al-Ṭabrisī and the *Baṣāʾir* of al-Ṣaffār. He started, 'I commend to you *al-Kāfī* [The sufficient], a work that corrects (*tahdhīb*) [the traditions] for one who has no jurist present (*man lā yaḥḍuruhu al-faqīh*) by the best of what appears to one's insight (*maḥāsin al-istibṣār*)'.[63] Thus, in the first sentence he mentions the titles of the four works and the early compilation of al-Barqī.

Al-Wāfī of Kāshānī is explicitly based on the four books, but more closely resembles the structure of *al-Kāfī*; it begins with the book on the intellect and comprises fifteen parts following the order of the earlier collection (that is, *al-Kāfī*). In the introduction, Kāshānī describes the work as

59 Najm al-Dīn al-Ḥillī, *Sharāʾiʿ al-islām*. There are over a hundred glosses and commentaries on this text of substantive Shīʿī law, which is divided into four sections: ritual worship (*ʿibādāt*), contracts (*ʿuqūd*), obligations and duties (*īqāʿāt*) and social precepts (*aḥkām*). It was popular in the Ṣafavid period because it was promoted as a school text according to the tradition of Shahīd II.

60 Al-Ḥurr al-ʿĀmilī, *Wasāʾil al-shīʿa*, 1:8–9.

61 Al-Ḥurr al-ʿĀmilī, *Wasāʾil al-shīʿa*, 1:12.

62 Al-Ḥurr al-ʿĀmilī, *Wasāʾil al-shīʿa*, 1:12.

63 Al-Ḥurr al-ʿĀmilī, *Wasāʾil al-shīʿa*, 1:13.

sufficient and extensive in the matters of faith, and bases it on the four principal works that were dominant 'in our time', namely, *al-Kāfī*, *al-Faqīh*, *Tahdhīb* and *Istibṣār*.[64] He then provides a short description of each of the works, starting with the 'noblest, the most reliable, the most comprehensive and the most complete' of them, *al-Kāfī*.[65] But this is not just a compilation of texts, as he explicitly states, it is a commentary. He then examines three preliminary points for understanding and engaging the texts: how to study religious texts, how to make sense of the chains of transmission (*isnād*s) and how to understand the technical terms (*muṣṭalaḥāt*) he has used.[66] He leaves the way open for a philosophical and mystical understanding of the text. In the first preliminary, he outlines the options starkly:

> A person must be [one] of two types: either a verifier possessing mystical intuition and certainty (*ṣāḥib kashf wa-yaqīn*), or a follower who attests and acquiesces (*ṣāḥib taṣdīq wa-taslīm*). The third option is misguidance leading to destruction, confusing what is right with what is wrong.[67]

Kāshānī goes further than al-Ḥurr. Kāshānī follows each hadith or set of hadiths with an explanation (*bayān*) that analyses the terms used and deploys his philosophical, theological and mystical training. In this sense, the commentary, especially the one on the first book of the intellect, seems to mirror much of the discussion of his teacher, Mullā Ṣadrā.

The Case Study: The Intellect

As is often the case, and especially with the recent interest in commentary culture, commentaries on a particular text become battlegrounds for conflicting conceptions of knowledge, scholarship and visions of reality. I interrogate this with respect to a case study of the commentaries on the hadiths relating to the intellect in *al-Kāfī*. The fundamental question at stake with respect to the notion of the intellect (*'aql*) was whether the hadiths were referring to (and could be reconciled with) philosophical notions of the higher intellects emanating from the One and the idea of the intellect as an immaterial substance both within and without the human person. Allied to this was the basic problem of terminology: (1) were technical terms in the hadith used in a conventional linguistic way, (2) could they be collated with usage and overlap in meaning with other disciplines (such as philosophy)

64　Kāshānī, *al-Wāfī*, 1:4.
65　Kāshānī, *al-Wāfī*, 1:5–7.
66　Kāshānī, *al-Wāfī*, 1:7–43.
67　Kāshānī, *al-Wāfī*, 1:12.

or (3) were they particular to hadith or scriptural language as such? If one opted for the third possibility, it becomes difficult to see how hadith could really be applied outside the very specific context of a particular report. If the first option, did this conform to ordinary linguistic usage? Naturally, philosophers opted for the first and the second options. For the scripturalists (such as Astarābādī), the *kitāb al-ʿaql* does not refer to the *nous* or any transcendent entity. Rather, the intellect is an innate faculty (*gharīza*), placed by God in humans as an inner guiding light (*nūr*) that motivates humans toward what is sound and appropriate to their nature and facilitates the distinction between what is right and what is wrong (*al-tamayyuz bayn al-ṣawāb wa-l-khaṭaʾ*), and as such it varies from person to person.[68] The scripturalists rejected a Neoplatonic reading of intellect and insisted that it was merely an internal faculty. Mullā Ṣadrā took this as a challenge to establish that intellect was both an internal human faculty as well as a transcendent reality and it was this position to which later commentators responded (positively or negatively).

Mullā Ṣadrā

Mullā Ṣadrā (d. 1045/1636), perhaps the most famous philosopher inclined to mysticism in the Ṣafavid period, and student of hadith specialists such as Mīr Dāmād and al-Shaykh Bahāʾ al-Dīn al-ʿĀmilī, wrote the first major commentary on the theological sections of *al-Kāfī*. Unfortunately the commentary remained incomplete; the last section extant was completed in 1045/1635 and is at the beginning of the book on the imamate (*kitāb al-ḥujja*). One might argue that the popularity of glossing the theological sections of *al-Kāfī* began with Mullā Ṣadrā, and that others then responded to him. We can see this in the many glosses and commentaries after him that have now been published. Certainly, it seems to have been a successful commentary as manuscript copies attest.[69]

Mullā Ṣadrā's commentary on the nature of the intellect is predicated on his approach of reconciling philosophy and scripture because both are geared toward the acquisition of knowledge about the nature of reality by those who seek to achieve happiness in this life and in the hereafter. The introduction to the text makes his approach quite clear: On the one hand he makes a conventional apophatic assertion of the inability of human intellects to grasp God, an assertion that necessitates the sending of messengers

---

68 Astarābādī, *al-Ḥāshiya*, 85.

69 According to the Iranian union catalogue, *Dinā*, 6:974–978, there are 110 copies in Iran. However, the most successful commentary, in terms of the sheer number of extant codices is that of Māzandarānī (see Dirāyatī (ed.), *Dinā*, 6:978–986), of which there are 249 copies. Al-Majlisī's *Mirʾāt al-ʿuqūl* states that there are only 69 extant copies (this may relate to the sheer size) – see Dirāyatī (ed.), *Dinā*, 9:353–356.

and revelation to allow humans to understand God sufficiently, and on the other hand, God's gift of the intellect allows humans to understand their reality – and ultimately God – in order that they may gain felicitous salvation.[70] Revelation acts as universal reason and the intellect reflects the inspired and revealed truths that God places within humans: The sound intellect (*al-ʿaql al-ṣaḥīḥ*) is supported by clear revelation (*al-naql al-ṣarīḥ*) and it is these practitioners of intellect – the godly scholars and wise people (*al-ʿulamā' al-rabbāniyyīn wa-l-ḥukamā'*) – who should explain the nature of the hadith.[71] The intellect is therefore the key instrument – the axis that allows the person to arrive at truth and avoid falsehood – and Mullā Ṣadrā is keenly aware of the need to gloss its meaning.[72] For him, *al-Kāfī* was the obvious and best repository of the hadith to gloss that sense of intellect, while recognising that many study both philosophy and hadith without understanding either, and he prays that he does not fall into that category.[73] His precise aim is not as clear: Was it to counter the simple Akhbārī acceptance of the entirety of the corpus without critical evaluation – and in a sense his critique of al-Kulaynī as compiler of the corpus suggests that he is no fan of 'simple' *muḥaddithīn* – or was it to make a claim for the superior ability and legitimacy of philosophers to claim the scriptural heritage central to their own pursuit?[74] He states that he wishes to dive into the sea of wisdom that is the hadith corpus and extract the pearls of meaning to unveil the true nature of faith and bring them together with the meanings of the Qur'an, aided and supported by God's favour and grace.[75] A humble topos, but one based on the clear homology of God's revelation in scripture and in the human intellect. Sometimes this homology is presented technically – for example, in the commentary on the sixth hadith (whoever has intellect has faith and whoever has faith enters paradise), he argues that the hadith is actually an assertoric syllogism in the first figure, and he proceeds to reconstruct the hadith in that manner.[76]

The commentary covers many aspects and glosses all the hadith in the *Kitāb al-ʿAql* (Book of intellect) including some elements on the chain of transmission and the philology. But his interest lies in the meaning. Four

70 Shīrāzī, *Sharḥ Uṣūl al-Kāfī*, 1:3–5.

71 Shīrāzī, *Sharḥ Uṣūl al-Kāfī*, 1:7–8.

72 Shīrāzī, *Sharḥ Uṣūl al-Kāfī*, 1:65.

73 Shīrāzī, *Sharḥ Uṣūl al-Kāfī*, 1:8–9.

74 For his critique of al-Kulaynī, see Shīrāzī, *Sharḥ Uṣūl al-Kāfī*, 1:12–13 and 63. Jari Kaukua has interestingly suggested that his intention may have been to provide philosophical foundations for the authority of the jurist to use and manipulate hadith and this may follow the approach of his teacher, Mīr Dāmād, but there is much more we need to consider to substantiate that; see Kaukua, 'The Intellect in Mullā Ṣadrā's Commentary'.

75 Shīrāzī, *Sharḥ Uṣūl al-Kāfī*, 1:10–12.

76 Shīrāzī, *Sharḥ Uṣūl al-Kāfī*, 1:101–102.

issues are central to this process: First, what is the nature of the intellect? Second, how can we relate the hadith on the intellect to the philosophical (Neoplatonic) account of the emanation of the cosmos mediated by intellects? Third, is the term intellect used univocally or is it a modulated concept? Finally, how does the function of the theoretical intellect relate to the practical – what is the connection between metaphysics and ethics?

The first question is expressed in a practical way in the commentary on the third hadith (what is intellect), where he explains that intellect can be taken in six senses, drawing on al-Fārābī's *al-Risāla fī al-ʿaql* (Treatise on the intellect):[77]

1. The first sense is an innate faculty (*gharīza*) that distinguishes humans from animals and prepares a person to receive theoretical knowledge and implement the rational arts – as a basic faculty in potentiality, this is equally present in the wise and the stupid, the unconscious and the conscious. This is our innate capacity to grasp first principles and is the sense used by philosophers in Aristotle's *Posterior Analytics* (*Kitāb al-Burhān*). This is the theoretical intellect.

2. The second sense is a loose sense of reason used by theologians in their appeal to the rationality of their argument; this seems to be a notion of common sense and as such can be both fallible and infallible in function. This is a faulty notion of the theoretical intellect.

3. The third sense is an ethical notion of the practical intellect that is part of the human soul, whereby moral beliefs are held and constructed and constitute the foundation for the will to moral agency. This faculty develops in a person over time and with age and experience.

4. The fourth sense is another theologians' common-sense approach to practical reason denoted by our concepts of a 'clever person' or a 'good thinker'. This is a faulty notion of the practical intellect.

5. The fifth sense is the intellect, as it is discussed in Ibn Sīnā's *al-Shifāʾ: Fī al-nafs*[78] (*De Anima*), with the four stages from potentiality to actuality that are faculties of the soul: the material intellect, the dispositional intellect, the actual intellect and the acquired intellect.

---

77 Shīrāzī, *Sharḥ Uṣūl al-Kāfī*, 1:84–89. Kaukua's discussion is pertinent and worth considering. Al-Fārābī's text is also cited in its entirety in Mullā Ṣadrā's philosophical summa: see Shīrāzī, *al-Ḥikma al-mutaʿāliya*, 3:455–465; for a discussion of al-Fārābī in Ṣafavid thought, see Pourjavady and Schmidtke, 'An Eastern Renaissance?'. See the text, translation, and its study in al-Fārābī, *Épître sur l'intellect*.

78 Ibn Sīnā, *al-Shifāʾ*, 1:5, 48–50.

6.   The final sixth sense is the metaphysical notion that comes from
     the *Theologia Aristotelis* of the higher transcendent intellects
     uncontaminated by matter that only desire and contemplate the
     One. These are pure, good lights above our material world.

The intellect is a term used in a modulated manner (*bi-l-tashkīk*) and
not univocally.[79] *'Aql* is sometimes a practical intellect and sometimes theoretical. It is sometimes a faculty of humans and what distinguishes humans
from animals, and at other times it is a celestial, eternal thing that emanates from the One. Crucially the sound intellect must be distinguished
from a cunning and satanic deviance – if it is oriented toward the Good,
the principles of the faith and mystical intuition of God in order to produce quietude of the soul and steadfastness, and if it is derived from the
moral psychology of the believer it can be separated from the actions and
thoughts of the followers of Satan, from whom even the simple-minded are
privileged.[80] The key feature that unites all of these instances and meanings of intellect is that they remain incorporeal and immaterial.[81] While
the intellect can be attached to a body, the intellect and the intellectual
faculty are decidedly not corporeal. Later commentators follow Mullā
Ṣadrā on the point that the intellect is an immaterial substance, an innate
faculty in the human that emerges from the higher intelligible world and
becomes the standard for discerning the truth and the good.[82]

The commentary on the first hadith (on the creation of the intellect)
pins Mullā Ṣadrā's clear reconciliation of the hadith with an emanationist
cosmology. For him the creation of the intellect and its speech and reasoning is the first creation, the first thing that issued from God – and he relates
this transcendent first creation to the hadith that states that the first creation was the intellect, the light of Muhammad (*awwal mā khalaq Allāhu
nūrī*) and the pen (*al-qalam*), which are meanings for a single referent.[83]
There are two aspects of this first creation: It is the first in a chain of ema-
nations that in particular populates the higher intelligible world and once
emanated, all these entities in their pure intelligible form have an erotic
desire to return to their origins, but it is also the case that since the intellect is associated with the Prophet's reality it becomes the pivotal mode

79 Shīrāzī, *Sharḥ Uṣūl al-Kāfī*, 1:84.
80 Shīrāzī, *Sharḥ Uṣūl al-Kāfī*, 1:90.
81 Shīrāzī, *Sharḥ Uṣūl al-Kāfī*, 1:91.
82 Aḥmad al-ʿAlawī, *al-Ḥāshiya*, 62, 64–65, 70; Shīrāzī, *al-Kashf al-wāfī*, 1:32–39. How-
    ever, his son Sayyid Badr al-Dīn disagreed and argued that the context and wording of
    the hadith that declare the intellect to be the first spiritual being created from the right
    side of the divine empyrean suggests that it had a location and hence was not devoid of
    any matter – see Badr al-Dīn al-ʿAlawī, *al-Ḥāshiya*, 40.
83 Shīrāzī, *Sharḥ Uṣūl al-Kāfī*, 1:73–74.

for expressing and fulfilling the moral obligations that believing creatures acquire.[84] The emanationist scheme – coupled with Mullā Ṣadrā's doctrine of motion in the category of substance as essential to the human rational soul – is further investigated in the long commentary on the famous fourteenth hadith on the armies of intellect and ignorance.[85] The motion of the intellect expressed in the hadith is associated with the Neoplatonic scheme of emanation and reversion through his notion of motion in substance: The *ʿaql* becomes a soul, in turn becoming nature, then form, then a body, and in reverse the rational embodied soul progresses in motion to become a form, then nature, then a celestial soul and then a pure intellect.[86] In the human soul this substantial motion is expressed by the transformation of the material intellect to the acquired intellect, which is capable of union with the active intellect.

However, this hadith also raises a problem, since the creation of ignorance seems to confer on it a positive, existential meaning – and usually in the Neoplatonism of Mullā Ṣadrā, non-existence, like evil and ignorance, is a privation.[87] He explains that what is meant by ignorance is not simple ignorance (*jahl basīṭ*), which is a privative matter since it is the absence of knowledge and hence cannot be created, nor is it compound ignorance (*jahl murakkab*), which is an accidental form in the mind that fails to correspond to mental or extra-mental reality.[88] Rather it is a psychic substance and a psychological aspect that adheres to the human soul; a false belief – an act of ignorance – is therefore a psychological state of a person with the propensity to accept falsehood.[89] He gives the analogy of pain that can be felt – a real evil so to speak – in the soul, and similarly the pain of being in error, which can also be felt in the soul.[90] The case of ignorance does pose a problem for Mullā Ṣadrā, as it challenges his metaphysics and in a sense, forces him to explain the hadith figuratively and deny its literal sense.

Considering the element of a person's moral psychology brings us to the final point about the nature of the practical intellect that is discussed in the commentary on the tenth hadith (and in more detail on virtues and vices and the range of moral psychology in hadith no. 14). It was quite common in the Ṣafavid period and beyond for ethical considerations to arise from engagement with hadiths. Here Mullā Ṣadrā's concern is with

---

84 Shīrāzī, *Sharḥ Uṣūl al-Kāfī*, 1:76–78.
85 Shīrāzī, *Sharḥ Uṣūl al-Kāfī*, 1:325–494. This is the largest section of the commentary on the *kitāb al-ʿaql*.
86 Shīrāzī, *Sharḥ Uṣūl al-Kāfī*, 1:330–331.
87 Shīrāzī, *Sharḥ Uṣūl al-Kāfī*, 1:341 (see also his commentary on the twelfth hadith on the virtues of the intellect, 1:307–318).
88 Shīrāzī, *Sharḥ Uṣūl al-Kāfī*, 1:331.
89 Shīrāzī, *Sharḥ Uṣūl al-Kāfī*, 1:333.
90 Shīrāzī, *Sharḥ Uṣūl al-Kāfī*, 1:334–335.

'satanic' temptation and whispering as a lapse in the rational soul, a lapse that is equated with ignorance in the revelation. This is an example of the homology of reason and revelation spelled out as lapse equals ignorance.[91] The context of hadith no. 10 (which deals with a rational person being misled by satanic whispering while performing ablutions) is performing one's ablutions and trying to engender tranquillity in the soul, which is disrupted by 'satanic' distraction (*waswās*). Mullā Ṣadrā's explanation of the moral psychology and the role of the practical intellect brings together insights from Sufi psychology and philosophy. His starting point is the subtle centre of the human, which is called the 'heart' (*al-qalb*) in the language of revelation and the 'rational soul' (*al-nafs al-nāṭiqa*) in the language of philosophy (once again this is a process of translating terms across contexts), and this mediates between the corporeal world and the spiritual and intelligible world (whence it came) and is the ground for all our moral actions. The motivations and perceptions that arise from the rational soul lead to actions, informed as they are by data that we have received from sense perception or from our inner psychological states whether positive (imagination for example) or negative (such as passionate vices and lusts). These aspects of data processed internally constitute 'thoughts' (*khawāṭir*) that move our intentions and desires. These thoughts constituting our internal will are therefore the basis of our intentions and deliberations to act. However, these thoughts that motivate our intentions and actions are of two types: those that motivate toward evil and hence harm our destination, and those that motivate toward the good, thus benefiting us in the hereafter. The former are known as 'satanic' distraction (*waswās*) and are propelled by a satan, and the latter are 'inspirations' (*ilhām*) that are guided by an angel.[92] In many ways this particular commentary is a good example of how Mullā Ṣadrā blends discourses from scripture, Sufism, philosophy and hadith, drawing on further texts on the human heart or soul as lying between the two 'fingers' of God. Thus, his commentary is not merely an act of eisegesis in which he attempts to make the hadith conform to philosophy but a creative approach to a holistic development of wisdom.

Ṣāliḥ Māzandarānī

Ḥusām al-Dīn Muḥammad Ṣāliḥ b. Aḥmad Māzandarānī (d. 1081/1670) was a student and son-in-law of Muḥammad Taqī al-Majlisī. He was known for his teaching of the theological parts of *al-Kāfī*, as attested by his (and Muḥammad Bāqir al-Majlisī's) student 'Abdallāh Afandī (d. c. 1130/1718).[93] Later biographers noted that he was famed for his expertise

91 Shīrāzī, *Sharḥ Uṣūl al-Kāfī*, 1:113.
92 Shīrāzī, *Sharḥ Uṣūl al-Kāfī*, 1:116–117.
93 Afandī, *Riyāḍ al-'ulamā'*, 5:110.

in hadith and philosophy and that his hadith commentary is one of the best and most complete.[94] At the beginning of his commentary, in his proemium, he uses the standard language of philosophy and mysticism, while later, when glossing the meaning of praise by engaging the arguments of Jalāl al-Dīn Dawānī, he shows his mastery of the philosophical theological tradition.[95] He states that he wrote a complete set of glosses on the hadith in the text, glosses that were sufficient based on all the disciplines the texts mention and allude to and based on his understanding of what was sufficient.[96] He does not mention why he chose to comment on *al-Kāfī* or whether he consulted earlier commentaries. At the end of the gloss on the proemium, he articulates his understanding of the nature of the intellect; he glosses the phrase on the axial nature of the intellect by explaining that it is the faculty that judges the nature of good and evil and helps a person fulfil his moral obligation and discern the nature of extra-mental reality, all the while being somewhat apophatic on the possibility of truly grasping the nature of external objects.[97]

The commentary on the book of the intellect is lengthy and comprehensive; it is almost three hundred pages, making it second only to that of Mullā Ṣadrā in size.[98] On the first instance of *ʿaql*, with respect to the first hadith (on the creation of the intellect), Māzandarānī begins by defining the intellect and establishing that it differs in degrees and states, of which he enumerates six.[99] The intellect is an immaterial substance that manages the body; when it is compared to the body it is called the rational soul (*nafs nāṭiqa*), when it is described with respect to matter it is called an intellect. As an immaterial substance it is associated with the higher intelligible (sacred) realm that it came from and where it yearns to return. The six states that it possesses are the following:

1. A state of pure preparedness to become perfected.
2. A state that is capable of discerning basic or self-evident truths (*awwaliyyāt*).
3. A state in which it is capable of discerning theoretical knowledge (*naẓariyyāt*) in the mirror of basic truths.
4. A state in which it can discern theoretical knowledge, even after it no longer perceives the forms in which they are manifest and it can recall those forms – this is the state of 'knowledge of

---

94 Khwānsārī, *Rawḍat al-jannāt*, 4:118–120.
95 Māzandarānī, *Sharḥ Uṣūl al-Kāfī* (based on the earlier edition of ʿAlī-Akbar Ghaffārī), 1:18–19.
96 Māzandarānī, *Sharḥ Uṣūl al-Kāfī*, 1:17.
97 Māzandarānī, *Sharḥ Uṣūl al-Kāfī*, 1:25–28, 63–64.
98 Māzandarānī, *Sharḥ Uṣūl al-Kāfī*, 1:65–332.
99 Māzandarānī, *Sharḥ Uṣūl al-Kāfī*, 1:66–67.

certainty' (*'ilm al-yaqīn*) since it is capable of perceiving purely intelligible forms in themselves.

5. A state of the 'essence of certainty' (*'ayn al-yaqīn*) in which it can perceive intelligible forms in their emanated form (that is, in the active intellect).

6. A final state that is the very 'reality of certainty' (*ḥaqq al-yaqīn*) in which it conjoins spiritually with the emanated intellect (that is, the active intellect) and continues to progress spiritually. This is the highest state of the creature, the state in which it is a pure perfected intellect.

This description of the progression of the human intellect from the material origins of the intellect as the first entelechy of the natural body (*kamāl awwal li-jism ṭabīī*) to the perfected intellect capable of acquiring infallible knowledge through conjunction with the active intellect, in which the intelligible forms of everything reside, recalls and reconciles the psychology of Ibn Sīnā with a Sufi understanding of the states of experiential and intuitive knowledge.[100]

But Māzandarānī goes on to say that by intellect we may also mean the transcendent immaterial intellects that are the first spiritual beings and first things that emanate from God. He does not cite the famous hadith, 'The first thing God created was the intellect', even though it was widely accepted by his colleagues who were similarly influenced by philosophy and mysticism.[101] The higher intelligible world is arranged in a hierarchy of intensity up to the light of lights, who is God; here Māzandarānī seems to invoke Mullā Ṣadrā's notion of the modulation of being when he argues that those intellects in the higher intelligible world are in degrees of being determined by intensity. But at the same time, he rejects that causal efficacy of those higher intellects with respect to engendering the spheres, for he insists that only God Himself creates those spheres; thus, Māzandarānī explicitly rejects the doctrine of 'some philosophers'.[102] It is important that he accepts that intellect applies to both a property in a human person and a

---

100 In the *De Anima* I.5 of Ibn Sīnā (d. 428/1037), these stages are the material intellect (*'aql hayūlānī*), the dispositional intellect (*'aql bi-l-malaka*), the actual intellect (*'aql bi-l-fiʿl*) and the acquired intellect (*'aql mustafād*) – once the intellect is at this final stage it can conjoin with the active intellect that transcends this world, and this is the closest stage of the emanation from God to the world; see Ibn Sīnā, *al-Shifāʾ*, 49–50. The language of stages of certainty goes back to classical Sufism, not least Aḥmad al-Ghazālī, but it is well established in the Ṣafavid period and constitutes an organising principle in the work of Māzandarānī's contemporary, Muḥsin Fayḍ Kāshānī, who sets out to reconcile the truth claims and visions of reality of the philosophers and the scriptures in his *'Ayn al-yaqīn*, 1:22.

101 For example, Kāshānī, *Maqāmāt al-qalb*, 12.

102 Māzandarānī, *Sharḥ Uṣūl al-Kāfī*, 1:67–68.

separable, immaterial substance, and that he also seems to accept elements of Mullā Ṣadrā's metaphysics and epistemology. He also raises a key moral point about the function of the intellect to discern good and evil and hence to acquire rewards and recompense appropriately – a point later reiterated by Muḥammad Bāqir al-Majlisī.[103]

In his commentary on the second hadith – in which Adam is presented by Gabriel with a selection of three 'things' (intellect, faith, shame) from which to choose – Māzadarānī clarifies that the inner light and psychological faculty of the person is intended. By this light and faculty, he may distinguish between good and evil, may discern metaphysical knowledge about the origins and the end of life, and may unveil the intelligible forms hidden within *sensibilia*.[104] He further emphasises that Adam's choice of intellect is not merely a parable for all humans, but is also a demonstration of the superiority and perfection of intellects – *qua* faculty – that prophets and friends of God have. The distinction of degrees is made clearer in the commentary on the three hadiths in which the Imams deny that Muʿāwiya had intellect; that is, a true intellect that is devoid of the contamination of material attachment, that yearns for the higher intelligible purity of truth and goodness and that should motivate a person to act in accordance with what he knows.[105] Therefore, the actions of Muʿāwiya – removed from truth and goodness – belie his possession of intellect. This focus on the actions – or the outer states – is also evident in Māzandarānī's acceptance of the two-fold nature of the intellect (from the Aristotelian tradition). He glosses his commentary on the hadith, 'when a person comes to you with good traits look to the soundness of his intellect', in terms of the Aristotelian division between the theoretical and the practical intellect.[106] Thus, consistent with the complementarity of what one knows and how one acts, the exoteric and esoteric states of the person's intellect (or of the theoretical and practical intellects) must also be in harmony. This complementarity is clarified in the way in which ignorance and 'satanic' distractions (*waswās*) are understood with respect to the sound intellect and angelic inspiration located in the struggles of the human heart or the rational soul (in the commentary on the tenth hadith especially).[107] Here we see that Māzandarānī's approach and language are rather like those of Mullā Ṣadrā, but Māzandarānī seems far less disturbed by the notion of the creation of ignorance and its substantiation.

In the commentary of Māzandarānī, we see the significant influence of the approaches to reconciling hadith with philosophical and mystical

<hr>

103 Māzandarānī, *Sharḥ Uṣūl al-Kāfī*, 1:72.
104 Māzandarānī, *Sharḥ Uṣūl al-Kāfī*, 1:73.
105 Māzandarānī, *Sharḥ Uṣūl al-Kāfī*, 1:74–76.
106 Māzandarānī, *Sharḥ Uṣūl al-Kāfī*, 1:84.
107 Māzandarānī, *Sharḥ Uṣūl al-Kāfī*, 1:75, 85–86.

learning that were evident in the exegesis of Mullā Ṣadrā, except that these approaches adhere more closely to the basic requirements of commentary, as they assess the *isnād* and the scholarly transmission apparatus (i.e. regarding the narrator's reliability and the status of the hadith as *ṣaḥīḥ*) alongside a serious reconsideration in which the scripture seems to contradict philosophical doctrine.[108] If a choice has to be made between philosophy and hadith, Māzandarānī clearly chooses the latter.

al-Majlisī

In the work of al-Majlisī, this approach to the hadith material, the careful philology and consideration of the transmission and the seriousness with which he takes the hadith are evident.[109] Before turning to the commentary, it is worth discussing al-Majlisī's position on the nature of the intellect and his critique of the philosophers' positions, which appear in two sections of *Biḥār al-anwār*, not least because we can discern the themes that appear in the commentary. His encyclopaedia shares with *al-Kāfī* the order of theological discussions, beginning with the book on intellect and ignorance and the book of knowledge (*kitāb al-ʿaql wa-l-jahl, kitāb al-ʿilm*). Later in the books on cosmology (*al-samā' wa-l-ʿālam*), he returns to the question of the intellect in cosmogony and discusses the incipience of the cosmos (*ḥudūth al-ʿālam*), including a critique of philosophers for maintaining that the cosmos is eternal and not created in time and also that it comes about through a process of emanation in which intellects feature as eternal mediating causes.[110] In particular, he attacks one report that is usually cited as a hadith: 'the first thing created was the intellect', saying that this is not a hadith in the Shīʿī tradition, and furthermore, it is contradicted by both the Shīʿī tradition and even the pre-Socratics. He also cites the tradition of Thales of Miletus, (ps-)Appolonius of Tyana, and Plutarch, mentioning that the first thing in fact was water.[111] He condemns the hadith as a Sunnī fabrication (and by implication he questions the Shīʿī credentials of Shīʿī philosophers).[112] This is a classic polemical stratagem to deploy the authorities of opponents against them. He concludes that section by conceding that the intellect was the

---

108 The similarity of language and at times particular interpretations certainly suggests that Māzandarānī had not only read Mullā Ṣadrā but may well have been influenced by him.

109 Note that there are studies in Persian comparing the approaches of al-Majlisī and Mullā Ṣadrā, not least on the question of the intellect. One of the better ones is al-Kāfī, 'Mafhūm-i ʿaql'.

110 Al-Majlisī, *Biḥār al-anwār*, 54:278–309.

111 Al-Majlisī, *Biḥār al-anwār*, 54:306–308.

112 Al-Majlisī, *Biḥār al-anwār*, 1:102.

first spiritual thing created, and was clearly posterior to water because the empyrean of God itself 'sits' on water.[113]

The discussion in the earlier part of the *Biḥār* is more extensive. One sees how the text is far more than just a selection; after the citation of Qur'anic verses on a topic and then the arrangement of hadith in topical sections, he concludes with a commentarial explanation (*bayān*). He praises the intellect as a faculty that is in close conformity – as the Shīʿī tradition held – with revelation and the law. In this world, both the intellect – as a capacity and faculty in the person – and the law are perfected to allow a person to enjoy the freedom to choose to believe in God and take on their moral obligation (*taklīf*).[114] He also affirms the existence of intelligibles and unlike earlier theologians, he is not a materialist. He states that there are intelligible entities and forms, and this is why the offer to Adam (in the first hadith in the section) to choose between faith, intellect and shame should not be read literally, because it was the intelligible forms of those notions that were presented to Adam.[115] He comes close to accepting that the intellect is a 'thing' when he states that intellects vary in different people according to the perfection of their rational faculty and their propensities and dispositions.[116] However, he discusses the nature of the intellect and puts forward the six conceptions of the intellect available to him, the first two being textually admitted, the next two textually possible, but the last two, which are associated with philosophers, are to be rejected as incompatible with tradition. These are the six:[117]

1. a faculty that is capable of perceiving good and evil and distinguishing them in order to facilitate the person's fulfilment of their moral obligation;
2. a property that resides in the soul, capable of acquiring good and evil and possessing the ability to act on that knowledge;
3. a faculty that is used by people in order to make sense of their world and arrange their affairs;
4. states of a property that reside in a soul that is capable of acquiring theoretical knowledge;
5. the rational soul of humans that differentiates them from other animals (following Aristotle); and
6. an eternal, immaterial substance whose relationship to the Active Intellect is like that of the body to the soul in the human.

The fundamental problem with the sixth option is two-fold: it means that the intellect is eternal while only God is eternal and the cosmos incipient,

113 Al-Majlisī, *Biḥār al-anwār*, 54:309.
114 Al-Majlisī, *Biḥār al-anwār*, 1:83–84.
115 Al-Majlisī, *Biḥār al-anwār*, 1:86.
116 Al-Majlisī, *Biḥār al-anwār*, 1:97–98.
117 Al-Majlisī, *Biḥār al-anwār*, 1:99–101.

created *ex nihilo*, and it presumes that the intellect is immaterial, but for al-Majlisī only God is wholly immaterial. Theologically, only the souls of the Prophet and the Imams exist prior to the cosmos that comes into being in space and time with the creation of bodies.[118] The positions of philosophers are therefore rejected as mere fantasies and strange imaginings (*muwahhimāt wa-khayālāt gharība*).[119]

Al-Majlisī's voluminous commentary on *al-Kāfī* is relatively concise on the question of the intellect, which is primarily seen as a faculty that brings a person into harmony with the divine law and suppresses his carnal desires and caprice.[120] In the introduction he makes it clear that the cacophony of claims and forms of deception and deviation in his time – and in particular he accuses the Sufis – have distracted people from the true guidance and wisdom of the Imams; he sees it as his duty to reorient people to those fonts of wisdom.[121] In the commentary on the first hadith, he reiterates the six senses of intellect that he mentioned in the *Biḥār*, insisting that the intended meaning was the linguistic meaning of a faculty of understanding and grasping.[122] He also repeats his rejection of the first hadith, that the first creation was the intellect. Similarly, he rejects the philosophical gloss that the hadith about the command of God for the intellect to approach and to retreat is a metaphor for the Neoplatonic procession from the One and reversion to the One. For him, intellect in the hadith does not denote the philosophical conception of the *nous* as the first emanated being from which the spheres emanate.[123] However, in his commentary on the fourteenth hadith (on the opposing armies of the intellect and ignorance), he seems to accept the esoteric philosophical account: the intellect represents what is luminous and immaterial from God, and ignorance is an expression of the problem of embodiment in matter and the attachment of the person with matter.[124] The brevity of the commentary and al-Majlisī's insistence on the evaluation of the transmission and on philological matters is part of a strategy, it seems, to deflect attention from a philosophical reading that on the whole he rejects, except in elements of the commentary on the fourteenth hadith. Unlike Mullā Ṣadrā, al-Majlisī cannot admit to a sense of intellect that is beyond the univocal as an innate capacity for cognition of moral truths and basic beliefs about the cosmos.

---

118 Again, this may be a concession to the conflation of the first creation as intellect and the light of the Prophet; al-Majlisī, *Biḥār al-anwār*, 1:103–104.
119 Al-Majlisī, *Biḥār al-anwār*, 1:101–102.
120 Al-Majlisī, *Mirʾāt al-ʿuqūl*, 1:25–98.
121 Al-Majlisī, *Mirʾāt al-ʿuqūl*, 1:1–3.
122 Al-Majlisī, *Mirʾāt al-ʿuqūl*, 1:25–28.
123 Al-Majlisī, *Mirʾāt al-ʿuqūl*, 1:30.
124 Al-Majlisī, *Mirʾāt al-ʿuqūl*, 1:65–67.

Qummī

In one sense Qāḍī Saʿīd Qummī (d. 1107/1696) is the outlier, as his works are not formally a commentary on *al-Kāfī* but an independent treatise in which he combines commentaries on various hadiths in *al-Kāfī* and his famous commentary on al-Shaykh al-Ṣadūq's *Kitāb al-Tawḥīd*. Completed in Qum on 10 Dhū al-Qaʿda 1084/February 1674, the treatise, entitled *Mirqāt al-asrār wa-miʿrāj al-anwār* ('Stepping stones of arcana and the ascension of lights'), is on the nature of the incipience of the cosmos and deals with the Neoplatonic hypostases of intellect, soul and matter.[125] The text covers emanation as well as the description of the material cosmos and its contrast with the intelligible higher world and indeed with the intermediary 'imaginal world', all the while it links his positions with hadiths.

In this text, we see three main claims; these reoccur in his commentary on *al-Tawḥīd*. The first is that the first entity – the first emanated thing – is the intellect (*ʿaql*) that arises from the Principle (*al-mabdaʾ*), that is God and God's self-intellection from which emanates the first in the chain of being that in turn, through the act of intellection and contemplation, produces the soul and then nature and matter and so forth. He affirms the validity of the hadith that the intellect is the first creation and that it is synonymous with the light of Muhammad, the calamus, and many other scriptural names.[126] The second claim is that the intellect is wholly immaterial and it desires its like; its very nature is intellecting and seeking out the intelligible.[127] The third claim is that the intelligible is superior to the sensible and constitutes the higher 'divine' realm of existence, and in that the influence of the *Theologia Aristotelis* is clear.[128] In fact on the chain of being that connects the three worlds – of *sensibilia*, of *imagibilia* and of *intelligibilia* – he cites the *Theologia* on how the plenitude and perfection of the higher intelligible world is reflected in a less perfect manner in the sensible world, and it is the function of the imaginal world (*ʿālam al-mithāl*) to link the sensible to the intelligible through the function and substance of the human intellect.[129] The existence of the *sensibilia* is preceded by matter; for *intelligibilia*, it is preceded by intellect – and matter itself is preceded by intellect, making the latter ontologically prior and privileged.[130]

In his commentary on one of the key hadith collections rediscovered in the Ṣafavid period, the *Kitāb al-Tawḥīd* of al-Shaykh al-Ṣadūq, Qummī discusses the nature of the intellect, the intelligible world and how knowledge

---

125 This is the fourth treatise in his collection; see Qummī, *al-Arbaʿīniyyāt*, 115–156.
126 Qummī, *al-Arbaʿīniyyāt*, 118–119, 131–133.
127 Qummī, *al-Arbaʿīniyyāt*, 120.
128 Qummī, *al-Arbaʿīniyyāt*, 134, 137–138.
129 Qummī, *al-Arbaʿīniyyāt*, 146–147.
130 Qummī, *al-Arbaʿīniyyāt*, 150–151.

is produced by the intellect. These matters are necessarily about the nature of intellect with respect to God. The first issue in the discussion of God's transcendent unity relates to the affirmation of the reality of a higher intelligible realm and the existence of higher immaterial intellects. The intelligible realm is immaterial and emanates from God, beginning with the first emanated thing which is the intellect, which Qummī articulates, following (as he explicitly says) Plato, in order to gloss the meaning of the hadith phrase that 'God has nothing prior to him'.[131] The procession from the One that proceeds through the *intelligibilia* through to the *sensibilia* of this world is reversed in the reversion to the One – eschatology so to speak – when Qummī comments on the hadith about the entities of the afterlife and the move from the *sensibilia* of this world to the *intelligibilia* of the afterlife and its perfection, once again mediated by the intellect.[132] The higher intelligible – divine – realm that is both prior and posterior to our material world is populated with immaterial substances and intellects arranged in a chain of being.[133] This comes primarily in the context of commenting on God's eternity and transcendence and the nature of His creative agency – and clearly, like most Neoplatonists, Qummī thinks the distinction between creation and emanation is that of theological and philosophical language alone.[134] Desire (*shawq*) is what connects the chain of being – matter for the immaterial, the pneumatic for the noetic, and the intelligibles for other intelligibles and ultimately God.[135] Nevertheless the apophaticism of his Neoplatonism remains clear: intellects (human and otherwise) yearn for God but there is no way in which they can truly arrive, in their creaturely, contingent, emanated nature, at the very plane of the majesty of the divine.[136]

The second issue Qummī discusses concerns the nature of divine knowledge and the intellect. In this, he takes an apophatic approach and categorically says what God's knowledge is not. After complaining about the ink spilt in vain on the question of knowledge and the function of the intellect, he outlines four main theories of knowledge: (Aristotelian) representational knowledge (*'ilm ḥuṣūlī*), knowledge by presence (*ḥuḍūrī*), knowledge through an illuminative annexation (*iḍāfa ishrāqiyya*) and knowledge by union (with the active intellect).[137] These are all modes of understanding human knowledge and given the element of contingency and passivity cannot possibly be entertained for God. They all entail an

---

131 Qummī, *Sharḥ tawḥīd al-Ṣadūq*, 1:132.
132 Qummī, *Sharḥ tawḥīd al-Ṣadūq*, 1:553.
133 Qummī, *Sharḥ tawḥīd al-Ṣadūq*, 1:202–207.
134 Qummī, *Sharḥ tawḥīd al-Ṣadūq*, 1:227–232.
135 Qummī, *Sharḥ tawḥīd al-Ṣadūq*, 1:216–217.
136 Qummī, *Sharḥ tawḥīd al-Ṣadūq*, 1:236.
137 Qummī, *Sharḥ tawḥīd al-Ṣadūq*, 2:443.

element of alterity and God's dependence on an external cause. The terms intellect and knowledge are used analogically for God, but He does not depend on 'forms' that are the principal intermediary in representational knowledge either for His knowledge before things come into existence (of potential entities in the mind of God so to speak) or for actual ones.[138] This is clearly a rejection of Aristotle and even of Ibn Sīnā's notion of 'God's knowledge of particulars in a universal sense'. There are two principal reasons that God's knowledge cannot be presential: first, presence entails the existence of another and is concomitant to it, thus making God dependent, and second, presence is the state of a thing and is contrary to the perfection of the divine essence, which includes the possibility of being in states.[139] Similarly, the annexational theory does not work because all relations are dependencies, which is also true of union.[140] These two points refute the positions of Suhrawardī and Mullā Ṣadrā. Qummī also does not approve of the ascription of a distinction between general and detailed knowledge with respect to God because God's knowledge of entities is the same before they came into existence as it is while they exist – God's knowledge knows no limit.[141] The apophatic approach is also used to make sense of the denial that God is a body since bodies entail dyads of matter and spirit and, especially, of matter and intellect in which each is a substance. In a broad sense, Qummī accepts that intellects are substances either within or without humans but that the divine intellect is not a substance (either in the sense of being a hylomorphic dyad of matter and form, or in the sense of being a substrate in which accidental properties inhere). Qummī similarly accepts the emanation of intellects from God's self-intellection and in that context, he affirms the hadith that the first thing created was the *nous* (contrary to al-Majlisī).[142] On the immanent intellect, he even cites Ibn Sīnā's famous use of the parable of light verse (Q. 24:35) to describe the states of the human intellect from material passivity to intellectual activity and conjunction with the transcendent active intellect.[143] As a Neoplatonist, Qummī holds firm to a strong principle of plenitude; that is, all that is possible comes into existence and all that exists in extra-mental reality was previously in God's knowledge.[144]

Qummī's Neoplatonic commitments are clear in his commentaries affirming the substantiality of the intellect – both the transcendent and the human. In fact, as we can see from his commentary on the *Theologia*

138 Qummī, *Sharḥ tawḥīd al-Ṣadūq*, 2:444.
139 Qummī, *Sharḥ tawḥīd al-Ṣadūq*, 2:446.
140 Qummī, *Sharḥ tawḥīd al-Ṣadūq*, 2:447–448.
141 Qummī, *Sharḥ tawḥīd al-Ṣadūq*, 2:449.
142 Qummī, *Sharḥ tawḥīd al-Ṣadūq*, 2:297–298, 419–420.
143 Qummī, *Sharḥ tawḥīd al-Ṣadūq*, 2:609–611.
144 Qummī, *Sharḥ tawḥīd al-Ṣadūq*, 2:457–460.

178   SAJJAD RIZVI

Aristotelis, in which he adduces hadiths as commentarial material, his Neoplatonism is more striking and dominant than that of any other thinkers on the intellect in the Ṣafavid period.[145] His is the most prominent example of hadith exegesis as philosophy.

Conclusion

As an activity, hadith commentary in the Shīʿī tradition is a Ṣafavid phenomenon and creation motivated by the desire to rediscover and revive the Shīʿī scriptural tradition. But as we have seen with the case study of the nature of the intellect in al-Kulaynī's *Uṣūl al-Kāfī*, the act of commentary was used by various thinkers to put forward their worldview and understanding of knowledge and the use of hadith. Mullā Ṣadrā's philosophical exegesis that was premised on a holistic understanding of the pursuit of wisdom, in which hadith, scripture and metaphysical learning were raw materials for the instrument of the human intellect to discern, was highly influential and effective. Many disagreed, and to an extent al-Majlisī's hostile response to the philosophical appropriation of hadith had precursors in Mīrzā Rafīʿā Nāʾinī (d. 1082/1672), a philosopher who resisted a straightforward equation of the intellect as a faculty in the hadith with the philosophical account of an immaterial substance. Nāʾinī insisted that the hadith referred to a state in the soul that is capable of discerning good and evil in order to facilitate the person's fulfilment of their moral obligation.[146] Some authors even attempted to combine the various positions and did not wish to adjudicate between them. This is the case of Muḥammad Hādī Shīrāzī (d. 1081/1670) and his eleven senses of the intellect that range from immaterial, higher celestial beings, to the immaterial human rational soul, the theoretical and the practical intellect, and the moral compass within the human.[147] A more intriguing example is the little known eleventh-/seventeenth-century figure Majdhūb-i Tabrīzī, the only commentator who extensively cites the positions of all the commentators before him but somewhat ironically (given his name, Majdhūb, which means 'enraptured' and suggests a Sufi state) was hostile to Sufi and philosophical interpretations of the nature of the intellect in the hadith; he cites Mullā Ṣadrā extensively, but critically.[148] To a large extent one might argue that al-Majlisī won the day – his commentary seems to be the most widely used and available today. Nevertheless, the commentary tradition on *al-Kāfī* demonstrates that the imprint of Mullā Ṣadrā's holistic approach won adherents –

145 For a discussion on this, see my 'Neoplatonism Revised in the Light of the Imams'.
146 Nāʾinī, *al-Ḥāshiya ʿalā uṣūl al-Kāfī*, 41–43.
147 Shīrāzī, *al-Kashf al-wāfī*, 1:32–39.
148 Majdhūb-i Tabrīzī, *al-Hadāyā*, 1:194–196.

and thinkers in the period continued to grapple with a central problem: how can one comment on scripture without imposing one's learning and preconceptions on it? In what sense can exegesis avoid the temptations of eisegesis? In this sense, we might say that the philosophically and mystically inclined, as well as the more exoteric-minded, were unable to extricate themselves from the very act of interpretation.

Bibliography

Afandī, ʿAbdallāh. *Riyāḍ al-ʿulamā' wa-ḥiyāḍ al-fuḍalā'*. Edited by Aḥmad al-Ḥusaynī. 6 vols. Qum: Maktabat Āyatullāh al-Marʿashī al-Najafī, 1981.

Ahmad, Saiyid Nizamuddin. 'Twelver Šīʿī ḥadīṯ: From Tradition to Contemporary Evaluations.' *Oriente Moderno* 82 (2002): 125–145.

al-ʿAlawī, Aḥmad. *al-Ḥāshiya ʿalā uṣūl al-Kāfī*. Edited by Ṣādiq Ḥusaynī Ashkiwarī. Qum: Dār al-Ḥadīth, 1387 Sh/2008.

al-ʿAlawī, Badr al-Dīn. *al-Ḥāshiya ʿalā uṣūl al-Kāfī*. Edited by ʿAlī al-Fāḍilī. Qum: Dār al-Ḥadīth, 1389 Sh/2010.

ʿAlī al-Riḍā. *Fiqh al-Riḍā*. Qum: Muʾassasat Āl al-Bayt li-Iḥyāʾ al-Turāth, 1406/1986.

ʿAlī al-Riḍā. *al-Risāla al-Dhahabiyya: Il Trattato Aurea sulla medicina attribuito all'Imām ʿAlī al-Riḍā*. Edited and translated by Fabrizio Speziale and Giorgio Guirini. Palermo: Officina di studi medievali, 2009.

ʿAlī al-Riḍā. *Ṣaḥīfat al-Riḍā*. Edited by Jawād Qayyūmī Iṣfahānī. Qum: Dalīl-i Mā, 1373 Sh/1995.

al-ʿĀmilī, Bahāʾ al-Dīn. *Arbaʿūna ḥadīthan li-Bahāʾ al-Dīn al-ʿĀmilī maʿ taʿlīqāt hāmma li-Muḥammad Ismāʿīl Māzandarānī Khājūʾī*. Edited by Mahdī Rajāʾī. Qum: Muʾassasa-yi ʿĀshūrā, 1384 Sh/2005.

al-ʿĀmilī, Bahāʾ al-Dīn. *Ḥāshiyat al-Faqīh*. Edited by Fāris Ḥassūn. Qum: Maktabat Āyatullāh al-Marʿashī al-Najafī, 1382 Sh/2003.

al-ʿĀmilī, Bahāʾ al-Dīn. 'al-Wajīza fī ʿilm al-dirāya.' Edited by Mājid al-Gharbāwī. *Turāthunā* 32–33 (1413/1992): 389–439.

al-ʿĀmilī, al-Ḥusayn b. ʿAbd al-Ṣamad. *Wuṣūl al-akhyār ilā uṣūl al-akhbār*. Edited by ʿAbd al-Laṭīf Kuhkamaraʾī. Qum: Majmaʿ al-Dhakhāʾir al-Islāmiyya, 1401/1981.

Amir-Moezzi, Mohammad Ali. *The Silent Qurʾan & the Speaking Qurʾan*. Translated by Eric Ormsby. New York: Columbia University Press, 2016.

al-Ardabīlī, Muḥammad b. ʿAlī. *Jāmiʿ al-ruwāt*. 2 vols. Qum: Maktabat Āyatullāh al-Marʿashī al-Najafī, 1403/1983.

Asatryan, Mushegh. *Controversies in Formative Shiʿi Islam: The Ghulāt Muslims and their Beliefs*. London: Tauris in association with the Institute of Ismaili Studies, 2017.

Astarābādī, Muḥammad Amīn. *al-Ḥāshiya ʿalā uṣūl al-Kāfī*. Edited by ʿAlī al-Fāḍilī. Qum: Dār al-Ḥadīth, 1387 Sh/2008.

Aʿzamī, Muhammad Muṣṭafā. *Studies in Early Hadith Literature*. Indianapolis: Muslim Trust Publications, 1972.

al-Baḥrānī, ʿAbdallāh. *ʿAwālim al-ʿulūm wa-l-maʿārif wa-l-aḥwāl min al-āyāt wa-l-akhbār wa-l-aqwāl*. 11 vols. Qum: Madrasat al-Imām al-Mahdī, 1404/1984.

al-Baḥrānī, Maytham. *Sharḥ Nahj al-balāgha*. 5 vols. Repr. Qum: Daftar-i Tablīghāt-i Islāmī, 1362 Sh/1983.

Bandy, Hunter. 'Beyond a Mountain of Light: Niẓām al-Dīn Gīlānī and Shīʿī Naturalism between Safavid Iran and the Deccan.' PhD dissertation, Duke University, 2019.

Bar-Asher, Meir. 'The Qurʾān Commentary Ascribed to Imam Ḥasan al-ʿAskarī.' *Jerusalem Studies in Arabic and Islam* 24 (2000): 358–379.

al-Barqī, Aḥmad. *Kitāb al-Maḥāsin*. Edited by Jalāl al-Dīn Ḥusaynī. Tehran: Dār al-Kutub al-Islāmiyya, 1370/1950.

al-Bursī, Ḥāfiẓ Rajab. *Mashāriq anwār al-yaqīn fī asrār Amīr al-muʾminīn*. Beirut: Muʾassasat al-Aʿlamī, 1971.

al-Bursī, Ḥāfiẓ Rajab. *Mashāriq anwār al-yaqīn fī asrār Amīr al-muʾminīn*. Edited by ʿAbd al-Ghaffār Māzandarānī. Qum: Intishārāt al-Sharīf al-Raḍī, 1384 Sh/2005.

Cook, Michael. 'The Opponents of Writing of Tradition in Early Islam.' *Arabica* 44 (1997): 437–530.

Dīmagār-Gurāb, Muḥsin. 'Rivāyat-i *Anā al-nuqṭa taḥta al-bā* dar tarāzū-yi naqd.' *ʿUlūm-i ḥadīs* 77 (Pāyīz 1394 Sh/2015): 81–103.

Dirāyatī, Muṣṭafā (ed). *Fihristvāra-yi dast-navisht-hā-yi Īrān (Dinā)*. 12 vols. Mashhad: Muʾassasa-yi farhangī u pazhūhishī-yi al-Jawād, 1389 Sh/2010.

Ehteshami, Amin. 'The Four Books of Shiʿi Hadith: From Inception to Consolidation.' *Islamic Law and Society* 29 (2022): 225–279. Online: doi:10.1163/15685195-28040002.

El-Shamsy, Ahmed. 'Al-Ghazālī's Teleology and the Galenic Tradition.' In Frank Griffel (ed.), *Islam and Rationality: Studies on al-Ghazālī*, vol. 2, pp. 90–112. Leiden: Brill, 2016.

al-Fārābī, Abū Naṣr. *Épître sur l'intellect (Risāla fī al-ʿaql)*. Edited and translated by Philippe Vallat. Paris: Les belles lettres, 2012.

al-Ḥasan al-ʿAskarī. *al-Tafsīr al-mansūb ilā al-Imām al-ʿAskarī*. Edited by Muḥammad Bāqir al-Abṭaḥī. Qum: Muʾassasat al-Imām al-Mahdī, 1433/2012.

al-Ḥillī, Najm al-Dīn. *Sharāʾiʿ al-islām fī masāʾil al-ḥalāl wa-l-ḥarām*. 4 vols. Tehran: Intishārāt-i Istaqlāl, 1409/1989.

al-Ḥurr al-ʿĀmilī. *Wasāʾil al-shīʿa*. 17 vols. Qum: Muʾassasat al-Nashr al-Islāmī, 1384 Sh/2005.

Ibn Abī al-Ḥadīd. *Sharḥ Nahj al-balāgha*. Edited by Muḥammad Abū al-Faḍl Ibrāhīm. 20 vols. Beirut: Dār al-Jīl, 1987.

Ibn Abī Jumhūr al-Aḥsāʾī. *Mujlī mirʾāt al-munjī fī al-kalām wa-l-ḥikmatayn wa-l-taṣawwuf*. Edited by Riḍā Yaḥyā Pūrfārmad. 5 vols. Beirut: Jamiʿat Ibn Abī Jumhūr al-Aḥsāʾī li-Iḥyāʾ al-Turāth, 2013.

Ibn Shahrāshūb. *Maʿālim al-ʿulamāʾ*. 4 vols. Najaf: al-Maṭbaʿa al-Ḥaydariyya, 1961.

Ibn Sīnā. *al-Shifāʾ: al-nafs*. Edited by Fazlur Rahman. Oxford: Oxford University Press, 1959.

Ibn Ṭāwūs, *Kashf al-muḥajja fī thamarat al-muhja*. Edited by Muḥammad al-Ḥassūn. Qum: Bustān-i Kitāb, 1371 Sh/1992.

Jaʿfar al-Ṣādiq. *Kitāb al-Ihlīlijā bi-riwāyat Abī Muḥammad al-Mufaḍḍal ibn ʿUmar al-Juʿfī wa-bi-dhaylihi shurūḥ wa-taʿlīqāt al-ʿAllāma al-Majlisī*. Edited by Qays al-ʿAṭṭār. Qum: Intishārāt-i Dalīl-i Mā, 1385 Sh/2006.

Ja'far al-Ṣādiq. *Kitāb al-Tawḥīd amlā'ahu ilā tilmīdhihi al-Mufaḍḍal ibn 'Umar.* Beirut: Dār al-Murtaḍā, 2010.

al-Jalālī, Muḥammad Riḍā. *Tadwīn al-sunna al-sharīfa.* Qum: Maktab al-I'lām al-Islāmī, 1413/1992.

al-Jazā'irī, Ni'matallāh. *Kashf al-asrār fī sharḥ al-istibṣār.* Edited by Ṭayyib al-Jazā'irī. 3 vols. Qum: Mu'assasat Dār al-Kitāb, 1408/1988.

al-Jazā'irī, Ni'matallāh. *Nūr al-anwār fī sharḥ al-Ṣaḥīfa al-sajjādiyya.* Beirut: Dār al-Maḥajja al-Bayḍā', 2000.

al-Kāfī, 'Abd al-Ḥusayn. ''Mafhūm-i 'aql az dīdgāh-i dū shāriḥ-i uṣūl-i Kāfī.' *'Ulūm-i ḥadīs* 26 (Zamistān 1381 Sh/2003): 96–119.

Kāshānī, Muḥsin Fayḍ. *'Ayn al-yaqīn.* Edited by Fāliḥ 'Abd al-Razzāq al-'Ubaydī. 2 vols. Qum: Anwār al-Hudā, 1428/2007.

Kāshānī, Muḥsin Fayḍ. *Maqāmāt al-qalb.* Qum: Dhawī al-Qurba, 1426/2005.

Kāshānī, Muḥsin Fayḍ. *al-Wāfī.* 24 vols. Isfahan: Madrasat Amīr al-Mu'minīn, 1430/2009.

Kaukua, Jari. 'The Intellect in Mullā Ṣadrā's Commentary on *Uṣūl al-Kāfī*.' In Saiyid Nizamuddin Ahmad and Sajjad Rizvi (eds), *Philosophy and the Intellectual Life in Shi'ah Islam*, 158–183. London: Shi'ah Institute, 2017.

Khwānsārī, Muḥammad Bāqir. *Rawḍāt al-jannāt fī tarājim al-'ulamā' wa-l-sādāt.* 9 vols. Qum: Maktaba-yi Ismā'īliyān, 1971.

Kohlberg, Etan. ''al-Uṣūl al-arba'umi'a.' *Jerusalem Studies in Arabic and Islam* 10 (1987): 128–166.

al-Kulaynī, Abū Ja'far. *al-Kāfī.* Edited by Muḥammad Ḥusayn Dirāyatī. 15 vols. Qum: Dār al-Ḥadīth, 1387 Sh/2008.

Mahdawī-Rād, Muḥammad 'Alī. *Tadwīn al-ḥadīth 'ind al-shī'a al-imāmiyya.* Tehran: Hastī-Numā, 1394 Sh/2015.

Majdhūb-i Tabrīzī, Muḥammad. *al-Hadāyā li-shī'at a'immat al-hudā.* Edited by Muḥammad Ḥusayn Dirāyatī and Ghulām-Ḥusayn Qayṣariyya-hā. 4 vols. Qum: Dār al-Ḥadīth, 1389 Sh/2010.

al-Majlisī, Muḥammad Bāqir. *Biḥār al-anwār al-jāmi'a li-durar akhbār al-a'imma al-aṭhār.* 110 vols. Beirut: Dār Iḥyā' al-Turāth al-'Arabī, 1983.

al-Majlisī, Muḥammad Taqī. *Lawāmi'-yi ṣāḥibqirānī.* 8 vols. Qum: Kitābfurūshī-yi Ismā'īliyān, 1414/1994.

al-Majlisī, Muḥammad Bāqir. *Mir'āt al-'uqūl fī sharḥ akhbār Āl al-rasūl.* 26 vols. Qum: Dār al-Kutub al-Islāmiyya, 1370 Sh/1991.

al-Majlisī, Muḥammad Taqī. *Rawḍat al-muttaqīn fī sharḥ Man lā yaḥḍuruhu al-Faqīh.* 20 vols. Qum: Dār al-Kitāb al-Islāmī, 1387 Sh/2008.

al-Majlisī, Muḥammad Taqī. *Sharḥ al-Ṣaḥīfa al-sajjādiyya.* Edited by 'Alī al-Fāḍilī. Qum: Pazhūhishgāh-i Bāqir al-'Ulūm, 1388 Sh/2009.

Maybudī, Mīr Ḥusayn. *Sharḥ-i dīwān mansūb bih Amīr al-mu'minīn.* Edited by Ḥasan Raḥmānī and Sayyid Ibrāhīm Ashk-Shīrīn. Tehran: Mīrāth-i Maktūb, 1379 Sh/2000.

Māzandarānī, Muḥammad Ṣāliḥ. *Sharḥ Uṣūl al-Kāfī.* Edited by 'Alī 'Āshūr. 20 vols. Beirut: Mu'assasat al-Tārīkh al-'Arabī, 2008.

Mīr Dāmād. *al-Rawāshiḥ al-samāwiyya.* Edited by Ghulām-Ḥusayn Qayṣarīya-hā and Ni'matallāh al-Jalīlī. Qum: Dār al-Ḥadīth, 1380 Sh/2001.

Mīr Dāmād. *Sharḥ al-Ṣaḥīfa al-sajjādiyya*. Edited by Mahdī al-Rajā'ī. Isfahan: Maktabat Walī al-ʿAṣr, 1422/2001.

Mīr Dāmād. *al-Taʿlīqāt ʿalā kitāb al-Kāfī*. Edited by Mahdī al-Rajā'ī. Qum: Sayyid Jamāl al-Dīn Mīrdāmādī/Maktabat Āyatullāh al-Marʿashī al-Najafī, 1403/1982.

Nā'inī, Rafīʿ al-Dīn. *al-Ḥāshiya ʿalā Uṣūl al-Kāfī*. Edited by Muḥammad Ḥusayn Dirāyatī. Qum: Dār al-Ḥadīth, 1387 Sh/2008.

Newman, Andrew. 'Bāqir al-Majlisī and Islamicate Medicine II: the *Risāla dhahabiyya* in the *Biḥār al-anwār*.' In Mohammad Ali Amir-Moezzi et al. (eds), *Le Shī'isme imāmite quarante ans après: hommage à Etan Kohlberg*, 349–361. Turnhout: Brepols, 2009.

Newman, Andrew. 'The Recovery of the Past, Ibn Bābawayh, Muḥammad Bāqir al-Majlisī and Safawid Medical Discourse.' *Iran: Journal of the British Institute of Persian Studies* 50 (2012): 109–127.

Pourjavady, Reza and Sabine Schmidtke. 'An Eastern Renaissance? Greek Philosophy under the Safavids (16th–18th Centuries AD).' *Intellectual History of the Islamicate World* 3 (2015): 248–290.

Qāsimī, Raḥīm. *Muḥaqqiq-i Majlisī*. 2 vols. Qum: Majmaʿ al-Dhakhā'ir al-Islāmiyya, 2015.

Quhpā'ī, ʿInāyatallāh. *Majmaʿ al-rijāl*. Edited by Ḍiyā' al-Dīn Iṣfahānī. 7 vols. Isfahan: N.p., 1384/1964.

Qummī, Qāḍī Saʿīd. *al-Arbaʿīniyyāt li-kashf anwār al-qudsiyyāt*. Edited by Najafqulī Ḥabībī. Tehran: Mīrāth-i Maktūb, 1381 Sh/2002.

Qummī, Qāḍī Saʿīd. *Sharḥ tawḥīd al-Ṣadūq*. Edited by Najafqulī Ḥabībī. 3 vols. Tehran: Wizārat al-Thaqāfa wa-l-Irshād al-Islāmī, 1380 Sh/2001.

Rizvi, Sajjad. 'Neoplatonism Revised in the Light of the Imams.' In Peter Adamson (ed.), *Classical Arabic Philosophy: Sources and Receptions*, 177–208. London: The Warburg Institute, 2007.

al-Ṣadūq, Ibn Bābawayh al-Qummī. *ʿIlal al-sharā'iʿ*. Edited by Muḥammad Ṣādiq Āl Baḥr al-ʿUlūm. Rept. 2 vols. Qum: al-Maktaba al-Ḥaydariyya, 1383 Sh/2004.

al-Ṣadūq, Ibn Bābawayh al-Qummī. *Maʿānī al-akhbār*. Edited by ʿAlī-Akbar Ghaffārī. Rept. Beirut: Dār al-Murtaḍā, 1979.

al-Ṣaffār al-Qummī. *Basā'ir al-darajāt*. Edited by Muḥammad Bāqir Abṭaḥī. Qum: Madrasat al-Imām al-Mahdī, 1431/2010.

al-Shahīd al-Awwal (I), Ibn Makkī al-Jizzinī. *Dhikrā al-shīʿa ilā aḥkām al-sharīʿa*. 2 vols. Qum: Mu'assasat Āl al-Bayt li-Iḥyā' al-Turāth, 1419/1998.

al-Shahīd al-Thānī (II), Zayn al-Dīn al-ʿĀmilī. *Rasā'il al-Shahīd al-thānī*. Edited by Riḍā Mukhtārī and Ḥasan Shāfiʿī. 5 vols. In *Mawsūʿat al-Shahīd al-thānī*. Qum: Markaz Iḥyā' al-Turāth, 1434/2013.

al-Shahīd al-Thānī (II), Zayn al-Dīn al-ʿĀmilī. *al-Riʿāya fī ʿilm al-dirāya*. Edited by ʿAbd al-Ḥusayn Muḥammad al-Baqqāl. Qum: Maktabat Āyatullāh al-Marʿashī al-Najafī, 1408/1988.

Shīrāzī, ʿAlī Khān Madanī. *Riyāḍ al-sālikīn fī sharḥ Ṣaḥīfat Sayyid al-sājidīn*. 7 vols. Qum: Mu'assassat al-Nashr al-Islāmī, 1385 Sh/2006.

Shīrāzī, Muḥammad Hādī. *al-Kashf al-wāfī fī sharḥ uṣūl al-Kāfī*. Edited by ʿAlī Fāḍilī. Qum: Dār al-Ḥadīth, 1387 Sh/2008.

Shīrāzī, Muḥammad Shāh Dārābī. *Riyāḍ al-ʿārifīn fī sharḥ Ṣaḥīfat al-Sājidīn*. Tehran: Dār al-Uswa, 1421/2000.

Shīrāzī, Mullā Ṣadrā. *al-Ḥikma al-mutaʿāliya fī al-asfār al-ʿaqliyya al-arbaʿa*. Edited by Muḥammad Khāminihī. 9 vols. Tehran: Intishārāt-i Bunyād-i Ḥikmat-i Islāmī-yi Ṣadrā, 1380–83 Sh/2001–4.

Shīrāzī, Mullā Ṣadrā. *Sharḥ Uṣūl al-Kāfī*. Edited by Riḍā Ustādī. 5 vols. Tehran: Bunyād-i Ḥikmat-i Islāmī-yi Ṣadrā, 1384 Sh/2005.

Shushtarī, Nūrallāh. *al-Ṣawārim al-muhriqa fī naqd al-Ṣawaʾiq al-muhriqa*. Edited by Jalāl al-Dīn Ḥusaynī. Tehran: Chāpkhāna-yi Nahżat, 1367 Sh/1988.

al-Ṭūsī, Abū Jaʿfar. *al-Istibṣār fī mā ikhtulifa min al-akhbār*. Edited by ʿAlī-Akbar Ghaffārī. 4 vols. Rept. Qum: Dār al-Ḥadīth, 1380 Sh/2001.

al-Ṭūsī, Abū Jaʿfar. *Tahdhīb al-aḥkām*. Edited by ʿAlī-Akbar Ghaffārī. 10 vols. Rept. Tehran: Dār al-Kutub al-Islāmiyya, 1385 Sh/2006.

al-Uṣūl al-sittat ʿashar. Edited by Ḥasan Muṣṭafawī. Qum: Muʾassasat al-Nashr al-Islāmī, 1415/1994.

Vilozny, Roy. *Constructing a Worldview: al-Barqī’s Role in the Making of Early Shīʿī Faith*. Turnhout: Brepols, 2017.

PART II

Modern Recollections and Reimaginings

CHAPTER 7

Contesting Ḥanafī Thought in a Twentieth-century Turkish Hadith Commentary

Susan Gunasti

In a widely circulated 2008 article the British Broadcasting Corporation (BBC) reported on a Turkish hadith project that promised to be 'a revolutionary reinterpretation of Islam'. This project, spearheaded by the Diyanet[1] and intended to be a hadith compilation suitable for the modern period, was still in the works at the time of the BBC story, which invoked the 'revolutionary nature' of the project and claimed that the compilation would bring about the 'reformation of Islam'.[2] The Diyanet responded to the story in two ways: in the short term, its head issued an official statement to counter and reject the claims of the BBC article and, in the long term, it reissued (in 2019) an early republican (1923–1938) hadith project, a Turkish translation entitled *Sahih-i Buhari Muhtasarı: Tecrid-i Sarih Tercümesi* (An Abridgement of *Ṣaḥīḥ* al-Bukhārī: A Translation of *al-Tajrīd al-Ṣarīḥ*), first published between 1928 and 1948.[3] The 'revolutionary' hadith project

---

1 The Diyanet is a governmental department charged with regulating religious affairs; its jurisdiction and power was dynamic over the period covered in this chapter. For this reason, I maintain the Turkish for Diyanet. For the pre-1950 period, 'Diyanet' is commonly translated as 'Directorate of Religious Affairs', but after 1950, it was infelicitously translated by the Diyanet themselves as 'Presidency of Religious Affairs'; on the nature of these changes, see Kara, *Cumhuriyet Türkiyesi'nde bir Mesele Olarak İslam*, 55–64. On the 'Directorate of Religious Affairs', s.v. 'Diyanet İşleri Başkanlığı,' in *Türkiye Diyanet Vakfı İslam Ansiklopedisi* (hereinafter *TDVİA*), (particularly 455–456 on the history of its early years).

2 Daniel Brown mentions this hadith project and the BBC report on it in his discussion of modern hadith reform efforts; Brown, 'Reappraisal', 315–316.

3 On the BBC report, see <http://news.bbc.co.uk/2/hi/europe/7264903.stm> (accessed 29 April 2018). For the text of the response to the BBC, see <http://www.hikem.net/basin-aciklamatr.pdf> (accessed 29 April 2018); for the Diyanet's report about the completion of its publication of the reissue of the Babanzade–Miras hadith work, see <http://www.

was completed in 2011; work to reissue the early republican hadith translation project began at the end of 2012.[4]

This incident reflects the BBC's and the Diyanet's understanding (or lack of understanding) of the relationship between texts and religion. The BBC story betrays a Protestant understanding of religion and a Western attitude that if only Muslims had access to the proper texts Islam would be compatible with modernity. The BBC's invocation of a reformation reinforces this textual attitude toward religion, an attitude that obscures the importance of the many vibrant religious cultures throughout the Muslim world; further, it overlooks the fact that while texts are important to its intellectual tradition, Islam is more than its texts. The Diyanet's defence, that is, its focus on an early republican project, is peculiar. With this response, the Diyanet sought to reassure its domestic audience by demonstrating that it was not embarking on a revision of the hadith, and that the Turkish state had already engaged in a similar compilation of the hadith for the modern period. The Diyanet invoked the authority of a twentieth-century text for its twenty-first-century project – the published hadith compilation made this continuity explicit – to assuage concerns about textual revisionism.[5]

In February 1925, the Turkish parliament approved a bill commissioning translation of the Qur'an and hadith to create a new canon in the recently established Turkish republic in the wake of the dissolution of the Ottoman Empire. The hadith translation project utilised the hadith collections of al-Bukhārī, Muslim and al-Tirmidhī for the translation.[6] Parliament's concern to commission these texts resulted from its desire to produce vernacular religious texts; this desire had been gaining momentum since the nineteenth century. The Diyanet managed the project and initially commissioned Babanzade Ahmet Naim (1872–1934) to translate the hadith and engaged two other men to translate and comment on the Qur'an (Mehmet Akif [d. 1936] and Elmalılı Muhammed Hamdi Yazır [d. 1942], respectively). The text that resulted from this commission, *Sahih-i Buhari Muhtasarı: Tecrid-i Sarih Tercümesi* (1928–1948), was based solely on the

diyanet.gov.tr/tr/icerik/unlu-hadis-kitabi-sahih-i-buhari-muhtasari-tecrid-i-sarihin-yeni-baskisinda-son-asamaya-gelindi/6855> (accessed 29 April 2018).

4 For six years a commission worked on the newer hadith compilation that was the subject of the BBC report. The seven-volume work was first published in 2011 and has been reissued several times since. On the start date of the work on the reissue of the early republican hadith translation project, see Ez-Zebidi, *Sahih-i Buhari Muhtasarı*, 1:20.

5 Komisyon, *Hadislerle İslam*, 1:42.

6 'İkinci Celse', in *Meclis-i Meb'usan Zabıt Ceridesi* 14 (year 2): 249–263. The debate was also summarised in 'Yeni Bir Heyet-i İlmiye', in *Sebil'ür-Reşad* 25, no. 640 (26 Şubat 1341) [26 February 1925], 249–251. The focus of the discussion was on translating the Qur'an; the translation of the hadith collections was only a secondary concern; no rationale was provided for the selection of these particular works.

work of al-Bukhārī. Babanzade died shortly after completing a draft of the third volume in 1934, at which point Kamil Miras (1875–1957) took over translation work on the project. Ultimately, the hadith compilation was more than a translation, it was a commentary described as a translation. In this chapter I use the translation of Babanzade and Miras as a vehicle with which to study hadith commentary in the late Ottoman and early republican periods.

Selecting a Scholar

The state had a great interest in vernacular religious text projects; the Diyanet oversaw these types of projects. In this case, the Diyanet selected Babanzade as the translator, a choice that was a little surprising because, though he had an excellent reputation (surpassing that of many non-Arab Ottoman scholars) for his knowledge of Arabic, he was not a specialist in hadith. Though Babanzade's publications included works of hadith, his main scholarly reputation derived from his knowledge of philosophy.

The real and perceived expertise of the author in the subject matter contributes to the religious authority of the work. From a scholarly perspective, a better choice for the project would have been Babanzade's contemporary, Muhammed Zahit Kevseri (Muḥammad Zāhid al-Kawtharī) (1879–1952), an Ottoman scholar who was foremost among hadith scholars in the Muslim world at the time. But the Diyanet was unlikely to choose Kevseri, who fled the empire before its collapse and eventually settled in Egypt (as did others from among the late Ottoman *ulamā*). Over the course of his professional career in the late Ottoman period, Kevseri had run into conflict with those who emerged to lead the republic, thus, the leadership at the Diyanet, which was a governmental department, did not choose Kevseri for the task.

Rather than choosing the most qualified individual for the task, it appeared that the Diyanet was treating this as a translation project. Though the Diyanet had reasons for making the decision it did, its emphasis on choosing a translator rather than a hadith specialist was in line with Ottoman approaches to hadith commentary. Much of the late Ottoman hadith commentary activity took place in translations rather than as line-by-line explications, interlinear annotations or marginal annotations. The most prominent examples of this translation approach can be seen in the numerous translations of the forty hadith (*arbaʿīn*) collections, many of which were translations from Persian into Ottoman Turkish.[7]

Babanzade would have agreed that he was not a scholar of hadith on a par with Kevseri, but at the time he accepted this commission he had been working on translating hadith for nearly two decades. His contributions

7 Karahan, *İslam-Türk Edebiyatında Kırk Hadis.*

to Ottoman hadith culture were important; apart from his many translations of hadith in journals, in 1925 he also translated Yaḥyā b. Sharaf al-Nawawī's *Arbaʿīn* into Ottoman Turkish.[8] He first began translating from Aḥmad b. Aḥmad al-Zabīdī's (d. 893/1488) *al-Tajrīd al-ṣarīḥ* for the Islamic journals *Sırat-ı Müstakim* in 1910 and, after it ceased publication in 1912, in *Kelime-i Tayyibe*. In this regard, Babanzade was part of and contributed to the two prominent strands of Ottoman hadith culture with his translations from al-Bukhārī and of the forty hadith genre.[9] Babanzade negotiated the position he found himself in – of not being an expert in hadith and yet having a strong interest in the corpus – by referring to himself as a *mütercim* (translator) in his hadith works.

Babanzade died in 1934 and the Diyanet sought a replacement to complete the project. The Diyanet's immediate need was to find someone to edit the incomplete draft of the third volume that Babanzade had submitted prior to his death. Miras was a high-ranking member of the late Ottoman *ʿulamāʾ* and had held many positions in the Istanbul madrasa system. He was a political veteran who did not have a reputation for his knowledge of hadith. However, at this point, the Diyanet must have been desperate to find a replacement for Babanzade. By 1935 – a decade after parliament approved the bill to commission vernacular religious texts – two of the three original men who had taken up commissions had dropped out (Akif by choice and Babanzade as a result of his death), and only two volumes of the hadith compilation and one volume of the Qur'an commentary and translation project had been published. The leadership at the Diyanet faced pressure from the government to see progress on the publication of the works;[10] this likely influenced their decision to hire Miras in the wake of Babanzade's death. Miras, who had been a member of parliament in 1925 and had voted in favour of commissioning translations of the Qur'an and hadith, now found himself working on one of those very projects.

Hadith in the Late Ottoman Empire and the Early Turkish Republic

In the late Ottoman period the madrasa was an important venue for hadith education. In the hierarchical organisation of the Istanbul madrasa system from the eleventh/seventeenth century to the reforms of 1914, there were twelve categories; the highest level for a madrasa teacher was that of

---

8 Babanzade, *Kirk Hadis.*

9 I will elaborate on these two trends in a future work.

10 See <http://www.yenisafak.com/hayat/tefsiri-birak-turkce-meal-yaz-2654024> (accessed 28 April 2018); the government sent a letter to pressure the Diyanet to publish the vernacular Qur'an commentary.

instructor at the Darü'l-hadis-i Süleymaniye.[11] In the Ottoman madrasa system, Ḥasan b. Muḥammad al-Ṣaghānī's (d. 650/1252) *Mashāriq al-anwār al-Nabawiyya*, Ḥusayn b. Mas'ūd al-Baghawī's (d. 510/1117 or 516/1122) *Maṣābīḥ al-sunna*, Muslim b. al-Ḥajjaj's (d. 261/875) *Ṣaḥīḥ Muslim* and Muḥammad b. Ismā'īl al-Bukhārī's *Ṣaḥīḥ al-Bukhārī*, and commentaries on these works, were variously read in the study of hadith.[12] And Ibn Ḥajar al-'Asqalānī's *al-Nukhbat al-fikr* was one of the main texts used for the study of *uṣūl al-ḥadīth* among the Ottomans.[13]

In order to understand the study of hadith in the late Ottoman context and the making of hadith specialists (*muḥaddiths*), it is not enough to look at the madrasa curriculum because there were numerous opportunities to study hadith beyond the formal setting of the madrasa. For example, there was a tradition of live recitations of hadith at mosques.[14] Libraries built in the twelfth/eighteenth century featured rooms specifically designated for hadith recitations.[15] And, as further evidence of the vibrancy of hadith study outside the madrasa system, we find *majālis* in which hadith were also studied.[16] The imperial palace was also a site for hadith study; in the reign of Sultan Abdülhamit II (r. 1876–1909), the Yıldız Palace (the vast

11 In the Ottoman madrasa system there were three broad divisions: the madrasas of Istanbul, the madrasas of Edirne and Bursa (early capitals of the empire) and all the other madrasas. On the twelve levels of the twentieth-century Istanbul madrasa system, and the eleven levels of the eleventh-/seventeenth-century Istanbul madrasa system, see Uzunçarşılı, *Osmanlı Devletinin İlmiye Teşkilatı*, 271–272. In the twelfth/eighteenth century, a new level was introduced to the Istanbul system, but the highest level from the eleventh/seventeenth century onward remained the Darü'l-hadis-i Süleymaniye (est. 1557). In the twentieth century, the Edirne and Bursa madrasa systems were organised in the same way as that of Istanbul, with the Darü'l-hadis being the highest (see Uzunçarşılı, *Osmanlı Devletinin İlmiye Teşkilatı*, 273). The twelve-part division of the Istanbul madrasa system was in place from the twelfth/eighteenth century until the madrasa reforms of 1914. For a general overview of the Ottoman Darü'l-hadis, see Gül, *Osmanlı Medreselerinde*. On the Darü'l-hadis-i Süleymaniye, see Çiftçi, *Süleymaniye Darulhadisi*.
12 Uzunçarşılı, *Osmanlı Devletinin İlmiye Teşkilatı*, 28–29.
13 On the role of *Nukhbat al-fikr* in the study of *uṣūl al-ḥadīth* among the Ottomans, see Sadık, 'Osmanlı Devrinde', 127–136.
14 Regarding recitations at mosques during the nineteenth century in Istanbul, see Karacabey, 'Osmanlı Madrasalerinin Son Dönemi'nde Hadis Öğretimi', 165. For an example from late nineteenth-century Konya, see Sadık, 'Les Lieux de L'Enseignement', 11.
15 On the construction of rooms specifically for hadith recitation at the Hagia Sophia and Fatih Libraries in twelfth-/eighteenth-century Istanbul, see Sezer, 'The Architecture of Bibiliophilia', 66 and 154 (respectively). This trend of library construction declined in the late nineteenth century (Sezer, 'The Architecture of Bibiliophilia', 264–266).
16 Al-Kawtharī, *Maqalāt al-Kawtharī*, 556–557. Kevseri provides several examples from the career of a renowned twelfth-/eighteenth-century scholar, Gelenbevi İsmail Efendi (d. 1791). He provides examples of various *majālis* that he and Muṣṭafā b. Muḥammad al-Safarjalānī (d. 1765) attended in the presence of leading officials.

complex that included the residences of the late Ottoman sultans) formally appointed a scholar to teach hadith from al-Bukhārī's collection.[17] Furthermore, informal scholarly networks were as important as formal pathways.

In the education of Zahit Kevseri, who published his *ijāza* for his Egyptian students' reference, we observe how these trends came together. From this *ijāza*, we can gain valuable and detailed information about the study of hadith in the late Ottoman context.[18] Kevseri was a typical late Ottoman scholar; he began his education in the provinces in his natal hometown of Düzce in northwestern Turkey under the tutelage of his father, a distinguished teacher, and then moved to Istanbul, where he continued his education and began his professional career. While in Istanbul, Kevseri was given instruction in both formal and informal settings; two teachers in particular exerted a profound influence on his learning: Alasonyalı Ali Zeynelabidin Efendi (d. 1917) and Eğinli İbrahim Hakkı Efendi (d. 1894).[19] From his *ijāza*, we know that he was authorised to transmit nearly twenty works relating to hadith: *Ṣaḥīḥ al-Bukhārī* (on Alasonyalı), *Nukhbat al-fikr, Ṣaḥīḥ Muslim, Sunan Abī Dāwūd, Jāmiʿ al-Tirmidhī, Sunan al-Nasāʾī, Sunan Ibn Mājah, Musnad Abī Ḥanīfa, Masānīd Abī Ḥanīfa al-sabʿat ʿashara, al-Muwaṭṭaʾ, Musnad al-Shāfiʿī, Musnad Aḥmad, Maṣābīḥ al-sunna, Mashāriq al-anwār, Mishkat al-maṣābīḥ, al-Mawāhib, al-Shifāʾ, al-Jāmiʿ al-kabīr* and *al-Jāmiʿ al-ṣaghīr*.[20] From Kevseri's example, we know that the study of hadith was exhaustive and that it relied on instruction in informal networks, which were as important as the formal madrasa and its curriculum.

We have little information about the hadith education of the two translators of *Sahihi-i Buhari Muhtasarı: Tecrid-i Sarih Tercümesi*. Kamil Miras, who was born into a scholarly family, was a product of the madrasa system in which the study of hadith was part of the curriculum. He completed his studies in his hometown of Afyonkarahisar in western Turkey, after which he moved to Istanbul to continue his studies. We do not have details about his study of hadith outside the madrasa system, but we do know that during his studies in Istanbul he received an *ijāza* from Alasonyalı Ali Zeynelabidin Efendi, one of the two scholars who figured prominently in Kevseri's hadith

---

17 Mardin, *Huzur Dersleri*, 2:326–237. The position, held by Rizeli İshak Nuri Efendi (d. 1927), was terminated with the event of March 31 (24 April 1909). Thereafter, he was appointed to recite hadith from al-Bukhārī in the Meşihat.

18 Given the limited details we have about late Ottoman hadith culture, it is not surprising that many Turkish scholars have analysed Kevseri's *ijāza*; see, for example, Özafşar, 'Osmanlı Eğitim', and Ayaz, 'Hadis İlimlerinin Tedrîsâtı', 50–52.

19 Al-Kawtharī, *al-Taḥrīr al-wajīz*, 59. For another example of his study of *Rāmūz al-aḥādīth* with Kastamanolu Hasan Efendi in an informal setting, see al-Kawtharī, *al-Taḥrīr al-wajīz*, 60.

20 Al-Kawtharī, *al-Taḥrīr al-wajīz*, 11–15. The *ijāza* then goes on to works of *fiqh, athbāt* (confirmation) and then a selective biographical dictionary.

education; presumably, Miras studied hadith with him, too.[21] Miras completed his course of study, passed the qualifying exams (*ruus imtihanları*) in 1907 and began his teaching career at the Beyazit Mosque. Over the course of his career, Miras taught on a range of subjects, including the history of jurisprudence, logic, the history of Islam and the history of religions.

Despite Babanzade's longstanding interest in hadith, we do not know anything about his education on the topic. We know that he began his studies in Baghdad, where he was born, and that he never attended a madrasa, so we cannot assume that he pursued a madrasa curriculum for the study of hadith. He came to Istanbul as a young man and continued his studies at Mekteb-i Sultani and later at Mekteb-i Mülkiye.[22] In 1914, he began teaching philosophy at Darü'l-Fünun, where he remained until the institution was closed in 1933.

Babanzade studied hadith independently; we have no information about what and with whom he studied. As noted above, Babanzade's earliest works of hadith translation were based on al-Zabīdī's *al-Tajrīd al-ṣarīḥ* and published in *Sırat-ı Müstakim* and *Kelime-i Tayyibe* beginning in late 1910. This journal ran for almost forty issues and covered approximately two hundred hadith in these two journals. Al-Zabīdī's text was likely instrumental in helping Babanzade study hadith, as it was for other beginners. He wrote a letter to the journal, and this served as the preface to the first article of the hadith translation; in it, after explaining why he translated the hadith, Babanzade mentioned the state of the Muslim community. He believed that the journal could play an important role in awakening readers and further, that for the Muslim community to improve its situation, it should be concerned with Qur'anic exegesis (*tafsīr*) and hadith. He pointed out the articles on *tafsīr* that *Sırat-ı Müstakim* published and singled out its publication of articles from İsmail Hakkı Bereketzade's (d. 1918) *Envar-i Kur'an* in particular. Despite the importance of the Qur'an and hadith in the Islamic tradition, the journal published very little on hadith. Babanzade went on to state that he was not an expert in *tafsīr* or hadith but, in order to remedy the problem of the journal's omission of articles on hadith, he could translate and thus help readers. He said that he would translate from al-Zabīdī's *al-Tajrīd al-ṣarīḥ* as he found the time.[23] Babanzade's explanation is striking for the way he situates his efforts on hadith in the context of calls for a 'new *tafsīr*' by invoking Bereketzade's Qur'an commentary.[24] And the fact that

---

21 *TDVİA*, s.v. 'Kamil Miras', 145.

22 Ergin, 'Babanzade Ahmed Naim', 129.

23 Babanzade, 'Sırat-ı Müstakim', 257.

24 Bereketzade İsmail Hakkı wrote two partial Qur'an commentaries: *Envar-i Kur'an*, a learned work written for a scholarly audience, and *Neca'ib-i Kur'aniye*, a popular work for laypeople. Both works were partially published in serial form in *Sırat-ı Müstakim*. The publication of these works in the *tafsīr* section of the journal, and others on the topic

Babanzade situates hadith at the heart of an Islamic revival aligns his hadith translation project with broader trends in the Muslim world, where the role of hadith in the period was being reappraised.[25] Babanzade wanted to see hadith gain at least some of the attention that was being shown to rejuvenate the other disciplines of the Islamic sciences.

In 1925, Babanzade published a translation of al-Nawawī's *Arbaʿīn*. His strategy was to provide a literal translation of the original, with footnotes to provide extra information. It was in the space of the footnotes that he selectively provided commentary. Babanzade utilised this practice to provide information on topics that he thought needed clarification or attracted his interest. He continued this practice in the *Sahih-i Buhari Muhtasarı: Tecrid-i Sarih Tercümesi* as well. Since he never approached any of his hadith projects with the formal intention of commenting on a hadith text, he was free to skip over material that also may have needed clarification. He modestly presented himself as a translator of hadith, a role that also gave him the freedom to comment as much or as little as he wanted.

The two men who worked on *Sahih-i Buhari Muhtasarı: Tecrid-i Sarih Tercümesi* spent their formative intellectual years in Ottoman institutions. Regarding the religious realm, the Ottoman Empire did not end abruptly with the establishment of the republic in 1923, rather, there was a great deal of continuity between the Ottoman Empire and the Turkish Republic in the religious realm. In the early years of the republic, Ottoman religious works were still being read and taught. For example, *Sahih-i Buhari Muhtasarı: Tecrid-i Sarih Tercümesi* was the only work on hadith published under the imprint of the Diyanet until 1952, when a Turkish translation of ʿAlī al-Qārī's (d. 1014/1605) *al-Aḥādīth al-qudsiyya* was translated as *Kırk Kudsi Hadis*.[26] The religious scholars who dominated the pre-1950s republican era had received their educational training in Ottoman religious institutions and began their careers in those institutions. Though the state sought to severely curtail opportunities for religious education, individual members of the ʿulamāʾ remained and trained others in the Islamic tradition through informal, personal networks. It was only after the Diyanet became stronger after the 1950 elections that more opportunities were available in Turkey for those seeking a systematic religious education; subsequently, new religious scholars trained in republican institutions emerged. The contributions of former members of the Ottoman ʿulamāʾ and the slow emergence of new Muslim scholars were key

of *tafsīr*, were related to Mehmet Akif's call for a 'new *tafsīr*' in the inaugural article of the *tafsīr* section; for more on the 'new *tafsīr*', see Gunasti, *The Qur'an*, 65, 72. The relationship between the study of hadith and calls for a 'new *tafsīr*', 'new theology' and 'new philosophy' fall beyond the purview of this chapter, but need further exploring.

25 Brown, *Rethinking Tradition*.

26 Al-Qārī, *Kırk Kudsi Hadis*.

factors that contributed to a continuity in the religious realm between the Ottoman Empire and the Turkish Republic.

Sahih-i Buhari Muhtasarı: Tecrid-i Sarih Tercümesi

We do not know why Babanzade chose to translate al-Zabīdī's *al-Tajrīd al-ṣarīḥ* for his commission. All we know is that he had already begun a translation of it a little over two decades prior, in an effort to revitalise the Muslim community. Perhaps he still thought the text could serve this role. Or the overwhelming nature of the task of translating al-Bukhārī's hadith compilation might have led him to prefer al-Zabīdī's abridgement of it rather than the original. In any case, the text served the purposes of study for beginners and provided opportunities for commentators to interpret *Ṣaḥīḥ al-Bukhārī*.

Even though the hadith project was commissioned as a vernacular translation for the public, the text was only accessible to specialists. One needed to know both Ottoman Turkish and Arabic to understand it. The first two volumes were published in 1928 in Ottoman Turkish; after the passage of the alphabet reform law of 1928 (which changed the alphabet from the Arabic-Ottoman script to Latin letters), the remaining volumes were published using Latin letters. Throughout the twelve volumes of the text, the chains of transmission and hadith reports are first provided in Arabic, followed by the translation (*tercemesi*) [*sic*]. Babanzade strove to provide a literal translation (*harfiyyen tercemeye itina etmekle*) but, where the translation warranted additional words to communicate the meaning of the original, he put the explanatory words in parentheses to indicate that they were not present in the original.[27] The distinction between the translation and the original was clear from the page layout.

The title page of the first volume contains the imprint indicating that it is an official publication of the Diyanet of the Turkish Republic (the fourth imprint to be published). The title of the book, *Sahih-i Buhari Muhtasarı: Tecrid-i Sarih Tercemesi*, is displayed prominently in large font, followed by the volume number and publication information (see Figure 7.1). The layout of the title page of the first volume presents the text as a translation: it does not mention the author of the *Tajrīd* (leaving specialists to infer al-Zabīdī's authority) or the identity of the translator, Babanzade. This information is provided later, from the third volume onwards. The title page of the first volume is followed by what could be considered the preface of the book, in which Babanzade provides information on al-Zabīdī and Babanzade's reasons for translating the book at the behest of the Diyanet.

27 Babanzade, *Sahih-i Buhari Muhtasarı: Tecrid-i Sarih Tercümesi* (hereinafter *SBM-TST*), 1:4–5.

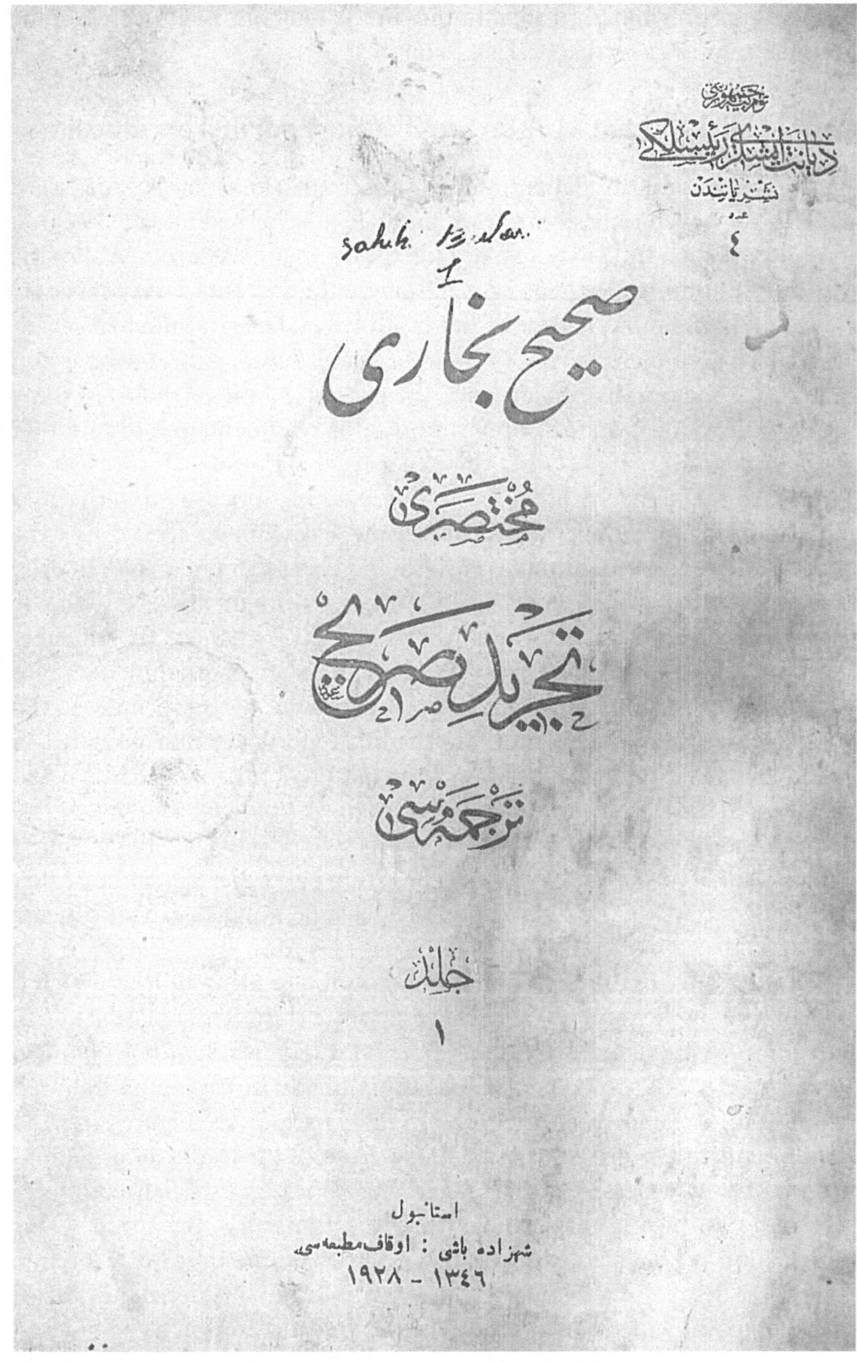

Figure 7.1   Title page of volume 1 of the first edition of *Sahihi-i Buhari Muhtasarı: Tecrid-i Sarih Tercümesi* (1928); photograph provided courtesy of McGill Islamic Studies Library.

He does not mention his reasons for choosing al-Zabīdī's *al-Tajrīd al-ṣarīḥ* for translation. At the end of the preface, we find 'Translator: Ahmet Naim'.[28] Thus, Bababzade's personal authority is minimised, while the Diyanet is closely associated with the project. Writing commentaries is a means through which religious authority is constituted and preserved; we can view this text as a way to establish the authority of the Diyanet in the early republican period.

Regarding writing commentaries, the choices ultimately fall to the individual writers; here it is significant that Babanzade had different goals for the project than did the Diyanet. If the Diyanet intended to create a Turkish canon and to minimise the relevance of the *'ulamā'*, Babanzade was interested in pursuing a particular classical tradition of reading al-Bukhārī and had no interest in the concerns of the state. Babanzade, intentionally or not, subverted the goals of the Diyanet because he had complete control over the content of the work.

The preface of the book is followed by a lengthy introduction that is close to five hundred pages long; this itself can be considered an independent work on *uṣūl al-ḥadīth*. In length, this introduction exceeds many works of this genre. The introduction positions the work in the context of premodern scholars, such as al-Zabīdī. In providing his sources for the introduction, the first text Babanzade identified was Ibn Ḥajar al-'Asqalānī's *Nukhbat al-fikr fī muṣṭalaḥ ahl al-athar*, followed by Ibn Ḥajar's commentary on it, *Nuzhat al-naẓar*, then followed by 'Alī al-Qārī's 'commentary on the commentary [of Ibn Ḥajar]'.[29] Babanzade's reliance on Ibn Ḥajar's contributions to hadith extended beyond his use of *Nukhbat al-fikr* to *Fatḥ al-Bārī fī sharḥ Ṣaḥīḥ al-Bukhārī*, Ibn Ḥajar's key work on reading al-Bukhārī.

Despite presenting the introduction as being grounded in *Nukhbat al-fikr*, Babanzade departs from it and adds a great deal. One of his stated goals in the introduction was to offer a methodological explanation on how hadith could be understood in the twentieth century.[30] He was very interested in methodology and in defending the methods of evaluating hadith. In one instance, he takes issue with the views of Leone Caetani (d. 1935), an Italian Orientalist who analysed and evaluated hadith based on historical critical methods and then rejected many hadiths that Muslims accepted as authentic. Babanzade defends the methodology of the 'hadith folk' (*ahl al-ḥadīth*) against Caetani by emphasising their different motivations for

---

28 Babanzade, *SBM-TST*, 1:6.

29 Babanzade, *SBM-TST*, 1:n.p. (the page follows immediately after p. 482). In addition to these three, he lists nineteen other sources that he also consulted by name. On the *Nukhbat al-fikr* and its commentaries and 'Alī al-Qārī's work, see Engin, 'Hadis Literatüründe Hâşiyeler', 76–98 and 84–85 respectively.

30 I am building on the observation made by his close friend, Muallim Mehmed Cevdet; Cevdet, *Müderris Babanzade Ahmed Naim*, 56–57.

evaluating hadith. Babanzade considered the hadith folk historians and their methods more comprehensive than the historical critical approach of modern historians. This was due, he said, to their objectives; historians like Caetani sought to clarify the historical record, whereas hadith folk had to be meticulous in evaluating hadith because accepting a hadith report as valid could influence the practice of religion, and therefore the stakes were higher.[31] Babanzade's goal was to preserve the methodology of *isnād* criticism, but also to leverage the method to different ends than classical hadith scholars.

From the very outset of the project, commentary on the hadith was an integral part of Babanzade's work. Babanzade explains that he found a 'bare translation' (*kuru bir terceme*) insufficient and therefore it was necessary to add a commentary.[32] In this regard, he said that he would try to provide alternative transmissions and other differences to the extent that he could. Yet, rather than dedicating a separate section to commentary, Babanzade's commentary appears in the footnotes that sometimes dominate the page. This choice of the page layout (we do not know whose choice it was) affected the religious authority of the text by downplaying the prominence of the commentary. In addition, Babanzade's commentary was not systematic; rather it included alternative narrations, information about transmitters and elaborations on themes that piqued his interest. In the commentary tradition, it is the exegete's prerogative to determine which parts he dwells on and which ones he ignores. Babanzade's commentary is less systematic in its presentation than that of Miras, which has a uniform presentation.

As noted, Babanzade died early in the project; the third volume was in draft form, and still required editing. The Diyanet assigned the editing project to Kamil Miras, who edited the third volume and preserved Babanzade's text. He formally took over the translation work of the project with the fourth volume, at which point he made changes to Babanzade's approach and page layout. For example, he changed the section labelled *tercemesi* (translation) to *Türkçesi* (Turkish); the change in labels is notable, given the prominent discussions about translations in the early republican period.

Miras made a significant change in the layout of the book. He provided a section labelled *izahı* (elucidation), in which he provided his commentary on the hadith. By designating a formal section for the commentary on each hadith, he shifted the location of the commentary from the footnotes to the body of the text. He began this section with a discussion of the transmitters of the hadith, then focused on issues raised in the hadith report, information on the narrators and other topics. Sometimes, he provided a separate

---

31 Babanzade, *SBM-TST*, 1:74–81.
32 Babanzade, *SBM-TST*, 1:5.

section for biographical information, or about the legal implications of the hadith. Thus, under Miras, the commentary on the hadith reports acquired more prominence.

The addition of this information transformed the work from a translation project into a full-fledged hadith commentary; this change was reflected in an addition to the title (*ve şerhi* [and its commentary]). For the commentary, Miras first refers to al-Bukhārī's *Ṣaḥīḥ* to explain hadith and then consulted al-ʿAynī's *ʿUmdat al-qārī fī sharḥ Ṣaḥīḥ al-Bukhārī*, a commentary on al-Bukhārī's *Ṣaḥīḥ*.[33] The reference to Badr al-Dīn al-ʿAynī (d. 855/1451), a prominent Ḥanafī jurist in the Mamlūk period, signalled Miras's desire to avoid what he perceived to be Babanzade's Shāfiʿī bias. Miras's choice was interesting because, as a Ḥanafī, he was clearly championing al-ʿAynī's interpretation over Babanzade's strong preference for the interpretations of Ibn Ḥajar, a Shāfiʿī scholar (Babanzade was himself a Shāfiʿī). Thus, the rivalry of the two classical scholars, al-ʿAynī and Ibn Ḥajar, manifested itself in the modern period.[34] In the pages of this twentieth-century commentary, we observe Miras and Babanzade drawing on different strands of the classical hadith commentary tradition that were in tension with one another; in this sense, they contested *madhhab* identity through their commentaries on al-Bukhārī.

Contestations over Religious Authority

The third volume of *Sahih-i Buhari Muhtasarı: Tecrid-i Sarih Tercemesi* is of particular interest because it is the only volume on which both Babanzade and Miras worked; in a sense, it was a one-sided monologue from Miras to Babanzade. In a few instances, Miras praised Babanzade's approach to the text,[35] but on other occasions he was very critical of it. Miras cautiously approached the task of correcting what he deemed points of error in Babanzade's commentary. Rather, he left Babanzade's original in the text, but provided his comments, criticisms and/or clarifications to these points in the notes. Miras explained that, in instances where he believed Babanzade had erred, he provided interpretations and/or translations that align with the Ḥanafī school.[36] One trend emerges particularly from Miras's

---

33 Miras, *SBM-TST*, 4:8.

34 On the rivalry between Ibn Ḥajar and al-ʿAynī, see Blecher, *Said the Prophet of God*, 57–79 and 100–108. On the invocation of their respective works in the context of scholarly rivalries in the context of the twentieth-century Indian subcontinent, see Blecher, *Said the Prophet of God*, 153. I thank Joel Blecher for drawing my attention to the parallels between the Turkish and Indian cases.

35 Babanzade and Miras, *SBM-TST*, 3:100, in which Miras praises Babanzade's discussion of multiple narrations for a report.

36 Babanzade and Miras, *SBM-TST*, 3:n.p. (the text is between pages 403 and 404).

edits; namely, he found Babanzade too partisan in his legal school affiliation. The intensity with which Miras criticised Babanzade on this point is surprising given that legal school boundaries were not an issue for the Diyanet at the time. But at the same time, in the modern period there were broader contestations over hadith commentary in which we observe commentators adopting the views of scholars of the same legal school.[37] In this regard, the third volume is important to understanding competing notions of religious authority with respect to Babanzade and Miras championing their particular readings of al-Bukhārī (along *madhhab* lines).

Miras expressed his differences with Babanzade through his portrayal of al-'Aynī's commentary. For example, Miras interjected notes to refer to al-'Aynī's opinion on the matter under discussion, to make clear that the Ḥanafīs carefully discussed the matter in their hadith works. In some places, Miras defends al-'Aynī from what he perceived to be Babanzade's misinterpretations of al-'Aynī's positions. We can see an example of this in the discussion of a hadith related to the Battle of the Trench (*al-khandaq*) in which Muhammad commanded the believers not to start the afternoon prayer until they had reached their destination; some obeyed and others did not:

> When Muḥammad, peace be upon him, returned from the confederates [who fought at the Battle of the Trench], he said to us that no one is to pray the afternoon prayer (*'asr*) until reaching the Banū Qurayẓa. While on the path [to the Banū Qurayẓa], some encountered [the issue of when to pray the prayer]. Some from among them said that they would not pray until they reached their destination. Others among them said that they would pray and that this is not what was being asked of them [i.e. not to pray *'asr*].[38]

After providing alternative transmission reports, Babanzade states that this hadith report does not belong in the section to which al-Bukhārī assigns it, *abwāb ṣalāt al-khawf* (chapters of the prayer of fear), because it does not deal with prayer in times of fear. However, he justifies al-Bukhārī's placement by linking the topic to that of the preceding one, relating to praying while on foot or mounted when one is outnumbered by enemies. Babanzade's discussion enabled him to focus on the previous report and on whether it is permitted to pray while mounted rather than to consider the specifics related to the one about the Battle of the Trench. The point of contention relates to Babanzade's reports of the views of al-'Aynī on praying while mounted and

---

37 On the Diyanet's reaching out, in 1937, to a Ḥanafī scholar for a *fatwā* on divorce according to a classical Ḥanbalī school, see <http://www.yenisafak.com/hayat/diyanetle-elmalilinin-fetva-tartismasi-2654917> (accessed 15 April 2018). On hadith, see Blecher, *Said the Prophet of God*, 153 and Zaman, 'Commentaries, Print, and Patronage'.
38 Babanzade and Miras, *SBM-TST*, 3:144.

in a dangerous situation.[39] In a footnote, Miras quotes al-ʿAynī extensively to claim that Babanzade misrepresented his position because he did not read al-ʿAynī's commentary on the topic thoroughly.[40] Miras's aim was to defend al-ʿAynī's reputation against Babanzade's censure.

We see Miras's interest in preserving the reputation of al-ʿAynī in another minor instance later in the text. In the translation of a hadith, Babanzade notes a discrepancy in the chain of transmission. It is unclear what source text he is using for al-Bukhārī's hadith, but Babanzade notes that the chain of transmission incorrectly includes the name of ʿUthmān, one of the rightly guided caliphs. Even though the chain of transmission includes a name it should not, Babanzade reproduces it in the text. In the comment on the translation, he attributes the error to al-ʿAynī's text. In a footnote, Miras notes that an Egyptian publication from 1348/1929–1930 did not include the name of ʿUthmān in the chain of transmission. With this correction, Miras indicated that the problem was in the text that Babanzade consulted and not with al-ʿAynī.

Miras's frustration with Babanzade's representation of al-ʿAynī's views appears in a long footnote in which he counters what he perceived to be Babanzade's attempts to criticise al-ʿAynī.[41] The topic in this case relates to *ṣalāt al-witr*, a prayer performed after the night prayers; whether it is compulsory is contested among the various legal schools. According to the consensus of the Ḥanafīs, *ṣalāt al-witr* is considered compulsory, though some of the school's followers consider its performance a matter of Sunna and thus not compulsory.[42] In the commentary on the hadith report, 'the Prophet, peace by upon him, said that you should establish *al-witr* as your last prayer of the evening', Babanzade brings up the obligatory nature of *ṣalāt al-witr* for the Ḥanafīs by referring to al-ʿAynī's commentary.[43] He alludes to differences of opinion on this hadith; some view it as a Ḥanafī position and others disagree. Al-ʿAynī vehemently critiques those who do not view it as a Ḥanafī position. Babanzade describes al-ʿAynī's defence, and mentions that al-ʿAynī cites another hadith report that states: 'one who does not pray *witr* is not from among us.' Babanzade notes that this hadith is a particularly strong one to make the Ḥanafī case but that al-ʿAynī does not interpret it in a particularly compelling manner. Babanzade accuses al-ʿAynī of misinterpreting this hadith because in fact he misunderstood what it means and says the hadith means 'they are not from among those who act according to our Sunna'.[44]

<hr>

39 Babanzade and Miras, *SBM-TST*, 3:149.
40 Cf., Babanzade and Miras, *SBM-TST*, 3:149 and al-ʿAynī, *ʿUmdat al-qārī*, 6:262–263.
41 Babanzade and Miras, *SBM-TST*, 3:225–226.
42 *TDVİA*, s.v. 'Vitir Namazı'.
43 Babanzade and Miras, *SBM-TST*, 3:223.
44 Cf. Babanzade and Miras, *SBM-TST*, 3:225 and al-ʿAynī, *ʿUmdat al-qārī*, 7:12. Miras does a better job of reporting on what al-ʿAynī wrote in *ʿUmdat al-qārī*.

Miras objects to Babanzade's criticism of al-'Aynī and accuses Babanzade of being overly partisan with respect to *madhhab*s (*mezheb taassubunun izlerini görüyor*). The irony of this comment is not lost on readers who have noted Miras's *madhhab* partisanship throughout his translation. Yet the comment also raises the issue that was at stake for Miras, who was frustrated by Babanzade's portrayal of al-'Aynī and the suggestion that al-'Aynī and the Ḥanafīs were not strong in hadith commentary. The Ḥanafīs were relative latecomers to hadith studies and, by defending al-'Aynī, Miras was upholding the Ḥanafī tradition of hadith interpretation in the twentieth century.

Another issue that emerges between Miras and Babanzade is their differing views on narrators. In a lengthy footnote in his introduction, Babanzade defends Nūḥ b. Abī Maryam Abū 'Isma al-Marwazī (d. 173/789), a Ḥanafī scholar who was known to fabricate hadith reports. Babanzade defends this maligned Ḥanafī scholar from the second/eighth century in order to make a larger point about Ḥanafīs and hadith scholarship. Babanzade mentions that misperceptions about Nūḥ b. Abī Maryam's role as a hadith transmitter were so entrenched that even Ḥanafī scholars such as 'Alī al-Qārī and 'Abd al-Ḥayy Laknawī (d. 1304/1886) did not correctly judge Nūḥ b. Abī Maryam as a reliable narrator. Babanzade's critique of prominent Ḥanafī scholars was a criticism of them as being weak in hadith.

After rehearsing the breadth of Nūḥ b. Abī Maryam's learning and scholarly reputation, Babanzade brings up the forged report in which Nūḥ b. Abī Maryam, upon seeing people reading works of *fiqh* by Abū Ḥanīfa and works of *maghāzī* by Ibn Isḥāq, speaks about the excellent qualities (*faḍā'il*) of the Qur'an. Babanzade focuses on the use of 'on the authority of' (*'an*) in one of the narrations of this report (Nūḥ b. Abī Maryam on the authority of 'Ikrima [d. 107/725] on the authority of Ibn 'Abbas). The use of 'on the authority of' is generally considered a less authoritative mode of transmission than 'was transmitted to us' (*ḥaddathanā*), and in this instance the use of 'on the authority of' in one of the chains of transmission leaves the particular mode by which the hadith was transmitted as ambiguous.[45] Babanzade then brings up another variation of the hadith that places an unknown individual (*rajul*) between Nūḥ b. Abī Maryam and 'Ikrima in the chain of transmission, and the transmission of this fabricated report is attributed to this unknown individual. With this step he clears Nūḥ b. Abī Maryam's name, and then Babanzade proceeds to mention the ways in which some hadith scholars have relied on Nūḥ b. Abī Maryam's transmission of hadith. Babanzade argues that, given that others have relied on Nūḥ b. Abī Maryam with respect to other hadith reports and because of his legal reputation, his narrations should be accepted.[46]

45 Blecher, *Said the Prophet of God*, 100.
46 Babanzade, *SBM-TST*, 1:276–279.

In a similar vein, Babanzade also defends the reputation of Muḥammad b. ʿUmar al-Wāqidī (d. 207/823), a historian who wrote about early campaigns.[47] The hadith folk (*ahl al-ḥadīth*) took issue with al-Wāqidī's loose approach to hadith. Babanzade went back to the sources and reevaluated the reputation of the narrators and accepted their transmissions as valid. Though Babanzade establishes a compelling defence of al-Wāqidī, his defence illustrates the late Shahab Ahmed's point that different genres have different methods and standards for evaluating and using hadith reports. Babanzade invokes al-Wāqidī's good reputation in the *maghāzī* genre, but conflates this good reputation to the realm of hadith. Babanzade ignored the different standards in the genres and, once he defended al-Wāqidī in the realm of history, surreptitiously sought to transfer that good standing from history to al-Wāqidī's reputation in the realm of hadith and its transmission.[48]

Miras, too, sought to defend Nūḥ b. Abī Maryam's reputation, but for different reasons and with different strategies.[49] Babanzade's critique of Ḥanafī scholars was not lost on Miras. Miras begins by providing the full hadith report in Arabic and then analyses the chain of transmission. He focuses on the use of 'on the authority of' in the chain of transmission and the introduction of the report with 'it was said' (*qīla*), highlighting the problem, namely, that the narrator remains ambiguous or unknown. He focuses on the disparity between the death dates of Nūḥ b. Abī Maryam and ʿIkrima (173/789 and 107/725, respectively), and notes the other narration that places an unknown individual between the two. Based on these two narrations, it is unclear from whom Nūḥ b. Abī Maryam narrated the hadith; Miras argues that the hadith report is weak because it is forged, though not by Nūḥ b. Abī Maryam. Significantly, Miras goes further than Babanzade and says that those close to Nūḥ b. Abī Maryam attributed this report to him and that it is unimaginable that Nūḥ b. Abī Maryam, who was a disciple of Abū Ḥanīfa, would ever say anything bad about his teacher, as this report implies. Miras sought to defend Nūḥ b. Abī Maryam's reputation, and beyond that, to preserve the reputation of Abū Ḥanīfa. Despite their differences, Miras shared Babanzade's modernist approach to the reevaluation of chains of transmission.

In his concluding remarks to his introduction we get a sense of Babanzade's reasons for rehabilitating the reputations of Nūḥ b. Abī Maryam and al-Wāqidī. Babanzade writes that one of the main reasons he went

---

47 Babanzade, *SBM-TST*, 1:481–482.

48 On the standards adopted by scholars in evaluating hadith reports in various genres in early Islam, see Ahmed, *Before Orthodoxy*.

49 On Babanzade's defense, see *SBM-TST*, 1:277–279 and 481. On Miras's refutation, see Babanzade and Miras, *SBM-TST*, 3:405–407. Later editions of the work also published Miras's refutation in the first volume.

into such a detailed discussion about the criteria for evaluating hadith was to show how, from the early Islamic period, Muslims – unlike any other religious community – subjected knowledge to strict criteria.[50] Babanzade adopted an all-encompassing approach that enabled him to incorporate the broad range of views held by Muslims. The lengthy introduction, with its painstaking efforts to show how hadith are evaluated, was meant to show that the Muslim world had internal standards by which to evaluate knowledge, and that these methods surpass those in the West.[51] The introduction can be seen as a reaction to arguments current at the time; these views presented the Muslim world as a civilisation in decline and encouraged the adoption of European disciplines and modes of learning.

Conclusion

The Turkish state's efforts to publish vernacular translations and commentaries on the two most important sources of scriptural authority in Islam demonstrates, as I have shown in this chapter, that the state was not indifferent to the practice of Islam in the early republican era. The commentary tradition and genre have their own style and expectations, and although individual authors had freedom within the constraints of the genre, they still had to work within these parameters. Although the state may have initially thought that it could dictate the terms of the book project, its goals ran into the considerable autonomy that Babanzade and Miras had over the project. Babanzade and Miras approached the interpretation of al-Bukhārī's *Ṣaḥīḥ* unfettered by the state and its interests. The Diyanet's inability to dictate the content of the texts it commissioned meant that the state could not play a role in shaping Islam in textual sources in the early republican period. The Diyanet, and by extension the state, could not control the final shape of the translation project they commissioned because they depended on scholars writing from within the hadith commentary tradition.

Under Babanzade, the project became an effort to reorient understandings of hadith methodology contra the evaluations of classical scholars and to serve as the basis of a revival of the Islamic intellectual tradition *vis-à-vis* the impact of European learning. In this regard, he was not alone in viewing hadith as a vehicle for religious reform and demonstrating to those who viewed Islam as an obstacle to progress that the Islamic tradition had internal standards for evaluating knowledge, standards that exceeded those of the Europeans. Miras, by contrast, had a more limited goal; he sought to

50 Babanzade, *SBM-TST*, 1:480.
51 Babanzade makes this point in his text on the study of Arabic; see Cemil and Babanzade, *Sarf-ı Arabi*, 1:3.

limit Babanzade's championing of Ibn Ḥajar, which he interpreted as coming at the expense of al-ʿAynī's influence and the Ḥanafī legal school more broadly. This dynamic mirrored similar trends in hadith commentary in other parts of the Islamic world at the time, including the Indian subcontinent. Miras transformed the third volume into a contestation over the authority of al-ʿAynī and Abū Ḥanīfa. The work of Babanzade and Miras, when taken together, demonstrates the range of interpretive debates over hadith, the tensions that animated these issues in early republican Turkey, and the commentarial opportunities that the medium of the translation afforded in defining and redefining the meanings of the sayings and practices of Muhammad.

Bibliography

Ahmed, Shahab. *Before Orthodoxy: The Satanic Verses in Early Islam*. Cambridge, MA: Harvard University Press, 2017.

Ayaz, Kadir. 'Hadis İlimlerinin Tedrisatı Açısından Osmanlı Darulhadisleri.' *Osmanlı Araştırmaları / Journal of Ottoman Studies* 47 (2016): 39–68.

al-ʿAynī, Badr al-Dīn. *ʿUmdat al-qārī fī sharḥ Ṣaḥīḥ al-Bukhārī*. 25 vols. Beirut: Idarat al-Tabāʿa al-Muniriyya, 1970.

Babanzade, Ahmet Naim. *Kirk hadis: İtikadan, Amelan, Ahlakan İnsanlara Rehber-i Kemalat Olacak Cevami ül-Kelam Ahmadiyeden*. Istanbul: Matbaa-i Amire, 1343/1925.

Babanzade, Ahmet Naim. *Sahihi-i Buhari Muhtasarı: Tecrid-i Sarih Tercümesi*. Vols. 1–2. Istanbul: Evkaf Matbaası, 1928.

Babanzade, Ahmet Naim. 'Sırat-ı Müstakim Ceride-i İslamiyesi Müessis-i Muhteremesine.' *Sebil'ür-Reşad* 5, no. 120 (9 Kanunıevvel 1326) [22 December 1910]: 257–258.

Babanzade, Ahmet Naim and Kamil Miras. *Sahihi-i Buhari Muhtasarı: Tecrid-i Sarih Tercümesi*. Vol. 3 Istanbul: Matbaai Ebüzziya, 1934.

Babanzade, Ahmet Naim and Kamil Miras. *Sahih-i Buhari Muhtasarı: Tecrid-i Sarih Tercümesi ve Şerhi*. 8 vols. Ankara: Diyanet İşleri Başkanlığı, 2019.

Blecher, Joel. *Said the Prophet of God: Hadith Commentary across a Millennium*. Oakland: University of California Press, 2018.

Brown, Daniel W. 'Reappraisal.' In Daniel W. Brown (ed.), *The Wiley Blackwell Concise Companion to the Hadith*, 315–333. Hoboken, NJ: John Wiley and Sons, 2020.

Brown, Daniel W. *Rethinking Tradition in Modern Islamic Thought*. Cambridge: Cambridge University Press, 1996.

Cemil, Mustafa and [Babanzade] Ahmed Naim. *Sarf-ı Arabi: Temrinat*. 3rd ed. Istanbul: Ibrahim Hilmi Matbaası, 1323 [/1907].

Cevdet, [Muallim] Mehmed. *Müderris Babanzade Ahmed Naim*. Edited by Fahrettin Gün. Istanbul: Beyan, 2016.

Çiftçi, Mehdin. *Süleymaniye Darulhadisi (XVI–XVII. Asırlar)*. Istanbul: Kitabevi, 2013.

Engin, Sezai. 'Hadis Literatüründe Haşiyeler: *Nuhbetü'l-fiker* ve *Nüzhetü'n-nazar* Üzerine Yapılan Haşiye Çalışmaları Bibliyografyası.' *Hadis ve Siyer Aramaştırmaları* 1, no. 1 (2015): 76–98.

Ergin, Osman Nuri. 'Babanzade Ahmed Naim, Şahsiyeti ve Eserleri.' In Muallim Mehmed Cevdet, *Müderris Babanzade Ahmed Naim*, edited by Fahrettin Gün. Istanbul: Beyan, 2016.

Gül, Ahmet. *Osmanlı Medreselerinde Eğitim-Öğretim ve Bunlar Arasında Daru'l-Hadislerin Yeri.* Ankara: Türk Tarih Kurumu, 1997.

Gunasti, Susan. *The Qur'an Between the Ottoman Empire and the Turkish Republic.* Abingdon: Routledge, 2019.

'İkinci Celse.' *Meclis-i Meb'usan Zabıt Ceridesi* 14 (year 2): 249–263.

Kara, İsmail. *Cumhuriyet Türkiyesi'nde bir Mesele Olarak İslam.* Istanbul: Dergah Yayınları, 2009.

Karacabey, Salih. 'Osmanlı Madrasalerinin Son Dönemi'nde Hadis Öğretimi.' *Uludağ Üniversitesi İlahiyat Fakültesi Dergisi* 8, no. 8 (1999): 149–169.

Karahan, Abdülkadir. *İslam-Türk Edebiyatında Kırk Hadis: Toplama, Tercüme ve Şerhleri.* Istanbul: İbrahim Horoz Basımevi, 1954.

al-Kawtharī, Muḥammad Zāhid al-Ḥasan. *Maqalāt al-Kawtharī.* Cairo: al-Maktaba al-Azhariyya li-l-Turāth, 1414/1994.

al-Kawtharī, Muḥammad Zāhid al-Ḥasan. *al-Taḥrīr al-wajīz fimā yabtaghīh al-mustajīz.* Aleppo: Maktabat al-Maṭbu'āt al-Islāmiyya, 1993.

Komisyon. *Hadislerle İslam.* 7 vols. Ankara: Diyanet İşleri Başkanlığı, 2013.

Mardin, Ebül'ula. *Huzur Dersleri.* 2 vols. Istanbul: İsmail Akgün Matbaası, 1956–1966.

Miras, Kamil. *Sahih-i Buhari Muhtasarı: Tecrid-i Sarih Tercümesi ve Şerhi.* Vols. 4–12. Istanbul: Matbaai Ebüzziya, 1938–1948.

Özafşar, Mehmet Emin. 'Osmanlı Eğitim, Kültür ve Sanat Hayatında Hadis.' In Hasan Celal Güzel et al. (eds), *Türkler*, 11:356–369. Ankara: Türkiye Yayınları, 2002.

al-Qārī, 'Alī. *Kırk Kudsi Hadis.* Translated by Hasan Hüsnü Erden. Istanbul: Diyanet, 1952.

Sadık, Cihan. 'Les Lieux de L'Enseignement de la Tradition et L'Importance Donne A La Science du Hadis A L'Epoque Ottomane' [*sic*]. *Ondokuz Mayis Üniversitesi İlahiyat Fakültesi Dergisi* 3 (1989): 1–41.

Sadık, Cihan. 'Osmanlı Devrinde Türk Hadiscileri Tarafından Yazılan Usulü Hadis Eserleri, Risaleleri ve *Nühbetü'l-Fiker* Üzerine Yapılan Şerh ve Tercümeler.' *Atatürk Üniversitesi İslami İlimler Fakültesi Dergisi* 1, no. 1 (1975): 127–136.

Sezer, Yavuz. 'The Architecture of Bibiliophilia: Eighteenth-Century Ottoman Libraries.' PhD dissertation, Massachusetts Institute of Technology, 2016.

Uzunçarşılı, İsmail Hakkı. *Osmanlı Devletinin İlmiye Teşkilatı.* Ankara: Türk Tarih Kurumu Basimevi, 1965.

Zaman, Muhammad Qasim. 'Commentaries, Print, and Patronage: *Hadith* and the Madrasas in Modern South Asia.' *Bulletin of the School of Oriental and African Studies* 62, no. 1 (1999): 60–81.

Ez-Zebidi, Zeynüddin Ahmed b. Ahmed b. Abdillatif [al-Zabīdī, Zayn al-Dīn Aḥmad b. Aḥmad b. 'Abd al-Laṭīf]. *Sahih-i Buhari Muhtasarı – Tecrid-i Sarih Tercümesi ve Şerhi.* Translated by Ahmet Naim Babanzade and Kamil Miras. 8 vols. Istanbul: Diyanet İşleri Başkanlığı, 2019.

CHAPTER 8

Debating Authority and Authenticity in Modern South Asian Hadith Commentaries: Muḥammad Zakariyyā Kāndhalawī's Awjaz al-masālik

*Ali Altaf Mian**

Introduction

In colonial India the hadith commentary genre saw a considerable rise in popularity among Muslim scholars, some of whom produced multi-volume works as a demonstration of their religious authority and authenticity.[1] This textual production coincided with a growing pedagogical investment in hadith in Indo-Muslim madrasas and the formation of new sectarian identities that continue to inform creedal distinctions and ritual differences among South Asian Muslims in the subcontinent but also in the diaspora.[2] The sectarian orientations (*masālik*) of late nineteenth-century India – the Ahl-i Ḥadīth, Deobandīs and Barelvīs – have deep historical roots.[3] The Deobandī and Barelvī division over the meaning of divine sovereignty and the theological status of the Prophet Muhammad arguably crystallised competing Indian responses to the classical mystical theologian Ibn ʿArabī (d. 638/1240).[4] Likewise, the colonial-era conflicts

---

* I would like to thank Joel Blecher, Ramon Harvey, Ebrahim Moosa and Muhammad Rafeeq Shinwari for their feedback on earlier versions of this chapter.

1 See Zaman, 'Commentaries, Print and Patronage'; Zaman, *The ʿUlama in Contemporary Islam*; Blecher, *Said the Prophet of God*. See also Karagözoğlu, 'Commentaries', 164; Qureshi, 'Reform'.

2 For an in-depth discussion of various, and often overlapping, rationalist and traditionist trends in South Asian madrasa cultures, especially over the last two hundred years, see Moosa, *What is a Madrasa?*

3 Much has been written on these sectarian orientations. For a salient overview, see Malik, *Islam in South Asia*, 397–401.

4 See Tareen, *Defending Muḥammad*. Tareen helpfully demonstrates the centrality of 'divine sovereignty' and the theological status of the Prophet Muhammad in the divisive polemics between the Deobandīs and Barelvīs. Yet, he does not contextualise their differences on these two issues in relation to the South Asian reception history of Ibn

between the Deobandīs and Barelvīs (both Ḥanafīs) on the one hand, and Ahl-i Ḥadīth scholars (South Asia's 'indigenous Salafi community'[5]) on the other hand, evoke earlier debates between 'reason-based jurists' and 'transmission-based jurists'.[6]

These intra-Muslim sectarian orientations also reflected the political and social realities of British India. The use of modern technologies (print and steam) allowed scholars to project their religious authority and the authenticity of their interpretive communities in unprecedented ways. Ḥanafīs and Salafīs also responded to the colonial division of social life into the private sphere of religious and domestic life versus the public order of secular reason and governance.[7] This meant that many religious authorities concentrated their revivalist and reformist efforts in certain seemingly depoliticised textual and institutional spaces (communal magazines and newspapers, the home, mosques, madrasas and Sufi lodges). This partitioning process had its own critics among colonial-era Muslims who called for unity and labelled jurisprudential differences the cause of Muslim political decay. This diagnosis in turn reflected the reformist and revivalist trends of the twelfth/eighteenth century across Muslim-majority societies.[8] Some scholars, however, resisted this diagnosis. For example, the Indo-Muslim historian Shiblī Nuʿmānī (1857–1914) argued that jurisprudential differences arise out of various legitimate reasons, such as changing social circumstances and competing approaches to legal hermeneutics.[9] Muslims

'Arabī. This contextualisation remains a desideratum in the scholarship on South Asian Islamic discursive traditions. For reference to this argument, see Malik, *Islam in South Asia*, 400.

5 I follow Zaman here in referring to Ahl-i Ḥadīth scholars as 'Salafīs': 'South Asia has its indigenous Salafi community, commonly known as the Ahl-i Hadith – a designation that underscores their desire to be guided by the Islamic foundational texts, the Qurʾan and the hadith-reports attributed to the Prophet Muhammad, rather than the norms of the medieval schools of law' (Zaman, *Modern Islamic Thought*, 40). On the Ahl-i Ḥadīth movement, see Siyālkōtī, *Tārīkh-i Ahl-i Ḥadīth*; Riexinger, *Sanaʾullah Amritsari*; Riexinger, 'A Study of the Ahl-i Hadīs'; Riexinger, 'Ibn Taymiya's Worldview'; Preckel, 'Ahl-i Ḥadīth'; Daniel W. Brown, 'Reappraisal', 319–321. See also Mian, 'South Asian Salafism'. For Amritsarī, see also al-Ḥasanī, *Nuzhat al-khawāṭir*, 8:105–106.

6 Jonathan Brown, *The Canonization of al-Bukhārī and Muslim*. Melchert uses the terms 'traditionist-jurisprudents' and 'rationalistic jurisprudents' to refer to the *fuqahāʾ aṣḥāb al-ḥadīth* and the *aṣḥāb al-raʾy*, respectively (Melchert, 'Traditionist-Jurisprudents'). See also Goldziher, *The Ẓāhirīs*, 3–5; Nuʿmānī, *Sīrat-un-Nuʿmān*, 141–142; Schacht, *The Origins of Muhammadan Jurisprudence*.

7 Numerous scholars have documented and analysed the colonialist division of social life into private religiosity and public secularity. For a recent, nuanced account, see Stephens, *Governing Islam*.

8 On this, see Dallal, *Islam without Europe*.

9 For his biography, see Sayyid Sulaymān Nadwī, *Ḥayāt-i Shiblī*; Muḥammad Akram al-Nadawī, *Shiblī Nuʿmānī*; al-Ḥasanī, *Nuzhat al-khawāṭir*, 8:189–191.

can keep their perspectival and practical differences, he further argued, and still collaborate on their communal interests. Thus, unity and difference were not necessarily mutually exclusive investments.[10]

This chapter turns to the hadith commentary genre to describe and critically analyse how Muslims in colonial India navigated the question of unity and difference *vis-à-vis* jurisprudential differences. This genre is salient for addressing this question, since many such differences arise directly out of divergent, if not always contradictory, reports about the Prophet's normative teaching and practice. Commentators thus seek to 'demonstrate the conformity of their reasoning with the Prophet's teachings'[11] and to posit their commentaries as a 'useful means of endorsing legal and theological positions in addition to providing a convenient ground to interpret and neutralize problematic traditions'.[12] In colonial India, both Ḥanafī and Salafī scholars cultivated authority and claimed authenticity by turning to the hadith commentary genre. In this chapter I examine this point by concentrating on a commentary on the *Muwaṭṭaʾ* of Mālik b. Anas (d. 179/796), authored by the Deobandī Ḥanafī scholar Muḥammad Zakariyyā Kāndhalawī.[13]

Kāndhalawī (1898–1982) was at once a Sufi master, hadith professor and Ḥanafī jurist.[14] His writings on hadith include a series of Urdu books on the 'virtues of good deeds', which preachers affiliated with the transnational missionary organisation, Tablīghī Jamāʿat, use as pedagogical texts.[15] This organisation was founded in the late 1920s in North India by Kāndhalawī's

---

10 Nuʿmānī, *Maqālāt-i Shiblī*, 1:220–229.

11 Karagözoğlu, 'Commentaries', 165.

12 Karagözoğlu, 'Commentaries', 165.

13 On Mālik and his approach to jurisprudence, see Abd-Allah, *Mālik and Medina*.

14 There are many sources for his biography, including his own multi-volume autobiography: Kāndhalawī, *Āp bītī*. For an analysis of this text, see Metcalf, 'The Past in the Present'. See also al-Kumillāyī, *al-Budūr al-maḍiyya*, 8:41–60; Sayyid Abū al-Ḥasan Nadwī, *Sawāniḥ Ḥazrat Shaykh al-Ḥadīth*; Nadwī, *Zikr-i Zakariyyā*; al-Nadawī, *al-Muḥaddith al-kabīr*; Sahāranpūrī, *Ḥayāt-i Shaykh*; Naqshbandī, *Shaikh al-ḥadīth Ḥazrat Mawlānā Muḥammad Zakariyyā*.

15 There is considerable scholarship on the Tablīghī Jamāʿat. For general overviews, see Masud (ed.), *Travellers in Faith*; Sikand, *The Origins and Development of the Tablighi-Jamaʿat*. Kāndhalawī's 'books of virtues' (*kutub-i Faẓāʾil*) document and discuss reports about the virtues of good deeds, such as 'virtues of prayer' (*faẓāʾil-i namāz*), 'virtues of remembrance of God' (*faẓāʾil-i zikr*), and so on. They were later collected in a single volume entitled, *Tablīghī niṣāb*, or 'preachers' curriculum', and are now published as *Faẓāʾil-i aʿmāl*. See Kāndhalawī, *Faẓāʾil-i aʿmāl*. For an analysis, see Metcalf, 'Living Hadith'. For his answer to the criticism directed at this body of work, see Kāndhalawī, *Kutub-i faẓāʾil*. For his defense of the Tablīghī Jamāʿat, see Kāndhalawī, *Tablīghī Jamāʿat*. He also authored a hagiography of the Sufi saints of the Chishtī order (Kāndhalawī, *Tārīkh-i mashāʾikh-i Chisht*).

paternal uncle, Muḥammad Ilyās Kāndhalawī (1885–1944).[16] Muḥammad Zakariyyā Kāndhalawī also authored a tract on the 'differences of the jurists', and a voluminous work on Muḥammad b. Ismāʿīl al-Bukhārī's 'chapter headings' (*abwāb*).[17] His most extensive scholarly contribution, however, is the *Awjaz al-masālik ilā Muwaṭṭaʾ Mālik* (lit., 'the most abridged path to Mālik's *Muwaṭṭaʾ*').[18] Note that the use of the word *masālik* in the title alludes to the intra-Muslim polemical context of colonial India. The *Awjaz* is a massive commentary on the *Muwaṭṭaʾ* that is comparable in depth and breadth to those compiled by the Andalusian scholars Ibn ʿAbd al-Barr (d. 463/1071) and Abū al-Walīd al-Bājī (d. 474/1081).[19] Kāndhalawī was occupied with the work from 1926 to 1956, and since the late 1950s numerous editions have been published in South Asia and the Middle East.[20]

The *Awjaz* defends the Ḥanafī tradition by balancing 'content-based' (*matn* or *dirāya*) and 'transmission-based' (*isnād* or *riwāya*) forms of criticism. Kāndhalawī differed from his contemporaries – both Ḥanafīs and Salafīs – who focused their commentaries on the third-/ninth-century Sunnī hadith canon.[21] Thus, the *Awjaz* shifts the terms of the debate from a canon whose compilers are rather critical of reason-based jurisprudence to a second-/eighth-century text whose contents and modes of transmission are more consistent with the Ḥanafī tradition.[22] Kāndhalawī navigates differences with a reverential comportment (*adab*), emphasising to his

16 On him, see Sayyid Abū al-Ḥasan Nadwī, *Sawāniḥ Ḥaẓrat Mawlānā Muḥammad Ilyās Kāndhalawī*; Haq, *The Faith Movement*; Hermansen, 'Said Nursi and Maulana Ilyas'.

17 Kāndhalawī, *Ikhtilāf al-aʾimma*; Kāndhalawī, *The Differences of the Imāms*; al-Kāndhalawī, *al-Abwāb wa-l-tarājim*. For his Urdu and Arabic commentaries on al-Bukhārī's *Ṣaḥīḥ*, see Kāndhalawī, *Taqrīr-i Bukhārī Sharīf*; al-Kāndhalawī, *al-Kanz al-mutawārī*.

18 Al-Kāndhalawī, *Awjaz al-masālik*. There is scant scholarship in Urdu on this hadith commentary. See Farmān and Iqbāl, '*Awjaz al-masālik*'.

19 Ibn ʿAbd al-Barr, *al-Istidhkār*; Ibn ʿAbd al-Barr, *al-Tamhīd*; al-Bājī, *al-Muntaqā*.

20 Al-Kāndhalawī, *Awjaz al-masālik*, 15:382. For the publication history of the commentary, see Sahāranpūrī, *Fihrist-i Taʾlīfāt-i Shaykh*, 1:35–36.

21 See al-Kashmīrī, *Fayḍ al-Bārī*; al-ʿUthmānī, *Fatḥ al-mulhim*; al-Sahāranfūrī, *Badhl al-majhūd*; Shams al-Ḥaqq al-ʿAẓīmabādī and Sharaf al-Ḥaqq al-ʿAẓīmabādī, *ʿAwn al-maʿbūd*; al-Mubārakfūrī, *Tuḥfat al-aḥwadhī*.

22 As Brown explains, 'The Ḥanafī school ... constituted the bulk of the reason-based school to which the transmission-based scholars remained in steadfast opposition. Just as Ḥadīth scholars like al-Bukhārī and al-Ḥākim had condemned Ḥanafīs for departing from the Prophet's true *sunna*, so did the Ḥanafīs like Abū Muṭīʿ Makhūl al-Nasafī (d. 318/930) consider the *ahl al-ḥadīth* brainless literalists, capable of merely parroting the Prophet's words but not of understanding his message' (Jonathan Brown, *The Canonization of al-Bukhārī and Muslim*, 237). Deobandī scholars, however, sought to pacify and reconcile the conflict between early Ḥanafī luminaries and hadith scholars such as al-Bukhārī. See Taqī al-Dīn Nadwī, *Muḥaddithīn-i ʿiẓām*, 161–162. See also Ṣafdar, *Maqām-i Abī Ḥanīfa*. For a more critical assessment by a non-Deobandī colonial-era Indo-Muslim scholar, see Nuʿmānī, *Sīrat-un-Nuʿmān*, 138–140.

contemporaries the advantages of embracing the legal pluralism that is immanent in the traditional law schools. While *adab* permits him to display his loyalty to the tradition and to claim an 'aura of authenticity', it allows the critical reader to observe the role played by tact and deference in neutralising contradictions and disagreements. Kāndhalawī also copiously cites from and builds on earlier hadith and jurisprudential sources and engages with the four Sunnī schools of law, as well as the extinct law schools. This feature of the *Awjaz* enables readers to discern how commentators construct authority and claim authenticity.

In the context of the hadith commentary genre, authority and authenticity are mutually constitutive and the Prophet Muhammad's normative teaching (Sunna) serves as a vintage source of both. Scholars such as Kāndhalawī cultivated religious authority by claiming that their beliefs and actions were authentic imitations of the Sunna. Yet claiming to be an authoritative representative of the Sunna is not merely contingent on intellectual exertion and personal piety. Such claims are realised within social rubrics of recognition and scales of value and are connected to sociopolitical privileges. Joel Blecher thus emphasises the methodological necessity of attending to 'lived experience, power, and interpretive excellences' while studying the hadith commentary genre.[23] Thus, we should examine how Kāndhalawī's commentary on Mālik's *Muwaṭṭa'* reflects his aesthetic and ethical sensibilities and how he deployed the honed interpretive strategies of a broader discursive tradition to intervene in polemics between Indian Ḥanafīs and Ahl-i Ḥadīth/Salafī scholars.

I argue that in the *Awjaz* Kāndhalawī deploys both 'content-based criticism' (*'ilm al-dirāya*) and 'narration- or transmission-based criticism' (*'ilm al-riwāya*) to elaborate on contradictions in reports and differences in legal doctrines.[24] This elaboration in turn justifies the necessity of legal reasoning (and therefore the soundness of the traditional law schools). Kāndhalawī's deployment of this interpretive strategy gives us the impression that he turns to the *Muwaṭṭa'* in the footsteps of an earlier Indo-Muslim hadith scholar, Shāh Walī Allāh of Delhi (1114–1176/1703–1762).[25] Yet here we must be careful not to conflate their overlapping but distinct approaches. Unlike Walī Allāh, Kāndhalawī is not interested in using the *Muwaṭṭa'* to reconcile intra-Sunnī differences in the service of elucidating a unified, capacious approach to the normative order. Rather, his interpretive strategy of using contradictions and differences enables him to simultaneously display his interpretive excellence and to defend the

---

23 Blecher, *Said the Prophet of God*, 15.

24 For an exposition of *'ilm al-dirāya* and *'ilm al-riwāya* on the part of an Indo-Muslim scholar, see Nuʿmānī, *Sīrat-un-Nuʿmān*, 166–178.

25 On Shāh Walī Allāh, see Baljon, *Religion and Thought*; Jalbani, *Life of Shāh Waliyullāh*.

Ḥanafī tradition. I provide evidence for my argument by considering how he interprets two legal controversies related to manual movement: Does touching the penis invalidate ritual purity? Should one raise one's hands to the shoulders before and after bowing in prayer? These were two of the many seemingly minor differences that animated public debates and textual contestations between Ḥanafīs and Salafīs in colonial India (and continue to do so today).[26]

Before proceeding further, note the structure of what follows. I begin by discussing Shāh Walī Allāh's eclectic vision, especially in relation to his engagement with Mālik's *Muwaṭṭaʾ*. I also illuminate how Deobandīs and Salafīs generally resist Walī Allāh's vision. In the next section I furnish readers with a biographical portrait of Kāndhalawī and a discussion of the *Awjaz*. I then offer two close readings that provide evidence for my argument; I also contrast Kāndhalawī's commentary style with that of his predecessor, Walī Allāh, and his contemporary Salafī scholar, ʿAbd al-Raḥmān Mubārakpūrī (d. 1935).[27] In the conclusion I pursue some open-ended ideas and questions about the significance of the hadith commentary genre for understanding modern intra-Muslim contestations of authority and authenticity.

Subtle Resistances

It is tempting to overemphasise Salafī and Deobandī Ḥanafī scholars as competing intellectual heirs of Shāh Walī Allāh of Delhi, since most of them trace their hadith authorisations back to the Prophet Muhammad through Walī Allāh. This singular framing, however, conceals some significant nuances. Salafīs and Deobandīs draw inspiration from a diverse set of scholars and texts to fashion their discursive and social trajectories. Two examples suffice to illustrate this point: Walī Allāh does not appear in the Sufi genealogies of Deobandī scholars and the Ahl-i Ḥadīth scholars also draw on reformist theologians such as the Yemeni scholar Muḥammad b. ʿAlī al-Shawkānī (c. 1173–1255/1760–1839).[28] To posit Salafīs and Deobandīs as competing intellectual heirs of Shāh Walī Allāh also obfuscates their critical, albeit deferential, reactions to his reconciliation of

---

26 Other key debates between South Asian Ḥanafīs and Salafīs concern the recitation of Sūrat al-Fātiḥa (Q. 1) in the prayer, the audible recitation of 'amen' by the congregants in the prayer and the issue of triple divorce (in which Salafīs hold that a husband pronouncing the divorce three times at once does not irrevocably terminate the marriage, while Ḥanafīs maintain that doing this does nullify the marriage contract).

27 For a biographical account, see Nawshahrawī, *Tarājim ʿulamāʾ*, 401–407; al-Ḥasanī, *Nuzhat al-khawāṭir*, 8:259–260.

28 On him, see Haykel, *Revival and Reform in Islam*; Dallal, *Islam without Europe*.

some of the divergent tendencies of Muslim discursive traditions. I will disentangle this point in some detail, since it directly relates to why Kāndhalawī wrote a commentary on Mālik's *Muwaṭṭa'*.

Shāh Walī Allāh was born during the last years of Emperor Aurang-zeb's reign and saw first-hand some of the splendour and glory of the Mughal imperium. Yet Walī Allāh also witnessed the destruction of Delhi in 1151/1739 by the armies of the Persian ruler Nādir Shāh (d. 1160/1747). The waning of Mughal sovereignty perturbed Walī Allāh but it also encour-aged him to think afresh about political change and its relationship to reli-gious thought and practice.[29] He also agonised over the disagreements of the jurists, viewing their divergent methodologies and interpretations as signs of an incoherent epistemological foundation. He approached these two problems – what he saw as his discursive tradition's disharmony and the political order's fragility – in a single analytical framework. His pro-posed solution was a complex moral theology that was also an idealistic political manifesto.[30] This solution seeks to bridge the epistemological gaps between the material world and metaphysical reality, paying special atten-tion to what he calls the 'supports of civilisation' (*al-irtifāqāt*). As was true for Ibn 'Arabī before him, Walī Allāh saw the daily actions of the Prophet Muhammad as the material manifestations of an imaginal unity.

How do the canonical law schools fit into this picture? Walī Allāh takes aim at the uncritical conformity to the law schools and argues that each Muslim must learn the wisdom behind the divine norms (*sharī'a*). For him, most Muslims fail to connect the dots between their meta-physical doctrines and their daily actions. For their part, learned reli-gious authorities such as jurists often fail to educate the masses about the higher objectives of the *sharī'a*. He argues, as a result, that most Muslims do not see the alignment between the immanent and the tran-scendent. Without the ability to see this alignment, practitioners find it hard to grasp how minor rituals, such as raising the hands in prayer, secure worldly benefit and otherworldly bliss.[31] Walī Allāh elucidates the secrets of the *sharī'a* in a hadith-based framework, since he consid-ers hadith to be the noblest of the Islamic sciences. He claimed to have received divine inspiration pointing him in the direction of Mālik's *Muwaṭṭa'*.[32] This mystical experience merged with his sharp analytical skills and afforded him the confidence to interpret the normative order in an original way.

<hr>

29 Zaman, 'Political Power, Religious Authority, and the Caliphate'.
30 Al-Dihlawī, *Ḥujjat Allāh al-Bāligha*; al-Dihlawī, *Shah Wali Allah of Delhi's* Hujjat Allah al-Baligha.
31 See Dallal's account in *Islam without Europe*, 245–274.
32 Al-Dihlawī, *al-Musawwā*, 1:17.

Walī Allāh proposes that Mālik's *Muwaṭṭa'* can help Muslims resolve their jurisprudential differences:

> My heart expanded and I gained certainty about the *Muwaṭṭa'* being the most authentic book on the face of the Earth after the book of God [the Qur'an]. Likewise, it became clear to me that the path to sound and independent reasoning (*ijtihād*) and the acquisition of jurisprudential understanding (*fiqh*) is blocked in this epoch except through a single approach, namely, to concentrate on the *Muwaṭṭa'*, and to interpret its interrupted reports (*marāsīl*) based on knowledge acquired from the sayings of the Companions and the Successors.[33]

Note that Walī Allāh does not encourage a literalist reading of prophetic texts. Instead, he upholds the necessity of legal reasoning and 'the method outlined by the master jurists',[34] which includes 'specifying the meanings of words and synthesising the proof texts by clarifying the various elements, prerequisites, and etiquette [of normative practices]'.[35] Here, he emphasises attending to both the *isnād* (chains of narration) and the *matn* (content) in hadith interpretation, thus forecasting one of the main reformist attitudes toward hadith in the nineteenth and twentieth centuries.[36] Walī Allāh proposes a middle path between adhering to what he deemed time-transcending interpretive methods and time-bound particular legal doctrines and positions. His reformist agenda is summed up in his statement that 'this method implies that *ijtihād* remains a collective obligation for each generation [of Muslims]'.[37]

Walī Allāh thus calls for an innovative approach to the normative order within the bounds of tradition. Yet his careful balancing of innovation and tradition has not been easy for many of his self-professed intellectual heirs. The Deobandīs honour his jurisprudential eclecticism but do not abandon the 'obligation to conform to a single school' (*al-iltizām bi-madhhab mu'ayyan*).[38] The Salafīs also hold him in high regard, but do not see much value in traditional reason-based jurisprudential methodologies. His South Asian 'heirs' have not explored his proposal to use Mālik's *Muwaṭṭa'* to resolve intra-Muslim normative differences. Here, Kāndhalawī's *Awjaz* is an exception, since the author explores contradictions and differences in the classical law schools at length. Yet, as I demonstrate in what follows,

---

33 Al-Dihlawī, *al-Musawwā*, 1:29.

34 Al-Dihlawī, *al-Musawwā*, 1:29.

35 Al-Dihlawī, *al-Musawwā*, 1:29.

36 See Daniel W. Brown, *Rethinking Tradition*, 112–116.

37 Al-Dihlawī, *al-Musawwā*, 1:29.

38 On this, see al-Tahānawī, *I'lā' al-sunan*, 19:9373–9375. See also Thānawī, *al-Iqtiṣād fī-l-taqlīd wa-l-ijtihād*.

Kāndhalawī does not use the *Muwaṭṭa'* to flesh out Walī Allāh's reconciliatory programme. Rather, the *Awjaz* is largely an apologetic effort by
a Ḥanafī traditionist to fortify the authority and authenticity of his legal
school against Salafī detractors. My argument makes it clear that while Walī
Allāh is interested in resolving contradictions between reports (a method
called *jam'* or *tawfīq*), Kāndhalawī prefers one set of reports over another
(a process called *tarjīḥ*, i.e. 'juristic preference').[39] This is not to suggest
that Walī Allāh does not occasionally engage in *tarjīḥ* or that Kāndhalawī
does not engage in jurisprudential reconciliation. Rather, I note that reconciliation is Walī Allāh's hermeneutic modus operandi, since it assists in his
elaboration of a unified, capacious normative order. Kāndhalawī, however,
is primarily invested in a 'juristic preference' that enables him to defend
the Ḥanafī school. In this way, the *Awjaz* amply documents the Deobandī
resistance to Walī Allāh's intra-Sunnī eclecticism. Before we examine
examples of how this happens in the pages of the *Awjaz*, a more detailed
portrait of Kāndhalawī and some further notes on this text are in order.

The Commentator and the Commentary

Muḥammad Zakariyyā Kāndhalawī was born in the United Provinces
of colonial India in a small town known as Kandhla on 3 February 1898
(11 Ramadan 1315).[40] His family was renowned for 'knowledge, righteousness, and piety'.[41] His father and grandfather, Muḥammad Yaḥyā and
Muḥammad Ismā'īl respectively, preoccupied themselves in the teaching
and preaching of the Qur'an, prophetic traditions and Ḥanafī jurisprudence. They were also practising Sufis and embodied strict personal discipline. Kāndhalawī's father, Muḥammad Yaḥyā, was a disciple of the Sufi
and jurist Rashīd Aḥmad Gangōhī (1826–1905), the first major Deobandī
hadith commentator.[42] Kāndhalawī later assisted his father in publishing
Rashīd Aḥmad's commentaries on the hadith collections of al-Bukhārī and
al-Tirmidhī.[43] Muḥammad Yaḥyā paid great attention to his son's religious
upbringing; he taught him Arabic and Persian primers as well as basic theological and jurisprudential texts at home. After memorising the Qur'an at a
young age, Kāndhalawī became a full-time student at a traditional madrasa
in Saharanpur, India.

---

39 See Turkmānī, *Dirāsāt*, 499–506. See also 'Abd al-Ṣamad, *Ta'āruḍ al-akhbār wa-l-tarjīḥ
    baynahā.*
40 Nadwī, *Sawāniḥ Ḥaẓrat Shaykh al-Ḥadīth*, 49.
41 Al-Banūrī, 'Kalima 'an al-mu'allif, 1:7.
42 For his biography, see Mīrathī, *Tazkirat-ur-Rashīd*; al-Ḥasanī, *Nuzhat al-khawāṭir*,
    8:163–167; al-Kumillāyī, *al-Budūr al-maḍiyya*, 7:283–287.
43 Gangōhī and al-Kāndhalawī, *Lāmi' al-darārī*; Gangōhī and al-Kāndhalawī, *al-Kawkab
    al-durrī.* See Zaman, 'Commentaries, Print and Patronage', 69–71.

The madrasa culture in which Kāndhalawī was trained as an adolescent was an amalgamation of a Qur'an memorisation school (*maktab*), a classical Muslim seminary, a colonial Indian British college, a hadith study circle and a Sufi lodge. He was intensely devoted to his studies; his biography states that sometimes six consecutive months would pass by without him stepping outside the walls of Maẓāhir al-ʿUlūm in Saharanpur, the madrasa from which he graduated in 1916.[44] This madrasa and the Dār al-ʿUlūm in Deoband shared an almost identical approach to theology, jurisprudence and Sufism.[45]

Scholars at Deoband and Maẓāhir al-ʿUlūm used a modified version of the twelfth-/eighteenth-century Indo-Muslim curriculum known as the *dars-i Niẓāmī* whose core subjects included Persian and Arabic language and literature, law and legal theory, and the rationalist sciences (*maʿqūlāt*).[46] While these two madrasas valued these subjects, they also transmitted to their students a hadith-centred approach to theology and law.[47] Thus, they modified the Niẓāmī curriculum by omitting some texts of philosophy and logic and adding a final year exclusively devoted to the 'six authentic books' and other classical hadith collections by Mālik, Muḥammad b. al-Ḥasan al-Shaybānī (132–189/750–805), and Abū Jaʿfar al-Ṭaḥāwī (c. 230–321/845–933).[48] Kāndhalawī excelled in his hadith studies to such an extent that his teacher, Khalīl Aḥmad Saharanpūrī (1852–1927), sought his help to complete his research on hadith.[49] Kāndhalawī's rigorous editorial efforts enabled Khalīl Aḥmad to publish his *Badhl al-majhūd*, a voluminous commentary on the *Sunan* of Abū Dāwūd.[50] In the book's initial manuscript, Khalīl Aḥmad wrote that Kāndhalawī 'is worthy of having this work attributed to him', but Kāndhalawī 'deleted this phrase out of respect and reverence [for his teacher]'.[51] When Khalīl Aḥmad died in 1927, Kāndhalawī succeeded him as 'Shaykh al-Ḥadīth'.

It is important to note that Khalīl Aḥmad was also Kāndhalawī's Sufi master. Hadith and Sufism merged in Kāndhalawī's life in a significant way. He likened his editorial work on Khalīl Aḥmad's *Badhl al-majhūd* to the Sufi

---

44 Nadwī, *Sawāniḥ Ḥaẓrat Shaykh al-Ḥadīth*, 59.

45 For scholarship on Deobandī Islam, see Metcalf, *Islamic Revival in British India*; Metcalf, *Islamic Contestations*; Zaman, *The Ulama in Contemporary Islam*; Zaman, *Modern Islamic Thought*; Moosa, *What is a Madrasa?*; Ingram, *Revival from Below*.

46 For a historical account of the Islamic sciences in precolonial India, see al-Ḥasanī, *al-Thaqāfa al-islāmiyya*.

47 For an overview of hadith in South Asia, see Isḥāq, *India's Contribution*; Aḥmad, "Ulūm-i Ḥadīth par Hindustān kī ʿArabī taʾlīfāt'; ʿUsmānī, 'Silsila-yi Shāh Walīullāh kī khidmat-i Ḥadīth'.

48 Mālik b. Anas, *al-Muwaṭṭaʾ*; al-Shaybānī, *Muwaṭṭaʾ*; al-Ṭaḥāwī, *Sharḥ maʿānī al-āthār*.

49 For his biography, see Mīrathī, *Tazkirat-ul-Khalīl*; al-Ḥasanī, *Nuzhat al-khawāṭir*, 8:145–148; al-Kumillāyī, *al-Budūr al-maḍiyya*, 7:158–162.

50 Al-Saḥāranfūrī, *Badhl al-majhūd*.

51 Taqī al-Dīn Nadwī, 'Muqaddima', 29.

ideal of annihilation. Note that in some strands of Sufi thought and practice, annihilation (*fanā'*) first begins with 'annihilation in the Sufi master', which is then transformed into 'annihilation in the Prophet Muḥammad'.[52] The act of compiling footnotes on his Sufi master's hadith commentary was at once a method for him to deepen his attachment to hadith *and* Sufism. By Kāndhalawī's time, this practice of combining the study of hadith and Sufism was a well-trodden path for South Asian jurists and Sufis.[53]

To annihilate oneself in the Sufi master, then in the person of the Prophet Muhammad and finally in God involves developing a highly reverential relationship with these objects of devotional love. In this regard, biographical sources draw attention to Kāndhalawī's adoration for and awe of his 'elders', the Prophet and God. In some of these sources, his students characterise his lectures on al-Bukhārī's *Ṣaḥīḥ* and Abū Dāwūd's *Sunan* as full of 'concentration, compassion, diligence, zeal, and cheerfulness'.[54] His student Taqī al-Dīn Nadwī writes, 'He ornamented the lecture hall of Dār al-Ḥadīth with his sweet-scented presence. The reverence, honour, and peace of mind we experienced in his presence made us feel as if the Prophet Muḥammad himself was in our midst.'[55] In some cases, commentary lectures involved physical lessons. For example, a report in the 'Book of Prayer' in al-Bukhārī's *Ṣaḥīḥ* is difficult to understand without a physical demonstration. According to this report, the Prophet

> stood up near a piece of wood in the mosque [after finishing the prayer], and leaned on it in such a manner [that it appeared that] he was quite upset. He then put his right hand over his left hand, and clasped his hands by interlacing his fingers, then he placed his right cheek in the palm of his left hand.

In his lectures on al-Bukhārī, Kāndhalawī would stand up to demonstrate this prophetic posture, acting out the report's content (*matn*), so to speak.[56]

Kāndhalawī also commented on intra-Sunnī jurisprudential differences in his hadith lectures. Taqī al-Dīn Nadwī notes that while Kāndhalawī often defended Ḥanafī legal doctrines, he did so without deriding opponents such as Ibn Ḥajar al-'Asqalānī (773–852/1372–1449). In fact, he

---

52 For a complication of this trajectory, see Ogunnaike, 'Annihilation in the Messenger Revisited'.

53 Some of the major exemplars of this trend in South Asian Islam include 'Alī al-Muttaqī (885–975/1480–1568), Muḥammad Ṭāhir al-Patanī of Gujarat (914–980/1508–1578), 'Abd al-Ḥaqq al-Dihlawī (958–1052/1551–1642) and Shāh Walī Allāh of Delhi (1114–1176/1702–1763).

54 Taqī al-Dīn Nadwī, 'Muqaddima', 31.

55 Taqī al-Dīn Nadwī, 'Muqaddima', 31.

56 Taqī al-Dīn Nadwī, 'Muqaddima', 34.

218 ALI ALTAF MIAN

'acknowledged the indebtedness of all hadith students to Ibn Ḥajar',[57] but noted that the latter 'pretended' that Ḥanafī jurists lacked scriptural proofs for their legal doctrines. Kāndhalawī sought ways to translate reports into modern idioms and shared his stories about his teachers and other Indo-Muslim religious luminaries with his students. Taqī al-Dīn states that his teacher paid special attention to reports that authenticate Ḥanafī legal doctrines, making the latter 'appear as closely aligned with hadith'.[58]

After teaching hadith in Saharanpur for over forty years, in 1973 Kāndhalawī permanently settled in Medina, where he died in 1982. His influence among Deobandīs, and among many South Asian Muslims more broadly, is largely due to two factors: (1) his hadith books, which have been popularised by the Tablīghī Jamāʿat and (2) the noteworthy madrasa network of his student disciples in India, Pakistan, Bangladesh, southern Africa, the United Kingdom and North America. His Sufi order is a vibrant global network with disciples and successors in places as diverse as London, Lahore and Lusaka. In this regard, one student disciple, Muḥammad Yūsuf Motālā (1946–2019), deserves special mention as the founder (in 1973) of the first Deobandī madrasa in the Western hemisphere; it is in Holcombe (near Bury, England). Muḥammad Yūsuf's students and disciples are active as imams, hadith teachers and spiritual guides, in mosques and madrasas, but also on social media.[59] We can now briefly examine the text at hand, namely, the *Awjaz al-masālik*.

In his 1972 preface to the *Awjaz*, Muḥammad Yūsuf al-Banūrī (1908–1977), a leading student of the Deobandī traditionist and jurist Anwar Shāh Kashmīrī (1875–1933) and a distinguished hadith scholar in his own right, lists various 'distinctions' (*khaṣāʾiṣ*) of Kāndhalawī's commentary.[60] To summarise his main points, the *Awjaz* comments on both the report itself (*matn*) and its chain of narration (*isnād*). It deals with *isnād*s in a concise manner and concentrates in greater depth on a tradition's meaning. Kāndhalawī identifies a report's phraseological variations and contextualises the report in the jurisprudential framework of the canonical Sunnī law schools. The *Awjaz* also includes abundant citations from earlier commentaries of the *Muwaṭṭaʾ*.[61]

---

57 Taqī al-Dīn Nadwī, 'Muqaddima', 32.

58 Taqī al-Dīn Nadwī, 'Muqaddima', 32–33.

59 Birt and Lewis, 'The Pattern of Islamic Reform in Britain'.

60 Al-Banūrī, 'Kalima ʿan al-muʾallif'.

61 According to Raḥmat Allāh al-Nadawī, Kāndhalawī's most trusted authorities include Ibn ʿAbd al-Barr's *al-Tamhīd* (on which he relies for debates concerning chains of narration, or *asānīd*), al-Bājī's *al-Muntaqā* (for jurisprudential interpretation and for the general sense of a report), al-Zarqānī's *Sharḥ* (for philology and for the biographies of narrators), and Khalīl Aḥmad's *Badhl al-majhūd*, which is especially instructive for insights into composition, argumentation and the biographies of narrators (al-Nadawī, *al-Muḥaddith al-kabīr*, 278).

For al-Banūrī, the *Awjaz* 'is the most comprehensive commentary on the *Muwaṭṭa'* in terms of hadith studies, jurisprudence, and philology'.[62] The *Awjaz* is also like 'a connective tissue between the luminaries of India and the notables of the Arab world'[63] since it draws on Indo-Muslim sources rarely consulted in the Arabic-speaking world. Moreover, the *Awjaz* adopts a clear and balanced method of exposition; it strikes a balance between verbosity and brevity. In this way, al-Banūrī highlights Kāndhalawī's 'interpretive excellences'. Yet the latter's commentary also addresses a broader social arena.

According to the broader logic that governs the *Awjaz*, the most effective defence of the Ḥanafī tradition involves demonstrating the authority and authenticity of the textual and non-textual types of the Prophet's practice (Sunna). Mālik's *Muwaṭṭa'* is especially useful for this objective, since it honours both types of Sunna. Kāndhalawī seeks to demonstrate the authority of 'the inherited tradition' (*al-sunnat al-mutawāratha*), especially in its non-textual forms (such as social institutions and embodied practices). This demonstration in turn bolsters the authority and authenticity of the Ḥanafī tradition, since many of its legal doctrines rely on an inherited tradition that was not always verified by the Sunnī hadith canon. Yet we should note that what Kāndhalawī offers in the *Awjaz* is not only an apologetic polemic directed at Ahl-i Ḥadīth scholars but also a subtle response to Shāh Walī Allāh's eclectic, capacious approach to the normative order. The following two illustrations from the *Awjaz* demonstrate this point.

Touching the Penis

At the beginning of the *Muwaṭṭa'* a cluster of six reports suggests that it is necessary to make ablution (*wuḍū'*) after touching the genitalia. These reports reflect the position of the Mālikīs, Shāfiʿīs, and Ḥanbalīs.[64] The Ḥanafīs, however, unambiguously state that touching the penis does not invalidate purity. Before exploring this matter further, let us first consider the report that Kāndhalawī focuses on in his commentary:

According to Mālik, ʿAbdallāh b. Abī Bakr reported from Ibn Muḥammad b. ʿAmr b. Ḥazm that he heard ʿUrwa b. al-Zubayr say, 'I met with Marwān b. al-Ḥakam, and we discussed what necessitates the performance of ablution. Marwān said, "Touching one's penis necessitates ablution." ʿUrwa said, "I did not know that." Marwān b. al-Ḥakam then said, "Busra bt. Ṣafwān informed me that she heard

---

62 Al-Banūrī, 'Kalima ʿan al-muʾallif', 9.
63 Al-Banūrī, 'Kalima ʿan al-muʾallif', 10.
64 On this issue, see Wheeler, 'Touching the Penis in Islamic Law'.

the Messenger of God say, 'If someone touches his penis, he should perform ablution.'"[65]

We can refer to this as 'the report of Busra.' Shāh Walī Allāh's commentary on this matter is quite brief:

According to al-Shāfiʿī, it is obligatory to perform ablution after touching the genitalia if this touching involves the palm of the hand or rubbing between fingers. For Abū Ḥanīfa, however, touching the genitalia does not invalidate *wuḍūʾ*, and his evidence for this position is the saying of the Prophet, 'Is it not only a part of your body?'[66]

Kāndhalawī's commentary starts by citing Ibn Qudāma's definition of 'genitalia': it is 'another name for those body parts that discharge impurities and can refer to the penis, vagina, and anus'.[67] Kāndhalawī problematises this definition:

It is clear that the author [Mālik] is only referring to the penis. As for touching the vagina and anus, none of the following reports address this, as is clear from these texts. According to the Mālikīs, touching the anus does not invalidate *wuḍūʾ*, even though there is much disagreement among jurists on this issue.[68]

Kāndhalawī then summarises numerous reports on this issue, allowing readers to see that there is significant disagreement among the Companions, the Successors and the master jurists of the four law schools. He presents the Ḥanafī position as remarkably consistent on the matter: 'touching the penis does not invalidate *wuḍūʾ*'.[69] However, the views of non-Ḥanafī jurists are not as clear. For example, some think that touching the genitalia invalidates one's ablution only when done intentionally. Others stipulate that it is only touching with the palm of one's hand that invalidates *wuḍūʾ*. Some say that purity is lost only if lust is involved. Kāndhalawī directs the reader to the Mālikī scholar Abū Bakr b. al-ʿArabī's commentary on al-Tirmidhī's *Jāmiʿ* for a fuller account of these differences.[70]

Kāndhalawī next turns his attention to the six reports on this matter in Mālik's *Muwaṭṭaʾ*. He starts with the observation that only the first of the

---

65 Mālik b. Anas, *al-Muwaṭṭaʾ*, 95.
66 Al-Dihlawī, *al-Musawwā*, 1:73.
67 Ibn Qudāma, *al-Mughnī*, 1:240.
68 Al-Kāndhalawī, *Awjaz al-masālik*, 1:268. For other Deobandī treatments of this issue in the context of the hadith commentary genre, see al-Banūrī, *Maʿārif al-sunan*, 1:356–361.
69 Al-Kāndhalawī, *Awjaz al-masālik*, 1:269.
70 Ibn al-ʿArabī, *ʿĀriḍat al-aḥwadhī*, 1:113–123.

six reports can be attributed to the Prophet (that is, only the first report is a *ḥadīth marfūʿ*). The other five reports are sayings of the Companions (*āthār al-Ṣaḥāba*). He then engages in an ingenious interpretive exercise called 'opposition of attributed reports' (*muʿāraḍa al-marfūʿ bi-l-marfūʿ*).[71] He informs us that the Ḥanafīs cite and support their position by means of another *ḥadīth marfūʿ* on this matter, namely: 'Ṭalq b. ʿAlī said, 'A person asked the Prophet about a man who touches his penis: should he perform ablution?' The Prophet replied, "Is it not only a part of your body?"'[72] (Note that Shāh Walī Allāh, as mentioned above, alludes to the same report.) Clearly, this report contradicts 'the report of Busra' (see above). Instead of letting the contradiction stand, as Walī Allāh did, Kāndhalawī demonstrates his mastery of 'narration- or transmission-based criticism' (*ʿilm al-riwāya*) to expose the weakness of the report of Busra and to establish the soundness of the *ḥadīth marfūʿ*, which supports the Ḥanafī position (the report of Ṭalq b. ʿAlī).

Kāndhalawī also cites earlier Ḥanafī authorities who dismissed the report of Busra on the grounds that she was not qualified to know this, since 'the issue pertains to the matters of men'.[73] Moreover, Kāndhalawī appeals to the Ḥanafī legal principle according to which a solitary report is insufficient to determine norms in matters of common hardship (*ʿumūm al-balwā*, i.e., requiring Muslim men to wash their bodies each time they touched their penis would amount to practical hardship). In short, the hermeneutical strategy of 'opposition of attributed reports' allows Kāndhalawī to use contradictions to defend the Ḥanafī position. As for the possibility that the report used by the Ḥanafīs is unreliable, Kāndhalawī refers his readers to the *Badhl al-majhūd* of his teacher Khalīl Aḥmad, which comments on the authenticity of this report.[74] Here we see how, without saying so, Kāndhalawī positions himself as a judge between the proof texts of the Ḥanafī school and those of the other law schools on this issue. And in his judgement, the Ḥanafīs are winners. We can also see, quite clearly, that he is not invested in eclecticism or reconciliation, but uses both *matn* and *isnād* tools to pursue his apologetic agenda.

Raising the Hands in Prayer

The *Muwaṭṭaʾ* contains a chapter titled 'Commencement of the Prayer (*Ṣalāt*)', which includes the following report:

According to Mālik, Ibn Shihāb reported from Sālim b. ʿAbdallāh, from ʿAbdallāh b. ʿUmar, that when the Messenger of God commenced the prayer, he would raise both of his hands to the level of his

---

71 Al-Kāndhalawī, *Awjaz al-masālik*, 1:273.
72 Al-Kāndhalawī, *Awjaz al-masālik*, 1:271.
73 Al-Kāndhalawī, *Awjaz al-masālik*, 1:272.
74 Al-Sahāranfūrī, *Badhl al-majhūd*, 2:53–63.

shoulders, and when he stood up after bowing, he raised them again in a similar manner and said, 'God hears those who praise Him. All praise belongs to You, our Lord!' He did not do that, however, when he stood up following prostration.[75]

This report contradicts the Ḥanafī position, which stipulates that the only time one raises the hands to the shoulders is at the beginning of the prayer. However, both Shāfiʿīs and Ḥanbalīs believe it is necessary to raise one's hands to the shoulders before and after bowing, as a recurring act *inside* the prayer. There are two Mālikī positions on the matter. The first is in accordance with the above report (and thus in accordance with the Shāfiʿīs and Ḥanbalīs), and the second, which is mentioned in the *Mudawanna* (another major Mālikī legal compendium), is in accordance with the Ḥanafīs. Note that in addition to the above report there are many others in the Sunnī hadith canon that support the non-Ḥanafī position.

With the weight of transmission-based proofs against his law school, Kāndhalawī deploys a clever interpretive strategy. He first lists all the reports that pertain to various types of 'raising of hands' (*rafʿ al-yadayn*). These reports mention raising the hands when one begins the prayer, raising the hands before and after bowing, raising the hands before and after prostration and raising the hands after completing two prayer cycles. After a lengthy discussion, Kāndhalawī addresses the reader: 'Perhaps you have understood from the aforementioned reports and sayings of scholars that various forms of raising the hands in prayer are proven from authentic traditions?'[76] Kāndhalawī thus assembles the contradictory reports about manual movements to argue for the necessity of legal reasoning, since following all the authentic reports on this issue means that one would perform the prayer without any formal consistency. In the presence of such contradictions, Ḥanafī jurists rely on 'juristic preference' (*tarjīḥ*) out of necessity.

Here we see how, for Kāndhalawī, the 'contradiction of reports' (*taʿāruḍ al-riwāyāt*) serves to invalidate the *sola scriptura* method advocated by the Salafīs. When one takes seriously the transmission-based archive of hadith, the logical conclusion is to use reason-based jurisprudence.[77] To make his case for 'juristic preference', Kāndhalawī argues that the Ḥanafīs and Mālikīs alone cannot be blamed for preferring one set of reports when the Shāfiʿīs and Mālikīs also engage in 'juristic preference' by abandoning reports about raising the hands before and after prostration.[78] Thus, with

---

75 Mālik b. Anas, *al-Muwaṭṭaʾ*, 113.

76 Al-Kāndhalawī, *Awjaz al-masālik*, 2:47. For other Deobandī treatments of this issue in the context of the hadith commentary genre, see al-Kashmīrī, *Fayḍ al-Bārī*, 2:321–331; al-ʿUthmānī, *Fatḥ al-mulhim*, 3:306–329; al-Banūrī, *Maʿārif al-sunan*, 2:453–506.

77 Al-Kāndhalawī, *Awjaz al-masālik*, 2:48.

78 Al-ʿUthmānī also makes this point; see *Fatḥ al-mulhim*, 3:327.

reference to this issue all law schools engage in some form of juristic preference.[79] Yet for Kāndhalawī it is important not to give readers the impression that in this matter the Ḥanafī position depends solely on 'forms of juristic preference' (*wujūh at-tarjīḥ*).[80]

Kāndhalawī offers ten prophetic reports to defend the Ḥanafī position, and in so doing displays his mastery of *isnād* criticism. He then presents several sayings of Companions, underscoring the idea that on the matter of raising one's hands during the prayer, we must clearly distinguish between 'textual reports' and 'communal practice'. It is in this context that he answers Salafis: 'It cannot be said that the reports I have mentioned are weak or that their narrators are compromised just because al-Bukhārī and Muslim do not include them in their books. Nor can someone who has insight into the science of hadith raise such objections.'[81] Kāndhalawī cites both Aḥmad b. Ḥanbal (164–241/780–855) and Jalāl al-Dīn al-Suyūṭī (849–911/1445–1505) to argue that the actual number of 'authentic' reports far exceeds the contents of the collections of al-Bukhārī and Muslim, saying: 'It is clear that authentic reports are not restricted to what is present in the extant circulating books.'[82] Kāndhalawī further suggests that al-Bukhārī and Muslim only recorded those reports that agreed with their personal jurisprudential positions. He also points out that while from the vantage of *isnād* criticism the collections of al-Bukhārī and Muslim are the most authentic books after the Qur'an, those familiar with hadith studies know that these two compilers and their narrators are not immune from scrutiny. Yet he does not say this to encourage hypervigilance in *isnād* criticism. Rather, his point is to restrict this form of criticism. Thus, he emphasises holistic interpretations and focuses on solving the practical issues faced by ordinary Muslims:

> There are entire archives (*dafātir*) that can be constructed to support both sides of this debate, and this is the secret behind why the Ḥanafīs, may God reward them for their efforts, do not pursue the extensive listing of reports ... and instead focus their efforts on the extraction of legal details, since that is what the blessed Muslim community requires for practical purposes.[83]

Kāndhalawī thus defends the Ḥanafī tradition by appealing to both reason-based and transmission-based forms of argumentation. He cites

79 Al-Kāndhalawī, *Awjaz al-masālik*, 2:48.
80 On the debates involved in *tarjīḥ* internal to Muslim legal traditions, see ʿAwwāma, *Athar al-ḥadīth al-sharīf*, 145–165; for a more precise account of these debates in the Ḥanafī tradition, see Turkmānī, *Dirāsāt*, 510–531.
81 Al-Kāndhalawī, *Awjaz al-masālik*, 2:52.
82 Al-Kāndhalawī, *Awjaz al-masālik*, 2:52.
83 Al-Kāndhalawī, *Awjaz al-masālik*, 2:52.

'Abd al-Wahhāb al-Shaʿrānī (897–973/1492–1565) to claim that 'it suffices for the authenticity of a report that it has formed the basis for the action of the major jurists'.[84] This point echoes the traditional Ḥanafī legal principle, according to which preference should be given to jurists' reports over non-jurists' reports.[85]

What reason-based interpretive strategies served Kāndhalawī's polemical purposes? First and foremost, he claims, Ḥanafī jurists prefer to read the normative order in light of the Qur'an.[86] Their position on not raising hands before and after bowing in prayer is extrapolated from the Qur'anic verse, 'and stand before God in sincere devotion' (2:38).[87] Ḥanafī jurists also entertain the likely possibility that the practice of raising one's hands in prayer was abrogated in the final years of the Prophet's mission, because many Companions, especially those based in Medina and Kufa, did not raise their hands. This position can be traced back to the fourth-/tenth-century jurist Abū Jaʿfar al-Ṭaḥāwī (d. 321/933). However, here Kāndhalawī differs from other Deobandī scholars, such as Anwar Shāh Kashmīrī, who defend the Ḥanafī position without endorsing al-Ṭaḥāwī's judgement about abrogation.[88] Kāndhalawī then discusses the rational proof, according to which '[the evolving form of] prayer transitioned [in the Prophet's lifetime] from movements to calmness, and so from among the contradictory reports on this issue, the Ḥanafīs choose what is closest to [achieving] calmness'.[89] Kāndhalawī also cites the argument from al-Ṭaḥāwī that raising the hands and turning one's face right and left are opening and closing gestures of the prayer. According to this line of reasoning, these two gestures are used exclusively in the prayer and differentiate it from other human actions.[90] In what follows, we see that Shāh Walī Allāh offers a different perspective on such 'forms of juristic preference'.

In the final analysis, Kāndhalawī seeks to demonstrate that one cannot read reports alone to determine the norm, even in something as minor as raising the hands (though this is not a trivial matter for him). The diversity of, and contradictions in, reports necessitates legal reasoning. The language he uses to make his case is at times quite apologetic and he

---

84 Al-Kāndhalawī, *Awjaz al-masālik*, 2:52–53.

85 On this, see al-Tahānawī, *Iʿlā' al-sunan*, 19:9398–9400. See also al-Kāndhalawī, *Awjaz al-masālik*, 1:9.

86 For an exposition of this Ḥanafī jurisprudential principle, see Nāṣir, 'Fiqh al-ḥadīth', 314–315.

87 Al-Kāndhalawī, *Awjaz al-masālik*, 2:53.

88 See al-Kashmīrī, *Nayl al-farqadayn*; ʿUsmānī, *Dars-i Tirmidhī*. For al-Kashmīrī's biography, see al-Banūrī, *Nafḥat al-ʿanbar*; al-Ḥasanī, *Nuzhat al-khawāṭir*, 8:90–94; al-Kumillāyī, *al-Budūr al-maḍiyya*, 5:87–127; Abū Ghudda, *Tarājim sitta*, 13–81.

89 Al-Kāndhalawī, *Awjaz al-masālik*, 2:53.

90 Al-Kāndhalawī, *Awjaz al-masālik*, 2:53.

sometimes lumps together the Ḥanafīs and Mālikīs without acknowledging the difference of opinion on this issue that had characterised the Mālikī tradition.[91] Kāndhalawī thus offers quite a different approach than what we find in Shāh Walī Allāh's extremely brief note on the same report, in which he says, 'this report serves to establish for most learned authorities the [legitimacy of] raising the hands at the beginning of the prayer as well as before and after bowing. However, for Abū Ḥanīfa, the hands are not raised except [i.e. raised only] at the beginning of the prayer.'[92] It is useful to dwell on this comparison to see how Kāndhalawī's exegetical aims differ from that of his twelfth-/eighteenth-century predecessor.

Walī Allāh addresses the question of raising the hands lucidly in his masterpiece, *Ḥujjat Allāh al-bāligha*. I cite his words at some length since they flesh out how he differs from Kāndhalawī's mode of reasoning:

> Raising the hands is a reverential act that alerts the self to abandon preoccupation with all that might distract from the prayer. This act also prepares the self to enter the field of supplication. The Prophet raised his hands at the beginning of each of the three major reverential parts of the prayer [standing, bowing, and prostration], so that the self might be reminded to be aware of the benefit [of these acts of reverence]. This act is one of those forms that the Prophet performed and abandoned, and both practices are validated by his *sunna*. This is why each position has its followers from among the Companions, the Successors, and those who came after them. This is in fact one of those matters on which the following two groups differed: the people of Medina and the people of Kufa. Each group has solid proof on its side. The truth of the matter, in my view, is that both practices are normative ... but I prefer those who raise their hands [before and after bowing] over those who do not, since their position is supported by more and sounder prophetic reports. However, it is not suitable for anyone to invite upon himself the wrath of his compatriots in such matters [by following the legal position that is not customary in one's locality].[93]

Note that Walī Allāh reconciles this jurisprudential difference to secure an eclectic approach to the normative order. He relies on content-based analysis to vindicate the non-Ḥanafī position ('reverential act that alerts the self'), but also mentions a transmission-based reason ('more and sounder reports'). In his view, the two vying groups are not Ḥanafīs and

91 For debates among Mālikī jurists on this question, see Fierro, 'La polemique'.
92 Al-Dihlawī, *al-Musawwā*, 1:142.
93 Al-Dihawī, *Ḥujjat Allāh al-Bāligha*, 1:16.

Mālikīs on one side, and Shāfiʿīs and Ḥanbalīs on the other side. Rather, the disagreement, as he sees it, is between the people of Medina and those of Kufa. Mālik's *Muwaṭṭa'* essentially upholds the position that was later taken to be normative by the Shāfiʿīs and Ḥanbalīs. Also note that Walī Allāh reveals his preference but creates room in the normative order for both interpretations, and so advises against the disruption of a local norm as long as it is based in the *sunna*.

A Salafi Commentary

How did Ahl-i Ḥadīth scholars comment on this issue? To answer this question, I briefly examine a commentary on al-Tirmidhī's *al-Jāmiʿ al-Ṣaḥīḥ* by the Ahl-i Ḥadīth scholar ʿAbd al-Raḥmān Mubārakpūrī (al-Mubārakfūrī). Al-Tirmidhī mentions reports about raising the hands before and after bowing in two chapters (*abwāb*). The main report is in the chapter titled 'Raising the hands while bowing', and has the following chain:

Tirmidhī – Qutayba – Ibn Abī ʿUmar [Muḥammad b. Yaḥyā] – Sufyān b. ʿUyayna – al-Zuhrī – Sālim – the latter's faith [the Companion ʿAbdallāh b. ʿUmar].[94]

In this report ʿAbdallāh b. ʿUmar describes the Prophet Muhammad as raising his hands to his shoulders when he began the prayer and doing the same before and after bowing. However, he did not raise his hands to his shoulders before and after the prostration. This first report does not support the Ḥanafī position. The second chapter, 'What has been transmitted from the Prophet as he only raised his hands the first time [while initiating the prayer]', mentions a report that supports the Ḥanafī position and has the following chain:

Hannād – Wakīʿ – Sufyān [al-Thawrī] – ʿĀsim b. Kulayb – ʿAbd al-Raḥmān b. al-Aswad – ʿAlqama – ʿAbdallāh b. Masʿūd.[95]

In his commentary al-Mubārakfūrī presents a detailed refutation of the second report attributed to the Companion ʿAbdallāh b. Masʿūd (hereafter Ibn Masʿūd). Al-Mubārakfūrī writes, 'This report is weak, as you will soon learn, and is not a trusted report with reference to raising the hands while bowing.'[96] He thus contradicts al-Tirmidhī, who said: 'This report

---

94 Al-Mubārakfūrī, *Tuḥfat al-aḥwadhī*, 2:118. In what follows, I use the Arabicised al-Mubārakfūrī instead of the Urdu Mubārakpūrī since the text is in Arabic.

95 Al-Mubārakfūrī, *Tuḥfat al-aḥwadhī*, 2:122–123.

96 Al-Mubārakfūrī, *Tuḥfat al-aḥwadhī*, 2:123.

is of good standing and forms the basis of [the position of] many learned authorities from the Prophet's Companions and the Successors. It is also the saying of Sufyān al-Thawrī and the people of Kufa.'[97] Al-Mubārakfūrī, however, argues to the contrary:

> While al-Tirmidhī deems this report 'good' and Ibn Ḥazm has authenticated it, indeed ʿAbdallāh b. Mubārak considers it 'weak' and does not confirm the report of Ibn Masʿūd. Moreover, after narrating this report, Abū Dāwūd says in his *Sunan*: 'This report abridges a longer report, and its wording here is not reliable.'[98]

Al-Mubārakfūrī accuses al-Tirmidhī of laxity (*tasāhul*) in *isnād* criticism, and with reference to Ibn Ḥazm, he writes, 'Here, Ibn Ḥazm cannot be taken seriously since numerous other hadith authorities have determined the report in question to be "weak"'.[99] Al-Mubārakfūrī also cites from al-Bukhārī's chapter on 'raising the hands' to refute the authenticity of the report attributed to Ibn Masʿūd.[100]

To further make his case, al-Mubārakfūrī cites at length from Ibn ʿAbd al-Barr's *al-Tamhīd*, underscoring that the most reliable report on raising the hands before and after bowing is the one attributed to ʿAbdallāh b. ʿUmar (see above), and its content is corroborated by reports of at least twelve additional Companions. On the report that supports the Ḥanafī position, al-Mubārakfūrī cites Ibn Ḥibbān's saying from Ibn Ḥajar al-ʿAsqalani's *al-Talkhīṣ*:

> This is the best report that has been narrated in favour of the position of the people of Kufa on the absence of raising of hands before and after bowing in prayer. Yet in reality it is the weakest [element] to depend on, since its various weaknesses [of the *isnād*] obliterate its authenticity.[101]

Al-Mubārakfūrī also considers sayings of the Companions (*āthār*). The first two *āthār* he presents, namely the sayings of ʿUmar and ʿAlī b. Abī Ṭālib, are used by al-Ṭaḥāwī to defend the Ḥanafī position. Al-Mubārakfūrī refutes the authenticity of the *āthār* that support the Ḥanafī position and in doing so censures modern Indian Ḥanafī scholars, such as ʿAbd al-Ḥayy al-Laknawī (1848–1886).[102] While al-Mubārakfūrī has a good grasp of

---

97 Al-Mubārakfūrī, *Tuḥfat al-aḥwadhī*, 2:124.

98 Al-Mubārakfūrī, *Tuḥfat al-aḥwadhī*, 2:124.

99 Al-Mubārakfūrī, *Tuḥfat al-aḥwadhī*, 2:125.

100 See al-Bukhārī, *Kitāb rafʿ al-yadayn*.

101 Al-Mubārakfūrī, *Tuḥfat al-aḥwadhī*, 2:125.

102 On him, see Abū al-Ḥājj, *al-Manhaj al-fiqhhī*; al-Ḥasanī, *Nuzhat al-khawāṭir*, 8:250–256.

Ḥanafī scholars' writings, he does not engage with those dimensions of their arguments that rely on extra-hadith jurisprudential methodology. For example, there is no mention of 'forms of juristic preference' (*wujūh al-tarjīḥ*) in his Salafī polemic.[103]

Al-Mubārakfūrī finally asks: What if we accept the authenticity of Ibn Masʿūd's report? Al-Mubārakfūrī does not raise this possibility to affirm legal pluralism but to further weaken his opponent's position. In doing so he attacks Ibn Masʿūd himself, claiming that his reports are tainted by his (Ibn Masʿūd's) forgetfulness. He also cites the Ḥanafī authority Badr al-Dīn al-ʿAynī (d. 855/1451) to make the point that in the case of contradictory reports, one must prefer the most authentic report. Finally, he relies on Ibn Ḥazm to argue that Ibn Masʿūd's report establishes the 'non-existence of obligation' (*ʿadam al-wujūb*) and not the abrogation (*naskh*) of the practice of raising one's hands before and after bowing.[104]

Al-Mubārakfūrī's criticism of the Companion Ibn Masʿūd tangentially echoes the views of Shāh Walī Allāh. Yet there is a substantial difference between the two commentators. Walī Allāh balances criticism and reverential comportment (*adab*). He explains that Ibn Masʿūd's views are based on his 'understanding that the purpose of the prayer is to calm the body parts, and he did not think that raising the hands is a reverential act'.[105] Note Walī Allāh's use of empathy: 'One must also consider that he might have thought that raising the hands signifies abandoning something [throwing it behind one's back] and that is why he saw it as inappropriate for this act to occur *inside* the prayer.'[106] This does not mean that Walī Allāh agrees with Ibn Masʿūd. Rather, he offers his own independent interpretation: 'It did not appear to Ibn Masʿūd that this act is [done] to alert the self to abandon everything besides God, and this [awareness] is desirable in every part of the prayer. And God knows best.'[107] In Walī Allāh's hands, transmission-based concerns about authenticity do not weaken the authority of Ibn Masʿūd's position. At the same time, he re-centres the spiritual objectives of the prayer in order to justify his own position. Thus, he models ecumenical cosmopolitanism and uses a method that balances the *matn* and *isnād*. Yet his vision for unity and difference does not sustain Deobandī Ḥanafīs or Ahl-i Ḥadīth Salafīs.

Conclusion

In this chapter I have explored the limitations of intra-Muslim eclecticism and the enduring anxieties of authority and authenticity among Salafīs

---

103 Al-Mubārakfūrī, *Tuḥfat al-aḥwadhī*, 2:129–133.
104 Al-Mubārakfūrī, *Tuḥfat al-aḥwadhī*, 2:125–126.
105 Al-Dihlawī, *Ḥujjat Allāh al-bāligha*, 1:16.
106 Al-Dihlawī, *Ḥujjat Allāh al-bāligha*, 1:16.
107 Al-Dihlawī, *Ḥujjat Allāh al-bāligha*, 1:16–17.

and Ḥanafīs in modern South Asia. My aim, in part, has been to illuminate the particular 'interpretive excellences' modelled by Indo-Muslim hadith commentators. I have also sought to show that their hermeneutic efforts take place in broader social frameworks, such as the contestations between the Salafī/Ahl-i Ḥadīth movement and Deobandī Ḥanafīs. Finally, I have attempted to highlight the salience of the hadith commentary genre for understanding how 'minor differences' of perspective and practice constitute major social fault lines. For both Ḥanafīs and Salafīs, hadiths are the surest link to the prophetic past, and are the source of authority and authenticity. Yet an analytical focus on hadith itself seldom reveals the precise contours of their sectarian fault lines. The latter can only be critically observed when we note divergent interpretive methodologies and conflicting uses of content-based (*matn*) and transmission-based (*isnād*) forms of investigation. It is here that the hadith commentary genre illuminates subtle intra-Muslim discursive differences quite effectively.

We saw above the significant extent to which al-Mubārakfūrī largely relies on *isnād* criticism without addressing his detractors' reason-based methodologies and arguments. *Isnād* criticism offers him ample ammunition to attack the Ḥanafī tradition. The Salafī valorisation of the *isnāds*, however, was challenged in colonial India. In addition to the Deobandīs, Muslim thinkers of other ideological persuasions also supported the Ḥanafī tradition. For example, Shiblī Nu'mānī wrote a long treatise on the distinguishing features of Abū Ḥanīfa's jurisprudential legacy and argued 'that the study of ḥadīth requires the participation of legal scholars, the *fuqahā*'.[108] Likewise, the Islamist ideologue Abū'l A'la Mawdūdī (1903–1979) called for renewed attention to *matn* criticism.[109] Yet Kāndhalawī's approach does not align with Nu'mānī and Mawdūdī, since for him the jurisprudential tradition provides knowledge of the 'forms of juristic preference' that require expertise in both *isnād* and *matn*.[110] In the hands of Kāndhalawī, the commentary genre becomes the best textual space in which to elaborate and authenticate the minor details that have already been stipulated by earlier Ḥanafī jurists. His conservative balance of *matn* and *isnād* continues to characterise more recent Deobandī hadith commentaries whose authors cite copiously from the *Awjaz*.[111]

Kāndhalawī's approach substantially differs from that of both his cosmopolitan predecessor, Shāh Walī Allāh, and his contemporary sectarian opponents, such as al-Mubārakfūrī. Shāh Walī Allāh reconciles intra-Sunnī

---

108 Daniel W. Brown, *Rethinking Tradition*, 114. See Nu'mānī, *Sīrat-un-Nu'mān*, esp. 233–280, where he elaborates on the five unique features of the Ḥanafī tradition.
109 Daniel W. Brown, *Rethinking Tradition*, 115.
110 'Awwāma, *Athar al-ḥadīth al-sharīf*, 147.
111 See Bijnawrī, *Anwār al-bārī*; Khān, *Kashf al-bārī*.

differences in order to align the material and metaphysical dimensions
of the normative order. Kāndhalawī concentrates on *isnād* criticism and
imagines a normative order that reproduces – in embodied and sociologi-
cal forms – the contents of the Sunnī hadith canon. Studying these con-
trasting approaches allows us to observe how the hadith commentary genre
becomes a site of imagining and contesting competing normative orders,
and therefore a site of vying Muslim selves and societies.

In conclusion, I would like to reflect, in an open-ended manner, on
some lingering thoughts and questions about the themes of authority and
authenticity, especially, the analytical purchase of the hadith commentary
genre and the promise and politics of intra-Muslim reconciliation (*taṭbīq*).
It seems that as early as the twelfth/eighteenth century, Shāh Walī Allāh
could vaguely sense the gathering storm of intra-Muslim conflict, the
incoming flood of perspectival and practical differences that would coincide
with the collapse of Muslim sovereignty in South Asia. His proposed solution to contemporary and future discord was the embrace of intra-Sunnī
ecumenism *vis-à-vis* the hadith canon, along with a renewed commitment
to critical-constructive reasoning and reconciliatory hermeneutics. His
textual support for this ambitious, and perhaps idealistic, reform project
was Mālik's *Muwaṭṭa'*, a collection of reports that balances communal cus-
toms, social welfare and transmission-based norms. Following Walī Allāh,
the most extensive commentary on the *Muwaṭṭa'* is Kāndhalawī's *Awjaz
al-masālik*, whose title ('the most abridged path') evokes Walī Allāh's hope
for intra-Sunnī unity. To some extent the *Awjaz* honours this hope. Yet
the polemical agenda of the *Awjaz* resists Walī Allāh's ecumenical vision.
Kāndhalawī pursues the realisation of an alternative hope.

Perhaps we should view Shāh Walī Allāh's hope for intra-Sunnī unity
as a reflection of a normative order that overlapped with Muslim sovereignty and lacked, for the most part, the kind of colonial-era social division
between the religious private and the secular public. For Walī Allāh, the
everyday norms of the *sharīʿa* were not only manifest in the public, political realm, but were also a link to the classical imaginary world of forms.
Kāndhalawī retained some elements of this aspirational moral theology-
cum-cosmology in his private style of piety and highly technical commentaries. Yet Walī Allāh's political world and imaginal cosmos did not exist
as stages of self-fashioning and world-making for Kāndhalawī. What was
Kāndhalawī's alternative hope?

In Kāndhalawī's biography we read that during his days as a student
in the madrasa, his father, Muḥammad Yaḥyā, strictly monitored his son's
behaviour, including whom he stood next to in congregational prayers in
the mosque, who greeted him with unwarranted affection and so on.[112] His

---

112 Nadwī, *Sawāniḥ Ḥaẓrat Shaykh al-Ḥadīth*, 59.

biographer, the Indian Muslim scholar Abū al-Ḥasan ʿAlī Nadwī (1914–1999), writes:

> The shaykh [Kāndhalawī] avoided social company altogether and concentrated all of his energy on his studies. He was not permitted to leave the madrasa or sit in someone's company without the supervision of his father or his paternal uncle, Mawlānā Muḥammad Ilyās. This occasioned in him a complete disinterest in sightseeing and entertainment. Seclusion became his second nature.[113]

These words illuminate how Kāndhalawī cultivated his aesthetic and ethical sensibilities through disciplinary practices, which, when coupled with colonial secularity, produced a compartmentalised sphere of private religiosity.

The kind of intra-Sunnī ecumenism imagined by Shāh Walī Allāh did not inspire Kāndhalawī's exegetical self and madrasa community. I suggest that this happened because the material and metaphysical union Walī Allāh took for granted was no longer tenable in Kāndhalawī's circumstances. Instead, the latter articulated and imagined a different hope, namely, that his tradition – in its jurisprudential, mystical and theological dimensions – would survive the onslaught of colonial modernity.[114] Thus, I am suggesting that for some Deobandīs personal predilection merged with colonial compartmentalisation, affording them the opportunity to unleash their creative and imaginative capacities to secure what they cherished most, namely, the aesthetics and ethics of asceticism and its institutional support networks (madrasas, Sufi lodges and the Tablīghī Jamāʿat). It might prove fruitful for future researchers to focus on representations of subjectivity – those lived, and often neglected, details that historian of Sufism Alexander Knysh terms 'innumerable nuances, personal predilections, pragmatic calculations of one's interest, pious reservations, and bet-hedging'.[115] While the Deobandīs did not take up Walī Allāh's invitation to bridge contradictory epistemological gaps to secure ontological unity, they managed to retain what Joel Blecher describes as 'the aura of a qualified religious scholar and exegete, and students' connection with his presence'.[116] As I conclude, I thus open this series of concerns in order to identify representations of subjectivity in genres such as hadith and Qur'an commentary as an investigative desideratum.

113 Nadwī, *Sawāniḥ Ḥaẓrat Shaykh al-Ḥadīth*, 59.
114 For an earlier version of this argument with reference to Deobandī jurists, see Mian, 'Troubling Technology'.
115 Knysh, *Ibn ʿArabi in the Later Islamic Tradition*, 277.
116 Blecher, *Said the Prophet of God*, 150. For an analysis of the erotic dimensions of the disciple-Sufi master relationship in Deobandī Islam, see Mian, 'Genres of Desire'.

Bibliography

Abd-Allah, Umar F. *Mālik and Medina: Islamic Legal Reasoning in the Formative Period*. Leiden: Brill, 2013.

'Abd al-Ṣamad, Abū Bakr Yaḥyā. *Taʿāruḍ al-akhbār wa-l-tarjīḥ baynahā: Dirāsa naẓariyya taṭbīqiyya taʾṣīliyya*. Cairo: Muʾassasat al-ʿAlyāʾ, 2010.

Abū Ghudda, ʿAbd al-Fattāḥ. *Tarājim sitta min fuqahāʾ al-ʿālam al-islāmī fī al-qarn al-rābiʿi ʿashara wa āthāruhum al-fiqhiyya*. Beirut: Dār al-Bashāʾir al-Islāmiyya, 1997.

Abū al-Ḥājj, Muḥammad Ṣalāḥ. *al-Manhaj al-fiqhhī li-l-Imām al-Laknawī*. Amman: Dār al-Nafāʾis, 2002.

Aḥmad, Zabīd. "Ulūm-i ḥadīth par Hindustān kī ʿArabī taʾlīfāt." *Maʿārif* 50, no. 6 (December 1942): 417–432.

'Awwāma, Muḥammad. *Athar al-ḥadīth al-sharīf fī ikhtilāf al-aʾimma al-fuqahāʾ*. Medina: Dār al-Yusr, 2007.

al-ʿAẓīmabādī, Shams al-Ḥaqq and Sharaf al-Ḥaqq Muḥammad Ashraf al-ʿAẓīmabādī, *ʿAwn al-maʿbūd sharḥ Sunan Abī Dāwūd*. Edited by Yūsuf al-Ḥājj Aḥmad. 7 vols. Damascus: Dār al-Fayḥāʾ, 2013.

al-Bājī, Abū al-Walīd. *al-Muntaqā fī sharḥ al-Muwaṭṭaʾ fī al-fiqh wa-l-maʿānī*. Edited by Maḥmūd Shākir. 10 vols. Beirut: Dār Iḥyāʾ al-Turāth al-ʿArabī, 2012.

Baljon, J. M. S. *Religion and Thought of Shāh Walī Allāh Dihlawī, 1703–1762*. Leiden: E. J. Brill, 1986.

al-Banūrī, Muḥammad Yūsuf. 'Kalima ʿan al-muʾallif.' In al-Kāndhalawī, *Awjaz al-masālik*, 1:7–10. 15 vols. Beirut: Dār al-Fikr, 2008.

al-Banūrī, Muḥammad Yūsuf. *Maʿārif al-sunan sharḥ Sunan al-Tirmidhī*. 6 vols. Karachi: Jāmiʿa al-ʿUlūm al-Islāmiyya, n.d.

al-Banūrī, Muḥammad Yūsuf. *Nafḥat al-ʿanbar fī ḥayāt imām al-ʿaṣr al-shaykh Anwar*. Karachi: al-Majlis al-ʿIlmī, 1969.

Bijnawrī, Sayyid Aḥmad Raẓā Khān. *Anwār al-bārī: Urdū sharḥ Ṣaḥīḥ al-Bukhārī*. 19 vols. in 9 bindings. Multan: Idāra-yi Taʾlīfāt-i Ashrafiyya, n.d.

Birt, Jonathan and Philip Lewis. 'The Pattern of Islamic Reform in Britain: The Deobandis Between Intra-Muslim Sectarianism and Engagement with Wider Society.' In Martin van Bruinessen and Stefano Allievi (eds), *Producing Islamic Knowledge: Transmission and Dissemination in Western Europe*, pp. 91–120. London: Routledge, 2010.

Blecher, Joel. *Said the Prophet of God: Hadith Commentary across a Millennium*. Oakland, CA: University of California Press, 2018.

Brown, Daniel W. 'Reappraisal.' In Daniel W. Brown (ed.), *The Wiley Blackwell Concise Companion to the Hadith*, pp. 315–333. Hoboken, NJ and Chichester: Wiley Blackwell, 2020.

Brown, Daniel W. *Rethinking Tradition in Modern Islamic Thought*. Cambridge: Cambridge University Press, 1996.

Brown, Jonathan. *The Canonization of al-Bukhārī and Muslim: The Formation and Function of the Sunnī Ḥadīth Canon*. Leiden: Brill, 2007.

al-Bukhārī, Muḥammad b. Ismāʿīl. *Kitāb rafʿ al-yadayn fī al-ṣalāh*. Edited by Badīʿ al-Dīn al-Rāshidī. Beirut: Dār Ibn Ḥazm, 1416/1996.

Dallal, Ahmad. *Islam without Europe: Traditions of Reform in Eighteenth-Century Islamic Thought*. Chapel Hill: University of North Carolina Press, 2018.

al-Dihlawī, Shāh Walī Allāh b. ʿAbd al-Raḥīm. *Ḥujjat Allāh al-bāligha*. Edited by al-Sayyid Sābiq. 2 vols. Beirut: Dār al-Jīl, 2005.

al-Dihlawī, Shāh Walī Allāh b. ʿAbd al-Raḥīm. *al-Musawwā sharḥ al-Muwaṭṭaʾ*. 2 vols. Beirut: Dār al-Kutub al-ʿIlmiyya, 1403/1983.

al-Dihlawī, Shāh Walī Allāh b. ʿAbd al-Raḥīm. *Shah Wali Allah of Delhi's* Hujjat Allah al-Baligha (*The Conclusive Argument from God*). Translated by Marcia Hermansen. Leiden: E. J. Brill, 1996.

Farmān, Mursal and Javēd Iqbāl. 'Awjaz al-masālik sharḥ al-Muwaṭṭaʾ Imām Mālik: Approach and Metholodogy.' *Hazara Islamicus* 5, no. 1 (2016): 39–50.

Fierro, Maribel I. 'La polemique à propos de rafʿ al-yadayn fī al-ṣalāt dans al-Andalus.' *Studia Islamica* 65 (1987): 69–90.

Gangōhī, Rashīd Aḥmad and Muḥammad Yaḥyā al-Kāndhalawī. *al-Kawkab al-durrī ʿalā Jāmiʿ al-Tirmidhī*. Edited by Muḥammad Zakariyyā al-Kāndhalawī. 4 vols. Karachi: Idārat al-Qurʾān wa-l-ʿUlūm al-Islāmiyya, 1987.

Gangōhī, Rashīd Aḥmad and Muḥammad Yaḥyā al-Kāndhalawī. *Lāmiʿ al-darārī ʿalā Jāmiʿ al-Bukhārī*. Edited by Muḥammad Zakariyyā al-Kāndhalawī. 10 vols. Mecca: al-Maktaba al-Imdādiyya, 1975.

Goldziher, Ignaz. *The Ẓāhirīs: Their Doctrine and their History: A Contribution to the History of Islamic Theology*. Edited and translated by Wolfgang Behn. Leiden and Boston: Brill, 2008.

Haq, M. Anwarul. *The Faith Movement of Mawlana Muḥammad Ilyās*. London: Allen and Unwin, 1972.

al-Ḥasanī, ʿAbd al-Ḥayy. *Nuzhat al-khawāṭir wa-bahjat al-masāmiʿ wa-l-nawāẓir*. 8 vols. Multan: Ṭayyab Academy, 1992.

al-Ḥasanī, ʿAbd al-Ḥayy. *al-Thaqāfa al-islāmiyya fī al-Hind*. Damascus: Maṭbūʿāt al-Majmaʿ al-ʿIlmī al-ʿArabī, 1958.

Haykel, Bernard. *Revival and Reform in Islam: The Legacy of Muḥammad al-Shawkānī*. Cambridge: Cambridge University Press, 2003.

Hermansen, Marcia. 'Said Nursi and Maulana Ilyas: Examples of Pietistic Spirituality among Twentieth-Century Islamic Movements.' *Islam and Christian-Muslim Relations* 19, no. 1 (2008): 73–88.

Ibn ʿAbd al-Barr, Abū ʿUmar Yūsuf. *al-Istidhkār li-madhāhib al-amṣār fī mā taḍammanahu al-Muwaṭṭaʾ min maʿānī al-raʾy wa-l-āthār*. Edited by ʿAbd al-Muʿṭī Amīn al-Qalʿajī. 30 vols. Cairo: Dār Qutayba li-l-Ṭibāʿa wa-l-Nashr, 1993.

Ibn ʿAbd al-Barr, Abū ʿUmar Yūsuf. *al-Tamhīd li-mā fī al-Muwaṭṭaʾ min al-maʿānī wa-l-asānīd*. Cairo: al-Fārūq al-Ḥadītha, 2008.

Ibn al-ʿArabī, Abū Bakr al-Ishbīlī al-Mālikī. *ʿĀriḍat al-aḥwadhī bi-sharḥ Ṣaḥīḥ al-Tirmidhī*. 13 vols. Beirut: Dār al-Kutub al-ʿIlmiyya, n.d.

Ibn Qudāma, Abū Muḥammad ʿAbdallāh b. Aḥmad. *al-Mughnī*. Edited by ʿAbdallāh b. ʿAbd al-Muḥsin al-Turkī and ʿAbd al-Fattāḥ Muḥammad al-Ḥilw. 15 vols. Riyadh: Dār ʿĀlam al-Kutub, 1997.

Ingram, Brannon D. *Revival from Below: The Deoband Movement and Global Islam*. Oakland: University of California Press, 2018.

Isḥāq, Muḥammad. *India's Contribution to the Study of Hadith Literature.* Dhaka: University of Dacca, 1955.

Jalbani, G. N. *Life of Shāh Waliyullāh.* Lahore: Sh. Muhammad Ashraf, 1978.

al-Kāndhalawī, Muḥammad Zakariyyā. *al-Abwāb wa-l-tarājim li-Ṣaḥīḥ al-Bukhārī.* Edited by Walī al-Dīn b. Taqī al-Dīn al-Nadawī. 6 vols. Beirut: Dār al-Bashā'ir al-Islāmiyya, 2012.

Kāndhalawī, Muḥammad Zakariyyā. *Āp bītī.* 7 vols. in 2 bindings. Karachi: Maʻhad al-Khalīl al-Islāmī, n.d.

al-Kāndhalawī, Muḥammad Zakariyyā. *Awjaz al-masālik ilā Muwaṭṭa' Mālik.* 15 vols. Beirut: Dār al-Fikr, 2008.

Kāndhalawī, Muḥammad Zakariyyā. *Faẓā'il-i aʻmāl.* Karachi: Maktaba al-Bushrā, 2006.

Kāndhalawī, Muḥammad Zakariyyā. *Ikhtilāf al-a'imma.* Karachi: Maktaba al-Shaykh, n.d.

al-Kāndhalawī, Muḥammad Zakariyyā. *al-Kanz al-mutawārī fī maʻādin Lāmiʻ al-darārī wa Ṣaḥīḥ al-Bukhārī.* 24 vols. Rawalpindi: Dār al-Khalīl, 1420[/1999–2000].

Kāndhalawī, Muḥammad Zakariyyā. *Kutub-i faẓā'il par ishkālāt aur unkē jawābāt.* Edited by Muḥammad Shāhid Sahāranpūrī. Karachi: Maktaba al-Shaykh, n.d.

Kāndhalawī, Muḥammad Zakariyyā. *Tablīghī Jamāʻat par chand ʻumūmī iʻtirāẓāt aur unkē mufaṣṣal jawābāt.* Lahore: Maktaba al-Khalīl, n.d.

Kāndhalawī, Muḥammad Zakariyyā. *Taqrīr-i Bukhārī Sharīf.* Karachi: Dār al-Ishāʻat, 1988.

Kāndhalawī, Muḥammad Zakariyyā. *Tārīkh-i mashā'ikh-i Chisht.* Karachi: Maktaba al-Shaykh, n.d.

Kāndhlawī, Muḥammad Zakariyyā. *The Differences of the Imāms.* Translated by Mawlānā Muḥammad Kadwa. Santa Barbara, CA: White Thread Press, 2004.

Karagözoğlu, Mustafa Macit. 'Commentaries.' In Daniel W. Brown (ed.), *The Wiley Blackwell Concise Companion to the Hadith,* pp. 159–185. Hoboken, NJ and Chichester: Wiley Blackwell, 2020.

al-Kashmīrī, Anwar Shāh. *Fayḍ al-bārī ʻalā Ṣaḥīḥ al-Bukhārī.* Edited by Badr ʻĀlam Mīrathī. 6 vols. Quetta: al-Maktaba al-Rashīdiyya, n.d.

al-Kashmīrī, Anwar Shāh. *Nayl al-farqadayn fī mas'alat raf al-yadayn.* In *Majmūʻa rasā'il al-Kashmīrī,* vol. 1, pp. 159–334. 4 vols. Karachi: Idārat al-Qur'ān wa-l-ʻUlūm al-Islāmiyya, 2004.

Khān, Salīmullāh. *Kashf al-bārī ʻammā fī Ṣaḥīḥ al-Bukhārī.* Edited by Ibn al-Ḥasan ʻAbbāsī. Karachi: Maktaba Fārūqiyya, 1432/2001.

Knysh, Alexander. *Ibn ʻArabi in the Later Islamic Tradition: The Making of a Polemical Image in Medieval Islam.* Albany: State University of New York Press, 1999.

al-Kumillāyī, Muḥammad Ḥifẓ al-Raḥmān. *al-Budūr al-maḍiyya fī tarājim al-Ḥanafiyya.* 20 vols. Cairo: Dār al-Ṣāliḥ, 2018.

[Mālik b. Anas.] *al-Muwaṭṭa'.* Edited and translated by Mohammad Fadel and Connell Monette. Cambridge, MA: Program in Islamic Law, Harvard Law School, 2019.

Malik, Jamal. *Islam in South Asia.* Leiden and Boston: Brill, 2020.

Masud, Muhammad Khalid (ed.). *Travellers in Faith: Studies of the Tablighi Jamaʻat as a Transnational Islamic Movement for Faith Renewal.* Leiden: Brill, 2000.

Melchert, Christopher. 'Traditionist-Jurisprudents and the Framing of Islamic Law.' *Islamic Law and Society* 8, no. 3 (2001): 383–406.

Metcalf, Barbara D. *Islamic Contestations: Essays on Muslims in India and Pakistan.* New Delhi: Oxford University Press, 2004.

Metcalf, Barbara D. *Islamic Revival in British India: Deoband, 1860–1900.* Princeton, NJ: Princeton University Press, 1982.

Metcalf, Barbara D. 'Living Hadith in the Tablighi Jamaat.' *Journal of Asian Studies* 52, no. 3 (1993): 584–608.

Metcalf, Barbara D. 'The Past in the Present: Instruction, Pleasure, and Blessing in Maulana Muhammad Zakariyya's *Aap Biitii*.' In *Islamic Contestations: Essays on Muslims in India and Pakistan*, pp. 67–95. New Delhi: Oxford University Press, 2004.

Mian, Ali Altaf. 'South Asian Salafism: Islamic Reform in the Ahl-i Ḥadīth Movement.' In Natana DeLong-Bas and Emad Hamdeh (eds), *Oxford Handbook on Islamic Reform*. New York: Oxford University Press (forthcoming).

Mian, Ali Altaf. 'Genres of Desire: The Erotic in Deobandī Islam.' *History of Religions* 59, no. 2 (2019): 108–145.

Mian, Ali Altaf. 'Troubling Technology: The Deobandī Debate on the Loudspeaker and Ritual Prayer.' *Islamic Law and Society* 24, no. 4 (2017): 355–383.

Mīrathī, Muḥammad ʿĀshiq Ilāhī. *Tazkirat-ul-Khalīl*. Karachi: Maktaba al-Shaykh, n.d.

Mīrathī, Muḥammad ʿĀshiq Ilāhī. *Tazkirat-ur-Rashīd*. Lahore: Idāra-yi Islāmiyyāt, 1986.

Moosa, Ebrahim. *What is a Madrasa?* Chapel Hill: University of North Carolina Press, 2015.

al-Mubārakfūrī, Muḥammad ʿAbd al-Raḥmān. *Tuḥfat al-aḥwadhī bi-sharḥ Jāmiʿ al-Tirmidhī*. Edited by Yūsuf al-Ḥājj Aḥmad. 10 vols. Damascus: Dār al-Fayḥāʾ, 2011.

al-Nadawī, Muḥammad Akram. *Shiblī Nuʿmānī ʿallāmat al-Hind al-adīb wa-l-muʾarrikh al-nāqid al-arīb*. Damascus: Dār al-Qalam, 2001.

al-Nadawī, Muḥammad Raḥmat Allāh Muḥammad Nāẓim. *al-Muḥaddith al-kabīr al-dāʿiyat al-jalīl al-Shaykh Muḥammad Zakariyyā al-Kāndhalawī: Ḥayātuhu wa-juhūduhu al-ʿilmiyya wa-l-taʿrīf bi-ahammi muʾallafātihi*. Beirut: Dār al-Bashāʾir al-Islāmiyya, 2012.

Nadwī, Fīroz Akhtar. *Zikr-i Zakariyyā*. Azamgarh: Markaz al-Shaykh Abī al-Ḥasan al-Nadwī, Jāmiʿa Islāmiyya Muẓaffarpūr, 2005.

Nadwī, Sayyid Abū al-Ḥasan ʿAlī. *Sawāniḥ Ḥaẓrat Mawlānā Muḥammad Ilyās Kāndhalawī*. New Delhi: Idāra-yi Ishāʿat-i Dīniyāt, n.d.

Nadwī, Sayyid Abū al-Ḥasan ʿAlī. *Sawāniḥ Ḥaẓrat Shaykh al-Ḥadīth Mawlānā Muḥammad Zakariyyā*. Karachi: Majlis Nashriyāt-i Islām, n.d.

Nadwī, Sayyid Sulaymān. *Ḥayāt-i Shiblī*. Azamgarh, India: Dār al-Muṣannifīn Shiblī Academy, 1993.

Nadwī, Taqī al-Dīn. *Muḥaddithīn-i ʿiẓām awr unkē kārnāmay*. Karachi: Majlis-i Nashriyāt-i Islām, 2000.

Nadwī, Taqī al-Dīn. 'Muqaddima.' In Kāndhalawī, *Taqrīr-i Bukhārī Sharīf*, 27–34. Karachi: Dār al-Ishāʿat, 1988.

Naqshbandī, Muḥammad Rūḥullāh. *Shaikh al-ḥadīth Ḥaẓrat Mawlānā Muḥammad Zakariyyā Ṣāḥib Sahānpūrī kī dīnī wa 'ilmī khidmāt.* Lahore: Maktabat ul-Ḥaramayn, 2013.

Nāṣir, Muḥammad 'Ammār Khān. 'Fiqh al-ḥadīth men a'imma-yi aḥnāf kā uṣūlī manhaj.' PhD dissertation, Punjab University, 2018.

Nawshahrawī, Abū Yaḥyā Imām Khān. *Tarājim 'ulamā'-yi Ahl-i Ḥadīth Hind.* Karachi: Maktaba-yi Ahl-i Ḥadīth, n.d.

Nu'mānī, Shiblī. *Maqālāt-i Shiblī.* 3 vols. Azamgarh, India: Dār al-Muṣannifīn Shiblī Academy, 1999.

Nu'mānī, Shiblī. *Sīrat-un-Nu'mān.* Agra: Maṭba' Mufīd-i 'Ām, 1892.

Ogunnaike, Oludamini. 'Annihilation in the Messenger Revisited: Clarifications on a Contemporary Sufi Practice and Its Precedents.' *Journal of Islamic and Muslim Studies* 1, no. 2 (2016): 13–34.

Preckel, Claudia. 'Ahl-i Ḥadīth', in *EI*[3]. <http://dx.doi.org/10.1163/1573-3912_ei3_COM_0107>, accessed 1 June 2020.

Qureshi, Jawad Anwar. 'Reform.' In Daniel W. Brown (ed.), *The Wiley Blackwell Concise Companion to the Hadith*, pp. 297–313. Hoboken, NJ and Chichester: Wiley Blackwell, 2020.

Riexinger, Martin. 'Ibn Taymiya's Worldview and the Challenge of Modernity: A Conflict Among the Ahl-i Ḥadīth in British India.' In Birgit Krawietz and Georges Tamer (eds), *Islamic Theology, Philosophy and Law: Debating Ibn Taymiyya and Ibn Qayyim al-Jawziyya*, pp. 493–517. Berlin: Walter de Gruyter, 2013.

Riexinger, Martin. *Sana'ullah Amritsari (1868–1948) und die Ahl-i Hadis im Punjab unter britischer Herrschaft.* Wurzburg: Ergon, 2004.

Riexinger, Martin. 'A Study of the Ahl-i Hadīs in Late Nineteenth/Early Twentieth Century South Asia.' In Gwilym Beckerlegge (ed.), *Colonialism, Modernity and Religious Identities: Religious Reform Movements in South Asia*, pp. 147–165. New Delhi: Oxford University Press, 2008.

Ṣafdar, Muḥammad Sarfarāz Khān. *Maqām-i Abī Ḥanīfa.* Gujranwala: Maktaba-yi Ṣafdariyya, 2001.

al-Sahāranfūrī, Khalīl Aḥmad. *Badhl al-majhūd fī ḥall Sunan Abī Dāwūd.* Edited by Taqī al-Dīn al-Nadawī. 14 vols. Azamgarh, India: Markaz al-Shaykh Abī'l-Ḥasan al-Nadawī, 2006.

Sahāranpūrī, Sayyid Muḥammad Shāhid. *Fihrist-i Ta'līfāt-i Shaykh.* 3 vols. Saharanpur: Maktaba-yi Yadgār-i Shaykh, 1997.

Sahāranpūrī, Sayyid Muḥammad Shāhid. *Ḥayāt-i Shaykh.* 2 vols. Saharanpur: Maktaba-yi Yādgār-i Shaykh, 2003.

Schacht, Joseph. *The Origins of Muhammadan Jurisprudence.* Oxford: Clarendon Press, 1979.

al-Shaybānī, Muḥammad b. al-Ḥasan. *Muwaṭṭa' al-Imām Mālik, riwāyat Muḥammad b. al-Ḥasan al-Shaybānī, ma'a al-ta'līq al-mumajjad 'alā Muwaṭṭa' Muḥammad sharḥ 'Abd al-Ḥayy al-Laknawī.* Edited by Taqī al-Dīn al-Nadawī. 3 vols. Damascus: Dār al-Qalam, 2011.

Sikand, Yoginder. *The Origins and Development of the Tablighi-Jama'at (1920–2000): A Cross-Country Comparative Study.* New Delhi: Orient Longman, 2002.

Siyālkōtī, Muḥammad Ibrāhīm Mīr. *Tārīkh-i Ahl-i Ḥadīth*. Lahore: Islamic Publishing Company, 1970.

Stephens, Julia. *Governing Islam: Law, Empire, and Secularism in Modern South Asia*. Cambridge: Cambridge University Press, 2018.

al-Tahānawī, Ẓafar Aḥmad al-ʿUthmānī. *Iʿlāʾ al-sunan*. 21 vols. Beirut: Dār al-Fikr, 2001.

al-Ṭaḥāwī, Abū Jaʿfar. *Sharḥ maʿānī al-āthār*. Edited by Muḥammad Zuhrī al-Najjār and Muḥammad Sayyid Jād al-Ḥaqq. 5 vols. Beirut: ʿĀlam al-Kutub, 1994.

Tareen, SherAli. *Defending Muḥammad in Modernity*. Notre Dame, IN: University of Notre Dame Press, 2020.

Thānawī, Ashraf ʿAlī. *al-Iqtiṣād fī al-taqlīd wa-l-ijtihād*. Karachi: Qadīmī Kutub Khāna, n.d.

Turkmānī, ʿAbd al-Majīd. *Dirāsāt fī uṣūl al-ḥadītā ʿalā manhaj al-Ḥanafiyya*. Karachi: Madrasa al-Nuʿmān, 2009.

ʿUsmānī, Muḥammad Taqī. *Dars-i Tirmidhī*. 3 vols. Karachi: Maktaba-yi Dār al-ʿUlūm Karāchī, 2001.

ʿUsmānī, Ẓafar Aḥmad. ʿSilsila-yi Shāh Walīullāh kī khidmat-i Ḥadīth.ʾ *Maʿārif* 53, no. 3 (May 1944): 340–354; 53, no. 6 (June 1944): 405–420.

al-ʿUthmānī, Shabbīr Aḥmad. *Fatḥ al-mulhim bi-sharḥ Ṣaḥīḥ al-Imām Muslim*. Edited by Nūr al-Bashar b. Nūr al-Ḥaqq. Karachi: Maktaba Dār al-ʿUlūm Karātshī, 1421/2000.

Wheeler, Brannon. ʿTouching the Penis in Islamic Law.ʾ *History of Religions* 44, no. 2 (2004): 89–119.

Zaman, Muhammad Qasim. ʿCommentaries, Print and Patronage: ʿHadithʾ and the Madrasas in Modern South Asia.ʾ *Bulletin of the School of Oriental and African Studies* 61, no. 2 (1999): 60–81.

Zaman, Muhammad Qasim. *Modern Islamic Thought in a Radical Age: Religious Authority and Internal Criticism*. Cambridge: Cambridge University Press, 2012.

Zaman, Muhammad Qasim. ʿPolitical Power, Religious Authority, and the Caliphate in Eighteenth-Century Indian Islamic Thought.ʾ *Journal of the Royal Asiatic Society* 30, no. 2 (2020): 313–340.

Zaman, Muhammad Qasim. *The Ulama in Contemporary Islam: Custodians of Change*. Princeton, NJ: Princeton University Press, 2002.

CHAPTER 9

'Allāma Ṭabāṭabā'ī and Exegetical Hadiths in al-Mīzān: A Contemporary Imāmī Commentary on Hadith?

*Shadi Nafisi**

'Allāma Muḥammad Ḥusayn Ṭabāṭabā'ī (1320–1402/1903–1981)[1] was a contemporary Iranian philosopher, mystic, theologian, exegete and prominent scholar on hadith. He was a master of the Islamic traditional sciences, received *ijāzas* in narrating and interpreting hadith, attained the rank of *mujtahid* and mastered Islamic philosophy according to the school of Mullā Ṣadrā.[2] He dedicated his scholastic life to teaching and writing on two subjects that had been overlooked in the traditional seminary curriculum: philosophy and exegesis. His lifetime effort in these fields sparked a revival of Islamic philosophy in contemporary Iran and led him to write the twenty-volume Qur'an commentary *al-Mīzān fī tafsīr al-Qur'ān*, a work that is considered the most important contemporary Shī'ī exegesis.[3]

---

* Associate professor at the Department of Hadith and Qur'anic sciences, University of Tehran (shadinafisi@ut.ac.ir). I would like to thank Stefanie Brinkmann and Joel Blecher for their constructive support.

1 For further information about Ṭabāṭabā'ī, see Medoff, 'Ṭabāṭabā'ī, Moḥammad-Ḥosayn', *EIr*, <http://www.iranicaonline.org/articles/tabatabai-mohammad-hosayn> (accessed 1 July 2020); Medoff, 'Ijtihad and Renewal', ii–vi, 1–20; Algar, "Allāma Sayyid Muḥammad Husayn Ṭabāṭabā'ī', 326–351; Kamaly, *God and Man in Tehran*, 138–144; Ṭabāṭabā'ī, *Shi'ite Islam*, 21–25; Ehteshami and Rizvi, 'Beyond the Letter', 444–448. For a list of primary sources on Ṭabāṭabā'ī's biography, see Medoff, 'Ijtihad and Renewal', 139–145.

2 That is, Ṣadr al-Dīn Muḥammad b. Ibrāhīm Shirāzī, best known as Mullā Ṣadrā Shirāzī (1045/1635–36?), a Shī'ī philosopher of the Ṣafavid period and arguably the most significant Islamic philosopher after Ibn Sīnā. For his ideas, see Rizvi, 'Mollā Ṣadrā Šīrāzi', *EIr*, <http://www.iranicaonline.org/articles/molla-sadra-sirazi> (accessed 1 August 2020).

3 Six volumes of this exegesis have been translated into English by Sayyid Saeed Akhtar Rizvi and published in twelve volumes. After Rizvi's death, his son finished the incomplete thirteenth volume. The remainder has been translated by Tawus Raja, including volumes 14 to 16 and 25 to 30. Rizvi's translation, although useful, is not very precise; see Medoff, 'Ijtihad and Renewal', x. Its popularity is clear from the number of dissertations (MA/PhD) focused

Ṭabāṭabā'ī is also considered an eminent hadith scholar. His approach and works on hadith were deeply influenced by his interest in philosophy and *tafsīr*. For Ṭabāṭabā'ī, philosophical knowledge is indispensable for the correct understanding of hadiths on creed. For ten years, he held classes on the hadiths in *Biḥār al-anwār* (lit., The seas of light), compiled by the Ṣafavid scholar Muḥammad Bāqir al-Majlisī (d. 1111/1700)[4] and supervised its new edition. He wrote glosses on the book, often providing further information or correcting al-Majlisī's misunderstanding of specific hadiths. He considered al-Majlisī's misunderstanding to be a result of his ignorance of hadiths with philosophical content; Ṭabāṭabā'ī's sharp criticism of al-Majlisī's hadith commentaries provoked discontent among religious authorities in Qum.[5] Ṭabāṭabā'ī's novel glosses were limited to the first six volumes and a part of the seventh volume. He also had a few brief comments on *al-Kāfī* of Muḥammad al-Kulaynī (d. 329/941)[6] in which he explained difficult concepts such as *badā'* (the appearance of change in the divine will), free will and predestination, and the difference between the divine will (*irāda*) and the divine wish (*mashiya*).[7]

Ṭabāṭabā'ī's works on *tafsīr* included hadith. In fact, hadith is the focus of concern in his brief (but incomplete) commentary on the Qur'an entitled *al-Bayān fī muwāfiqat bayn al-ḥadīth wa-l-Qur'ān* (The elucidation on consistency [between] hadith and the Qur'an). This commentary, which reaches Surat Yūsuf (12:57),[8] was published after his death. His most important work on hadith is 'the hadith discussion' (*baḥth rivāyī*) in his Qur'an exegesis, *al-Mīzān fī tafsīr al-Qur'ān*. The *Mīzān* is Ṭabāṭabā'ī's major project, on which his reputation largely rests. In contrast with some of his predecessors who commented on the Qur'an verse by verse, Ṭabāṭabā'ī divides the verses into several groups according to the length of the chapter. He then clarifies the apparent meaning of each group of verses in a section entitled 'explanation' (*bayān*), which is usually followed by separate 'discussions' (*baḥth*) on relevant hadiths or social, scientific, historical, philosophical and ethical implications of the verses.

In his exegesis, the 'hadith discussion' (*baḥth rivāyī*) occurs most frequently, following the 'explanation' (*bayān*). These sections on hadith

---

on his views. In the largest repository for Iranian theses (irandoc), 1,057 dissertations have been registered under the keyword 'al-Mīzān', and 304 appear under the keyword "Allama Ṭabāṭabā'ī'; see <https://ganj.irandoc.ac.ir/#/> (accessed 12 August 2020).

4 'Ābidī, 'Nigāhī bi ta'līqāt-i 'Allāma Ṭabāṭabā'ī', 670.

5 Ṭabāṭabā'ī's annotations have also been subject to criticism; see 'Ābidī, 'Nigāhī bi ta'līqāt-i 'Allāma Ṭabāṭabā'ī', 669–685.

6 For the book and his author, see Amir-Moezzi and Ansari, 'Perfecting a Religion', 125–160.

7 Sayyid 'Alavī, 'Mitud-i naqd', 21–25; Ḥusaynī Ṭihrānī, *Mihr-i tābān*, 36; Algar, "Allāma Sayyid Muḥammad Ḥusayn Ṭabāṭabā'ī', 340–341.

8 Al-Ṭabāṭabā'ī, *al-Bayān*, 28.

cover about one-sixth of the twenty-volume commentary of *al-Mīzān fī tafsīr al-Qurʾān* and make up 530 specific sections[9] in which he refers to numerous Shīʿī and Sunnī hadith collections.[10] Among Shīʿī sources, Ṭabāṭabāʾī quotes *al-Kāfī* most frequently (in 730 references), while *al-Durr al-manthūr fī al-tafsīr bi-l-maʾthūr*, compiled by Jalāl al-Dīn al-Suyūṭī (d. 911/1505),[11] is the most frequently quoted Sunnī hadith source (with 1,058 references). The hadith section comprises hadiths that, without exception, pertain to Qurʾanic verses or phrases.

Ṭabāṭabāʾī frequently cites hadiths without further comment. In many instances (nearly 2,500 occasions)[12] he provides explanatory notes that are brief and mainly fall into one of the three following categories:[13]

1. Variations of a hadith with alternative isnāds and sources (this is the most frequent information given). Without discussing the content in detail, Ṭabāṭabāʾī simply states that the relevant hadith has other versions that were transmitted by Shīʿī or Sunnī narrators and/or that the hadith has numerous chains of transmission.[14]

2. Explanations of the meaning of the hadith. Here, Ṭabāṭabāʾī seldom discusses the lexical meaning[15] or gives grammatical explications, instead he provides explanatory comments on numerous hadiths, pointing out their implications and/or clarifying difficult and at times controversial topics. Among these topics[16] are the hadiths on the greatest name of God and His speaking;[17] seeing God;[18] the throne (*ʿarsh*) and its description;[19] the angels and Satan and their nature;[20] the world of pre-existence (*ʿālam al-dahr*);[21] the ascension of the Prophet (*miʿrāj*)[22] and his

---

9 Nāṣiḥ, 'Pajūhishī', 56.

10 Awsī counts up to 135 sources: Awsī, *Ravish ʿAllāma Ṭabāṭabāʾī*, 124–129.

11 For the author, see Geoffroy, 'al-Suyūṭī', in *EI²*, 9:913–916.

12 His annotations usually begin with an introductory 'I say' (*aqūlu*).

13 In the first volume alone, there are forty hadith discussions with more than 140 comments. In nearly ninety cases he explains the hadith; his criticism is limited to two instances on the story of Hārūt and Mārūt and on the hadiths concerning *insāʾ* (postponing the sacred month). In the remaining cases, he mentions the variants of the hadiths.

14 For a few examples, see al-Ṭabāṭabāʾī, *al-Mīzān*, 1:39, 2:438, 3:143, 16:281, 18:13.

15 For some of these rare instances, see al-Ṭabāṭabāʾī, *al-Mīzān*, 2:58 and 146.

16 For a study on Ṭabāṭabāʾī's view on these topics, see Nafisi, *ʿAllāma Ṭabāṭabāʾī va ḥadīth*, 294–401. The references in the following footnotes are only the most important instances of this.

17 Al-Ṭabāṭabāʾī, *al-Mīzān*, 2:254–255.

18 Al-Ṭabāṭabāʾī, *al-Mīzān*, 8:256–258, 260; 19:34–35.

19 Al-Ṭabāṭabāʾī, *al-Mīzān*, 10:180; 14:128–134.

20 Al-Ṭabāṭabāʾī, *al-Mīzān*, 1:237, 8:62–66, 9:109, 14:36–41, 17:13.

21 Al-Ṭabāṭabāʾī, *al-Mīzān*, 8:324–331.

22 Al-Ṭabāṭabāʾī, *al-Mīzān*, 8:30–35; 19:36.

intercession (*shafāʿa*);[23] the problematic hadiths concerning the nature of those enjoying felicity and the wretched in the hereafter;[24] free will and predestination (*ikhtiyār, jabr*).[25] Although hadiths addressing theological issues are significant in Ṭabāṭabāʾī's hadith discussions, they are not the only issues on which he has written glosses. Legal hadiths are also addressed and glossed briefly.[26] Contemporary Shīʿī scholars consider his annotations on exegetical hadiths[27] referring to the Shīʿī Imams greatly significant. As they are esoteric in nature, this group of hadiths has generally been accepted by scholars and not discussed further. Thus, Ṭabāṭabāʾī's interpretation of this group of hadiths was something new and changed the status of these hadith in relation to the Qurʾan (see below).

3. Criticism of exegetical hadiths mentioned in other Qurʾanic commentaries. Emphasising *matn* criticism, Ṭabāṭabāʾī offers his opinion on the authenticity of a wide range of hadiths, particularly regarding their possible conflict with the teachings of the Qurʾan, the confirmed (*qaṭʿī*) Sunna, reason (*ʿaql*), history (*tārīkh*), science (*ʿilm*), and reality (*wāqiʿ*).[28] At times, he evaluates the isnād but he never refutes or accepts a hadith solely based on its *isnād* (see more below). Among the various exegetical traditions discussed in the *Mīzān*, those concerning Qurʾanic stories and the occasions of the revelation (*asbāb al-nuzūl*) have been largely refuted. Although there is a long history[29] of Shīʿīs writing

---

23 Al-Ṭabāṭabāʾī, *al-Mīzān*, 1:174–183.

24 Al-Ṭabāṭabāʾī, *al-Mīzān*, 1:121, 1:290–291, 8:95–109.

25 Al-Ṭabāṭabāʾī, *al-Mīzān*, 1:97–105.

26 Al-Ṭabāṭabāʾī, *al-Mīzān*, 2:252 (on divorce); 5:234 (on ablution); 4:289–311 (on temporary marriage).

27 'Exegetical hadith' refers to hadiths that explain one or several Qurʾanic verses, either by explicitly quoting the verse or by implicitly referring to its subject.

28 For a detailed study of his hadith criticism, see Nafisi, *ʿAllāma Ṭabāṭabāʾī va ḥadīth*, 477–523.

29 One might argue that the practice of hadith commentary is applied in three of the four canonical Shīʿī hadith collections (fourth/tenth to fifth/eleventh century); see Gleave, 'Between *Hadith* and *Fiqh*', 353. In addition to these books, one of the earliest commentaries on hadith is that of Sharīf al-Murtaḍā (d. 436/1044), *Amālī al-Murtaḍā*. Among the numerous works of Shaykh al-Mufīd (d. 413/1022) there are three books (no longer extant) on the meaning of a particular hadith: the prophetic hadith about the Companions being like stars, the status of ʿAlī for the Prophet being like that of Aaron for Moses and the two weighty things; see Najāshī, *Rijāl al-Najāshī*, 401. Ibn Rāvandī (d. 573/1177) was a pioneer who wrote the first commentary on *Nahj al-balāgha*. Finally, in the Ṣafavid era (907–1135/1501–1722), writing commentaries on hadith collections gained popularity; see Blecher 'Ḥadīth Commentary', in *EI*³, <http://dx.doi.org/10.1163/1573-3912_ei3_COM_32080> (accessed 6 February 2021).

commentaries on hadith collections, criticising the *matn* of hadiths is not a well-established Shīʿī practice. Hence, Ṭabāṭabāʾī's methodological approach gained much attention.

The first two approaches, discussing versions of hadiths and their *isnād*s as well as the meaning, implications and difficulties, related to their content are common in hadith commentaries.[30] Although some commentators might assume that the hadiths they discuss are authentic and they depend on the compilers in relation to this, others critically examine the *matn*s and *isnād*s. Such (sometimes) exhaustive and detailed critical examinations of transmissions and their subsequent evaluation of hadiths usually fall under the category of hadith criticism. Hence, to what extent can we consider hadith criticism a part of hadith commentary?

We can find hadith criticism, to a certain extent, in some hadith commentaries. One of these is *Mirʾāt al-ʿuqūl* (a multi-volume commentary on *al-Kāfī*) by Muḥammad Bāqir al-Majlisī (d. 1111/1700). In his *sharḥ*, al-Majlisī evaluates *isnād*s that are often deemed weak, and then discusses the content of the hadiths.[31] Despite his evaluations, he almost never criticises the text (*matn*), and it would seem that he does not refute hadiths. This kind of *isnād* criticism and evaluation can be found in other Shīʿī hadith commentaries.[32] In the *Manhaj al-naqd fī ʿulūm al-ḥadīth*, Nūr al-Dīn ʿItr (1937–2020) introduces what can be considered a *sharḥ*. Although he does not specifically mention hadith criticism (*naqd*) as a branch of *sharḥ*, he includes books on conflicting (*mukhtalaf*)[33] hadiths as one kind of *sharḥ*. In these works on *mukhtalaf*, the author's intention is to resolve the apparent contradiction between diverging hadiths. Abrogation (*naskh*) is one method of resolving these apparent contradictions. Another method involves refuting the authenticity of a hadith or preferring one hadith over another based on its *isnād*. Among the *mukhtalaf* books in jurisprudence (*fiqh*) is *al-Istibṣār fīmā ikhtulifa min al-akhbār* and the second is *Tahdhīb al-aḥkām* both by Muḥammad b. al-Ḥasan al-Ṭūsī (d. 460/1067); these are two of the four canonical hadith books in the Shīʿī tradition. Al-Ṭūsī himself criticises the authenticity of some

---

30 Blecher 'Ḥadīth Commentary', in *EI³*, <http://dx.doi.org/10.1163/1573-3912_ei3_COM_32080> (accessed 6 February 2021).

31 In 4,830 instances he considers the hadiths weak.

32 *Isnād* criticism can be seen in many hadith commentaries on the four canonical Shīʿī hadith collections; among these commentaries are Muḥammad b. al-Ḥasan b. al-Shahīd al-Thānī al-ʿĀmilī's (d. 1030/1620) *Istiqṣāʾ al-iʿtibār fī sharḥ al-istibṣār* and Muḥammad Taqī al-Majlisī's (d. 1070/1660) *Rawḍa al-muttaqīn fī sharḥ man lā yaḥḍarahū al-faqīh*.

33 He mentions that it is also called a 'difficult hadith' (*mushkil al-ḥadīth*). He defines it as a hadith that shows an apparent conflict with principles, with other hadiths, or the Qurʾanic texts. ʿItr, *Manhaj al-naqd*, 337.

of the hadiths collected in these works;[34] later commentators have made the same criticism.[35] In this sense, commentary on hadiths includes material typically understood as hadith criticism.

Regarding the quantity and the nature of his comments, Ṭabāṭabā'ī's annotations on the exegetical hadiths in the *Mīzān* can be considered a *sharḥ*. The *Mīzān* is not the only *tafsīr* that includes and discusses hadiths. In terms of hadith commentary within Qur'an commentary, we must distinguish between the various ways hadiths are included in *tafsīr*. Many traditional exegeses (*tafāsīr*) gather a great number of hadiths; these works are known as *tafsīr bi-l-ma'thūr*. Examples of this type of Qur'an commentary include works written by the Sunnī Ibn Abī Ḥātim al-Rāzī (d. 327/938) and the Shī'ī scholar Sayyid Hāshim al-Baḥrānī (d. 1107/1695). But often these authors do not comment on the hadiths collected in these exegeses, and the absence of any commentary on the hadiths makes them, at most, a selective collection of hadith, but not a hadith commentary. Like hadith collections, these exegeses only demonstrate their authors' choice of hadiths. Yet the classification of hadiths under the topic of a particular Qur'an verse may be considered a commentarial activity, like a hadith compiler who classifies hadiths under a specific chapter heading (*tarājim*).[36] By contrast, exegetes such as Muḥammad b. Ḥasan al-Ṭūsī (d. 460/1067),[37] Ibn Kathīr (d. 774/1373), Maḥmūd al-Ālūsī (d. 1270/1854),[38] and others discuss (exhaustively) the meaning or the authority of specific exegetical hadiths. Because they usually adopt a critical stance, these comments can be considered hadith analysis, or commentary. However, identifying these discussions in the often voluminous Qur'an commentaries is not an easy task. The *Mīzān* is unique for including a large number and variety of comments on hadith, and for separating the hadith discussion from other parts of his *tafsīr*; this means it is possible to discern and separate Ṭabāṭabā'ī's commentaries on hadiths.

Should Ṭabāṭabā'ī's separate hadith discussions and this kind of commentary on exegetical hadiths be classified under *tafsīr* or hadith? Each hadith has at least two aspects. It can be discussed under the general topic of hadith, but its subject may also include other disciplines,[39] such as

---

34 See, for example, al-Ṭūsī, *Tahdhīb al-aḥkām*, 1:18, 6:168, 7:361, 9:204; al-Ṭūsī, *al-Istibṣār*, 1:237, 2:36, 3:351, 4:89.

35 In reconciling the conflicting hadiths, the commentators do not necessarily adopt the same method as al-Ṭūsī; see, for example, al-'Āmilī, *Istiqṣā' al-i'tibār*, 7:13.

36 This classification has been considered a kind of commentary; see Blecher, *Said the Prophet of God*, 5.

37 For some examples, see al-Ṭūsī, *al-Tibyān*, 1:384, 2:422–423, 8:554.

38 For some examples, see al-Dhahabī, *al-Isrā'īliyyāt*, 107–147.

39 'Itr, *Manhaj al-naqd*, 198–199. The line between these disciplines is not necessarily clear; there are overlaps, particularly concerning exegetical hadiths that address relevant Qur'anic verses.

theology, law, history or Qur'an commentary. These, in turn, can be divided into more specific sub-categories. Hence, in varying degrees, the integration, application and discussion of hadiths is part of a discipline other than hadith. Examining the authenticity of hadiths and their meanings is a core part of the discipline of hadith; Yet similar questions and approaches can be found in other disciplines, such as Qur'an commentary, theology, law or ethics. Exegetes such as Ibn Taymiyya, who saw hadith as key to many disciplines, including *tafsir*, referred to hadith in their exegesis to a significant extent.[40] Others approached *tafsir* and included fewer discussions of hadiths in their argumentation.[41] This interrelation of hadith and *tafsir* has been noted by modern scholars.[42]

In relation to Ṭabāṭabā'ī's commentaries on hadith, he does not define his hadith discussions as one of his objectives for writing the *Mīzān*. Nevertheless, his hadith analysis has been considered a great contribution to the field of hadith comprehension (*fiqh al-ḥadīth*), and many studies have been written on it.[43] But to properly understand his approach to hadith, it is essential to understand his principles of exegesis. Thus, I discuss two of his basic exegetical principles, as they have a critical impact on his hadith analysis and are distinct even among his Shī'ī counterparts.

The Principles of Ṭabāṭabā'ī's Commentary on Hadith in the *Mīzān*

Ṭabāṭabā'ī does not outline his principles and methods of hadith commentary in the *Mīzān* (or in any of his other books), rather his statements on the above-mentioned topics are scattered throughout his books,

---

40 See Ibn Taymiyya, *Muqaddama fī uṣūl al-tafsīr*, 38–79. He discusses the authoritative hadiths and their implications for Qur'anic exegesis.

41 As an example, see al-'Ak, *Uṣūl al-tafsīr*, 123–135. Of his nearly five-hundred-page book, he dedicates only a few pages to a discussion of interpreting the Qur'an through hadiths.

42 For example, see Herbert Berg's discussion of early exegesis: Berg, *The Development of Exegesis*. Chapter 2 (6–65) is devoted to hadith; the other chapters relate to exegetical hadiths as the prominent form of *tafsir* in early Islam. Also see Marston R. Speight's article, 'The Function of Hadith'.

43 His hadith commentaries have been discussed with a focus on three aspects: his principles of hadith comprehension (his premises); his methods (the measures he takes to reach the correct meaning of the hadith); and his interpretations. (There is not necessarily a sharp line between these three aspects, but the emphasis in publications on this issue differs.) Studying Ṭabāṭabā'ī's interpretation of a specific issue in the framework of hadith and Qur'an (separately or together) is a common focus among modern scholars. His methods have been scrutinised in several studies, though studies dedicated to his principles are less common. In Western studies of this *tafsir*, Medoff, and Ehteshami/ Rizvi have also discussed Ṭabāṭabā'ī's position about the role of hadith in the interpretation of the Qur'an; see Medoff, 'Ijtihad and Renewal', 45–60; Ehteshami and Rizvi, 'Beyond the Letter', 463–467.

notably in the 'hadith discussion' (*baḥth riwāyī*) of his *Mīzān*. 'A. Zāri'ī discusses the principles of Ṭabāṭabā'ī's use of hadith in the interpretation of the Qur'an and notes the following six principles: (1) the importance of *ahl al-bayt*[44] to commentaries on the Qur'an, (2) the interpretation of the Qur'an by hadith, (3) the interpretation of the Qur'an by the Qur'an itself, (4) adaptation (*taṭbīq*) of exegetical hadiths (on *taṭbīq* see more below), (5) prioritising the *matn* of a hadith over its *isnād* and (6) prioritising the Qur'an over the hadith.[45] In general, Ṭabāṭabā'ī's principles have also been addressed (to various degrees) in other studies dedicated to hadith in *al-Mīzān*.[46]

Among the most basic principles in Ṭabāṭabā'ī's use of hadith are his rejection of the authority of isolated hadith (*khabar al-wāḥid*),[47] and his view about the Prophet and the *ahl al-bayt* and their role as interpreters of the Qur'an. His view on isolated hadith has been subject to much debate as it is not accepted by most contemporary Shī'ī scholars.[48] This first principle determines many of his other principles, and is discussed below.

*Rejecting the Probative Proof (*ḥujjiya*) of Isolated Hadith (Khabar Al-wāḥid) in Fields other than Islamic Law (Fiqh)*

Like most Muslim scholars, Ṭabāṭabā'ī maintains the probative force (*ḥujjiya*) of *mutawātir* traditions and those hadiths in which further evidence leads scholars to consider them authentic in the field of Islamic law (*fiqh*) and creed (*'aqā'id*).[49] By contrast, the authority of isolated hadiths has been the subject of much debate throughout the history of Shī'ī thought. Some generally dismiss them as invalid,[50] while others only

---

44 The *ahl al-bayt* are the Twelve Shī'ī Imams along with the Prophet's daughter Fāṭima; see Howard, 'Ahl-e Bayt', *EIr*, I/6, 635.

45 Zāri'ī, 'Barrisī mabānī 'Allāma Ṭabāṭabā'ī'. This is the only study that explicitly mentions Ṭabāṭabā'ī's principles in his approach to hadith.

46 For example, see Ma'ārif, 'Ḥadīth'; Naṣīrī and Naṣīrī, 'Dīdgāh-hayi'; Mīrī, 'Darāmadī'.

47 *Khabar al-wāḥid* and *khabar al-mutawātir* are quantitative criteria for assessing transmissions. A hadith that is *khabar al-wāḥid* falls short of the predicate *mutawātir* (a hadith with multiple chains of transmission), in that it has only one or a few transmitters in every *ṭabaqa* (stage) of its *isnād*; see Juynboll, 'Khabar al-wāḥid', in *EI²*, 4:896; Juynboll, 'Tawātur', in *EI²*, 10:381; Wensinck and Heinrichs, 'Mutawātir', in *EI²*, 7:781. There is no agreement on the English equivalent for the term *khabar al-wāḥid*. Many scholars use the transliterated form of the phrase, while others use 'solitary' or 'single'. Schacht defines it as a hadith transmitted by 'isolated individuals' and thus shortens it to 'isolated'. Although 'solitary' and 'single' correspond more closely to the literal meaning of the word, 'isolated' is more consistent with the technical usage of the term in the hadith sciences; see Schacht, 'Ahl al-Ḥadīth', in *EI²*, 1:258.

48 For example, see Qāḍīzādi and al-Ja'farī, 'Ḥujjiyya al-ḥadīth'.

49 Al-Ṭabāṭabā'ī, *al-Mīzān*, 10:351, 14:133.

50 Ḥubbullah, *Naẓariyat al-sunna*, 67–97.

prohibit their use in the realm of creed.[51] Ṭabāṭabāʾī is considered the most prominent scholar in the contemporary Shīʿī world to confine the application of *khabar al-wāḥid* hadith exclusively to Islamic law.[52] He briefly explains that in relation to the rules pertaining to a Muslim's deeds a probable (*ẓannī*) hadith is granted the same authority as a definite (*qaṭʿī*) hadith in order to facilitate the identification of duties imposed by God.[53] Beyond the realm of law, certainty (*yaqīn*) in knowledge is essential. Therefore an isolated hadith that is probable (*ẓannī*), and therefore may be true or false, is insufficient for issues of creed (*ʿaqāʾid*), history (*tārīkh*), Qurʾanic interpretation (*tafsīr*), the virtues (*faḍāʾil*) of prominent personalities and the stories (*qiṣaṣ*) of the Qurʾan.[54] Ṭabāṭabāʾī concludes that isolated hadiths do not have any rational or religious authority in fields beyond jurisprudence.[55]

Accordingly, an isolated hadith cannot be considered authoritative unless its content is somehow verified. In fact, the validity of non-jurisprudential hadiths is based on the text (*matn*). In Ṭabāṭabāʾī's view, agreement between the text and the Qurʾan is one of the main criteria to determine the validity of the hadith[56] and is the basis for endorsing or rejecting traditions.[57]

Furthermore, if the content of a hadith agrees with the Qurʾan, the weakness of its *isnād* is harmless, and its soundness is merely additional evidence of its validity. By contrast, if the content conflicts with the Qurʾan, the soundness of its *isnād* is of no value, and its possible weakness, in turn, is just additional evidence for its rejection.[58] Ṭabāṭabāʾī criticises commentators, whom he does not identify by name, for giving precedence to the soundness of the *isnād* in their evaluation of hadith. These commentators neglect the text (*matn*) of the hadith and its agreement with the Qurʾan, and thus subordinate the Qurʾan to the hadith.[59] In accordance with this argument, Ṭabāṭabāʾī only occasionally refers to the *isnād*s being

---

51 Ḥubbullah, *Naẓariyat al-sunna*, 700–702.

52 Ḥubbullah, *al-Ḥadīth al-sharīf*, 2:210.

53 Al-Ṭabāṭabāʾī, *al-Mīzān*, 10:351, 14:205–206.

54 Al-Ṭabāṭabāʾī, *al-Mīzān*, 8:141, 9:211.

55 Al-Majlisī, *Biḥār al-anwār*, 6:336 n.2; for other Shīʿī scholars' view on isolated hadith, see Ḥubbullah, *al-Ḥadīth al-sharīf*, 2:189–310; for this debate among other Muslim scholars, see al-Sarhānī, *Ḥadīth al-āḥād*, 1:67–185; and al-Ghusn, *Mawqif al-mutakallimīn*, 1:163–230.

56 Al-Ṭabāṭabāʾī, *al-Mīzān*, 9:212, 5:265.

57 In contemporary Sunni thought we find a similar stress on the text (*matn*) in the evaluation of hadith; see Brown, *Rethinking Tradition*, 112–122.

58 Al-Ṭabāṭabāʾī, *al-Mīzān*, 1:293, 9:212.

59 Al-Ṭabāṭabāʾī, *al-Mīzān*, 9:212.

interrupted (*mursal*),[60] and rarely mentions their weakness (*ḍaʿf*).[61] Yet he never evaluates a hadith with its *isnād* and seldom, if ever, refers to the soundness (*ṣiḥḥa*) of the *isnād*.[62] In contrast to isolated hadiths, a hadith with multiple chains of transmission maintains its probative force (*ḥujjiya*) for Ṭabāṭabāʾī. Although he includes in his *Mīzān* fewer than thirty hadiths deemed *mutawātir*,[63] hadiths that he classified as well-known (*mashhūr*) are significantly greater in number. He emphasises that they are *mashhūr*, as he finds them in Shīʿī,[64] Sunnī[65] or both Shīʿī and Sunnī sources.[66] He then points to other variants of the hadith.[67] It seems that hadiths with numerous transmitters, even when they fall short of the necessary qualification to be *mutawātir*, still have important qualifications that can lead to some degree of certainty, as compared to isolated hadiths. Regarding the content of the hadith, Ṭabāṭabāʾī occasionally mentions that it is consistent with the Qurʾan,[68] but there are many instances in which he does not clarify the reliability of the hadith's *isnād* or content. Though his exact position in these cases is not clear, it seems that generally, unless he explicitly mentions their defect, then he approves them.

Due to Ṭabāṭabāʾī's *matn*-oriented approach to hadith, Sunnī traditions were well integrated into his exegesis and have gained a comparatively prominent place. In this issue, his commentary differs from that of most Shīʿī scholars, who assess the reliability of a hadith by referring to the *isnād* and examining Sunnī or non-Imāmī transmitters based on Shīʿī *rijāl* works.[69] In these Shīʿī biographies, non-Imāmī transmitters often fall short

60 For contemporary Shīʿī scholars, the term *mursal* indicates that the chain of transmission has been interrupted and one or more transmitters is missing: al-Māmqānī, *Miqbās al-hidāya*, 1:338. In Sunnī terminology, *mursal* usually indicates a tradition quoting the Prophet but with a transmitter who never met him; that is, the Companion is missing. See Juynboll, 'Mursal', in *EI*², 7:631. Al-Ṭabāṭabāʾī uses the word *mursal* or *mursalan* 128 times in his *tafsīr*; about half of which refer to the *isnād*. See al-Ṭabāṭabāʾī, *al-Mīzān*, 2:26, 38; 3:214, 233; 4:385; 5:125.

61 Al-Ṭabāṭabāʾī mentions the category of weak hadith thirteen times with the term *ḍaʿf* and *ḍaʿafahu*; of these only four are his own judgements, the others are citations of judgements put forward by other scholars. For examples, see al-Ṭabāṭabāʾī, *al-Mīzān*, 5:389, 6:214, 7:148.

62 For an exception, see al-Ṭabāṭabāʾī, *al-Mīzān*, 10:328.

63 I searched for *tawātur* and *mutawātir* in the 'hadith discussion' section of al-Ṭabāṭabāʾī, *al-Mīzān*; for some examples see: 1:183, 2:107.

64 For examples, see al-Ṭabāṭabāʾī, *al-Mīzān*, 1:23; 2:258; 7:306.

65 For examples, see al-Ṭabāṭabāʾī, *al-Mīzān*, 2:88, 189; 9:217; 15:50.

66 For examples, see al-Ṭabāṭabāʾī, *al-Mīzān*, 6:169; 14:308.

67 As noted, these kinds of comments appear frequently in hadith discussions. A well-known (*mashhūr*) hadith is one with more than two transmitters in one level (*ṭabaqa*); see Robson, 'Ḥadīth', in *EI*², 3:25.

68 For examples, see al-Ṭabāṭabāʾī, *al-Mīzān*, 1:124, 3:163, 12:148, 20:117.

69 Al-Māmqānī, *Miqbās al-hidāya*, 1:168.

of the required qualifications, but since Ṭabāṭabāʾī's point of contention is the content of the hadith, he accepts Sunnī hadiths.

The Teachings of the Prophet and Ahl al-Bayt in the Context of the Qur'an

Ṭabāṭabāʾī's second principle is his view that the Prophet and the *ahl al-bayt* are the teachers of the Qur'an. Muslim scholars generally maintain that the Qur'an explicitly gives authority to the statements, actions and tacit approvals of the Prophet, whether in the field of interpretation, creed or law. The verses cited as proof for this status are those introducing the Prophet as the one who elucidates the verses[70] and teaches the Book.[71] Furthermore, he is to be obeyed in whatever he forbids or proscribes.[72] In Ṭabāṭabāʾī's view, these verses identify two roles of the Prophet. One group of verses introduces the Prophet Muhammad as a legislator,[73] according to which he specifies the details of the regulations that are not mentioned in the Book (i.e. the Qur'an).[74] Thus, his sayings or deeds on some matters of Islamic law (*fiqh*) cannot necessarily be confirmed by the Qur'an. The second group of verses designates the Prophet as a teacher[75] who explains the Qur'an so that it is properly understood. Therefore, the role of the Prophet and the *ahl al-bayt* as his spiritual successors[76] is to educate, meaning that they facilitate clear understanding for students. Ṭabābabāʾī cites verses and traditions in support of his argument. The Qur'an calls on Muslims and infidels to contemplate the Qur'an, and accept it because '[i]f it had been from other than God, surely they would have found in it much inconsistency' (Q. 4:82). For Ṭabāṭabāʾī, this verse implies that Qur'anic teachings can be understood by contemplation and rational reasoning, and obtaining this understanding does not depend on the explanations of the Companions, the Successors or even the Prophet and the *ahl al-bayt*. This does not mean that he prohibits one from drawing on the hadith or other extra sources to clarify Qur'anic verses, but for sources to

70 Q. 16:44. For translations of Qur'anic quotations, I used Arberry, *The Koran Interpreted*, with slight modifications.

71 Q. 2:129, 3:164, 62:1.

72 Q. 59:7; for this argument see ʿAbd al-Khāliq, *Ḥujjiya al-sunna*, 291–308; he refers to five groups of verses to prove the authenticity of the hadith. The ones mentioned are in the second and third group.

73 Q. 59:7.

74 Al-Ṭabāṭabāʾī, *al-Mīzān*, 3:84, 19:204.

75 According to the above-mentioned verses of suras al-Naḥl (16), al-Baqara (2), Āl-ʿImrān (3), al-Jumuʿa (62).

76 Al-Ṭabāṭabāʾī, *al-Mīzān*, 1:11; Ṭabāṭabāʾī, *Qur'an dar Islam*, 44; this book is also available in English: *The Qur'an in Islam*. For the conception of the imamate in Shīʿī Islam, see Sobhani, *Doctrines of Shi'i Islam*, 119–137.

have interpretive properties for the Qur'an, they must have certain qualifications. The decisive criterion for this is their accordance with the Qur'an.

To justify his position, Ṭabābabā'ī cites hadiths that call on Muslims to follow the teachings of the Qur'an, and others that stress agreement with the Qur'an as the central criterion for evaluating the authenticity of hadiths. Following the Qur'an and using it as a point of reference for evaluating hadiths can only be realised if their meanings are properly understood.[77]

Ṭabātabā'ī's view concerning the Qur'an as self-contained and not in need of hadith to be correctly understood resembles the perspective of those who claim that the Qur'an should be the sole, or at least the central point of reference, but in fact his view differs greatly.[78] First, Ṭabātabā'ī clearly approves of considering hadith, including the teachings of the Prophet and the *ahl al-bayt*, in the interpretation of the Qur'an. Second, he devotes a significant part of his *tafsīr* to hadith discussion, because to practise this method properly, one must be fully acquainted with the hadiths.[79]

The Qur'an as the Criterion of Hadith Assessment

According to the two above-mentioned principles, consistency with the Qur'an is the main criterion for evaluating hadith. This point is also mentioned in various hadiths transmitted on the authority of Prophet Muhammad, and also those transmitted from five of the twelve Shī'ī Imams: the first Imam, 'Alī b. Abī Ṭālib (d. 40/661); the fifth, Muḥammad b. 'Alī al-Bāqir (d. 117/733); the sixth, Ja'far b. Muḥammad al-Ṣādiq (d. 148/765); the seventh, Mūsā b. Ja'far al-Kāẓim (d. 183/799); and the ninth, Muḥammad b. 'Alī al-Jawwād (d. 220/835).[80] Some of these traditions mention two aspects, consistency with the Qur'an as a prerequisite for acceptance, and contradiction with the Qur'an as a reason for rejection. Among the better-known examples of these is one transmitted on the authority of the Prophet. It states that he said in a sermon in Mina: 'Whenever a hadith is revealed to you on my authority, it is mine if it is in agreement with the Book and it is not mine if it is in opposition with the Book.'[81] Although similar traditions have been narrated in Sunnī sources, generally they have been considered

---

77 Al-Ṭabāṭabā'ī, *al-Mīzān*, 3:84–86. For a detailed study of his interpretive method, see Medoff, 'Ijtihad and Renewal'; for a critical review, see Paya, *Islam*, 110–133; Ehteshami and Rizvi, 'Beyond the Letter'.

78 Ilāhī Bakhsh, *al-Qur'āniyūn*, 210–257.

79 Al-Ṭabāṭabā'ī, *al-Mīzān*, 3:87.

80 Al-Majlisī, *Biḥār al-anwār*, 2:225, 227, 237, 242, 244, 250; for a classification of these hadiths and a detailed discussion of them, see Nurūzī and Naqīzādih, 'Mafhūm shināsī', 37–66; Naṣīrī, *Ravishshināsī-i naqd-i aḥādīth*, 344–384.

81 Al-Majlisī, *Biḥār al-anwār*, 2:227; al-Ḥimyarī, *Qurb al-asnād*, 92.

invalid.[82] There is an ongoing debate in Shīʿī Islam on the interpretation of the first phrase as well, that is, agreement with the Qurʾan. As the Qurʾan does not address all the issues mentioned in the traditions, the criterion of agreement with the Qurʾan may lead to the rejection of many traditions. Therefore, the predominant interpretation of this criterion is that both criteria refer to one element, namely disagreement with the Qurʾan. Thus, if a hadith disagrees, it should be rejected, and if it does not disagree, it should be accepted. According to this dominant view, every hadith does not need to be in agreement with the Qurʾan.[83] By contrast, Ṭabāṭabāʾī continued to emphasise a hadith's consistency with the Qurʾan as a precondition for its verification, as mentioned above, while sharing the dominant view that a hadith's contradiction with the Qurʾan is a criterion for rejection.[84] This also implies that hadiths whose content does not relate to the Qurʾan, and for which the criterion of agreement with the Qurʾan cannot be applied, must be rejected – at least for disciplines beyond *fiqh*.

In the cases of traditions in which the apparent meaning of a hadith seems to contradict the Qurʾan, Ṭabāṭabāʾī might offer interpretations to resolve the problem to some extent. In the section on hadith discussion in his *Mīzān*, he often points out that a tradition might confirm the same meaning clarified in the explanation (*bayān*) through the textual analysis of the Qurʾan,[85] and at times, he refers the reader to the explanation section for further elucidation of the hadith.[86] He also might specify that an exegetical hadith does not qualify as authoritative if it lacks consistency. For example, the Qurʾan verse (2:259) mentions the story of a man passing a ruined city, wondering if and how God could give life to the dead. God causes the man to die for one hundred years and then raises him to show the man His power to resurrect. In both Shīʿī and Sunnī sources,[87] traditions suggest that the man in the verse may refer to ʿUzayr or Irmīyā. Ṭabāṭabāʾī does not accept these traditions as the correct interpretation for the above-mentioned Qurʾan verse because they are isolated, with weak *isnād*s, and there is no evidence supporting them from the Qurʾan, or even from the Torah.[88] His explanation for the identification of the addressee

<hr>

82 ʿAbd al-Khāliq, *Ḥujjiya al-sunna*, 474–475.

83 Shaykh Murtaḍā al-Anṣārī (d. 1281/1864) and Muḥammad Bāqir al-Ṣadr (d. 1400/1980) are two of the most eminent Shīʿī scholars to support this view. Nurūzī and Naqīzādih, 'Mafhūm shināsī', 48–52; Naṣīrī, *Ravishshināsī-i naqd-i aḥādīth*, 368–372.

84 He does not discuss this particular hadith, but he repeatedly mentions that it is necessary for the text (*matn*) to be consistent with the Qurʾan, beyond the subject matter of Islamic law (*fiqh*).

85 See, for example, al-Ṭabāṭabāʾī, *al-Mīzān*, 7:209; 8:324; 19:269.

86 Al-Ṭabāṭabāʾī, *al-Mīzān*, 1:255, 306; 2:99, 378; 10:220.

87 Al-Ṭabarī, *Jāmiʿ al-bayān*, 3:19–20; al-Baḥrānī, *al-Burhān*, 1:534.

88 Al-Ṭabāṭabāʾī, *al-Mīzān*, 2:378.

as 'Uzayr or Irmīyā is not a concrete identification of the man passing the ruined city. Instead, Ṭabāṭabā'ī advocates a general interpretation, that the man must have been pious, or probably a prophet, since he was used to conversing with God and receiving revelations from Him.[89]

Regarding legal issues, Muslim scholars generally use hadith for the specification (*takhṣīṣ*) of general (*'āmm*) expressions[90] in the Qur'an; this illustrates the explanatory role of the Prophet and *ahl al-bayt*. Ṭabāṭabā'ī accepts such hadiths for specification in the context of *fiqh*, but he rejects *takhṣīṣ* for exegetical hadiths. For example, the Qur'an verse (23:101) states that there will be no kinship on the Last Day. Nevertheless several prophetic traditions assert that all kinship, by blood or marriage, will be broken on that day *except* those related to the Prophet.[91] Ṭabāṭabā'ī rejects this exclusion of the Prophet's kinship because it conflicts with the general meaning of the verse. He suggests that the hadith may indicate that belonging to the Prophet's family could prompt them to do good deeds for which his kin will benefit on the day of resurrection.[92]

Ṭabāṭabā'ī applies the principle of consistency with the Qur'an to several themes of hadiths. Two of these are illustrated in hadiths on the occasions of revelation, and those hadiths that interpret certain verses as referring to the Imams.

Hadiths on the Occasions of Revelation

It is generally agreed that knowledge about the occasions of revelation can only be obtained from traditions that were reported on the authority of the Companions as eyewitnesses, or on the authority of the Successors, who were informed by the Companions.[93] The reliability of these reports has been the subject of debate by modern scholars.[94] Ṭabāṭabā'ī is among those who are generally suspicious about these reports on the occasions of revelation. Like many Shī'ī scholars, he does not regard the Companions' and Successors' Qur'an commentary as having more impact than that of any exegete. Because of their contradictory reports about the occasions

89 Al-Ṭabāṭabā'ī, *al-Mīzān*, 2:362–363.
90 For further explanation, see Weiss, "Umūm wa-Khuṣūṣ', in *EI²*, 10:866–867.
91 Al-Suyūṭī, *al-Durr al-manthūr*, 6:117.
92 Al-Ṭabāṭabā'ī, *al-Mīzān*, 15:75–76; for other examples, see al-Ṭabāṭabā'ī, *al-Mīzān*, 2:259; 7:148, 396; 8:62, 231, 288; 11:239.
93 Traditions on the authority of the Successors who were informed by the Companions are usually called *athar* (pl. *āthār*). Sunnī scholars consider these traditions on the occasions of revelation like those attributed to the Prophet; see al-Suyūṭī, *Tadrīb al-rāwī*, 1:215–216. See also al-Wāḥidī, *Asbāb nuzūl al-Qur'ān*, 10; al-Suyūṭī, *al-Itqān*, 1:126.
94 For a general introduction to this genre of exegetical literature, see Rippin, 'Occasions of Revelation', *EQ*, 3:569–573.

of revelation, Ṭabāṭabāʾī refutes them as eyewitnesses.[95] He questions the authenticity of the chronological list of the suras[96] attributed to the famous Companion and early Qurʾan commentator, Ibn ʿAbbās (d. 68/687), since according to Ṭabāṭabāʾī, he was too young[97] to have been a witness for the revelation of many suras. Moreover, Ibn ʿAbbās's report on the chronological order of the suras is an isolated one and therefore not authoritative.[98] Although Ṭabāṭabāʾī does not rule out the possibility of conscious forgery of the reports on the occasion of revelation, he considers most of these narrations to be the well-meaning interpretations of Companions, Successors or later commentators, whose reports were intended to reconcile historical events with Qurʾan verses and clarify the occasions of revelation.[99] In order to identify reliable hadiths related to the topic of the occasions of revelation, he considers it important to scrutinise the content of these traditions.[100]

For instance, quoting from hadith collections, Ṭabāṭabāʾī mentions a variety of possible events for the occasion of revelation of Surat al-Tawba (Q. 9:64–74).[101] These verses describe some of the features and deeds of the hypocrites (*munāfiqūn*). Among the numerous reports of the occasion of revelation for this group of verses, Ṭabāṭabāʾī holds that the one that mentions a group of hypocrites who intended to assassinate the Prophet on his return from the battle of Tabuk (9/630–631) as the most likely. The other reports mostly mention instances in which the hypocrites had mocked or insulted the Prophet.[102] As the Qurʾan mentions that 'They [the hypocrites] swear by God that they said nothing, but they indeed said the word of unbelief and disbelieved, after they had surrendered; They planned what they never attained to …' (Q. 9:74), Ṭabāṭabāʾī deduces that the hypocrites had concocted a plot, and that this conspiracy is what was meant by 'the word of unbelief' in the Qurʾanic verse, not the mocking and insulting of the Prophet. God revealed their plot to the Prophet, and thus, according to the tradition, they were not able to achieve their goal.[103]

<hr>

95 Al-Ṭabāṭabāʾī, *al-Mīzān*, 1:294.

96 This list is the main source for the chronological order of the suras in the standard Egyptian version of the Qurʾan; see Böwering, 'Chronology and the Qurʾān', in *EQ*, 1:321–322.

97 He was a boy of ten, thirteen or fifteen when the Prophet died; see Ibn Ḥajar al-ʿAsqalānī, *al-Iṣāba*, 9:122.

98 Ṭabāṭabāʾī, *Qurʾān dar Islam*, 144–145.

99 Ṭabāṭabāʾī, *Qurʾān dar Islam*, 135–136.

100 For other criteria on the evaluation of this genre of hadith, see Nafisi, "Allāma Ṭabāṭabāʾī va-miʿyārhā-yi fahm', 86–100.

101 Al-Ṭabrisī, *Majmaʿ al-bayān*, 5:70–71 and 78–79; al-Suyūṭī, *al-Durr al-manthūr*, 3:254–261.

102 Al-Ṭabarī, *Jāmiʿ al-bayān*, 10:127–130; al-Ṭabrisī, *Majmaʿ al-bayān*, 5:78–79.

103 Al-Ṭabāṭabāʾī, *al-Mīzān*, 9:325, 344–345.

Another example is Ṭabāṭabā'ī's view on the reports about the occasion of revelation of Surat al-Luqmān, which states: 'But if they [your parents] strive with you to make you associate with Me that of which you have no knowledge, then do not obey them. Keep them company honourably in this world but follow the way of those who turn to Me …' (Q. 31:15). Sa'd b. Abī Waqqāṣ (d. between 51/669 and 58/678)[104] claims that this verse was revealed about him.[105] Ṭabāṭabā'ī questions the validity of this claim and points out that it is a continuation of the preceding verse in which human beings are ordered to be kind to their parents, as part of a general command (wa-waṣṣayna al-insāna bi-wālidayhi iḥsānā) regardless of religion or law, with no specific occasion for it.[106]

Exegetical Hadiths on the Imams

Shī'ī sources report many traditions in which different verses of the Qur'an were interpreted as referring to the Imams of the *ahl al-bayt*. These traditions are of various types: some are classified as belonging to the occasions of revelation, such as the tradition on Surat al-Insān (76:8). In this verse, the Qur'an praises those who 'give food, for the love of Him, to the needy, the orphan, the captive (*asīr*)'.[107] According to a hadith, 'Alī b. Abī Ṭālib (d. 40/661) and his wife Fāṭima (d. 11/632) (the daughter of the Prophet) had prepared some food when a poor man came to their home and asked for provisions. They gave him one-third of their food. When an orphan, and then a captive came and asked for food, 'Alī and Fāṭima gave them the

---

104 *He died between 51/669 and 58/678*; see Ibn Ḥajar al-'Asqalānī, *al-Iṣāba*, 3:62; *al-Ziriklī, al-A'lām, 3:87 has 55/675 as the date of death*. His will has been a subject of debate; see Speight, 'The Will of Sa'd b. a. Waqqāṣ', 249–267; Powers, 'The Will of Sa'd b. Abî Waqqâṣ', 33–53.

105 No other occasion of revelation has been mentioned for this verse; see al-Ṭabarī, *Jāmi' al-bayān*, 21:45; al-Suyūṭī, *al-Durr al-manthūr*, 5:165–166; al-Wāḥidī, *Asbāb nuzūl al-Qur'ān*, 357.

106 Al-Ṭabāṭabā'ī, *al-Mīzān*, 9:15; for further examples, see al-Ṭabāṭabā'ī, *al-Mīzān*, 2:99, 163, 405, 407; 6:60, 112, 155; 10:40; 13:216; 15:105, 334; 16:241; 18:52, 317, 320; 19:337; 20:47, 58, 157.

107 Muslim commentators give a variety of interpretations of *asīr*. Al-Ṭabarī explains it as an infidel captured in a war against Muslims or a Muslim who has been justly imprisoned; see al-Ṭabarī, *Jāmi' al-bayān*, 29:129. Fakhr al-Dīn al-Rāzī gives five possible meanings for it: a slave, a captured infidel, a debtor, a Muslim prisoner or a wife; see al-Rāzī, *al-Tafsīr al-kabīr*, 30:747–748. Ṭabāṭabā'ī considers it someone captured in a war against Muslims; see al-Ṭabāṭabā'ī, *al-Mīzān*, 20:126. He does not explain how a captive could move about freely in the town. However, it is reported on the authority of Ḥasan that when the Prophet took captives, he would turn them over to Muslims for two or three days, and advise them to be kind to the captives; see al-Zamakhsharī, *al-Kashshāf*, 4:669.

rest of the food. After this event, the verse was revealed.[108] Sunnī sources also reported this event as the occasion of revelation for the verse. Some scholars accepted this hadith as the correct interpretation of the verse, while others challenged it.[109]

The second type of tradition refers to those hadiths in which ʿAlī and the other Imams are the intended meaning of a Qurʾanic verse, or parts of the verse. An example is the expression *ahl al-dhikr* (the people of remembrance; Q. 16:43 and 21:7), which is interpreted as referring to the Imams.[110] Traditions of this type, which are numerous, are rejected by Sunnī scholars and considered evidence of the Shīʿa imposing sectarian views on the Qurʾan.[111] Shīʿī commentators generally quote these traditions, but do not explain their relation to the Qurʾan. Most of these traditions were considered esoteric interpretations of the verses, part of the knowledge that was given to the *ahl al-bayt*.[112] According to some Shīʿī hadiths such interpretations of the Qurʾan are beyond the understanding of the human intellect,[113] and Shīʿī commentators consider their explanation unnecessary.

Unlike most of his predecessors, Ṭabāṭabāʾī offers an explanation for this second type of hadith because he believes, according to his second principle, that exegetical *ḥadīth*s must agree with the Qurʾan. In order to understand his line of argumentation, it is necessary to consider the terms he uses to differentiate between two basic types of exegetical hadith. The first type of exegetical hadith is called *tafsīr*[114] (interpretation), and the second type is called *taṭbīq* (adaptation) and/or *jary* (flowing [movement]). By *tafsīr*, he means the exoteric explanation of a verse that can be reached by observing its literal and historical context. The occasions of revelation are also considered a *tafsīr* since they clarify the specific occasion to which the verse refers historically. Therefore, ʿAlī and his wife are considered the *tafsīr* for Qurʾan 76:8. By *jary* and *taṭbīq*, he means those hadiths that explain a Qurʾanic verse in a figurative sense. The two distinct concepts of

108 Al-Qummī, *Tafsīr al-Qummī*, 2:398–399; this event has been reported in various sources but they differ in details; see al-Majlisī, *Biḥār al-anwār*, 35:237–255.

109 Al-Wāḥidī, *Asbāb nuzūl al-Qurʾān*, 470; al-Suyūṭī, *al-Durr al-manthūr*, 8:371; and see al-Qurṭubī, *al-Jāmiʿ*, 19:131–135, where he discusses this case in detail.

110 This hadith is very well known among the Shīʿa and is widely cited. See al-Qummī, *Tafsīr al-Qummī*, 2:68; al-Baḥrānī, *al-Burhān*, 3:423; al-Majlisī, *Biḥār al-anwār*, 23:179, 180, 183, 184.

111 Al-Dhahabī, *al-Tafsīr*, 2:87–96, 138, 139.

112 Al-Kāshānī, *Tafsīr al-ṣāfī*, 1:26; Sayyidān, *Tafsīr*, 1:16. For a discussion of the esoteric interpretation of Ṭabāṭabāʾī, see Ehteshami and Rizvi, 'Beyond the Letter'; I do not address Ṭabāṭabāʾī's view on the esoteric (*bāṭin*) interpretation of Qurʾan verses in this chapter.

113 Al-Baḥrānī, *al-Burhān*, 1:3–6.

114 For another category of *tafsīr/taṭbīq* in which, according to Ṭabāṭabāʾī, *taṭbīq* is considered unsuitable, see Ehteshami and Rizvi, 'Beyond the Letter', 453.

tafsīr and *taṭbīq* should not be understood as mutually exclusive; instead, in Ṭabāṭabā'ī's thought, they are regarded as complementary. For instance, any believer who helps the needy for the sake of God is an example of Qur'an 76:8, although this does not accord with the historical context of the verse (which is based on the first decade after the *hijra*), nor does it reflect the literal wording (namely giving to a needy person, an orphan or a captive). Ṭabāṭabā'ī borrows the term *jary* from a simile employed by the fifth Shī'ī Imam, Muḥammad b. 'Alī al-Bāqir (d. 117/733), and the sixth Imam, Ja'far b. Muḥammad al-Ṣādiq (d. 148/765). These two Imams compare these adaptations of Qur'anic verses to the sun and moon pursuing their course (*kamā yajrī al-shams wa-l-qamar*).[115] Thus, such new explanations of Qur'anic verses are considered a sign of the continuous presence of the Qur'an, something that is, in turn, illustrated by the simile of the sun and the moon.

How can these two types of hadith (*tafsīr* and *taṭbīq/jary*) be identified?[116] According to Ṭabāṭabā'ī, a hadith is only accepted as *tafsīr* of a verse if it is in accordance with the literal meaning and historical context of the verse. By contrast, when several hadiths identify Imams or various personalities as the intended interpretation of the same verse, it shows that this is not *tafsīr*, but *taṭbīq*; in this case, they are considered new examples of the ongoing rereading of the Qur'an.[117]

For example, Ṭabāṭabā'ī refutes hadiths that interpret the term *ahl al-dhikr* (the people of remembrance) as referring to the Imams. The word *dhikr* (lit., remembrance) is used in the Qur'an to refer to divine books, including the Qur'an and the Torah.[118] The term *ahl al-dhikr* occurs twice in the Qur'an. In both verses, it invites the people to ask *ahl al-dhikr* about the previous men to whom God sent revelations.[119] According to Ṭabāṭabā'ī, these verses refer to Christian and Jewish scholars who were considered knowledgeable; thus, the *tafsīr* of this term is the people of the book (*ahl al-kitāb*).[120] If the people at the time of the revelation were advised to ask Christian and Jewish

---

115 Al-'Ayyāshī, *al-Tafsīr*, 1:11, hadith nos. 4 and 5; al-Ṣaffār, *Baṣā'ir al-darajāt*, 1:196, hadith 7; al-Kulaynī, *al-Kāfī*, 1:191, 192.

116 Some hadiths explicitly distinguish between these two types of interpretation, but this is very rare. One of the few instances is a hadith transmitted on the authority of Imam al-Bāqir about Q. 22:40, saying that the verse was revealed about the Prophet, 'Alī, Ḥamza and Ja'far, but was applied to Ḥusayn (*nazalat fī … wa-jarat fī …*); see al-Kulaynī, *al-Kāfī*, 8:337–338.

117 Al-Ṭabāṭabā'ī, *al-Mīzān*, 1:41.

118 Lane, *Arabic-English Lexicon*, 1:968–969.

119 Q. 16:43 and 21:7; there is a very slight difference in the wording of the two verses, and Arberry's translation also differs slightly. The translation given here is the one for sura 21:7: 'And We sent none before you, but men to whom We made revelation; question the people of the Remembrance, if you do not know.'

120 Al-Ṭabāṭabā'ī, *al-Mīzān*, 14:254.

scholars, this was because of their knowledge. After the revelation, the last part of the verse, 'question the people of the remembrance, if you do not know', also implies a general rule; in this case, the Imams could become the interpretation of the knowledgeable.

Traditions associated with Qur'an 17:4–5 about the Israelites are another example of this line of argumentation:

> And We decreed for the Children of Israel in the Book: You shall cause corruption in the earth twice, and you shall ascend exceedingly high [in corruption]. So, when the promise of the first of these came to pass, We sent against you servants of Ours, men of great might, and they went through the habitations and it was a promise fulfilled. (Q. 17:4–5)

Some Shī'ī hadiths state that the two corruptions mentioned in the verse refer to the assassination of 'Alī b. Abī Ṭālib (d. 40/661) and the murder of Imam Ḥasan b. 'Alī (d. 50/670). The expression 'ascending high' is said to refer to the martyrdom of Imam Ḥusayn b. 'Alī (d. 61/680). And the 'men of the great might' are interpreted as a group of followers of the Imams who rise up before the coming of the last Imam, and take revenge for the martyred Imams.[121] For Ṭabāṭabā'ī, these are just events in the history of Islam in which Muslims committed corrupt acts (in this case the murders of Imams 'Alī and Ḥasan), just as the Israelites did, but they are not the *tafsīr* of the verse; they are the *jary* and *taṭbīq* of this verse.[122] Muslims are said to have followed the Israelites, as mentioned in a prophetic hadith quoted by both the Shī'ī and Sunnī sources: the Prophet predicted that Muslims would follow the Children of Israel (Banū Isrā'īl) in all their deeds, and this adherence would be so slavish that if they entered a lizard's nest, Muslims would do the same.[123] Thus, the murders of the two Imams are examples of such corrupt acts.[124]

Ṭabāṭabā'ī uses his division of *tafsīr* and *taṭbīq/jary* for other themes of hadiths beyond those that refer to the *ahl al-bayt*.[125] According to a tradition, the believers praised in the Qur'an ('But those who believe, and do deeds of righteousness, the gardens of paradise shall be their hospitality' [18:107])

---

121 Al-Baḥrānī, *al-Burhān*, 3:502.

122 Al-Ṭabāṭabā'ī, *al-Mīzān*, 4:256–257.

123 This is a prophetic hadith that has been narrated with different wordings and in a variety of sources. See al-Hilālī, *Kitāb Sulaym*, 2:599 (the last part of a very long tradition); al-'Ayyāshī, *al-Tafsīr*, 1:303; al-Bukhārī, *Ṣaḥīḥ*, 1808, hadith no. 7320; Muslim, *Ṣaḥīḥ Muslim*, 1230–1231, hadith no. 2669.

124 Al-Ṭabāṭabā'ī, *al-Mīzān*, 13:44.

125 See al-Ṭabāṭabā'ī, *al-Mīzān*, 17:252 for the followers of Imams; see 17:394 for Iblīs and Cain; see 5:94 for loans; and see 1:153 for fasting.

are Abū Dharr, Salmān, Miqdād, and 'Ammār.[126] But since this verse is from the Meccan period, and Salmān converted to Islam in Medina, the tradition cannot correspond to the historical context of the verse. Emphasising the apparent meaning of the verse, Ṭabāṭabā'ī says that it honours the righteous in general, and does not imply specific people; consequently, he considers the above-mentioned four people as examples of the numerous people who may be intended by the verse, and thus, this hadith is its *taṭbīq*, and not its *tafsīr*.[127]

Ṭabāṭabā'ī's explanation of Shī'ī hadith on *ahl al-bayt* is considered of great significance and is discussed separately.[128] For the contemporary Shī'ī community, which tends toward a rational justification of Islamic teachings, including the interpretation of hadiths, Ṭabāṭabā'ī's understanding of these hadiths is important because he explicates the variant hadiths on a given verse and resolves their conflict with the apparent meaning of the Qur'an.

Conclusion

As a contemporary commentator of Shī'ī hadith, Ṭabāṭabā'ī developed specific lines of thought that stirred great interest and were echoed among scholars. His uncommon standpoint regarding isolated hadiths as beyond the field of law, and his justification of interpretive hadiths of the Prophet and *ahl al-bayt*, made *matn* the focus of his evaluation of hadiths. Among the many different criteria of content evaluation, he emphasises the consistency of the hadith with the Qur'an as the most essential principle. A hadith can have exegetical authority if it agrees with the apparent meaning of the verse(s) of the Qur'an, even though its transmission might be weak. On the other hand, he refutes hadiths that fall short of the qualification of agreement, even though it might have a sound *isnād*.

In order to comprehend and justify the variety of hadiths that he uses to interpret verses of the Qur'an in somewhat divergent ways, Ṭabāṭabā'ī introduces a classification of types of hadiths (I have not addressed all of them in this chapter). That is, *tafsīr* hadiths refer only to the concrete, documented historical context at the time of the revelation, and must accord with the literal wording of the verse. The other type, *taṭbīq* or *jary*,

---

126 Al-Qummī, *Tafsīr al-Qummī*, 2:46.
127 Al-Ṭabāṭabā'ī, *al-Mīzān*, 13:402; for further discussion on its underlying principles, see Nafisi, 'Mabānī jary va taṭbīq'.
128 Many articles in Persian and Arabic discuss the issue of *jary*. The following are just a few: Daqīq, 'Naẓarīya al-jary'; Yazdān-panāh, 'Jary va taṭbīq'; Mu'min-nizhād and Rād, 'Mabānī adabī'.

encompasses the numerous traditions that do not fulfil these qualifications; they offer new applications and partly diverging interpretations of the assumed intended meaning. Ṭabāṭabā'ī does not dismiss these; on the contrary, such traditions reflect the ongoing presence of the Qur'an through the centuries, and its applicability to contemporary needs.

The example of the commentary on hadith in Ṭabāṭabā'ī's *tafsīr al-Mizān* might serve as one illustration of the fluid boundaries of the genre. If we consider Qur'anic exegesis and hadith commentary as two distinct genres, the following issues might be addressed. Often, the study of hadith in *tafsīr* has been conducted by specialists of *tafsīr* whose analytical focus was directed toward Qur'anic exegesis, with little consideration of hadith commentary as a genre unto itself. To contextualise hadith as part of *tafsīr* in the analytical framework of hadith commentary would involve a closer examination and consideration of the hadith commentary tradition, something some *tafsīr* experts might prefer to avoid. Future research should at least identify the differences between these two exegetical traditions, and examine how hadith commentary operates in *tafsīr* and how Qur'anic exegesis might be operating in hadith commentary, taking into consideration the relative amount of material, intertextuality, argumentative strategies, as they connect to the respective tradition.

Bibliography

'Abd al-Khāliq, 'A. *Ḥujjiya al-sunna*. Cairo: Dār al-Sa'dāwī, n.d.

'Ābidī, A. 'Nigāhī bi ta'līqāt-i 'Allāma Ṭabāṭabā'ī bar biḥār al-anwār.' In *Marzbān vaḥy va khirad*, edited by Daftar-i Tablīghāt-i Islāmī, pp. 669–685. Qum: Būstān-i Kitāb, 2002.

al-'Ak, Kh. *Uṣūl al-tafsīr wa-qawā'iduhū*. Beirut: Dār al-Nafā'is, 1986.

Algar, H. "Allāma Sayyid Muḥammad Ḥusayn Ṭabāṭabā'ī: Philosopher, Exegete and Gnostic.' *Journal of Islamic Studies* 17, no. 3 (September 2006): 326–351.

al-'Āmilī, Muḥammad b. al-Ḥasan b. al-Shahīd al-Thānī. *Istiqṣā' al-i'tibār fī sharḥ al-istibṣār*. Qum: Mu'assassat Āl al-Bayt, 1998.

Amir-Moezzi, M. and H. Ansari. 'Perfecting a Religion: Remarks on al-Kulaynī and His Summa of Traditions.' In Amir-Moezzi Mohammad (ed.), Eric Ormsby (trans.), *The Silent Qur'an and the Speaking Qur'an: Scriptural Sources of Islam Between History and Fervor*, pp. 125–160. New York: Columbia University Press, 2016.

Arberry, A. J. *The Koran Interpreted*. New York: Touchstone, 1996.

Awsī, 'A. *Ravish 'Allāmah Ṭabāṭabā'ī dar tafsīr al-mizān*. Translated by Ḥ. Mīr Jalīlī. Tehran: Sāzman Tablighāt Islāmī, 2002.

al-'Ayyāshī, M. *al-Tafsīr*. Edited by H. Rasūlī. 2 vols. Tehran: Maktabat al-'Ilmiyyat al-Islāmiyya, 1960.

al-Baḥrānī, H. *al-Burhān fī tafsīr al-Qur'ān*. 5 vols. Qum: Mu'assassat al-Ba'tha, 1994.

Berg, H. *The Development of Exegesis in Early Islam.* London: Routledge Curzon, 2000.

Blecher, J. 'Ḥadīth Commentary', in *EI³*. <http://dx.doi.org/10.1163/1573-3912_ei3_COM_32080>, accessed 6 February 2021.

Blecher, J. *Said the Prophet of God.* Oakland: University of California Press, 2018.

Böwering, G. 'Chronology and the Qur'ān', in *EQ*, 1:316–335.

Brown, D. *Rethinking Tradition in Modern Islamic Thought.* Cambridge: Cambridge University Press, 1996.

al-Bukhārī, M. *Ṣaḥīḥ al-Bukhārī.* Damascus and Beirut: Dār Ibn Kathīr, 2002.

Daqīq, M. 'Naẓarīya al-jary wa-l-taṭbīq 'alā ḍaw' tafsīr al-Mīzān: al-mafhūm wa-l-thamarāt.' *al-Minhāj* 64 (2011): 301–323.

al-Dhahabī, M. Ḥ. *al-Isrā'īliyyāt fī al-tafsīr wa-l-ḥadīth.* Cairo: Maktaba al-Wahba, 1990.

al-Dhahabī, M. Ḥ. *al-Tafsīr wa-l-mufassirūn.* 2 vols. Cairo: N.p., 1976.

Ehteshami, A. and S. Rizvi. 'Beyond the Letter: Explanation (*tafsīr*) versus Adaption (*taṭbīq*) in Ṭabāṭabā'ī's *al-Mīzān*.' In A. Keller and S. Rizvi (eds), *The Spirit and the Letter: Approaches to the Esoteric Interpretation of the Qur'an*, pp. 443–473. London: Oxford University Press in association with the Institute of Ismaili Studies, 2016.

Geoffroy, E. 'al-Suyuti', in *EI²*, 9:913–916.

al-Ghusn, S. *Mawqif al-mutukalimīn min al-istidlāl bi-nuṣūṣ al-kitāb wa-l-sunna.* 2 vols. Riyadh: Dār al-'Āṣim, 1996.

Gleave, R. 'Between *Ḥadīth* and *Fiqh*: the 'Canonical' Imāmī Collections of *Akhbār*.' *Islamic Law and Society* 8, no. 3 (2001): 350–382.

al-Hilālī, Sulaym b. al-Qays. *Kitāb Sulaym b. al-Qays al-Hilālī.* Edited by M. Anṣārī Zanjānī. Qum: al-Hādī, 1984.

al-Ḥimyarī, 'A. *Qurb al-asnād.* Qum: Mu'assasat Āl al-Bayt li-Iḥyā' al-Turāth, 1992.

Howard, I. K. A. 'Ahl e bayt', in *EIr*, I/6: 635.

Ḥubbullah, H. *al-Ḥadīth al-sharīf.* Beirut: al-Intishār al-'Arabī, 2017.

Ḥubbullah, Ḥ. *Naẓariyat al-sunna fī al-fikr al-imāmī al-shi'ī.* Beirut: al-Intishār al-'Arabī, 2006.

Ḥusaynī Ṭihrānī, M. Ḥ. *Mihr-i tābān.* Qum: Bāqir al-'Ulūm, 1982.

Ibn Ḥajar al-'Asqalānī, A. *al-Iṣāba fī tamyīz al-ṣaḥāba.* Edited by 'A. A. 'Abd al-Mawjūd and 'A. M. Mu'awwaḍ. 8 vols. Beirut: Dār al-Kutub al-'Ilmiyya, 1995.

Ibn Taymiyya. *Muqaddama fī uṣūl al-tafsīr.* Edited by 'Adnān Zarzūr. Kuwait: Dār al-Qur'ān al-Karīm, 1972.

Ilāhī Bakhsh, Kh. Ḥ. *al-Qur'ānīyūn wa-shubahatuhum ḥawl al-sunna.* Taif: Maktaba al-Ṣidīq, 1989.

'Itr, Nūr al-Dīn. *Manhaj al-naqd fī-'ulūm al-ḥadīth.* Beirut Dār al-Fikr al-Mu'āṣira and Damascus: Dār al-Fikr, 1992.

Juyboll, G. H. A. 'Khabar al-wāḥid', in *EI²*, 4:896.

Juynboll, G. H. A. 'Mursal', in *EI²*, 7:631.

Juynboll, G. H. A. 'Tawātur', in *EI²*, 10:381–382.

Kamaly, H. *God and Man in Tehran.* New York: Columbia University Press, 2010.

al-Kāshānī = M. al-Fayḍ al-Kāshānī. *Tafsīr al-ṣāfī.* Edited by Ḥ. A'lamī. 5 vols. Tehran: Maktabat al-Ṣadr, 1994.

al-Kulaynī, M. *al-Kāfī*. Edited by ʿA. A. Ghaffarī and M. Ākhūndī. 8 vols. Tehran: Dār al-Kutub al-Islāmiyya, 1986.

Lane, E. W. *Arabic-English Lexicon*. 8 vols. New York: Frederick Ungar Publishing, 1956.

Maʿārif, M. ʿHadīth, jāygāh va kārkard-i ān dar tafsīr al-Mīzān.ʾ *Pajūhish dīnī* 11 (2005): 47–64.

al-Majlisī, M. B. *Bihār al-anwār al-jāmiʿat li-durar akhbār al-aʾimmat al-athār*. 110 vols. Beirut: Dār Ihyāʾ al-Turāth al-ʿArabī, 1982.

al-Majlisī, Muhammad Taqī. *Rawda al-muttaqīn fī sharh man lā yahdarahū al-faqīh*. Edited by S. H. Mūsavī Kirmānī and ʿA. P. Ishtihārdī. 12 vols. Qum: Bunyād Farhang Islāmī Kushānpūr, 1985.

al-Māmqānī, ʿA. *Miqbās al-hidāya fī ʿilm al-dirāya*. Qum: Muʾassassat Āl al-Bayt li-Ihyāʾ al-Turāth, 1990.

Medoff, L. ʿIjtihad and Renewal in Qurʾanic Hermeneutics: An Analysis of Muhammad Husayn Tabātabāʾīʾs *al-Mīzān fī tafsīr al-Qurʾān*.ʾ PhD dissertation, University of California–Berkeley, 2007.

Medoff, L. ʿTabātabāʾi, Mohammad-Hosaynʾ, in *EIr*. <http://www.iranicaonline.org/articles/tabatabai-mohammad-hosayn>, accessed 1 July 2020.

Mīrī, S. S. ʿDarāmadī bar maktab-I hadīthī-yi ʿAllāma Tabātabāʾī dar tafsīr.ʾ MA dissertation, Usūl al-Dīn Institute of Higher Education, Qum, 1999.

Muʾmin-nizhād, A. and ʿA. Rād. ʿMabānī adabī va zabān sināsī-yi jary va tatbīq dar tafsīr Qurʾān.ʾ *Tahqīqāt-i ʿulūm-i Qurʾān va hadīth* 33 (2017): 57–79.

al-Murtadā, Sharīf. *Amālī al-Murtadā: Ghurar al-fawāʾid wa-durar al-qalāʾid*. Edited by M. A. Ibrāhīm. 2 vols. Cairo: Dār al-Fikr al-ʿArabī, 1998.

Muslim b. al-Hajjāj al-Qushayrī al-Nīsābūrī. *Sahīh Muslim*. Edited by N. M. al-Fāryābī. Riyadh: Dār Tayyiba, 2006.

Nafisi, Sh. *ʿAllāma Tabātabāʾī va hadīth*. Tehran: Shirkat Intishārāt ʿIlmī va Farhangī, 2010.

Nafisi, Sh. "Allāmah Tabātabāʾī va miʿyārhā-yi fahm va naqd ahādith-i asbāb nuzūl.ʾ *Amūzihā-yi Qurʾānī* 4–5 (2002): 69–100.

Nafisi, Sh. ʿMabānī jary va tatbīq az didgāh-i ʿAllāma Tabātabāʾī.ʾ *Qurʾān Shinākht* 12 (2014): 5–26.

Najāshī, A. *Rijāl al-Najāshī*. Qum: Muʾassassat al-Nashr al-Islāmī al-Tābiʿa li-Jāmiʿa al-Mudarrisīn, 1986.

Nāsih, ʿA. A. ʿPajūhishī dar iʿtibār-i rivāyāt tafsīrī.ʾ *Pajūhishnāmah Qurʾān va Hadīth* 1 (2006): 49–63.

Nasīrī, ʿA. *Ravishshināsī-i naqd-i ahādīth*. Qum: Vahy va Khirad, 2011.

Nasīrī ʿA. and M. H. Nasīrī. ʿDīdgāh-hāyi hadīthī-i ʿAllāma Tabātabāʾī dar tafsīr al-Mīzān.ʾ *Dānishnāma ʿulūm al-Qurʾān va hadīth* 1 (2014): 109–122.

Nurūzī, M. and H. Naqīzādih. ʿMafhūm shināsī mukhālifat va muvāfiqat-i hadīth ba Qurʾān.ʾ *Ulūm Hadīth* 55 (2010): 37–66.

Paya, A. *Islam, Modernity and a New Millennium*. London: Routledge, Taylor and Francis, 2018.

Powers, D. S. ʿThe Will of Saʿd b. Abî Waqqās: A Reassessment.ʾ *Studia Islamica* 58 (1983): 33–53. doi: <https://doi.org/10.2307/1595341>

Qādīzādi, K. and M. al-Jaʿfarī. ʿHujjiyya al-hadīth fī tafsīr al-Qurʾān: Dirāsa fī nazariyya al-ʿAllāma al- Tabātabāʾī.ʾ *Nusūs muʿāsira* 30–31 (2013): 375–394.

al-Qummī, 'A. *Tafsīr al-Qummī*. Edited by Ṭ. Jazāyirī. 2 vols. Qum: Dār al-Kitāb, 1984.

al-Qurṭubī, M. *al-Jāmi' li-aḥkām al-Qur'ān*. Edited by H. Samīr al-Bukhārī. 20 vols. Riyadh: Dār al-'Ālam al-Kutub, 2002.

al-Rāzī, Fakhr al-Dīn M. *al-Tafsīr al-kabīr*. 32 vols. Beirut: Dār Iḥyā' al-Turāth al-'Arabī, 1999.

Rippin, A. 'Occasions of Revelation', in *EQ*, 3:569–573.

Rizvi, 'Mollā Ṣadrā Širāzi', *in eIr*. <http://www.iranicaonline.org/articles/mollasadra-sirazi>, accessed 1 August 2020.

Robson, J. 'Ḥadīth', in *EI²*, 3:23–28.

al-Ṣaffār, M. Ḥ. *Baṣā'ir al-darajāt fī faḍā'il Āl Muḥammad (SA)*. Edited by M. Kuchi Bāghī. Qum: Maktabat Āyatullāh Mar'ashī Najafī, 1983.

al-Sarhānī, 'A. *Ḥadīth al-āḥād wa-ḥujjīyatuhū fī ta'ṣīl al-i'tiqād*. Riyadh: Maktabat al-Rushd, 2006.

Sayyid 'Alavī, S. I. 'Mitud-i naqd va taḥqīq-i ḥadīth az naẓar-i 'Allāma Ṭabāṭabā'ī.' *Kiyhān Andīshi* 38 (1991): 12–30.

Sayyidān, S. J. *Tafsīr āyāt al-'aqā'id*. Mashad: Vilāyat, 2013.

Schacht J. 'Ahl al-Ḥadīth', in *EI²*, 1:258–259.

Sobhani, J. *Doctrines of Shi'i Islam: A Compendium of Imami Beliefs and Practices*. Translated and edited by Reza Shah-Kazemi. London: I. B. Tauris, 2001.

Speight, M. 'The Function of Hadith as Commentary on the Qur'an.' In A. Rippin (ed.), *Approaches to the History of the Interpretation of the Qur'ān*, pp. 63–82. Oxford: Clarendon Press, 1988.

Speight, R. Marston. 'The Will of Sa'd b. a. Waqqāṣ: The Growth of a Tradition.' *Der Islam* 50, no. 2 (1973): 249–267.

al-Suyūṭī, 'A. *al-Durr al-manthūr fī al-tafsīr bi-l-ma'thūr*. 6 vols. Beirut: Dār al-Fikr, 2000.

al-Suyūṭī, 'A. *al-Itqān fī 'ulūm Qur'ān*. Edited by F. A. Zumarlī. 2 vols. Beirut: Dār al-Kitāb al-'Arabī, 2002.

al-Suyūṭī, 'A. *Tadrīb al-rāwī fī sharḥ taqrīb al-Nawāwī*. Edited by N. M. al-Fāryābī. 2 vols. Beirut: Dār al-Kalim al-Ṭayyib, 1996.

al-Ṭabarī, M. *Jāmi' al-bayān fī tafsīr al-Qur'ān*. 30 vols. Beirut: Dār al-Ma'rifa, 1994.

al-Ṭabāṭabā'ī, M. Ḥ. *al-Mīzān fī tafsīr al-Qur'ān*. 20 vols. Beirut: Mu'assasat al-A'lamī li-l-Maṭbu'āt, 1970.

Ṭabāṭabā'ī, M. Ḥ. *Shi'ite Islam*. Translated and edited by S. H. Nasr. New York: State University of New York Press, 1975.

Ṭabāṭabā'ī, M. Ḥ. *Qur'an dar Islam*. Qum: Daftar Intishārāt Islāmī, 2000.

al-Ṭabāṭabā'ī, M. Ḥ. *al-Bayān fī muwāfiqat bayn al-ḥadīth wa-l-Qur'ān*. Edited by A. Irādatī. Beirut: Dār al-Ta'arruf, 2006.

al-Ṭabrisī, F. *Majma' al-bayān fī tafsīr al-Qur'ān*. Edited by F. Yazdī Ṭabāṭabā'ī and H. Rasūlī. 10 vols. Tehran: Nāṣir Khusru, 1993.

al-Ṭūsī, M. *al-Istibṣār fī ma ikhtalafa min al-aḥkām*. Edited by Ḥ. Khirsān. Tehran: Dār al-Kutub al-Islāmiyya, 1970.

al-Ṭūsī, M. *Tahdhīb al-aḥkām*. Edited by Ḥ. Khirsān. Tehran: Dār al-Kutub al-Islāmiyya, 1986.

al-Ṭūsī, M. *al-Tibyān fī tafsīr al-Qur'ān*. Edited by A. Ḥ. al-'Āmilī, Qum: Mu'assassat Āl al-Bayt li-Iḥyā' al-Turāth, 1992.

al-Wāḥidī, ʿA. *Asbāb nuzūl al-Qurʾān*. Beirut: Dār al-Kutub al-ʿIlmiyya, 1990.

Weiss, B. G. "Umūm wa-Khuṣūṣ', in *EI²*, 10:866–867.

Wensinck, A. J. and W. F. Heinrichs. 'Mutawātir', in *EI²*, 7:781–782.

Yazdān-panāh, S. Y. 'Jary va taṭbīq, ravish-hā va mabānī-yi ān.' *Anvar-i maʿrifat* 4 (2012): 7–32.

Zāriʿī, ʿA. 'Barrisī mabānī ʿAllāma Ṭabāṭabāʾī pīrāmūn bahrigīrī az rivāyāt dar tafsīr al-Mīzān.' *Pajūhish-hāyi Nahj al-balāgha* 49 (2016): 135–151.

al-Zamakhsharī, M. *al-Kashshāf ʿan ḥaqāʾiq ghawāmiḍ al-tanzīl wa-ʿuyū al-aqāwīl fī wujūh al-taʾwīl*. Edited by ʿA. al-Mahdī. 4 vols. Beirut: Dār Iḥyāʾ al-Turāth al-ʿArabī, 2001.

al-Ziriklī, Khayr al-Dīn. *al-Aʿlām*. 8 vols. Beirut: Dar al-ʿIlm li-l-Malāyīn, 2002.

CHAPTER 10

Studying Hadith Commentaries in the Digital Age

*Maroussia Bednarkiewicz, Aslisho Qurboniev
and Gowaart Van Den Bossche**

'[Hadith] is the most eminent of sciences' (*min mukhtārāt al-ʿulūm ʿaynhā*), writes Badr al-Dīn al-ʿAynī (d. 855/1451) in the introduction to *ʿUmdat al-qārī*, his voluminous commentary on al-Bukhārī's (d. 256/870) *Ṣaḥīḥ*. His remark is part of a long rhetorical acclamation of prophetic traditions; it expresses the idea that hadith and its auxiliary disciplines occupied a central position in the Islamic oral and written tradition. This centrality has continued in the digital age, and various apps, forums and video channels devoted to the teaching and commentary of hadith have appeared. Many classical hadith texts are now also available in digital editions in online libraries such as Shamela or ShiaOnlineLibrary (al-Maktaba al-Shīʿiyya). The digitised texts from these collections can be used for traditional close reading but also for computational analysis. The advent of such online libraries facilitates the navigation and extraction of text to build corpora tailored to new research questions, thus radically changing historians' workflow. Yet there are still significant obstacles to the digital availability of hadith literature and these obstacles inhibit the building of large corpora for computational analysis.

In this essay we reflect on the challenges involved in corpus building for hadith studies as well as the advances already made. We specifically focus on the Open Islamicate Texts Initiative (OpenITI), a large, academically curated corpus of Arabic texts sourced from various online libraries. This corpus is continuously vetted and expanded by scholarly contributions.

* The authors have received funding from the European Research Council (ERC) under the European Union's Horizon 2020 research and innovation programme (grant agreement no. 772989) and the Deutsche Forschungsgemeinschaft under Germany's Excellence Strategy (EXC number 2064/1 – Project number 390727645). They would like to thank members of the KITAB team, Stefanie Brinkmann, Ramon Harvey and the anonymous reviewers for their insightful comments on earlier iterations of this essay.

We discuss its advantages for computational macro-analysis and for more traditional close reading, and survey recent research in digital hadith studies. As an example of the possibilities of computational macro-analysis, we focus on assessing the output of the software 'passim', which has identified millions of instances of text reuse – places where texts share materials with one another – across the OpenITI corpus by employing a set of algorithms to detect and align similar passages of text.[1] These instances of reuse may be the result of citation, plagiarism, use of common sources and many other forms of intertextuality. Text reuse is used in this chapter as a broad analytical category that may account for all these forms. In the final part of this essay we present examples of this text reuse data, specifically as it applies to the study of hadith commentaries.

Corpus Building

Despite the advantages of working with digital libraries (accessibility, full-text search, the possibility of computational analysis), few researchers would give online collections serious credit as research tools in their own right. After locating the information in a digitised text, they often crosscheck with the published physical editions on which it is based, and only cite the latter in their critical apparatus. In short, researchers' workflows have arguably changed in the digital age, but their general attitude toward digital corpora often remains one of adamant mistrust, mitigated by using long established historical-critical methods. To be sure, this is often a healthy attitude considering the number of mistakes in digital texts, the absence of critical apparatus and the inconsistent editorial methods employed in generating them, but these deficiencies do not discredit the efforts of those developing digital corpora and methods. Rather, the aim should be to strive for a representative premodern corpus that can be reliable and used for many different ends, both traditional and computational, complementary to manuscripts and printed editions.

There is no single definition of a corpus, as research questions call for various types of corpora, and the norms that exist in fields differ. While small corpora essentially support more traditional micro-analytical approaches, the progress in computational text analysis increasingly encourages scholars to take into consideration macro-analytical research questions on larger datasets.[2] As we see below, the OpenITI corpus belongs to the generation of large digital corpora inspired by historical linguistics that aims to represent historical textual culture.

---

1 See the discussion below and the description online at <https://github.com/dasmiq/passim> (accessed October 2022). For an application of these algorithms to another textual corpus, see Cordell and Smith, *Viral Texts*.
2 Jockers, *Macroanalysis*, 17–18.

Large digital corpora, like OpenITI, can be used for various kinds of computational analyses. Automated text analysis often renders traditional analyses more efficient and enables users to ask new research questions that were impossible to imagine before we had the computational power to process large datasets. Indeed, individual researchers, no matter how well read they are, can only approach the texts in a pixel-like way. They search *pars pro toto*, for the whole is usually far too large to be studied in any detail by a single scholar. By contrast, algorithms perform best with large text collections. In this regard, hadith commentaries are an ideal corpus for computational approaches, as they are for historians. As Joel Blecher has shown in his study of commentaries of *Ṣaḥīḥ al-Bukhārī* through the ages, these texts represent a great but understudied source of information for historians interested in Muslim societies, religious practices, law, cultures and traditions.[3] Furthermore, they are a living practice; Muslims have continuously transmitted, compiled and commented on hadith.[4] Despite the preponderance of hadith literature in most corpora of digitised Arabic texts, studies of hadith with digital tools remain scarce or largely limited to the canonical collections, especially the *Ṣaḥīḥayn* of al-Bukhārī (d. 256/870) and Muslim (d. 261/875).

There are three main reasons for the slow emergence of comprehensive digital analysis of hadith. First, it is difficult to precisely define and create a comprehensive corpus. In fact, building a digital corpus for macro-analysis poses several challenges, so many researchers turn to already digitised corpora that were usually limited to a few (canonical) hadith collections. Furthermore, digital texts tend to be riddled with mistakes and inconsistencies. The more they are edited, the more errors they accrue; these include typos, omissions, repeated information and so on.[5] Editorial tendencies to 'correct' them also sometimes take the text further away from the forms in which they have been transmitted historically. The fact that a digital version usually omits the critical apparatus of editions makes evaluating manuscript transmission and variance even more challenging. A corpus of texts reflecting manuscript attestation and variation, while technically possible, remains a desideratum in the field.[6]

---

3   Blecher, *Said the Prophet of God*.

4   On the continuous tradition of Qur'an interpretation, see Sinai, 'Die klassische islamische Koranexegese'. For a snapshot of the social practice of hadith transmission in late Mamlūk Damascus, see Hirschler, *A Monument to Medieval Syrian Book Culture*, and more generally, Davidson, *Carrying on the Tradition*.

5   A recent study on the computational analysis of a hadith corpus discusses part of the painstaking correction work necessary: Syed et al., 'Verifying Source Citations'.

6   The exception to this is two projects showcasing the manuscript transmission history of the Qur'an: www.corpuscoranicum.de and www.qurangateway.org (accessed 14 January 2021). While these two projects display exemplary results, their source codes are not public, so they fall short in terms of reproducibility.

Second, genre classifications in digital collections are rarely consistent. To create a corpus with hadith commentaries, one would first need to define what is meant by hadith commentaries. As the introduction to this volume makes abundantly clear, this is no trivial question, as there are many types of relationships between hadith texts that may or may not be defined explicitly as commentary. A text may also fit the definition of a commentary in a broader sense even without an explicit acknowledgement on the part of the author, or the use of the terms *sharḥ* (commentary), *ḥāshiya/taʿlīqa* (gloss) and so on in the title.[7] Most online libraries were built without taking these nuances into consideration and, as we see, addressing these genre classifications in academic corpora such as Open-ITI is also painstaking and iterative.[8]

Finally, the sources of the materials in online libraries can be difficult to obtain or may be wrongly or inconsistently attributed. Consider the following case that combines the challenges of corpus building and the digital reproduction of Arabic-Islamic books in a way that reflects the history of their transmission. The work of Ayatollah Ruhollah Khomeini (d. 1989) entitled *al-Taʿlīqa ʿalā al-fawāʾid al-raḍawiyya* is a gloss of Qāḍī Saʿīd al-Qummī's[9] (d. 1107/1695) commentary on reports of a short dialogue between the eighth (Twelver) Shīʿī imam ʿAlī b. Mūsā al-Riḍā (d. 203/818) and a Jewish Exilarch (Raʾs al-Jālūt).[10] The debates with the participation of the Shīʿī imam were first reported by the fourth-/tenth-century (Twelver) Shīʿī traditionist Ibn Bābawayh (known as al-Shaykh al-Ṣadūq, d. 381/991) in his *Kitāb al-Tawḥīd* and *ʿUyūn akhbār al-Riḍā*.[11] The commentary tradition is, however, centred on this particular dialogue known as 'ḥadīth Raʾs al-Jālūt', which begins with al-Qummī. Unlike Ibn Bābawayh's version, al-Qummī's popular version omits the chain of

---

7 Cornelis van Lit defines commentary in terms of 'structural textual correspondence' between hypotext and hypertext. Thus, a broad range of texts, including but not limited to *sharḥ*, *ḥāshiya/taʿlīqa* and so on, are included in the 'commentary tradition' that can be referred to, independently, as commentary. Van Lit, 'Commentary and Commentary Tradition'.

8 See also Lorenz Nigst's blog 'Preserving Pre-Modern Terminologies'.

9 Muḥammad Saʿīd b. Muḥammad Mufīd, known as Qāḍī Saʿīd al-Qummī and known as al-Ḥakīm al-Ṣaghīr (The lesser sage), was a Ṣafavid-era polymath like his famous teacher, Mullā Muḥsin al-Fayḍ al-Kāshānī (d. c. 1091/1680). Al-Qummī's magnum opus, *Sharḥ Tawḥīd al-Ṣadūq*, is a three-volume commentary on Ibn Bābawayh's hadith collection (entitled the *Kitāb al-Tawḥīd*) and has recently been added to the OpenITI corpus.

10 The famous *majālis* of ʿAlī b. Mūsā al-Riḍā, who was appointed heir apparent by the ʿAbbāsid caliph al-Maʾmūn (d. 218/833) before his premature death, have been analysed by several scholars. See Wasserstrom, *Between Muslim and Jew*; Wasserstein, 'The "Majlis of al-Riḍā"'; Cooperson, *Classical Arabic Biography*, 70–106; see also Sahner, 'A Zoroastrian Dispute in the Caliph's Court', 69–70.

11 Al-Qummī, *Kitāb al-Tawḥīd*, 1:139–182.

transmitters.[12] Despite this, the enigmatic nature of the questions raised by the Jewish scholar and the Imam's answers left them open to interpretation and thus have continuously provided occasions for elucidation and commentary by later scholars.[13]

In the ShiaOnlineLibrary the digital edition of the book is solely attributed to the first commentator, Qāḍī Saʿīd al-Qummī. While not incorrect *per se*, doing so fails to highlight Khomeini's important intervention in clarifying, expanding and challenging al-Qummī's interpretation of the hadith. It also presents an ahistorical picture of a commentary tradition that in fact continues to the present day.

When preparing digital texts, these kinds of complex relationships should be recorded in metadata, so that key information about the transmission of a text, as well as its authorship, provenance and relationship to other texts in a corpus can be easily and reliably accessed. Having this information available facilitates further research, including the distant reading (that is, computational reading and analysis of textual metadata, as opposed to traditional close reading)[14] and analysis of the corpus and the study of intertextual networks. Thus, upon including these texts in the OpenITI corpus, the KITAB team addressed this metadata issue. In OpenITI, authorship is principally attributed to the latest commentator (in this case Khomeini), whereas various relationships to other books are recorded in the metadata.[15] For example, a similar situation exists for *Nahj al-balāgha*, which some online libraries attribute to ʿAlī b. Abī Ṭālib (d. 40/661), because it is a compilation of his speeches, letters and sayings, though certainly the compilation itself was not made by him. In fact, the compilation was only undertaken in the late fourth/tenth to the early fifth/eleventh century by al-Sharīf al-Rāḍī (d. 406/1015), or, less likely, by his brother al-Sharīf al-Murtaḍā (d. 436/1044).[16] These cases illustrate some challenges

12 See Qāḍī Saʿīd al-Qummī's introduction to his commentary, where he notes the popularity of the hadith among his Shīʿī colleagues. Khomeini, *al-Taʿlīqa*, 40.

13 There are fifteen known commentaries on this hadith preserved in at least 132 manuscripts, mostly in Iranian libraries. *Al-Fawāʾid al-raḍawiyya* is part of al-Qummī's incomplete *Arbaʿīniyyāt*, and was published alongside Khomeini's *taʿlīqa* (gloss). See KITAB's blogpost for a detailed account: Qurboniev, 'Between Manuscripts and Digital Texts'; see also Ḥusaynī, 'Sharḥ-i Ḥadīth-i Raʾs al-Jālūt', 234–236.

14 See Moretti, *Distant Reading*.

15 In practice, these issues need to be addressed on a case-by-case basis. For instance, another commentary discussed in this chapter, al-Māzandarānī's *Sharḥ Uṣūl al-Kāfī* (on which, see below) was published with glosses by Abū al-Ḥasan al-Shaʿrānī, but because these *taʿlīqāt* are not so significant that they alter the general composition of the text, it makes sense to list the first commentator as the main author in the metadata. Moreover, in the printed edition, the glosses are appended as footnotes, which are normally removed (alongside editorial sections and the critical apparatus) when a text is added to the corpus.

16 Hassan, 'A Critical Study of Nahj al-Balāgha', 20–24.

of corpus building and the digital reproduction and referencing of Islamic texts in a way that reflects the history of their reception and transmission. Yet these cases also highlight the nature of hadith commentary as a living and discursive Islamic tradition.

Methods and Reproducibility

Once a digital corpus is established, the challenge lies in choosing appropriate analytic methods. A crucial consideration in this regard is that digital corpora and computational tools will only attain their full potential in the service of the scholarly community if the results can be reproduced and the tools can be repurposed for other datasets or research questions.[17] These considerations can be addressed by furnishing comprehensive metadata for the texts and making the tools available with well-documented, open-source codes. More importantly, reproducible results are required for intersubjective verifiability (that is, what cannot be reproduced, cannot be verified and remains subjective; just like any article ought to have an accurate bibliography, computational analyses must be presented with detailed documentation to allow other scholars to confirm or refute the results).[18] As the number of projects in Islamic studies increases, and these projects invest resources in the development of technologies to perform computational analysis on textual materials, the reproducibility of results becomes a primary concern and is now regularly required by funding institutions.

The issue with the absence of reproducible results can be illustrated with reference to an issue faced by many scholars working with hadith literature, namely, *isnād* recognition. While humans can easily distinguish a chain of transmitters, for computers, an *isnād* is a string of characters like any other. Scholars who want to automate the traditional *isnād* analysis on a given hadith corpus must find a way for computers to distinguish between *isnād* and non-*isnād* textual data. Over the past ten years or so, several computer scientists have developed methods to address this issue. However, generally, their metrics, tools or both, were not made available, so their methods do not allow for cross-checking and have not been used outside a single paper.[19]

---

17 Alger, *Defense of the Scientific Hypothesis.*

18 See the discussion of 'intersubjectivity' in Alger, *Defense of the Scientific Hypothesis*, 9 and 41.

19 Moath Najeeb has explored two methods with Muslim's *Ṣaḥīḥ*: In 2016 he used a particular statistical model (the so-called Hidden Markov Model) (see Najeeb, 'Processing of "Hadith Isnad"') and in 2020, he used an algorithm borrowed from genetic studies (see Najeeb, 'A Novel Hadith Processing Approach' and 'XML Database'). In 2018 and 2019, Maraoui Haddar and Romary developed a hadith schema for TEI and an undescribed (hence unreproducible) system to segment hadith automatically. See Maraoui et al., 'Encoding Prototype'; and Maraoui et al., 'Segmentation Tool for Hadith Corpus'.

This deficit in reproducibility has forced scholars who want to automatically isolate *isnād*s to constantly start over. While the primary concern for many of these studies has ultimately been the authentication of 'sound' hadith or *isnād*s,[20] automatically recognising *isnād*s is also necessary when studying patterns of reuse, as is done in the KITAB project with the passim software (see below). Chains of transmitters as text reuse should be distinguished from other instances of text reuse that indicate direct and indirect quotations, paraphrases, etc. In order to qualitatively highlight these instances in the OpenITI corpus, the passim software must be able to distinguish the chains of transmitters from other forms of text reuse.

To tackle these issues, members of the OpenITI-related KITAB project have been working on a new approach: Ryan Muther has trained a machine learning model on a manually annotated corpus extracted from OpenITI that is much larger than the *Ṣaḥīḥayn* or even hadith collections in general.[21] The primary goal of this project was to automatically mark the *isnād*s in texts, so they can either be excluded from a given text, or can be compiled in a separate corpus. The task is complex, however, as *isnād*s are much more diverse than initially thought, and the algorithm designed by Muther et al. only succeeded in identifying the beginning of the *isnād*. In the latest study on the topic, Alkaoud and Syed used different algorithms and could identify all *isnād*s in a small corpus. These are significant steps forward toward the automation of *isnād* recognition.[22] The close collaboration between scholars in Islamic studies and computer scientists exemplified in the studies of Muther and Alkaoud and Syed remains exceptional in the field, but is highly desirable for future projects.

The OpenITI Corpus

OpenITI is a corpus of digital texts from the premodern Islamic world created as a joint venture by research teams at various institutions. It aims to become as comprehensive as possible and in doing so provide the basic infrastructure for digital reading and information retrieval, and provide more complex forms of computational analysis, both with the entire corpus and with smaller sub-corpora based on period, genre or

20 Examples of models developed to authenticate hadith can be found in Harrag et al., 'Vector Space Model'.

21 Muther and Smith, 'Tracing Traditions'. The model is open source and was developed in public to guarantee reproducibility; the training data annotated by members of the KITAB team is stored in a GitHub repository, <https://github.com/kitab-project-org/training-data> (accessed October 2022).

22 Alkaoud and Syed, 'Learning to Identify Narrators', 335–342. This study builds on previous work by the team: Syed et al., 'Verifying Source Citations' and Alkaoud and Syed, 'On the Importance of Tokenization'.

region.[23] While the aim of the project is to eventually develop corpora for several relevant languages – Ottoman Turkish, Chaghatay, Urdu and so on – at the moment only Arabic and to a much lesser degree Persian are represented. The Arabic content is curated and managed by members of the KITAB Project.[24] They curate texts included in other online corpora and evaluate their quality by cross-checking the digital versions with the physical editions on which they are based, identifying issues in the digital texts; these issues range from missing parts to typos and residual mark-ups or footnotes. This is done at the same time as structural annotation of the texts is undertaken to make them more navigable and machine readable.[25] Further quality control and correction takes place in a second stage when texts are vetted by other annotators.

The corpus is hosted on GitHub and snapshots are periodically made available in ready-to-use form through Zenodo with a DOI to make them citable.[26] A digital reading environment is also being developed to enable researchers to visually query parts of the corpus. As of February 2020, the OpenITI corpus consisted of 4,129 unique texts – that is, not counting different versions of the same text. Most of the texts were sourced from three major digital libraries: Shamela, al-Jāmiʿ al-Kabīr and ShiaOnlineLibrary. Various new texts from these digital libraries and from other online libraries are gradually being added. Additionally, texts that constitute gaps in the corpus are being digitised and researchers are invited to submit texts they have typed or digitised through OCR.[27]

23 Romanov et al., 'Open Islamicate Texts Initiative'. An example of computational analysis of a small corpus extracted from OpenITI can be found in the blogpost of Syed, 'An Experiment'. Two further examples of smaller corpora based, at least in part, on OpenITI texts are first, a corpus of late mediaeval Syro-Egyptian historiographic texts compiled for the 'Mamlukisation of the Mamluk Sultanate II' project directed by Jo Van Steenbergen, and second, a corpus of texts from four broad genres ('jurisprudence, inter-faith literature, early modern and modern journalism, and Arabic poetry') for the 'Senses of Islam' project directed by Christian Lange.

24 KITAB is an acronym for 'Knowledge, Information Technology and the Arabic Book'. The project is funded by the European Research Council and led by Sarah Savant. In the project, the OpenITI corpus is used to study Arabic book history through large-scale text reuse data. The Persian side of OpenITI is managed by Matthew Miller and focuses on developing Optical Character Recognition (OCR) technology for premodern Persian and Arabic, and on developing the 'Persian Digital Library', which is currently heavily dominated by poetry. See <https://persdigumd.github.io/PDL/corpus-stats.html> (accessed October 2022).

25 For the description of the basic markup language used for the annotation see Romanov, 'OpenITI mARkdown', <https://maximromanov.github.io/mARkdown/> (accessed October 2022).

26 The most recent snapshot of the corpus is Nigst et al., *OpenITI*.

27 Currently, there is no formal procedure to contribute new texts; interested researchers contact team members. For a guide to the IDs for collections currently in OpenITI as well as general documentation on the corpus, see <https://openiti.github.io/documentation> (accessed October 2022).

Figure 10.1 Hadith classification in the OpenITI corpus, OpenITI: 4,129 unique texts (2,379 non-hadith texts; Digital libraries: 1,649 texts labelled as 'hadith' in digital libraries) (360 in digital libraries and GAL). GAL: 461 texts labelled 'hadith' in GAL (101 texts *not* labelled hadith in digital libraries).

Adding detailed metadata for texts in the corpus is an important goal. This includes information about authors, books, book relationships and also genre classifications. As noted above, scholars often disagree on genre classifications, and finding a system that works across the corpus, taking account of premodern classifications, is a work in progress. The tagging system adopted for genre classification in OpenITI is a good example of a combination of automated and manual approaches. In the case of hadith literature (see Figure 10.1), OpenITI currently contains two types of texts tagged as 'hadith': the texts that were labelled hadith in the digital libraries from which they were extracted (tag: HADITH) and the titles that Carl Brockelmann classified as hadith in his *Geschichte der arabischen Literatur* (tag: GAL@hadith).[28] The existence of two tags ('HADITH' and 'GAL@ hadith') allows scholars to choose their preferred classification or to combine the two, as GAL identified 101 hadith titles that are not recognised as such in the digital libraries. Scholars can even add their own classification in order to match the needs of their research, for instance, hadith texts from Iraqi scholars or a combination of hadith and philosophical texts. This system offers great flexibility for a variety of types of research and can be continually improved.

The representativeness of the hadith corpus remains an issue, although in general it is more balanced and undergoes higher quality control than comparably large digital collections of other Arabic texts. For hadith particularly, major Sunnī collections and commentaries are represented, and many others have been prepared to be added to the corpus. By contrast, while there are numerous commentaries on canonical Shīʿī hadith collections, only a few have been added to OpenITI so far. Even the especially rich tradition related to *Nahj al-balāgha* is only represented by the original compilation by al-Sharīf al-Rāḍī, Ibn Abī al-Ḥadīd's important *Sharḥ* and Muḥammad ʿAbduh's twentieth-century commentary, though hundreds

28 The collation of data from *GAL* with the OpenITI corpus was done by Walid A. Akef.

of commentaries on this text exist.[29] Similarly, more than twenty *sharḥs* and thirty *ḥāshiyas* have been written on al-Kulaynī's *al-Kāfī*,[30] but only four Ṣafavid-era commentaries have been added to the corpus so far, while the equally rich commentary tradition on other collections is still underrepresented.[31] Moreover, there are numerous addenda, supplements, indices and translations of Shīʿī hadith works, most notably into Persian, which must also be considered within the perimeters of hadith commentary as a literary and living tradition. Significant gaps such as these are being identified and addressed.

Examples of Text Reuse in Hadith Commentaries from OpenITI

Text reuse has been an important focus of research into historical texts for centuries. Indeed, it is an essential element of the historical and philological method, and many classical studies of Islamic history have been built around painstaking comparisons of reports to establish stemmas of filiation. This kind of research typically requires scholars to read widely and very closely to discern patterns of intertextuality, allusion, copying, plagiarism and so on. The data provided by passim on the OpenITI corpus do not aim to replace this part of the research process, but provide additional information and perspectives to aid the enquiry into textual relationships, while casting a much wider net to consider more candidates for text reuse or closer analysis.[32]

Several research questions in the study of hadith commentaries can be explored with a text reuse approach. For example, to what extent do commentators quote hadith collections and how do they define what to quote and what not to quote? Where do commentaries adhere to the textual structure of hadith collections and where do they diverge? Which texts are quoted or reused most in hadith commentaries and which other texts quote

---

29 For issues, reuse data and visualisations of this commentarial tradition, see Van Den Bossche, 'On Commentaries'. The complicated situation of *Nahj al-balāgha* outlined in this blog post has now been solved by deleting the footnotes of *Nahj al-balāgha* (this version is now filed as the work of al-Sharīf al-Rāḍī), and a separate version that includes the footnotes has been created and is now filed as the work of Muḥammad ʿAbduh.

30 See Muḥammad Ḥusayn al-Dirāyatī's editorial introduction to al-Nāʾilī, *al-Ḥāshiya*, 5. Aghā Buzurg al-Ṭihrānī lists 27 commentaries and 10 *ḥāshiyas* in his bibliography of Shīʿī works; al-Ṭihrānī, *al-Dharīʿa*, 13:95–99.

31 The commentaries currently available in the corpus are al-ʿĀmilī, *al-Ḥāshiya*; Mīr Dāmād, *al-Rawashiḥ al-samāwiyya*; al-Māzandarānī, *Sharḥ Uṣūl al-Kāfī*; al-Nāʾilī, *al-Ḥāshiya*.

32 For some observations on how passim works, as well as some pitfalls, see Barber, 'Adventures in Alignments'.

or reuse hadith commentaries the most? How closely related are two different commentaries on the same text? How widely attested are particular hadiths across the corpus? While scholars researching a project using physical books must select one textual type or characteristic or must restrict themselves to one period for a project to be manageable, the text reuse algorithm works better when given a large amount of data. Such passim data is extremely helpful in examining the broader picture, confirming known relationships and highlighting unexpected discrepancies and similarities between the most famous commentaries as well as lesser-known ones.

It will be no surprise that of the texts showing the most reuse in the OpenITI corpus the majority are hadith works (both collections and commentaries) or works containing a great number of hadiths.[33] The expansive commentary tradition is partially responsible for these high numbers but more generally, the prevalence of hadith in the Arabic written tradition is such that overlapping traditions are found in many texts. Furthermore, as noted, because of the prevalence of similar strings of names (especially in chains of transmitters) across the corpus, some of the reuse detected by passim is not meaningful and thus requires closer analysis. We must also keep in mind the caveats noted above concerning representativeness and the fact that such statistics are snapshots of a corpus in constant evolution. Nevertheless, the kind of raw statistics on text reuse provided now already help situate a given work in the tradition as a whole.

One of the texts with the highest level of reuse in the OpenITI corpus is Badr al-Dīn al-ʿAynī's (d. 855/1451) ʿUmdat al-qārī, with 224,735 instances recorded for it by passim, across 2,210 individual books. While extremely valuable insights on its make-up and its relationship to other commentaries of the period, notably Ibn Ḥajar al-ʿAsqalānī's (d. 852/1449) *Fatḥ al-Bārī*, have been formulated recently by Joel Blecher, the sheer length of the work and of works with which it shares materials, largely precludes an in-depth study. One way to study its relationship to the wider corpus can be seen in Figure 10.2, which visualises the instances of reuse in al-ʿAynī across time.

The graph in Figure 10.2 shows the strong continuity of the hadith commentary tradition, and particularly of al-Bukhārī's *Ṣaḥīḥ*, across time. The highest instances of text reuse of al-ʿAynī's ʿUmdat al-qārī are apparent in

---

33 For the following observations, we use the statistics generated based on the run of passim in February 2020. Of the top six reusers (based on number of instances of reuse with texts across the corpus) three are directly related to hadith (two collections and one commentary): Ibn Ḥanbal's *Musnad*, ʿAlā al-Dīn al-Hindī's *Kanz al-ʿummāl*, and al-ʿAynī's ʿUmdat al-qārī. The three remaining works in the list are two historical works and one *tafsīr*, all heavily reliant on hadith: Ibn ʿAsākir's *Tārīkh madīnat Dimashq* (the number one reuser), Ibn Kathīr's *al-Bidāya wa-l-nihāya*, and Shams al-Dīn al-Qurṭubī's (d. 671/1273) *al-Jāmiʿ li-aḥkām al-Qurʾān*.

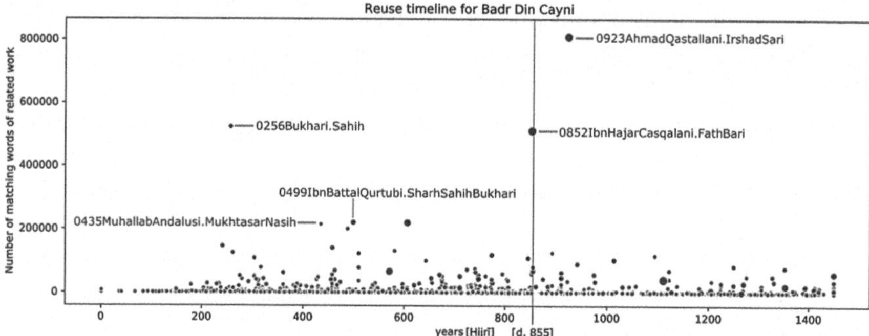

Figure 10.2   Reuse timeline for Badr al-Dīn al-'Ayni's *'Umdat al-qārī*. The abscissa sorts books by the death date of their author in the Hijrī calendar. The ordinate shows the number of word matches – in other words, instances of text reuse – with *'Umdat al-qārī*. The dot's area is proportional to the length of the text (in words).

Aḥmad al-Qasṭallānī's (d. 923/1517) *Irshād al-sārī* (914,038 word matches), followed by al-Bukhārī's *Ṣaḥīḥ* (490,455 word matches) and Ibn Ḥajar's *Fatḥ al-Bārī* (498,267). We then find two commentaries from Andalusian scholars: the *Sharḥ Ṣaḥīḥ al-Bukhārī* (191,179 word matches) by Ibn Baṭṭāl al-Qurṭubī (d. 449/1057) and *al-Mukhtaṣar al-naṣīḥ* (159,615 word matches) by al-Muhallab b. Abī Ṣufra (d. c. 435/1044). With the insights provided by Joel Blecher's research in mind, these names are not surprising, as they represent some of the best received commentaries on al-Bukhārī across the ages. However, the statistics do call attention to al-Qasṭallānī's *Irshād al-sārī* as a major commentary that should be considered. Indeed, the reuse between al-'Aynī and al-Qasṭallānī greatly exceeds the total word count of al-Bukhārī's *Ṣaḥīḥ* (593,471), which suggests that al-Qasṭallānī did not just quote the same traditions from al-Bukhārī as al-'Aynī did, but must have reused al-'Aynī's work and his sources extensively. This relationship is not explicitly stated by al-Qasṭallānī, who in his introduction to *Irshād al-sārī* diligently notes the various commentaries on al-Bukhārī that preceded his own, but does not name *'Umdat al-qārī* as more important than other commentaries. He assesses the accusations that al-'Aynī plagiarised Ibn Ḥajar, but avoids intervening forcefully in the discussion. Instead, he notes that al-'Aynī also added many beneficial insights on the rhetorical aspects of the traditions.[34] Throughout the remainder of the text he reproduces many of those insights, citing both al-'Aynī and Ibn Ḥajar hundreds of times. The

34 Al-Qasṭallānī, *Irshād al-sārī*, 1:59–60. The digital edition in OpenITI is based on the ten-volume 1905 Būlāq printing of the text, edited by Ibrāhīm 'Abd al-Ghaffār al-Dusūqī. The first printing of the text at the same press was in 1850.

statistics and his position on this controversy indicate that al-Qaṣṭallānī's work deserves a more extensive study in the context of the continued commentary tradition on al-Bukhārī in the late Mamlūk period, and given the reception and evaluation of the great works of generations immediately preceding and following al-Qaṣṭallānī.[35]

The data for al-ʿAynī's and al-Qaṣṭallānī's commentaries are insightful because the relevant corpus, while certainly not complete, is large enough to be meaningful and contains commentaries that have generally been less studied.[36] If we look at the Shīʿī tradition, however, the limitations of this approach become clear. While OpenITI is still useful in identifying a high number of reuse instances for texts present in OpenITI, as noted above, most important Shīʿī commentaries have not yet been included in the corpus, so the data has obvious gaps and a reuse timeline like that in Figure 10.2 would be notably less representative. However, as long as at least two relevant texts are included in the corpus, meaningful observations about reuse can be made. The passim output in the form of paired alignments of shared passages between texts (that is, passages identified in any given two texts that show enough overlap of words to be considered text reuse) can be used to explore intertextuality in any given corpus, to compare variant transmissions of a text and to determine direct and indirect relationships between books. For commentaries in particular, this type of visualisation highlights the 'structural textual correspondence' that Eric van Lit uses to define a commentary. Various blog posts by KITAB team members are devoted to case studies using this type of visualisation that are of broad interest to the study of hadith commentaries. These include Sarah Savant's study of the relationship of three known transmissions of Mālik's *Muwaṭṭaʾ*,[37] Aslisho Qurboniev's study of the relationship between a number of Shīʿī hadith collections,[38] and Gowaart Van Den Bossche's already noted exploration of *Nahj al-balāgha* and its *Sharḥ* by Ibn Abī al-Ḥadīd.

As a further example, we consider the case of *Sharḥ Uṣūl al-Kāfī* by Muḥammad Ṣāliḥ al-Māzandarānī (d. 1081/1669), a commentary on

---

35 Despite remaining an important reference work in the centuries following its first dissemination, it appears that al-Qaṣṭallānī's commentary has not received much modern scholarly attention since Brockelmann's entry devoted to him in *EI²*. Brockelmann, 'al-Ḳasṭallānī'. For very brief comments about al-Qaṣṭallānī's commentary, see Tokatly, 'The *Aʿlām al-ḥadīth* of al-Khaṭṭābī', 54 n.4.

36 At least three important works were not included in the February 2020 passim run: al-Suyūṭī's *al-Tawshīḥ ʿala al-Jāmiʿ al-ṣaḥīḥ*, Shams al-Dīn al-Kirmānī's (d. 786/1384) *al-Kawākib al-darārī fī sharḥ Ṣaḥīḥ al-Bukhārī* and Ibn Mulaqqin's (d. 803/1401) *al-Tawḍīḥ li-sharḥ al-Jāmiʿ al-ṣaḥīḥ*. All of these have since been added to the corpus and will be included in future passim runs.

37 Savant, 'A Tale of Three "Versions"'.

38 Qurboniev, 'Algorithmic Reading of Shīʿī Hadith Collections'.

Muḥammad b. Yaʿqūb al-Kulaynī's (d. 329/941) *Uṣūl al-Kāfī*, visualised below in Figure 10.3. The graph shows a clear alignment of *Sharḥ Uṣūl al-Kāfī* with *Uṣūl al-Kāfī* and with its final part (commonly known as *Rawḍat al-Kāfī*).[39] The large gap in the alignments corresponds to the *Furūʿ al-Kāfī*, the middle section of *al-Kāfī*. It is said that al-Māzandarānī did not comment on this part, because someone had questioned his competence and reminded him that he was not a *mujtahid*. While there is some evidence that in fact, al-Māzandarānī did comment on the *furūʿ* part of the *Kāfī*, these alignments confirm the general supposition of the relationship between the two texts.[40] Thus, a distant reading of the text confirms that *Sharḥ Uṣūl al-Kāfī* is a systematic commentary on the *Uṣūl al-Kāfī* and on the *Rawḍat al-Kāfī*, but not on *Furūʿ al-Kāfī*.

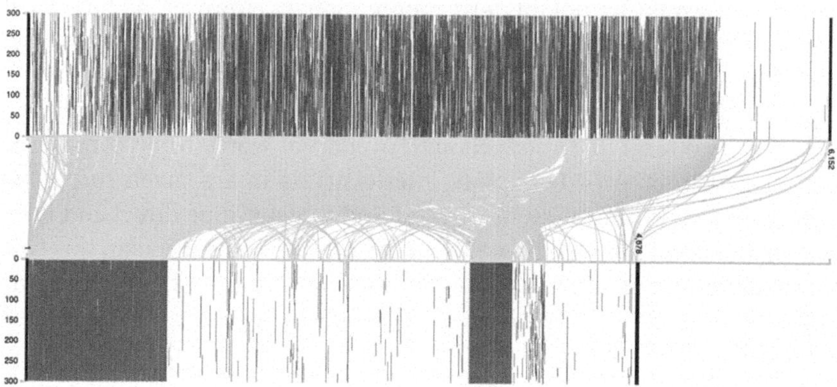

Figure 10.3   Pairwise alignment plot of text reuse between al-Māzandarānī's commentary, *Sharḥ ʿUṣūl al-Kāfī* (upper) and al-Kulaynī's *Uṣūl al-Kāfī* (lower). The dark grey lines mark the position of reuse passages (up to 300 words) within the individual texts and the light grey lines mark their links. This is a screenshot from the KITAB visualisation app developed by Sohail Merchant.

39   The actual final parts of both digital texts which show little alignment consist of endnotes. In principle these sections should be excluded, but in this case, they were preserved because neither text had yet been annotated.

40   The Indian Shīʿī scholar al-Sayyid Ḥāmid Ḥusayn al-Lakhnawī (d. 1306/1888) claimed to have had access to 'one of the volumes of [al-Māzandarānī's] commentary on the *furūʿ* part', and informed his Persian colleague Mīrzā Ḥusayn al-Nūrī al-Ṭabarsī (d. 1902) of this in his letters. This would contradict the above notion. See al-Shaʿrānī's introduction to al-Māzandarānī's *Sharḥ Uṣūl al-Kāfī*, 8. Aghā Buzurg al-Ṭihrānī, who consulted several manuscripts of the work in Iranian and Iraqi libraries, also mentions his partial commentary on the *furūʿ* part of *al-Kāfī*, but, as we see, the passim alignments do not indicate any significant textual overlap with this part. See al-Ṭihrānī, *al-Dharīʿa*, 13:97–98, 297.

The relationship thus represents an 'intentional' and 'structural textual correspondence', as per van Lit's definition cited above, but only with these parts of the compilation.

Experiments are also being undertaken to navigate the data in other ways, from large scale 'big data' to discern corpus-wide trends, to more fine-grained analysis of common passages in a small sub-corpus. A promising approach is what is referred to as studying the 'DNA' of one large book that reuses material from across a wide variety of sources. This DNA approach is especially useful for studying the patchwork of reused texts in such vast multi-volume works as al-Nuwayrī's (d. 733/1333) *Nihāyat al-arab* or al-Ṭabarī's (d. 310/923) *Tārīkh al-rusul wa-l-mulūk*. The next in line for such analysis should be hadith commentaries of especially wide-ranging contents, such as Ibn Ḥajar's *Fatḥ al-Bārī*, al-ʿAynī's *ʿUmdat al-qārī* or Ibn Abī al-Ḥadīd's *Sharḥ Nahj al-balāgha*.

Conclusion

Text reuse identification and the macro-analytical approach it facilitates have potential to advance the study of premodern Arabic literature generally and especially hadith commentaries. The case studies presented here can be easily multiplied, while a corpus-wide analysis can also be undertaken in much more detail. With the ever-increasing number of digital texts available online, the corpus on which computational analysis can be performed will become more representative. To accelerate this process, scholars can proactively identify the gaps and work together to digitise missing texts. Improving quality control and better reporting of metadata will also help this process. While combining several sources of metadata and automatically cross-validating them shows signs of success, much work remains to be done before a full-scale and reliable study of the OpenITI corpus can be undertaken. Ideally, scholars will contribute their knowledge to improve this metadata. Gaps notwithstanding, the case of the hadith commentary tradition aptly illustrates the ways computational methods and the macro-analytical approach can potentially advance modern hadith studies with relatively straightforward corpus building and statistical methods that can be easily understood and manipulated. Quality-controlled digital corpora, advanced statistical methods, high standards for reproducibility and user-friendly software can support and advance traditional research on premodern Arabic literature in the digital age. For hadith commentaries this means that scholars will be able to better map professional and textual networks relevant for the texts they study. It will also be possible to identify sources more easily across a wide-ranging corpus. Digital methods as such can help us to gain better insights into the evolution of hadith commentary, its working methods and, indeed, its practice in general.

Bibliography

Alger, B. *Defense of the Scientific Hypothesis: From Reproducibility Crisis to Big Data*. New York: Oxford University Press, 2020.

Alkaoud M. and M. Syed. 'On the Importance of Tokenization in Arabic Embedding Models.' In *Proceedings of the Fifth Arabic Natural Language Processing Workshop*, pp. 119–129. Barcelona: Association for Computational Linguistics, 2020.

Alkaoud, M. and M. Syed. 'Learning to Identify Narrators in Classical Arabic Texts.' *Procedia Computer Science, AI in Computational Linguistics* 189 (1 January 2021): 335–342.

al-ʿĀmilī, Badr al-Dīn b. Aḥmad al-Ḥusaynī. *al-Ḥāshiya ʿalā Usūl al-Kāfī*. Edited by ʿAlī al-Fāḍilī. Qum: Dār al-Ḥadīth li-l-Ṭibāʿa wa-l-Nashr, 1383/2004.

Barber, M. 'Adventures in Alignments.' Kitab Project (2020). <https://kitab-project.org/Adventures-in-Alignments-Training-an-Algorithm-to-Recognise-Text-Reuse/>, accessed 7 August 2020.

Blecher, J. *Said the Prophet of God: Hadith Commentary Across a Millenium*. Oakland: University of California Press, 2018.

Brockelmann, C. 'al-Ḳasṭallānī', in *EI²*, 4:736–737.

Cooperson, M. *Classical Arabic Biography: The Heirs of the Prophet in the Age of al-Maʾmūn*. Cambridge: Cambridge University Press, 2004.

Cordell R. and D. Smith. *Viral Texts: Mapping Networks of Reprinting in 19th-Century Newspapers and Magazines*. Viral Texts Project Blog (2017): http://viraltexts.org, accessed 12 August 2020.

Davidson, G. *Carrying on the Tradition: A Social and Intellectual History of Hadith Transmission across a Thousand Years*. Leiden: Brill, 2019.

Harrag, F., A. Hamdi-Cherif, and E. El-Qawasmeh. 'Vector Space Model for Arabic Information Retrieval – Application to 'Hadith' Indexing.' In *2008 First International Conference on the Applications of Digital Information and Web Technologies (ICADIWT)*, pp. 107–112, 2008. <https://doi.org/10.1109/ICADIWT.2008.4664328>.

Hassan, S. M. W. 'A Critical Study of Nahj al-balāgha.' PhD dissertation, University of Edinburgh, 1979.

Hirschler, K. *A Monument to Medieval Syrian Book Culture: The Library of Ibn ʿAbd al-Hādī*. Edinburgh: Edinburgh University Press, 2019.

Ḥusaynī, Sayyid Muḥammad Riḍā. 'Sharḥ-i Ḥadīth-i Raʾs al-Jālūt.' *Mīrāth-i Ḥadīth-i Shīʿa* 2 (1378/1999): 233–254.

Jockers, M. L. *Macroanalysis: Digital Methods and Literary History*. Baltimore: University of Illinois Press, 2013.

Khomeini, R. *al-Taʿlīqa ʿalā al-fawāʾid al-raḍawiyya*. Tehran: Muʾassassat Tanẓīm wa-Nashr Āthār al-Imām al-Khumaynī, 1378/1999.

Maraoui, H., K. Haddar, and L. Romary. 'Encoding Prototype of al-Hadith al-Shareef in TEI.' In A. Lachkar et al. (eds), *Arabic Language Processing: From Theory to Practice*, pp. 217–229. Cham, Switzerland: Springer, 2018.

Maraoui, H., K. Haddar, and L. Romary. 'Segmentation Tool for Hadith Corpus to Generate TEI Encoding.' In K. Shaalan et al. (eds), *Proceedings of the International*

Conference on Advanced Intelligent Systems and Informatics 2018, pp. 252–260. Cham, Switzerland: Springer International Publishing, 2019.

al-Māzandarānī, Muḥammad Ṣāliḥ. *Sharḥ Uṣūl al-Kāfī*. Edited by Mīrzā Abū al-Ḥasan al-Shaʿrānī. 12 vols. Beirut: Dār Iḥyāʾ al-Turāth al-ʿArabī li-l-Ṭibāʿa wa-l-Nashr wa-l-Tawzīʿ, 1421/2000.

Mīr Dāmād, Muḥammad Bāqir al-Ḥusaynī al-Astarabādī. *al-Rawashiḥ al-samāwiyya fī sharḥ aḥadīth al-imāmiyya*. Edited by Ghulāmḥusayn Qayṣariyyahā and Niʿmatullāh al-Jalīlī. Qum: Dār al-Ḥadīth li-l-Ṭibāʿa wa-l-Nashr, 1380 Sh/ 1422 [2001].

Moretti, F. *Distant Reading*. London: Verso, 2013.

Muther, R. and Smith, D. 'Tracing Traditions: Automatic Extraction of Isnads from Classical Arabic Texts.' In *Proceedings of the Fifth Arabic Natural Language Processing Workshop*, pp. 130–138. Barcelona: Association for Computational Linguistics, 2020.

al-Nāʾilī, Rafīʿ al-Dīn Muḥammad b. Haydar. *al-Ḥāshiya ʿalā Uṣūl al-Kāfī*. Edited by Muḥammad Ḥusayn al-Dirāyatī. Qum: Dār al-Ḥadīth li-l-Ṭibāʿa wa-l-Nashr, 1383 Sh/1424/[2003].

Najeeb, M. M. A. 'A Novel Hadith Processing Approach Based on Genetic Algorithms.' *IEEE Access* 8 (2020): 20233–20244.

Najeeb, M. M. A. 'Processing of "Hadith Isnad" Based on Hidden Markov Model.' *International Journal of Engineering and Technology* 6, no. 1 (2016): 50–55.

Najeeb, M. M. A. 'XML Database for Hadith and Narrators.' *American Journal of Applied Sciences* 13, no. 1 (2016): 55–63.

Nigst, L. 'Preserving Pre-Modern Terminologies.' Kitab Project (2020): https://kitab-project.org/Preserving-Pre-Modern-Terminologies/, accessed 6 August 2020.

Nigst, L., M. Romanov, S. Bowen Savant, M. Seydi, and P. Verkinderen. *OpenITI: A Machine-Readable Corpus of Islamicate Texts* (Version 2020.1.2) [Data set] (Zenodo, 2020), <http://doi.org/10.5281/zenodo.3891466>.

al-Qasṭallānī, Aḥmad b. Muḥammad b. Abī Bakr. *Irshād al-sārī ilā sharḥ Ṣaḥīḥ al-Bukhārī*. Edited by Muḥammad ʿAbd al-ʿAzīz al-Khālidī. 15 vols. Beirut: Dār al-Kutub al-ʿIlmiyya, 1416/1996.

al-Qummī, Muḥammad b. ʿAlī b. al-Ḥusayn b. Bābawayh. *Kitāb al-Tawḥīd*. Edited by Sayyid Hāshim al-Ḥusaynī al-Ṭihrānī. Qum: Manshūrāt Jamāʿat al-Mudarrisīn fī al-Ḥawzat al-ʿIlmiyya, n.d.

al-Qummī, Muḥammad b. ʿAlī b. al-Ḥusayn b. Bābawayh. *ʿUyūn akhbār al-Riḍā*. 2 vols. Qum: Intishārāt al-Sharīf al-Raḍī, 1378/1999.

al-Qummī, Muḥammad b. ʿAlī b. al-Ḥusayn b. Bābawayh. *al-Arbaʿīniyyāt li-kashfi anwār al-qudsiyyāt*. Edited by Najafqulī Ḥabībī. Tehran: Mīrās-i Maktūb, 1381/2002.

Qurboniev, A. 'Algorithmic Reading of Shīʿī Hadith Collections: Direct Borrowing and Common Sources.' Kitab Project (2020). https://kitab-project.org/Algorithmic-Reading-of-Shi%CA%BFi-Hadith-Collections-Direct-Borrowing-and-Common-Sources/, accessed 26 June 2020.

Qurboniev, A. 'Between Manuscripts and Digital Texts: Commentaries on Hadith Raʾs al-Jalut.' https://kitab-project.org/Between-Manuscripts-and-Digital-Texts-Commentaries-on-Hadith-Ra%CA%BEs-al-Jalut/, accessed 13 January 2021.

Romanov, Maxim. 'OpenITI mARkdown.' https://maximromanov.github.io/mARkdown/, accessed 13 January 2021.

Romanov, Maxim, Matthew Thomas Miller, Sarah Bowen Savant and Masoumeh Seydi. 'Open Islamicate Texts Initiative: A Machine-Readable Corpus of Texts Produced in the Premodern Islamicate World (Poster).' In *Digital Humanities 2019 Conference Papers: Book of Abstracts*. Utrecht: Utrecht University, 2019. https://dev.clariah.nl/files/dh2019/boa/0838.html, accessed 4 January 2022.

Sahner, C. C. 'A Zoroastrian Dispute in the Caliph's Court: The Gizistag Abāliš in its Early Islamic Context.' *Iranian Studies* 52, nos. 1–2 (2019): 61–83.

Savant, S. B. 'A Tale of Three "Versions": Measuring Variation in the Early Arabic Tradition.' Kitab Project (2017): https://kitab-project.org/A-Tale-of-3-Versions/, accessed 26 June 2020.

Sinai, N. 'Die klassische islamische Koranexegese: Eine Annäherung.' *Theologische Literaturzeitung* 136 (2011): 123–134.

Syed, M. 'An Experiment in Natural Language Processing, Machine Learning, and Islamic Law.' Islamic Law Blog (2020): https://islamiclaw.blog/2020/06/02/an-experiment-in-natural-language-processing-machine-learning-and-islamic-law-part-1/, accessed 31 July 2020.

Syed, M., Danny Halawi, Behnam Sadeghi and Nazmus Saquib. 'Verifying Source Citations in the Hadith Literature.' *Journal of Medieval Worlds* 1 no. 3 (2019): 5–20.

al-Ṭihrānī, Aghā Buzurg. *al-Dharīʿa ilā taṣānīf al-Shīʿa*. 25 vols. Beirut: Dār al-Aḍwāʾ, 1403/1983.

Tokatly, V. 'The *Aʿlām al-ḥadīth* of al-Khaṭṭābī: A Commentary on al-Bukhārī's *Ṣaḥīḥ* or a Polemical Treatise?' *Studia Islamica* 92 (2001): 53–91.

Van Den Bossche, G. 'On Commentaries, Digressions, Transtextualities, and Rabbit Holes.' Kitab Project (2019). <https://kitab-project.org/On-Commentaries,-Digressions,-Transtextualities,-and-Rabbit-Holes>, accessed 13 January 2021.

van Lit, L. W. C. 'Commentary and Commentary Tradition: The Basic Terms for Understanding Islamic Intellectual History.' *Mélanges de l'institut dominicain des études orientales* 32 (2017): 3–26.

Wasserstein, D. J. 'The "Majlis of al-Riḍā": A Religious Debate in the Court of the Caliph al-Maʾmūn as Represented in a Shīʿī Hagiographical Work about the Eighth Imām ʿAlī ibn Mūsā al-Riḍā.' In H. Lazarus-Yafeh et al. (eds), *The Majlis: Interreligious Encounters in Medieval Islam*, pp. 108–119. Wiesbaden: Harrassowitz Verlag, 1999.

Wasserstrom, S. M. *Between Muslim and Jew: The Problem of Symbiosis Under Early Islam*. Princeton, NJ: Princeton University Press, 1995.

Afterword
More Comments, Further Questions

Joel Blecher

The preceding chapters have presented rich illustrations of continuity and change in the hadith commentary tradition across sectarian divisions and genres, over a period dating back more than a millennium and spanning a region from the Mediterranean littoral to Persia and India. Before mapping out some future directions for the field, I first discuss one final example I encountered recently that aptly captures this interplay between continuity and change in the tradition of hadith commentary.

Tucked away in the Ambrosiana Library in Milan is, at first glance, an unremarkable manuscript of *Ṣaḥīḥ al-Bukhārī*. It was originally copied in 827/1424, during the very heyday of Mamlūk-era commentaries on hadith. And yet in the margins of this text we find notes from four separate hands. These reflect the practices of scholarly communities from the ninth/ fifteenth, tenth/sixteenth, twelfth/eighteenth, and nineteenth centuries (see Figure A.1).[1] These readers, though separated by long stretches of time, nevertheless returned to the margins of these delicate pages, to this very same paper, ink and glue to recite the text aloud, add their corrections and offer novel comments on the sayings of Muhammad. In places throughout this manuscript, these various marginal comments from different eras and places intertwine, with the notes of the twelfth-/eighteenth-century reader decorating either side of those of their tenth-/sixteenth-century predecessors.[2]

---

1 *Ṣaḥīḥ al-Bukhārī*, Bibliotheca Ambrosiana, MS D347 fol. 251. The first hand records a series of hadith sessions (*majālis*) that ended on a Thursday during the fall of 891/1486; the second hand, which preserved the most detailed marginal notes, concluded during Ramadan in 964/1556; a third annotated reading occurred during Ramadan in 1192/1778. The fourth hand is described below.

2 *Ṣaḥīḥ al-Bukhārī*, Bibliotheca Ambrosiana, MS D 347, fol. 54a.

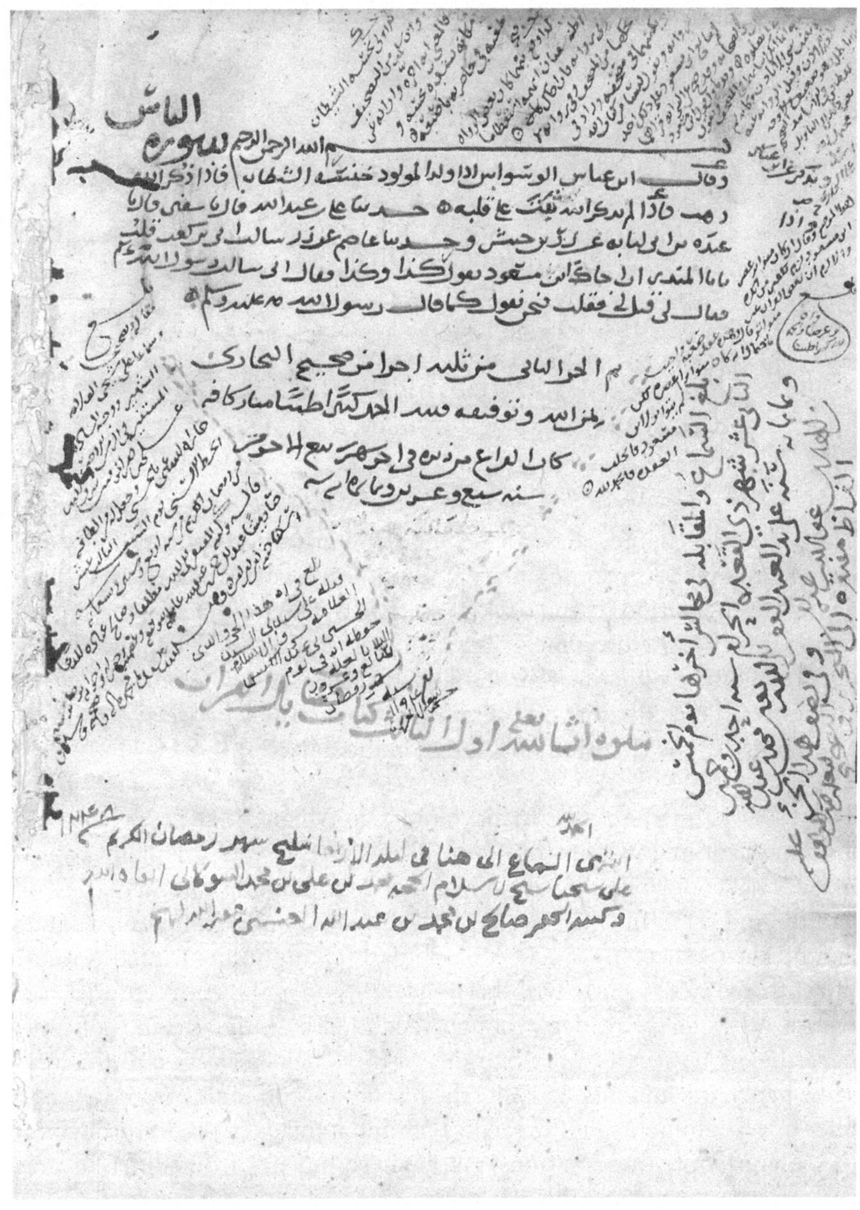

Figure A.1 *Ṣaḥīḥ al-Bukhārī*, Bibliotheca Ambrosiana, MS D 347, fol. 251b, dated 827/1424. The first annotation (right of centre) records a series of hadith sessions (*majālis*) that concluded Thursday, 12 Dhū al-Qaʿda 891/9 November 1486; the second annotation (left of centre) concluded during Ramadan 964/1556; a third annotation (centre) reading occurred during Ramadan 1192/1778; a fourth annotation (below centre) is that of al-Shawkānī's student, who dated the reading to Ramadan 1248/1833. Photo © Veneranda Biblioteca Ambrosiana.

The most modern hand to have read and annotated the text is the sparest, but also the most intriguing. This layer of commentary is attributed to a student who testified that, during Ramadan, he heard the text from the lips of the ageing iconoclastic hadith scholar from Yemen, Muḥammad al-Shawkānī, a year or so before al-Shawkānī's death in 1248/1833.[3] Al-Shawkānī was best known for his barbed commentaries and his call to revive bold methods of interpretation that mandated a direct interface with the hadith, a view that challenged the entrenched orthodoxies undergirding Islamic legal institutions in the nineteenth century.[4] And yet the periodic annotations preserved in this volume and attributed to al-Shawkānī are somewhat mundane. For instance, al-Shawkānī typically paused his student's recitation to ask that the student note that a variant of a hadith might be found in another section of *Ṣaḥīḥ al-Bukhārī*.

In the following Ramadan, of 1249/1834, just months from al-Shawkānī's impending death, the student returned to al-Shawkānī to hear the second volume of this same ninth-/fifteenth-century copy of *Ṣaḥīḥ al-Bukhārī* read aloud. Several times al-Shawkānī struggled to sign his name at the end of the manuscript – the ink failed him twice. On the third try, al-Shawkānī succeeded in stating clearly: 'In the name of God, the most compassionate, most merciful. This is correct. Signed by Muḥammad b. ʿAlī al-Shawkānī, God grant us forgiveness' (see Figure A.2).[5] As the final Ramadan of al-Shawkānī's life elapsed, this is the only comment he offered his student on this volume of the text.

Examining the manuscript on this scale, that is, at the instant when al-Shawkānī struggled to put ink to the manuscript's paper, and his growing reticence as he approached his own death – underscores that the simple embodied presence of the master and the physical labour he performed was susceptible to interruption, and these changes – however minute – set the very conditions for the practice of interpreting hadith.

And yet, at the broadest scale of time – the four hundred years of commentary this manuscript was subjected to – the list of political, social and economic upheavals that transformed the world was likewise dramatic: trans-oceanic mobility expanded, a global economic order dominated by Western European powers ascended, and print culture and literacy rose and spread, among many other phenomena. And yet readers of hadith who spanned these disparate temporal, cultural, political and economic orders returned to this text – indeed, to this very same manuscript – to employ

---

3 Al-Shawkānī's student's name was Ṣāliḥ b. Muḥammad b. ʿAbdallāh al-ʿAinsī (later Ṣanʿānī). Al-Shawkānī affirms in his biographical dictionary that the student heard *Ṣaḥīḥ al-Bukhārī* from him; al-Shawkānī *Badr al-ṭāliʿ*, 199.

4 Haykel, *Revival and Reform in Islam*, 234.

5 *Ṣaḥīḥ al-Bukhārī*, Bibliotheca Ambrosiana, MS D 348, fol. 222b.

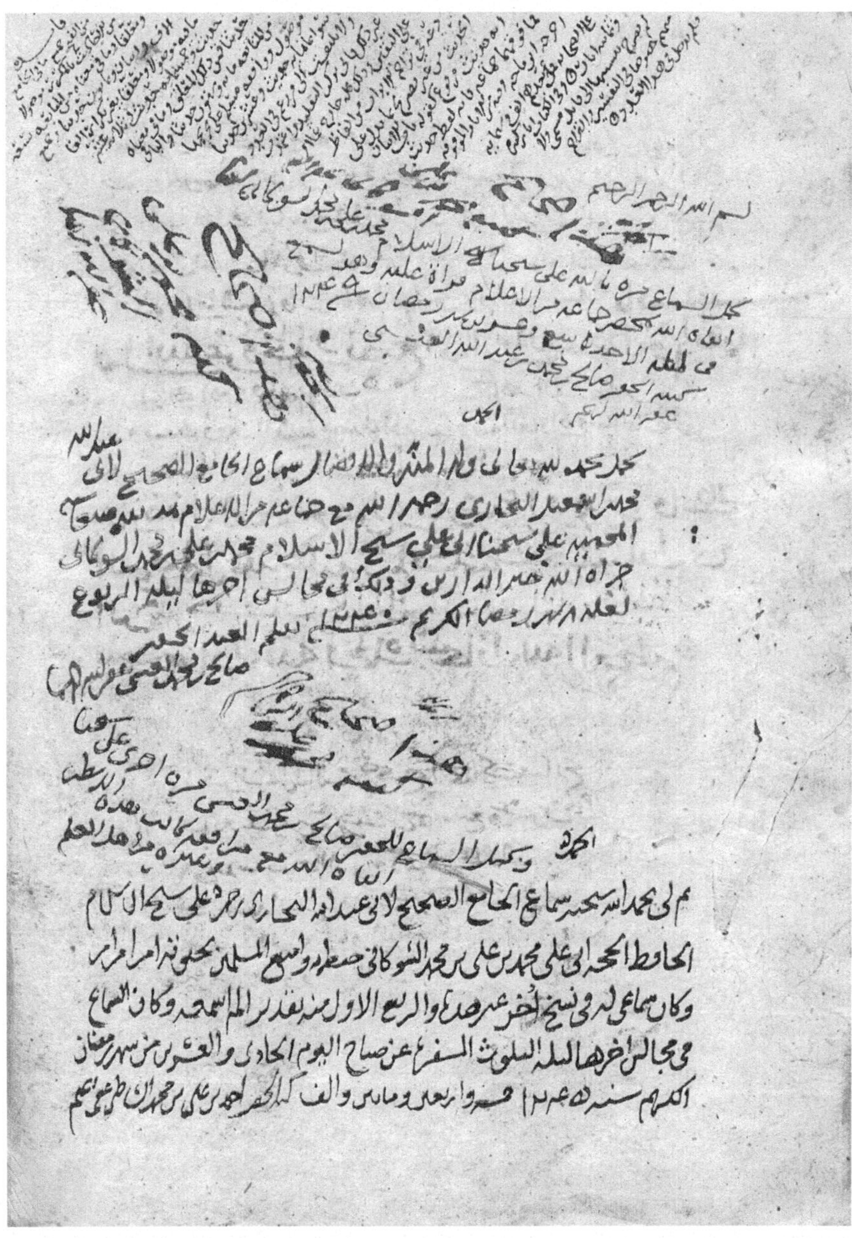

Figure A.2　*Ṣaḥīḥ al-Bukhārī*, Bibliotheca Ambrosiana, MS D 348, fol. 222b. Al-Shawkānī's two failed attempts to sign his name are evident, but the third attempt (upper left) al-Shawkānī succeeded in writing: 'In the name of God, the most compassionate, most merciful. This is correct. Signed by Muḥammad b. 'Alī al-Shawkānī, God grant us forgiveness'. Photo © Veneranda Biblioteca Ambrosiana.

shared practices of reading and interpretation, even as they sought to high-light different facets of the text's meaning. As a physical artefact, this manuscript offers us, as many examples in the preceding chapters of this book do, a profound lesson about the interplay of continuity and change that emerged in and across the centuries spent continuously reading and interpreting this book, in weekly sessions, over months, years, centuries, even a millennium and longer.

By bringing together diverse studies that cover an array of places and times, this volume opens new perspectives from which to explore and analyse continuity and change in the history of hadith commentary. This volume has taken us on a whirlwind tour from the caliph al-Ma'mūn in third-/ninth-century Khurāsān, to the networks of Sunnī and Shī'ī scholars from al-Andalus to Iraq in the fifth/eleventh century, to the Mamlūk and Tīmūrid-era thinkers of Egypt, Syria, and Iran in the seventh/thirteenth to ninth/fifteenth centuries, to the Shī'ī scholars of Ṣafavid Persia during the tenth/sixteenth to the twelfth/eighteenth centuries, to the modern Muslim scholars of nineteenth- and twentieth-century Turkey, Iran and India. In many cases, these contributions represent the first sustained scholarly engagement with the culture and tradition of hadith commentary in these places, times, disciplines and texts. In this regard, this volume opens the known universe of hadith commentary very wide indeed. While these case studies reveal many differences, we can also begin to identify numerous patterns of continuity in interpretive techniques, scholarly practices, intellectual debates, religious aims and adherence to certain discursive rules, and in the contexts of various social and political spaces.

Still, our map of the field, as wide as it is in scope, remains incomplete, at least in terms of places and periods that have yet to be explored. Deeper research into the thriving communities of hadith commentators of al-Andalus and North Africa must be undertaken.[6] Ethnographies that document and analyse contemporary practices and live sessions of hadith commentaries are needed in general, but particularly in contemporary Malaysia and Indonesia. This requires research into commentaries proper as well as translation as a form of commentary, a preliminary task that Mark Woodward laid the groundwork for nearly thirty years ago.[7] Scholars may also be able to cull evidence of commentary on hadith from the earliest surviving Islamic texts from the Indo-Malay world (some of which were handbooks on ethics), and from anthologies that contained hadith

---

6 The recent work of Khaoula Trad and Ömercan Kaçar in this area is most welcome. Trad, 'The Impact of Maghribi *Ḥadīth* Commentaries on the Mashriq' and Kaçar, 'Muhallab b. Abī Ṣufra and His Method of *Ḥadīth* Commentary.' See also Blecher, *Said the Prophet of God*, 19–46.

7 Woodward, 'Textual Exegesis as Social Commentary', 565–583.

translated into Javanese and Malay for local audiences who were encountering Islamic traditions for the first time in the ninth/fifteenth, tenth/sixteenth and eleventh/seventeenth centuries.[8] While Deobandī contributions to hadith commentary in South Asia are addressed in this volume and elsewhere, we do not know enough of the commentarial literature circulating among Deobandī scholars of South Africa.[9] Moreover, studies of hadith commentaries in Nigeria and other parts of sub-Saharan Africa have yet to be undertaken.

Scholars of Islam in America may also seek to collect and analyse modern American forms of hadith commentary, such as those circulating online or those in CD format in storefront mosques in Philadelphia, East Orange, Toronto and other cities across North America. In these contexts, we might ask whether the commentary tradition offers a forum for mediating questions of race, identity and political agency.[10] Practices of hadith commentary are likewise thriving in Muslim communities across the United Kingdom and Europe; certainly recordings and live sessions of these meetings would also be ripe for fresh analyses and ethnographic studies.

There is, lastly, the question of how non-Muslim cultures translated, recompiled and interpreted hadith. The recent study of a tenth-/sixteenth-century Arabic to Judaeo-Arabic translation of a collection of maxims that includes prophetic hadith suggests 'the strong attraction that this literature held for non-Muslim readers, in this case Karaite Jews'.[11] The translation itself could be studied as a form of hadith commentary. While rare, this discovery suggests that there may be more of this kind of literature, and that scholars of Jewish studies may also contribute to this field. Future studies of Anglo-Muhammadan Law and early Dutch attempts to translate the Islamic legal corpus may lead to further insights into the interpretation of hadith literature outside the Islamic tradition.[12] Moreover, placing early Orientalist and philological translations and interpretations of hadith in the Western academy (notably the work of Ignác Goldziher, Gustav Weil and more recently G. H. A. Juynboll) in the comparative context of other non-Muslim audiences of hadith may likewise help us better understand the state of the field and question the assumptions that have shaped our own enquiries.

---

8 Drewes, *Een Javaanse Primbon*; also see Abdul Majid et al., 'Hadith Written in Early Islam [the] Malay Region'; this is an analysis of a commentary and translation of al-Nawawī's *Arbaʿīn* in Malay by an eleventh-/seventeenth-century scholar named ʿAbd al-Raʾūf al-Jāwī al-Sinkilī.

9 On Deobandī networks in South Africa, see Ingraham, *Revival from Below*.

10 Blecher and Dubler, 'Overlooking Race and Secularism in Muslim Philadelphia', 122–150.

11 Fenton, 'K. ad-Durr al-Manzûm'.

12 Kooria, 'The Dutch Mogharaer', and Kugle, 'Framed, Blamed and Renamed'.

Our goal must not simply be to analyse hadith commentaries from disparate parts of the world, but to examine in depth the way in which hadith commentary relates to audiences entangled in local and global social, political and economic contexts. In understanding how power, tradition and experience are woven together in the form of the commentary, future studies could offer readers a three-dimensional view of this practice that is too often flattened within the folios of a manuscript or constrained to the four corners of a printed page.

This volume largely draws on print sources as evidence, although future researchers, taking their cue from Gunasti's study of a Turkish translation of *Ṣaḥīḥ al-Bukhārī*, may seek to shed greater light on the intersection of hadith commentary and the politics of print culture itself.[13] Likewise, there is much more to be understood about the production, transmission and reception of hadith commentary in manuscript culture. Early analyses of manuscript revisions and drafts of works offer insight into the craft of hadith commentary, but many more sit on library shelves waiting patiently for a curious researcher to examine them.[14] Such is the case with al-Zarkashī's autographed draft of his *Tanqīḥ*, a well-known commentary on *Ṣaḥīḥ al-Bukhārī*, heavily marked with his edits and revisions (see Figure A.3).[15]

Commentaries that are transmitted in the form of new media likewise offer novel archives for researchers. These include book stores and street vendors that sell hadith commentary on cassette tapes, DVDs and CDs; networks of websites that stream audio and video commentaries on hadith; and the robust archive of hadith commentary already present on social media. To what extent do these novel forms of media attract new audiences, and in doing so reshape the scope and effect of the commentary that they convey? How do these various media, in comparison to manuscripts and print works, shape the form of commentaries? And what patterns of continuity and change can be found in these different forms?

This book breaks new ground (in the chapters by Aghaei, Rizvi, and Nafisi) by examining Shīʿī hadith commentaries for the first time. As further elaboration of these particular intellectual traditions continues, I invite future researchers to undertake comparative studies that examine continuities and differences in the reception of hadith literature as they are glossed and interpreted across sectarian lines.[16] Likewise, this volume also examines hadith commentary in multiple genres and disciplines

13 See also Zaman, 'Commentaries, Print and Patronage', and El Shamsy, *Rediscovering the Islamic Classics.*
14 Blecher, 'Revision in the Manuscript Age'.
15 Al-Zarkashī, *Tanqīḥ Alfāẓ al-Jāmiʿ al-Ṣaḥīḥ*, Orientabteilung, Sprenger 499, fol. 22a.
16 Pamela Klasova's recent study of the 'Creation of the Intellect' hadith across sectarian lines explores the literary dimension of hadith commentary. Klasova, '*Ḥadīth* as Common Discourse'.

Figure A.3　　A folio from al-Zarkashī's commentary on *Ṣaḥīḥ al-Bukhārī* in the author's own hand. Cancellations with marginal and interlineal insertions and even some marginal cancellations illustrate the writing and revision process of what later became a well-known and widely circulated hadith commentary. See al-Zarkashī, *Tanqīḥ Alfāẓ al-Jāmiʿ al-Ṣaḥīḥ*, Orientabteilung, Sprenger 499, fol. 22a.

of knowledge: philology (Brinkmann), theology (Patel), law (Gunasti, Gharaibeh, and Mian), Sufism (Dajani), *isnād* criticism (Aghaei) and *tafsīr* (Nafisi). Preliminary studies of hadith commentary in the genre of prophetic medicine, published elsewhere, likewise pave the way for future researchers to build comparative studies of the practice of hadith commentary across genres and disciplines of knowledge.[17] To put it more generally, the field still needs comparisons of commentary on hadith in legal versus medical works, as well as studies comparing hadith commentary with Qur'an commentary.

Such comparative studies of hadith commentary would enable researchers to explore broader questions of hermeneutics across the Islamic sciences and in the humanities. This requires not only comparing the reception of hadith across genres and disciplines of knowledge, but also comparing patterns of interpretation between hadith commentary and other commentary traditions in which hadith are not the central focus. How might studies of hadith commentary contribute to conversations across the humanities about the interpretation of scriptures, canonical works and foundational philosophical and political documents?[18] And what might studies of hadith commentary teach scholars of hermeneutics working in other, more mature fields of Islamic studies, or those in the rapidly growing academic studies of *uṣūl al-fiqh* and *tafsīr*?[19] Alternatively, what might students of hadith commentary learn from the insights and methods used in these fields in Islamic studies? For example, in the present volume Samer Dajani uses existing debates in the category of 'Sufi *tafsīr*' to help us make sense of the category of Sufi hadith commentary. Future collaborations across these subfields and disciples are bound to yield further insights.

The coming decade will only increase the innovative forms of digital analyses that open researchers' eyes to distant reading, a big-data analytical approach that complements the traditional 'close reading' of the philologically inclined. This includes analyses of 'digital text reuse' (how commentaries quote and reuse the texts of their predecessors in the tradition) highlighted in our volume's final chapter (Bednarkiewicz, Qurboniev and Van Den Bossche) but also leaves room for the kinds of methods from the digital humanities that are being practised and developed elsewhere.[20] The material is also ripe for social network analyses

17 Stearns, *Infectious Ideas*; Eich, 'Patterns in the History of the Commentation'.

18 In addition to the foundational works of theorists such as Schleiermacher, Gadamer and Ricouer, researchers of hadith commentary should be encouraged to engage with comparative volumes such as those by Henderson, *Scripture, Canon, and Commentary*; Cabezón, *Scholasticism*; and Pelikan, *Interpreting the Bible & the Constitution*.

19 Keeler, *Sufi Hermeneutics*; Lowry, 'The Legal Hermeneutics'; Vishanoff, *The Formation of Islamic Hermeneutics*.

20 Muhanna, *The Digital Humanities*; Eich, 'Patterns in the History of the Commentation'.

of hadith commentators themselves. The very aspect of hadith commentary that has proven to be the greatest barrier for so long – its voluminousness – may yet prove to be its greatest asset.

Finally, it is paramount that we make progress on our understanding of women, gender and sexuality in this tradition. In her ethnographic work, Saba Mahmood has briefly explored women's pedagogy concerning the interpretation of hadith.[21] In an earlier publication, our contributor Ali Altaf Mian has opened the door for inquiry into the intersection of the erotic and hadith culture.[22] We hope the field builds on these studies by offering a critical-theoretical framework for analysing the scholarly networks dominated by male commentators, even as women were important transmitters of hadith at certain historical moments, especially in the first Islamic century, in the Ḥanbalī communities of Mamlūk-era Damascus, and once again in the contemporary era.[23] Here our volume's ambitious scope falls short, but I will conclude with a series of questions that I hope will stimulate future research in this still nascent dimension of the field. To what extent were the earliest transmitters of hadith, such as ʿĀʾisha, Umm Salama and others, also positioned as the interpreters of the very *matn* of the hadith text? What can we learn about the questions and modes of clarification attributed to them? How did later hadith commentators discuss women and women's issues? Does the extent of women's participation in hadith transmission in certain eras alter the scope of commentary? We know that women transmitters of hadith compiled digests and collections of 'forty hadith' – can a 'hermeneutics of compilation' be discerned in their works? What about women religious authorities in the modern world – what continuities and differences emerge in the way they approach the commentary of hadith?[24] And might hadith commentaries resolve problems of grave import to the trans and gender non-binary community?[25] And to what extent do these hadith commentaries serve as a forum for the performance of masculinity and the construction of male virtue?

In writing *Said the Prophet of God* in 2018, I had only intended to unlock the door to future studies of this tradition. When Stefanie Brinkmann and

---

21 Mahmood, *Politics of Piety*, 79–117.

22 Mian, 'Genres of Desire'.

23 Studies in this area should begin with Sayeed, *Women and the Transmission of Knowledge in Islam*; Geissinger, 'The Portrayal of the *Ḥajj*'; Nadwī, *al-Muḥaddithāt*.

24 Nuṣrat Amīn (1308–1423/1886 or 1887–1983), for instance, a well-known and well-respected *mujtahida* in twentieth-century Shīʿī Iran, is remembered for her *Arbaʿīn al-hāshimiyya* (published in 1931), in which she collected and commented on forty hadith and their lines of transmission; see Rutner, 'Religious Authority'.

25 For a range of hadiths that address these matters, see Kugle, *Islam and Homosexuality*.

Ali Zaherinezhad first told me of a workshop on hadith commentaries that they were organising at the University of Hamburg, I was delighted, and saw an opportunity to help shape the contours of future studies – to help others open the door and cross the threshold, so to speak. But as my afterword points out, our scholarly conversation has only just begun. Through the tireless efforts of my co-editor Stefanie Brinkmann and the inspiration of our colleague Ali Zaherinezhad, as well as the learned and original insights of our contributors from Gainesville to Exeter to Berlin to Tehran, our volume seeks not only to shed light on the patterns of continuity and change in the hadith commentary tradition, but also to lay the groundwork for other scholars with new voices and concerns to step into the foyer, and enter the garden beyond.

Bibliography

Abdul Majid, Latifah, Haziyah Husain, Mazlan Ibrahim, and Jawiah Dakir. 'Hadith Written in Early Islam in the Malay Region.' *Advances in Natural and Applied Sciences* 6, no. 3 (2012): 472–477.

al-Bukhārī, Muḥammad ibn Ismāʿīl. *Ṣaḥīḥ al-Bukhārī*. Milan, Bibliotheca Ambrosiana, MS. D 347 ar.

Blecher, Joel. 'Revision in the Manuscript Age: New Evidence of Early Versions of Ibn Ḥajar's *Fatḥ al-Bārī*.' *Journal of Near Eastern Studies* 76, no. 1 (2017): 39–51.

Blecher, Joel. *Said the Prophet of God: Hadith Commentary Across a Millenium*. Oakland: University of California Press, 2018.

Blecher, Joel and Josh Dubler. 'Overlooking Race and Secularism in Muslim Philadelphia.' In Vincent Lloyd and Jonathan S. Kahn (eds), *Race and Secularism in America*, pp. 122–150. New York: Columbia University Press, 2016.

Cabezón, José. *Scholasticism: Cross-Cultural and Comparative Perspectives*. Albany: State University of New York Press, 1998.

Drewes, G. W. J. *Een Javaanse Primbon Uit De Zestiende Eeuw*. Leiden: Brill, 1954.

Eich, Thomas. 'Patterns in the History of the Commentation on the So-Called Ḥadīth Ibn Masʿūd.' *Journal of Arabic and Islamic Studies* 18 (2018): 137–162.

El Shamsy, Ahmed. *Rediscovering the Islamic Classics: How Editors and Print Culture Transformed an Intellectual Tradition*. Princeton, NJ: Princeton University Press, 2020.

Fenton, Paul. '*K. ad-Durr al-Manzûm*: A Sufi Collection of Moral Aphorism in Judaeo-Arabic.' In Naoya Katsumata and Wout van Bekkum, *Giving a Diamond: Essays in Honor of Joseph Yahalom on the Occasion of His Seventieth Birthday*, pp. 213–242. Leiden: Brill, 2011. doi: <https://doi.org/10.1163/ej.9789004203815.i-328.57>.

Geissinger, Aisha. 'The Portrayal of the *Hajj* as a Context for Women's Exegesis: Textual Evidence from al-Bukhārī's (d. 870) *Ṣaḥīḥ*.' In Sebastian Günther (ed.), *Ideas, Images, and Methods of Portrayal: Insights into Classical Arabic Literature and Islam*, pp. 153–179. Leiden and Boston: Brill, 2005.

Haykel, Bernard. *Revival and Reform in Islam: The Legacy of Muhammad al-Shawkānī*. Cambridge: Cambridge University Press, 2003.

Henderson, John. *Scripture, Canon, and Commentary*. Princeton, NJ: Princeton University Press, 1991.

Ingraham, Brendan. *Revival from Below: The Deoband Movement and Global Islam*. Oakland: University of California Press, 2018.

Kaçar, Ömercan. 'Muhallab B. Abī Ṣufra and His Method of Ḥadīth Commentary.' MA Thesis, Marmara University, 2021.

Keeler, Annabel. *Sufi Hermeneutics: The Qur'an Commentary of Rashīd al-Dīn Maybudī*. Oxford: Oxford University Press, 2017.

Klasova, Pamela. 'Ḥadīth as Common Discourse: Reflections on the Intersectarian Dissemination of the Creation of the Intellect Tradition.' *al-ʿUṣūr al-Wusṭā* 28 (2020): 297–345.

Kooria, Mahmood. 'The Dutch Mogharaer, Arabic Muḥarrar, and Javanese Law Books: A VOC Experiment with Muslim Law in Java, 1747–1767.' *Itinerario, European Journal of Overseas History* (2018): 202–219.

Kugle, Scott. 'Framed, Blamed and Renamed: The Recasting of Islamic Jurisprudence in Colonial South Asia.' *Modern Asian Studies* 35, no. 2 (2001): 257–313.

Kugle, Scott. *Islam and Homosexuality: Critical Reflection on Gay, Lesbian, and Transgender Muslims*. London: Oneworld, 2010.

Lowry, Joseph. 'The Legal Hermeneutics of al-Shāfiʿī and Ibn Qutayba: A Reconsideration.' *Islamic Law and Society* 11, no. 1 (2004): 1–41.

Mahmood, Saba. *Politics of Piety: The Islamic Revival and the Feminist Subject*. Princeton, NJ: Princeton University Press, 2005.

Mian, Ali Altaf. 'Genres of Desire: The Erotic in Deobandī Islam.' *History of Religions* 59, no. 2 (2019): 108–145.

Muhanna, Elias. *The Digital Humanities and Islamic & Middle East Studies*. Berlin: DeGruyter, 2016.

Nadwī, Muhammad Akram. *al-Muḥaddithāt: The Women Scholars in Islam*. Oxford: Interface Publications, 2016.

Pelikan, Jaroslav. *Interpreting the Bible & the Constitution*. New Haven: Yale University Press, 2004.

Rutner, Maryam. 'Religious Authority, Gendered Recognition, and Instrumentalization of Nusrat Amin in Life and after Death.' *Journal of Middle East Womens Studies* 11, no. 1 (2015): 24–41.

Sayeed, Asma. *Women and the Transmission of Knowledge in Islam*. Cambridge: Cambridge University Press, 2013.

al-Shawkānī, Muḥammad. *Badr al-ṭāliʿ bi-maḥāsin man baʿd al-qarn al-sābiʿ*. Beirut: Dār al-Kutub al-ʿIlmiyya, 1998.

Stearns, Justin. *Infectious Ideas: Contagion in Premodern Islamic and Christian Thought in the Western Mediterranean*. Baltimore, MD: Johns Hopkins University Press, 2011.

Trad, Khaoula. 'The Impact of Maghribi Ḥadīth Commentaries on the Mashriq.' In Maribel Fierro and Mayte Penelas (eds), *The Maghrib in the Mashriq: Knowledge, Travel and Identity*, pp. 213–236. Berlin: De Gruyter, 2021. doi: <https://doi.org/10.1515/9783110713305-008>.

Vishanoff, David. *The Formation of Islamic Hermeneutics: How Sunni Legal Theorists Imagined a Revealed Law*. New Haven: American Oriental Society, 2011.

Woodward, Mark R. 'Textual Exegesis as Social Commentary: Religious, Social, and Political Meanings of Indonesian Translations of Arabic Ḥadīth Texts.' *Journal of Asian Studies* 52, no. 3 (1993): 565–583.

Zaman, Muhammad Qasim. 'Commentaries, Print and Patronage, "Ḥadīth" and the Madrasas in Modern South Asia.' *Bulletin of the School of Oriental and African Studies* 62, no. 1 (1999): 60–81.

al-Zarkashī, Badr al-Dīn. *Tanqīḥ Alfāẓ al-Jāmiʿ al-Ṣaḥīḥ*. Berlin, Staatsbibliothek, Orientabteilung, Sprenger 499, fol. 22a.

Index

The article 'al-', diacritics, the letters *'ayn* and *hamza* as well as 'b' are disregarded in the alphabetical order

The letter *f* following an entry indicates a page with a figure